Three Worlds of Relief

PRINCETON STUDIES IN AMERICAN POLITICS: HISTORICAL, INTERNATIONAL, AND COMPARATIVE PERSPECTIVES

Ira Katznelson, Martin Shefter, and Theda Skocpol, SERIES EDITORS

A list of titles in this series appears at the back of the book.

Three Worlds of Relief

RACE, IMMIGRATION, AND THE AMERICAN
WELFARE STATE FROM THE PROGRESSIVE
ERA TO THE NEW DEAL

Cybelle Fox

PRINCETON UNIVERSITY PRESS
PRINCETON AND OXFORD

Copyright © 2012 by Princeton University Press
Published by Princeton University Press, 41 William Street,
Princeton, New Jersey 08540
In the United Kingdom: Princeton University Press, 6 Oxford Street,
Woodstock, Oxfordshire OX20 1TW

press.princeton.edu

Jacket Art: John Langley Howard. *California Industrial Scenes, Coit Tower Mural*, 1934.
San Francisco. Public Works of Art Project. Photo © D.Godliman (www.dgphotos.co.uk)

Library of Congress Cataloging-in-Publication Data

Fox, Cybelle.
 Three worlds of relief : race, immigration, and the American welfare state
from the Progressive Era to the New Deal / Cybelle Fox.
    p. cm. — (Princeton studies in American politics: historical, international,
and comparative perspectives)
 Includes bibliographical references and index.
 ISBN-13: 978-0-691-15223-3 (cloth : alk. paper)
 ISBN-10: 0-691-15223-3 (cloth : alk. paper)
 ISBN-13: 978-0-691-15224-0 (pbk. : alk. paper)
 ISBN-10: 0-691-15224-1 (pbk. : alk. paper) 1. Immigrants—United States—
Social conditions—20th century. 2. Immigrants—Government policy—
United States—History—20th century. 3. Welfare state—United States—History—
20th century. 4. United States—Race relations—History—20th century. I. Title.
 JV6455.F69 2012
 362.89′9125650973—dc23
                     2011034395

British Library Cataloging-in-Publication Data is available

This book has been composed in Sabon

Printed on acid-free paper. ∞

Printed in the United States of America

10 9 8 7 6 5 4 3 2 1

Contents

Contents

Acknowledgments

IN THE COURSE OF RESEARCHING AND WRITING this manuscript I have accumulated debts too numerous to count. This book began as a doctoral dissertation in Harvard's Multidisciplinary Program in Inequality and Social Policy. I am especially grateful to my advisor, Lawrence Bobo. Over the years he has encouraged me, guided my professional development, and gently pushed me to sharpen my theoretical arguments. William Julius Wilson was especially supportive, giving me constructive and thoughtful feedback through each stage of the process. Jennifer Hochschild has a passion and enthusiasm for ideas that is contagious. She made strong intellectual demands of me but never let me feel defeated or overwhelmed. Theda Skocpol convinced me that this project was worth undertaking and pressed me to take politics seriously. Christopher "Sandy" Jencks listened patiently to my ideas, asked me tough questions, and painstakingly line-edited my work. Katherine Newman inspires me with her drive and determination. She urged me to write clearly and helped shepherd this book to the press. I could not have embarked on this project without the support of these generous mentors.

A Robert Wood Johnson Health Policy Postdoctoral Fellowship gave me the time and resources necessary for follow-up archival research and to work on my writing. I want to thank John Ellwood, Seana Van Buren, Stacy Gallagher, the scholars, the executive committee, and my mentors, Margaret Weir and Taeku Lee, for helping make my two years there so productive and enjoyable.

I finished the manuscript while an assistant professor at the University of California, Berkeley. I could not hope for a more supportive department. Many of my colleagues there and elsewhere read versions of this manuscript in part or in full. I owe an enormous debt of gratitude to Margaret Weir, Robert Lieberman, Desmond King, Katherine Newman, Tom Guglielmo, Helen Fox, and Martín Sánchez-Jankowski who each read some version of the manuscript in full. Others read portions of my work, shared data, or helped me puzzle through especially thorny issues. For this I thank Adam Berinsky, Irene Bloemraad, Tony Chen, Claude Fischer, Marion Fourcade, Luis Fraga, Heather Haveman, Luisa Heredia, Rodney Hero, Tomás Jiménez, Jennifer Johnson-Hanks, Taeku Lee, Sam Lucas, Helen Marrow, Isaac Martin, Rob Mickey, Maria Rendon, Dylan Riley, Eric Schickler, Jessica Trounstine, Cihan Tugal, Loïc Wacquant, and Mary Waters.

Many thanks to Rudy Garcia, Lissett Lopez, Leticia Mata, Katherine Trujillo, and Carmen Ye for spending a semester in Doe Library, reading and copying news articles from *La Opinión*. Your excellent memos and our biweekly conversations were indispensible to this project.

Over the years, I presented pieces of my work in various workshops. I received especially valuable feedback from participants in the Race, Ethnicity and Immigration workshop at UC Berkeley's Institute for Governmental Studies, the IGERT workshop at the Goldman School of Public Policy, the Stanford-Berkeley Seminar on Stratification, the Comparative Historical Workshop at UC San Diego, and the Interdisciplinary Immigration Workshop at UC Berkeley.

Much-needed financial support came at just the right times from Harvard's Multidisciplinary Program in Inequality and Social Policy, the National Science Foundation, Harvard's Center for American Political Studies, the Radcliffe Institute for Advanced Study, and the Berkeley Sociology Department. In addition, many people housed me, cooked meals for me, or loaned me a car while I was dissertating or working in archives far from home. For this and more, I owe special thanks to Jeanne Koopman, Mr. and Mrs. Rendon, the Montoya family, the Heredia family, Diane Gregorio, Therese Leung, Elisabeth Jacobs, Sam Walsh, Tom Guglielmo, Michal Kurlaender, and Bryce Vinokurov.

I am very grateful to Chuck Myers, my editor at Princeton University Press, for his support and expert editorial advice. Jennifer Backer and Hope Richardson, my copyeditors, saved me from innumerable mistakes. And I am indebted to Karen Fortgang and the entire production team at Princeton for the care with which they prepared the manuscript for publication. Portions of chapters 2 and 3 appeared in earlier form in Cybelle Fox, "Three Worlds of Relief: Race, Immigration, and Public and Private Social Welfare Spending in American Cities, 1929," *American Journal of Sociology* 116, no. 2 (2010): 453–502.

New friends and old have encouraged, supported, and motivated me during my writing. I cannot possibly mention them all, but a few deserve special recognition: David Almeling, Rene Almeling, Robin Chalfin, Diane Gregorio, Tom Guglielmo, Karena Heredia, Luisa Heredia, Elisabeth Jacobs, Nick Kopple-Perry, Michal Kurlaender, Therese Leung, Jal Mehta, Meena Munshi, Jeff Ostergren, Meenesh Pattni, Maria Rendon, Sandra Smith, Natasha Warikoo, Robb Willer, and Chris Wimer. Thank you.

I am incredibly fortunate to have an inspiring extended family. By example, they have encouraged my intellectual pursuits and interest in social justice, and with their love, they have sustained me during this long journey. A special thanks to my parents, who encouraged my curiosity and instilled in me a love of learning. My mother responded to my eleventh-hour plea to read the manuscript before I sent it out for review. Thank you for dropping everything for me. My aunt, Rebecca, has supported me in all of my endeavors. My sister Nondini and niece, Sarah, remind me to follow my passions. I share my joys and frustrations with my sister Maria. Maria, Mark, Devyn, and Kendall opened their home to me and cheered me on through it all.

Berkeley, California
March 2011

Abbreviations

ADC	Aid to Dependent Children
CCC	Civilian Conservation Corps
CCIH	California Commission of Immigration and Housing
CES	Committee on Economic Security
CSO	Community Service Organization
CWA	Civil Works Administration
ERB	Emergency Relief Bureau
FDR	Franklin Delano Roosevelt
FERA	Federal Emergency Relief Administration
FLIS	Foreign Language Information Service
GA	General Assistance
INS	Immigration and Naturalization Service
IPL	Immigrants' Protective League
NAACP	National Association for the Advancement of Colored People
OAA	Old Age Assistance
OAI	Old Age Insurance
PECE	President's Emergency Committee for Employment
PWA	Public Works Administration
SRA	State Relief Administration
SSB	Social Security Board
WPA	Works Progress Administration

Three Worlds of Relief

CHAPTER 1

Race, Immigration, and the American Welfare State

IN NOVEMBER 1994 more than five million California voters went to the polls and sent a message to Washington. Frustrated about the alleged costs of undocumented immigration, they passed Proposition 187, also known as the "Save Our State" initiative, by an overwhelming margin. "S.O.S." barred undocumented immigrants from access to welfare and other non-emergency services and required social welfare providers to report suspected undocumented immigrants to immigration officials. While the measure was overturned by the courts before it was implemented, a number of states subsequently passed similar legislation.[1]

Proposition 187's most enduring legacy, however, came in 1996. That year, as part of its overhaul of welfare, the federal government barred states from using federal funds to provide welfare coverage to most *legal* immigrants who had lived in the United States fewer than five years. Congressman E. Clay Shaw (R-FL) explained the logic behind this move: "Quite frankly . . . when we're cutting benefits and cutting welfare for our citizens, I don't see why we should stretch and say that we have an obligation to those that aren't even citizens of our own country." Twelve years later, as the Great Recession that began in 2008 deepened, many communities looked to further cull non-citizens from their public assistance rolls. The assumption that immigrants are less deserving, that they should be the first to be cut from the social welfare rolls when budgets are tight, now appears virtually unquestionable in many circles.[2]

Opponents of these legislative efforts have argued that the federal restrictions in 1996 were unprecedented and represented a major departure from previous federal policy, denoting the emergence of a "new nativism" that blatantly targets Mexican immigrants in particular. State-level restrictions on unauthorized immigrants, they claim, were redundant since undocumented immigrants had never been granted welfare assistance.[3] Others disagree, claiming that these exclusions represent nothing more than simple cost considerations or a continuation of America's historic unwillingness to extend welfare benefits to non-citizens.[4]

These debates led me to wonder: exactly how did immigrants fare historically? After all, the modern welfare state was born on the heels of the largest surge in immigration in American history. Between 1890 and

1930, more than twenty million people arrived on our shores. By the eve of Franklin Roosevelt's New Deal, fourteen million immigrants were living in America. Like today, these immigrants represented 12 percent of the population. Did these immigrants, many of them from Europe and Mexico, find their way to local social assistance when they arrived? Were they entitled to assistance in the midst of the Great Depression? How important was citizenship or legal status for access to New Deal programs and the nascent welfare state?[5]

When I began my search for answers to these questions, I found there was little published information on the subject. The vast literature on race and welfare focuses overwhelmingly on relations between blacks and whites. It demonstrates that racial divisions have profoundly affected the size and character of the American welfare state. Yet European immigrants, Mexicans, and Mexican Americans do not figure in this tale.

This book recounts the untold story of the politics of race and immigration in the development of the American social welfare system from the Progressive Era to the New Deal. It compares the incorporation of Mexicans,[6] European immigrants, and blacks into our social welfare system and examines the influence of race and immigration on the scope, form, and function of social welfare provision across three separate regions: the North, South, and Southwest. By looking across groups, it tries to tease apart the relative influence of race, formal citizenship, and legal status for access to the social safety net.

Understanding how different groups were treated by our early welfare system is important because access to or exclusion from the welfare state can have immediate and long-term consequences on group outcomes like wealth accumulation.[7] But the welfare state can also reflect a particular set of social relations, so the study of welfare state incorporation can also tell us something about where Mexicans fit into America's racial hierarchy, a subject of recent vigorous scholarly and public debate. Are Mexicans following the path of southern and eastern European immigrants, groups once thought to be racially distinct and inferior but now assimilated and treated simply as white? Or is theirs a path of blocked mobility due to enduring discrimination, an experience more akin to that of African Americans?[8]

Welfare scholars have often taken sides in this debate, at least implicitly. Some work suggests that the experiences of Mexicans and other minorities with the welfare state differ only in degree, not in kind, from the experiences of blacks. Authors who take this view slip comfortably between talking about "blacks" and "minorities," sometimes allotting a line or two to the treatment of Mexicans, Puerto Ricans, Filipinos, or Native Americans without investigating the similarities and differences in treatment across groups. Other scholars endorse a black exceptionalism perspective, which assumes that the welfare state's treatment of blacks is unique and that understanding black-white relations is sufficient to explain why the welfare state evolved as it did. In this line of thinking, the experiences of other minority groups are either politically insignificant or assumed to closely hew to the experiences of European immigrants and their descendants. Most social welfare scholars, however, simply ignore groups other than native-born blacks and whites. While there is much important work yet to be done on the black-white divide, the silence of the literature as a whole on other groups nonetheless reflects and reinforces a binary vision of American race relations. This book questions whether that vision—of an American welfare state in black and white—is truly warranted.[9]

This book demonstrates that blacks, Mexicans, and European immigrants were treated quite differently by both the Progressive Era relief system and the New Deal welfare state. European immigrants were largely included within the contours of social citizenship, while blacks were largely excluded. Mexicans straddled the boundaries of social citizenship precariously until relief officials forced them out—expelled from the boundaries of social citizenship *and* the nation.

By the eve of the Depression, when relief spending was still a local—not federal—responsibility, cities with more blacks or Mexicans typically invested the least in social assistance and relied more heavily on private money to fund their programs. Cities with more European immigrants, by contrast, invested more in relief and relied more heavily on public funding—even more, as it turns out, than cities with more native-born white residents. This was true even after taking into account differences across cities in levels of urbanization, need, or a city's financial ability to fund programs. The source of funding was an important feature of a relief system because private relief officials were more likely than their public counterparts to blame individuals for their poverty and believe that charity was a gift, not an entitlement; that the poor should be supervised while on the "dole"; and that the able-bodied should be forced to work for assistance. A city's choice to fund relief with public or private funds, therefore, might have a substantial effect on the treatment poor individuals would receive.

Disparities within communities mattered, too. Prior to the New Deal, blacks had less access to welfare assistance than any other group. Mexicans were often barred from Mothers' Pensions, the cash welfare programs for needy and deserving mothers, but they had greater access than blacks to less generous forms of relief like food baskets and clothing. But Mexicans were also sometimes expelled from the nation simply for requesting assistance. Relief offices in the Southwest cooperated with the Immigration Service to deport individuals who applied for welfare, and relief offices throughout the country used their own funds to forcibly expel dependent Mexicans and Mexican Americans from the nation. Relief officials rarely behaved so aggressively toward European immigrants. They often refused to cooperate with the Immigration Service and sometimes even protected destitute European immigrants from being deported. European immigrants could also rely on relief officials to access Mothers' Pensions and other vital sources of assistance.

After FDR came into office in 1933, the federal government got involved in the business of relief, and federal non-discrimination provisions opened up forms of social protection to blacks and Mexicans. Greater access to welfare, however, brought with it greater stigma, especially for blacks who, unlike Mexicans, had previously escaped the label of being "overly dependent" on the dole. Yet despite the advent of nationalizing reforms meant to standardize relief policies across the country, disparities in access did not disappear because state and local welfare offices were charged with implementing many of the federal programs. Blacks typically lived in communities with low benefit levels for all programs, and local relief officials often limited black access. Mexicans, meanwhile, often lived in communities with a stratified benefits system: very high benefits for Old Age Assistance, from which they were excluded, and low benefits for General Assistance, upon which they were forced to rely.

European immigrants, by contrast, typically lived in areas with uniformly high benefit levels, and they received generous access to the least demeaning social insurance programs. Indeed, when it first passed, Social Security did not cover agricultural and domestic workers, thereby excluding the vast majority of blacks and Mexicans from social insurance. But European immigrants were more likely than even native-born whites to work in occupations covered by Social Security, and they were also more likely to be nearing retirement when the program was instituted. Consequently, they ended up contributing little to the system but by design benefited almost as much as those who would contribute their whole working lives. For retirees of European origin, Social Security was more akin to welfare than insurance but without the means test and without the stigma.

The Myth of the Bootstrapping White Ethnic

The broad inclusion of European immigrants in the early social welfare system stands in contrast to our national mythology that European immigrants worked their way up without any help from the government. That view implicitly—and sometimes explicitly—suggests that differences in individual initiative explain persistent economic and social disparities between whites and blacks. Indeed, since 1994, when the question was first asked by the General Social Survey, between two-thirds and three-quarters of American residents have agreed with the following statement: "Irish, Italian, Jewish, and other minorities overcame prejudice and worked their way up. Blacks should do the same without special favors." Similarly, more than 80 percent agreed that "today's immigrants" should work their way up like their European counterparts did a century ago without any assistance. Many native-born white Americans believe that today's immigrants—especially Mexicans—are less self-sufficient than their own European ancestors. In the run-up to welfare reform in 1996, Representative Bill Archer (R-TX) said, "My ancestors, and most of our ancestors, came to this country not with their hands out for welfare checks." Writing a letter to the editor of the *Buffalo News*, a reader expressed a similar attitude: "Our ancestors came here legally and did not place great demands on government services." Even some of the best historical scholarship has helped perpetuate the myth that European immigrants did not benefit much from early social welfare programs.[10]

Given this lore, it is surprising how much European immigrants benefited from welfare programs and how little their formal citizenship or legal status impeded their access to relief. Contrary to T. H. Marshall's view that social citizenship or social rights always followed civil and political rights,[11] formal citizenship was not a prerequisite for social citizenship. Non-citizens were generally entitled to care in almshouses, to outdoor relief, and to Mothers' Pensions. While there were public charge provisions built into immigration law that allowed for the deportation of some recent immigrants, such provisions were rare until the 1890s, unevenly applied during the first third of the twentieth century, and hardly ever enforced after FDR took office in 1933. Moreover, non-citizens were granted wide access to New Deal programs such as Federal Emergency Relief, Social Security, Unemployment Insurance, Aid to Dependent Children, and many others. Federal officials even ensured that the Social Security Board would not cooperate with immigration officials to locate deportable aliens, assuring immigrants that they could apply for Social Security cards even if they had entered the country illegally.

Given that immigration to the United States was severely curtailed by the 1921 and 1924 Immigration Acts and was virtually blocked in 1929 at the onset of the Depression, it might be tempting to assume that questions about the inclusion of non-citizens in the New Deal had been rendered moot. This was not the case. It was a matter of serious concern to policymakers, social workers, congressmen, the general public, and especially non-citizens and their families. Rumors circulated in the press that there were a million or more aliens on relief and that FDR's administration refused to collect and share data on aliens' use of welfare programs. There was intense debate about whether non-citizens should be included in the welfare state, and letters sent to the White House, local news stories, and early public opinion polls all make clear that nativism was very strong during the Depression. A Chicago resident complained in 1935, for example, that "the majority of Foreigners think its [sic] smart to get on relief, drive a car, have two, or three others in the family working and live off of a big-hearted Uncle Sam. They should kick them all back to Europe as the majority of them are absolutely nogood [sic]."[12] Indeed, immigration officials speculated that nativism had become even more widespread and pronounced than in the period that spawned immigration quotas. Most Americans concluded that aliens should not receive relief and that those who did should be expelled from the country.

Impelled by catastrophic economic conditions and nativist sentiments, politicians passed citizenship requirements for a few state and federal relief programs. But despite strong opposition to alien inclusion, work relief programs—especially the WPA—and Old Age Assistance were the only programs that were limited to U.S. citizens. These restrictions, however, were generally short-lived and unevenly applied. Even when non-citizens were formally barred from assistance, European immigrants often found ways to overcome these barriers. Mexicans, however, were not as fortunate. Citizenship restrictions were more enduring in areas with more Mexicans, and where citizenship restrictions existed, Mexicans found them harder to circumvent. The presumption that all Mexicans were foreign even when they were American citizens also limited their access to relief in many places. This presumption became a mechanism not just for denying benefits but also for allowing relief officials to expel more than forty thousand Mexicans and Mexican Americans from the nation in the first few years of the Depression.

Explaining Disparities in Treatment

What explains these three different trajectories of inclusion, exclusion, and expulsion? There are reasons, in fact, why we might not have expected big differences in treatment across groups. Each group contained many members who were desperately poor and reviled, and blacks, Mexicans, and southern and eastern European immigrants each suffered from significant discrimination at the hands of native-born whites. Some historians, including David Roediger, have argued, in fact, that southern and eastern European immigrants were neither perceived nor treated as "white" when they first arrived in large numbers in the 1890s. It was only after the United States closed its doors to mass migration from southern and eastern Europe in 1924, perhaps even as late as World War

II, that the boundaries of whiteness even began to expand to include Italians, Poles, and Jews.[13] What, then, explains the stark differences in treatment?

Scholarship on the role of race in the development of the early welfare state points to several possible explanations, including the role of politics and institutions, regional economies and labor relations, attitudes of elite reformers, and mass opinion. Some scholars, for example, call attention to the state and the role that organizational arrangements, policy decisions, and institutional legacies play in welfare state development. According to Robert Lieberman, Jill Quadagno, and Ira Katznelson, in the years between Reconstruction and the Voting Rights Act in 1965, poll taxes and literacy tests excluded most blacks from voting, ensuring that there was little competition for public office. As a result, white southern senators gained control of key congressional committees. During the deliberations over the 1935 Social Security Act, these southern senators ensured that the final bill excluded the vast majority of African Americans from Social Security and Unemployment Insurance, and relegated blacks to "decentralized, often racist, public assistance programs." White workers, on the other hand, were given access to a wide array of social insurance programs that would help them weather the hazards of old age or temporary unemployment. By examining differences in the institutional structure of Unemployment Insurance, Old Age Insurance, and Aid to Dependent Children, Lieberman shows that these early disparities had a lasting effect: "By keeping poor blacks at arm's length while embracing white workers, national welfare policy helped construct the contemporary political divisions—middle class versus poor, suburb versus city, and white versus black—that define the urban underclass."[14]

These studies have made a strong case for the influence of the South and mass disenfranchisement on national welfare policy. Yet the focus on black exclusion has obscured the concurrent battles over the inclusion of non-citizens in New Deal programs. Indeed, the inclusion of non-citizens in the Social Security Act was not a foregone conclusion. The principal competing old age insurance bill—the Townsend Plan—excluded non-citizens. Even after the Social Security Act had passed, some congressmen tried to drop non-citizens from the benefits of the act. The omission of these debates from scholarship has left us ill equipped to historicize contemporary efforts to limit welfare to American citizens. And it has also prevented us from properly questioning whether the broad inclusion of European immigrants in New Deal programs had a lasting effect on their descendants, too.[15]

The black-white frame, moreover, has led scholars to focus too narrowly on the North and South, either ignoring the Southwest altogether or dividing it awkwardly between the two. I make no claim that the

Southwest's influence on federal policy matched the influence of the South, at least for the period under study here. Nevertheless, the political context of the Southwest—where the vast majority of Mexicans lived— was distinctive and left its own legacy on the scope, form, and function of the social welfare system that developed there.[16]

Instead of politics, other scholars argue that labor arrangements explain early welfare disparities. Lee Alston and Joseph Ferrie argue that the reason southerners sought to limit the "scope and scale" of the Social Security Act was to maintain their system of labor control. Southern senators did not push for the exclusion of agricultural and domestic workers and greater control over welfare programs because they did not want blacks to receive any type of social assistance. During this time, many southern blacks and poor whites who were loyal, productive, and displayed the "appropriate" measure of deference had access to a wide range of benefits, provided privately by their employer. What southern planter elites feared was that *federally funded* social benefits would undermine employers' paternalistic authority and jeopardize their access to cheap, dependable labor.[17]

These authors point to a crucial feature of the southern labor regime. However, their study is limited to the South—a region distinctive along many dimensions—making it difficult to ascertain that paternalism is truly the key. They gain causal leverage by examining the decline in southern resistance to federal control as planters' use of paternalism waned with greater mechanization. Comparing across regions of the United States, however, can reveal how different types of farm-labor arrangements— paternalistic versus migratory labor systems, for example—influenced the scope of welfare provision before and after federal intervention.

Instead of politics or labor, Linda Gordon and Gwendolyn Mink trace the origins of racial and gender inequality in the American welfare state to the attitudes of the white women reformers who helped pass and implement Mothers' Pensions—the forerunner to Aid to Dependent Children. Mink and Gordon argue that one of the primary purposes of Mothers' Pensions was to facilitate the cultural assimilation of southern and eastern European immigrants. Reformers extended pensions—or regular cash grants—to immigrant women and in return, the reformers expected the women to conform to Anglo norms about child-raising and housekeeping. But the social worker's emphasis on cultural and gender conformity "prescribed not only [women's] separate incorporation into the welfare state but also [their] subordination within it." Black women were not fully incorporated into the reformist agenda because prevailing stereotypes defined black women as workers, not mothers—permanently outside the Anglo cult of domesticity. Exclusion and enforced conformity to Anglo norms tarnished the early welfare agenda and shaped the possibilities for subsequent programs, restricting their vision and scope.[18]

Mink and Gordon's attention to social reformers is well placed, and they are among the few scholars of this period to consider immigrants, but they focus little attention on Mexicans. Did social workers try to assimilate Mexicans as they did European immigrants? Or did they exclude them from their reform efforts as they did blacks? Perhaps more important, how do we adjudicate between theories that focus on political or labor arrangements and those that focus on the agency of welfare elites? Should we think of social workers as operating independent of these contextual forces? Or are social workers largely controlled by state and capitalist interests, as some scholars maintain?[19]

Finally, a host of studies focus on how public opinion shapes our social policies. Some of these studies focus on demographic context and find that people are more generous in homogeneous societies and more likely to support redistributive policies that benefit members of their own group. Support for the welfare state, according to Joseph Carens, originates from a "sense of common bonds, from mutual identification by the members of the community." These attachments are "more likely to emerge when people share a common language and a common culture and when they belong to groups that have developed habits of cooperation with other groups." Studies consistently show that in communities with more blacks, white support for redistribution and actual spending on redistributive programs is lower. And states with more blacks and Latinos tend to adopt more punitively oriented welfare programs. Inspired by this research, some scholars have argued that there may be a universal tradeoff between diversity—whether racial, ethnic, religious, or linguistic—and redistribution. According to this argument, the increasing diversity that comes with immigration may decrease class consciousness, social solidarity, levels of trust, or generosity among members of the host society, all factors presumed necessary for the development and preservation of a generous welfare state. But if immigration hampers redistribution, as some of these scholars maintain, how do we explain the generous treatment of European immigrants and the high social spending in cities with large numbers of foreign-born whites?[20]

Instead of demographic context, some public opinion scholars argue that whites are ambivalent about welfare because of their negative stereotypes about the work ethic of subordinate groups, especially blacks. Martin Gilens famously argued that whites' stereotypes about black work ethic have driven much white opposition to welfare spending since the War on Poverty. Studies also show that people who are prejudiced against Mexicans or those with "cool" feelings toward Asians and Latinos are more likely to support a one-year delay or even an outright ban in the provision of benefits to certain immigrants. But we know less about how or even whether stereotypes about welfare dependence influenced social welfare provision in the past, nor do we have a clear idea about which groups were stereotyped as especially dependent in the early twentieth century.[21]

Moving beyond Black and White

The existing scholarship has done much to advance our understanding of the determinants of welfare state development. But the literature's heavy reliance on a black-white framework has left us ill equipped to understand the treatment of groups like Mexicans, Mexican Americans, and European immigrants. It has also led welfare scholars to focus on too narrow a set of outcomes: studies of benefit levels and support for or actual spending on redistributive programs tend to dominate the field. But as the sociologist Gøsta Esping-Andersen reminds us, the "amount of money spent" on the welfare state "may be less important than what it does." Toward that end, some scholars have studied the welfare state's function as a mechanism of social control, where it works to quell social unrest or racial insurgency and where it is deployed to scrutinize and manage the behavior of the poor by telling them what they can buy, how many children they can have, how they should spend their days, or how they should raise their children.[22] Along these lines, this book argues that in certain times and places, the welfare state may be best viewed as an extension of the Immigration Service, where one of its functions becomes not the provision of assistance but rather the expulsion of individuals or even segments of an entire population from the nation. In the most extreme cases, the welfare office quite literally turned into an immigration bureau or became an extralegal arm of the Immigration Service, expelling those immigration laws could not touch.

Ignoring citizenship and legal status restrictions may have even led scholars to underestimate the role of Mexican-Anglo relations on more traditional welfare outcomes. We see this most clearly when we look at welfare benefit levels. Scholars have long noted the uniformly low welfare benefits in the South, a fact often blamed on southern whites' reluctance to provide benefits to poor blacks. But we do not find uniformly low benefit levels across the Southwest. In fact, in some southwestern states, Old Age Assistance benefits were among the most generous in the nation. It would be a mistake, however, to conclude that Mexican-Anglo relations were unimportant in shaping the southwestern relief system. Indeed, southwestern states could offer generous Old Age Assistance benefits to white residents and withhold them from Mexicans because

Mexicans were largely excluded by citizenship restrictions that southwestern states were particularly slow to drop. We need to pay closer attention to citizenship and legal status restrictions in social welfare provision, and we should be especially mindful of how these restrictions may interact with more traditional welfare outcomes.

Moving beyond black and white may even help us better understand the treatment of African Americans or the role of the South in welfare state development. The inclusion of white non-citizens in the American welfare state certainly puts the exclusion of black Americans in stark relief and raises important questions about the relationship between formal citizenship, substantive citizenship, and social citizenship that we have not yet fully resolved. What is more, one of the challenges of understanding southern resistance to black inclusion has been finding a way to adjudicate between competing theories that highlight politics, class, race, or other factors. The South was different from the rest of the country on so many dimensions that it is hard to know with any certainty which factor or combination of factors made the difference. Comparing across groups and regions gives us another point of traction on some of these thorny questions.

Three Worlds

This book offers a new perspective that focuses on the intersection of labor, race, and politics, an approach that yields important insights into the role of both race and immigration in welfare state development. Blacks, Mexicans, and European immigrants inhabited three separate worlds in the first third of the twentieth century, each characterized by its own system of race and labor market relations and its own distinct political system. From these worlds—and each group's place within them— three separate perspectives emerged about each group's propensity to become dependent on relief. The distinct political systems, race and labor market relations, and ideologies about each group's proclivity to use relief, in turn, influenced the scope, reach, and character of the relief systems that emerged across American communities.

These three worlds were defined as much by regional political economies as by each group's social position. In 1930, 90 percent of European immigrants lived in the North, 69 percent of blacks lived in the South, and 87 percent of Mexicans lived in the Southwest. Regional differences in labor markets and politics were, in turn, partly products of the differing racial and immigrant concentrations in each region. European immigrants, especially from southeastern Europe, settled in large industrial sections of the Northeast and Midwest and worked primarily in skilled and unskilled manufacturing jobs. Blacks and Mexicans lived largely in rural areas and worked disproportionately in agriculture. But the regions in which blacks and Mexicans lived were governed by starkly different systems of farm-labor relations. The relationship between black tenants and white landlords in the South was shaped by both debt peonage and an ethos of paternalism. Both of these practices developed after emancipation as a way for planters to retain their labor force. Paternalistic landlords provided non-monetary assistance—housing, garden plots, medical care, assistance in old age, and intercession with legal authorities—to loyal and productive workers who displayed the appropriate amount of deference. Though such paternalistic relations could be found in some sections of Texas, much of the West either had never developed such relations or had long abandoned them. Mexicans were more often migrant laborers, unattached to any single employer, and therefore largely outside the system of debt peonage and paternalistic relations.

Blacks, Mexicans, and European immigrants also occupied different positions in America's racial and color hierarchy. Blacks were unambiguously non-white and deemed racially inferior and inassimilable and were subject to exclusion and segregation. Southern and eastern European immigrants were seen as racially distinct from and inferior to northern and western European immigrants. And racism against southern and eastern Europeans led directly to national origin quotas designed to exclude them from the nation. Yet however racially inferior these "new" immigrants were deemed to be, they were nonetheless treated by most American institutions—including the courts, the census, political parties, unions, schools, realtors, and social workers—as white.[23] Race and color at the turn of the twentieth century were not perfect synonyms as they were at the turn of the twenty-first. As a result, southeastern European immigrants could be both white *and* racially inferior to other whites. To the extent that their racial fitness was suspect and their patriotism and allegiance to America questioned, many native-born whites thought these deficiencies required the new immigrants' immediate and thorough assimilation. Mexicans, by contrast, occupied a more liminal position in America's racial and color hierarchy. Guaranteed many of the privileges of whiteness by law, they nonetheless increasingly suffered from many of the liabilities of non-whiteness in practice: separate neighborhoods, separate schools, and separate accommodations, to name a few. But the color line they faced in the Southwest was not as insidious as the one blacks faced in the South. This early liminal status and the growing hardening of opinion that Mexicans were not "really" white and perhaps forever "alien" had important implications for their experience with relief.

Finally, the political context in which each of these groups lived—itself also partly a product of each region's racial and immigrant context—varied significantly and helped shape access to and the development of welfare services. Northeastern cities were often rife with machine politics and other institutions—like settlement houses, unions, and schools—that encouraged the political incorporation of immigrants and sometimes mediated access to relief. Mexicans were far less likely to live in machine cities or in areas with other institutions bent on their assimilation. Cities in the Southwest were more likely to be run by Anglo municipal reformers who worked to pass progressive structural reforms designed to eliminate the "evil" influences of machine politics and especially the power of the immigrant vote. In the South, blacks were largely disenfranchised by poll taxes, literacy tests, and white primaries, tools that were also sometimes used to disenfranchise Mexican Americans. Disenfranchisement led to one-party rule and the election of racially conservative southern Democrats who did their best to maintain the racial, political, and economic status quo.

Because these three groups lived in such distinct worlds, federalism and the local control of relief had profoundly different consequences for each.[24] Blacks and Mexicans had far greater access to services provided directly by the federal government. Whenever local government provided or even administered benefits, blacks and Mexicans were often shut out. In addition, the communities in which Mexicans and especially blacks lived set benefits lower and spent less on welfare. Relief offices in communities with more Mexicans were more prone to cooperate with the Immigration Service and to establish more rigid and unyielding restrictions based on citizenship. Local control did not present problems for European immigrants—even aliens. While the federal government and northern states sometimes passed laws excluding non-citizens from benefits, local administration and control often led to *greater* overall welfare spending, protection from immigration agents and discriminatory legislation, as well as access to quite generous relief assistance, at least by the standards of the day. The consequences of decentralized policymaking were thus not the same for all disadvantaged groups.

The racial, political, and labor market context had a direct influence on access to assistance and on the scope of welfare provision. For example, western grower and southern planter interests influenced local social welfare spending as well as individual access to assistance but in different ways. While southern planters were reluctant to subsidize local relief provision and saw relief as a threat to their labor supply, western growers saw relief as a subsidy to the agricultural industry because it allowed a large pool of migrant workers to remain nearby and at the ready between harvests. As such, western growers sometimes encouraged Mexican migratory laborers to get on the "dole" prior to the New Deal, profoundly influencing the politics of relief provision in the Southwest. Western and southern agricultural elites' attitudes toward relief eventually converged but only after the advent of federal relief drastically altered their incentives. The regional contrast brings the importance of labor market context into strong relief. In addition, differences in political incorporation influenced access to assistance via naturalization rates, as well as through patronage. Because political parties and other institutions failed to incorporate Mexicans, their naturalization rates were extremely low, ensuring that citizenship restrictions, where adopted, would disproportionately affect them. European immigrants were not only encouraged and assisted to naturalize but sometimes rewarded for doing so with patronage jobs or access to social services.

The Role of Social Workers in These Three Worlds

These racial, political, and labor market differences also had a strong indirect effect on access and on welfare state development through its influence on the views and actions of social welfare workers, including caseworkers, relief officials, and reformers. Social workers during this period were typically white, native-born men and women. Many were college educated and had received specialized training volunteering in settlement houses, on the job, or, increasingly, in schools of social work. Social work was in the midst of professionalization in the Progressive Era, as social workers endeavored to carve out their own areas of expertise. As the gatekeepers of relief, they played a crucial role in this story.[25]

Regional political economies and racial regimes influenced public and private social workers' perceptions and characterizations of the three groups. Because planters opposed blacks' use of relief and because white social workers believed they could not assimilate racially, blacks were generally excluded from a host of social services or relegated to underfunded, segregated charities prior to the New Deal. Because of this exclusion, social workers came to see blacks as the group least likely to depend on the dole in the first third of the twentieth century, a belief that was often rationalized on cultural or biological grounds.

Social workers saw Mexicans in a very different light. Because growers were content to let them use relief and because social workers were initially cautiously optimistic that Mexicans could assimilate, Mexicans had greater access to relief than did blacks. But this access came at a price. As social workers grew increasingly pessimistic about the prospect of Mexican assimilation, they also came to believe that Mexicans were lazy, thriftless, and disproportionately dependent on relief. They began to frame Mexicans' use of relief as an illegitimate burden on "American taxpayers" and as a subsidy to the agricultural industry. Social workers exaggerated their use of relief, lobbied for Mexicans' exclusion from the country, and worked with immigration officials to deport those who sought assistance. A lack of political power made it difficult for Mexicans to challenge these constructions and their poor treatment.

Though the public often saw southern and eastern European immigrants as welfare dependent, too, social workers firmly rejected these characterizations. Partly because of the new immigrants' socioeconomic mobility and high naturalization rates, social workers were convinced that these immigrants were capable of assimilation and, with appropriate intervention—even coercion—they would develop into fine Americans. Social workers did not frame the provision of relief to European immigrants as an illegitimate burden; rather, they framed it as the natural humanitarian response, perhaps even necessary for their full Americanization. They lobbied against immigration restrictions that targeted southern and eastern Europeans, selectively cited data to try to convince the public that these immigrants were not dependent on relief, lobbied against citizenship restrictions for assistance, found loopholes in laws that barred non-citizens from work relief, and protected destitute European immigrants from immigration agents.

Though Progressive and New Deal era social workers were profoundly influenced by the worlds in which they lived, they were not simply passive products of their environment, blindly responsive to local public opinion, business interests, or political pressure, although these forces certainly influenced their actions at times. Nor should we think of them simply as "street-level bureaucrats" remaking policies handed down to them. Of course, public relief workers were, in some sense, arms of the state— officials charged with implementing local, state, and, after 1932, federal policies. Whether appointed through patronage or the civil service system, public relief workers often had to answer to elected officials. Elected officials, therefore, had the power to shape the public relief force, not to mention many of the rules and regulations under which they would operate. Yet many relief agencies, especially in the South and Southwest where most blacks and Mexicans lived, were funded by private—not public— funds prior to the Depression. Moreover, public and private relief officials not only tried to resist political interference, they actively constructed populations as deserving or undeserving, wielded data to prove their preconceptions, and made sustained efforts to convince local and national legislators and the broader public of their "expert" opinions. In addition, federal relief officials like Frances Perkins and Harry Hopkins had tremendous influence over the shape of federal legislation. Rather than simply street-level bureaucrats, Progressive and New Deal social workers were also poverty experts, public opinion shapers, advocates, and policymakers. They could be powerful allies or tireless opponents. Which role they chose to adopt often made the difference in which groups got benefits and which groups did not.[26]

One advantage of this three worlds approach is that it helps us think about racial, political, and labor market contexts as whole systems rather than separate, mutually exclusive variables. Previous attempts to explain racial disparities in social welfare provision have sometimes been framed in stark either/or terms: race or class, individual attitudes or institutions. These debates have helped advance our understanding of the determinants of social welfare provision and racial inequality. But they can also at times mask the ways in which race, labor, and politics were so thoroughly entangled in this period. For example, racial attitudes about group welfare use were not simply a reflection of their position in the racial hierarchy. Rather, these attitudes were also informed by local labor relations and the extent of their political incorporation. Mexicans were perceived to be especially "dependent" and an illegitimate burden because assistance was seen as a subsidy to the agricultural industry that encouraged migratory workers to get on relief between harvests. Low naturalization rates confirmed to social workers that Mexicans would never become true Americans and that expulsion was a natural solution. Low rates of naturalization, however, were products of the municipal reform movement's refusal to politically incorporate Mexicans, as well as the severe racism that they faced.

The three worlds approach also highlights the cumulative disadvantages that blacks and Mexicans faced, especially compared to European immigrants. Mexicans and blacks were treated so differently from European immigrants because so many forces were set against them. During the Depression, social workers, politicians, planters, and eventually growers all conspired to exclude them from social assistance—or in the case of Mexicans, expel them from the nation. Not so for European immigrants. Social workers and elected officials often fought for their inclusion, and industrial employers made no special effort to exclude them from relief.

To be clear, this is not a simple story about regional variation; it is that, but it is also much more. Esping-Andersen used the concept of *three worlds* to discuss qualitative differences in the scope, form, and function of welfare provision across three types of countries: liberal, corporatist, and social democratic.[27] Here *three worlds* refers to local and regional differences in political and labor market contexts *as well as* group-level differences in labor market position, political incorporation, and racial or color status. Indeed, while most blacks, Mexicans, and European immigrants lived in different regions of the country, their experiences usually differed markedly from those around them, even within those regions. These differences were sometimes even more pronounced when their co-ethnics represented a large fraction of their community. So while social welfare spending was very low in the South, it was lowest in communities with the most blacks, and poor southern whites still had much greater access to assistance than did poor blacks. Furthermore, their differential treatment was not always confined within the regions in which most of their compatriots lived. Blacks in the North were often served in segregated charities. Midwestern relief agencies joined their southwestern colleagues in targeting Mexicans for repatriation. And European immigrants were not targeted for expulsion in the Southwest.

THE STUDY

This book focuses on blacks, Mexicans, and European immigrants because they were the three largest minority groups in the United States during the Progressive and New Deal eras when the modern American welfare system was coming into being. Much of the debate about immigrants and welfare today remains focused on Mexicans, so understanding their historical treatment is crucial to placing current debates about immigration and welfare in historical context. Comparing Mexicans against blacks and European immigrants, moreover, can help disentangle the effects of race and color from citizenship and legal status. There are important stories to be told about the incorporation of Puerto Ricans, Filipinos, Chinese, Japanese, and Native Americans in the Progressive and New Deal eras, but I must leave those for other scholars to tell.

The conclusions in this book are drawn from analyses of census, public opinion, and city-level relief spending data, alongside in-depth investigation of materials in national, state, and local archives, relief agency reports, congressional hearings and debates, social welfare conference proceedings, and the contents of contemporary journals, popular magazines, and newspapers. The book aims to be national in scope. By aiming for breadth and generalizability, however, I risked losing some of the rich nuance, detail, and traction on causal narrative that comes with case studies of local communities. This proved especially important in investigating the treatment of non-citizens since the subject has received so little scholarly attention. Therefore I sometimes pay special attention in this book to two cities: Los Angeles and Chicago. Each city contained significant numbers of blacks, Mexicans, and European immigrants, helping me further tease apart group- and region-level effects. I chose not to highlight any single southern city because there were no southern cities with sizable Mexican and European immigrant populations. Moreover, though Mexicans in the Southwest often lived in rural areas and worked as migrant laborers, many spent the winter months in cities like Los Angeles, and it was there that they came to the attention of social workers. As my research progressed, however, I discovered that what transpired in these cities was not always representative of what happened in cities within each region. In some ways, Los Angeles and Chicago represent polar extremes of treatment on key issues. I highlight this fact whenever warranted using evidence from other cities.

The story begins in chapter 2, with a detailed description of the three worlds, focused on the factors—labor, race, and politics—that will best explain the differential incorporation of blacks, Mexicans, and European immigrants into the American welfare state and the scope, form, and function of relief provision across regions. Chapter 3 explores the relief systems that had emerged in different parts of the country by the eve of the Great Depression. It describes and explains the racial patterning of local social welfare provision across the 295 largest cities, focusing not only on spending levels but also on the sources of funding. Chapters 4 and 5 examine social workers' views about the welfare dependence of each group prior to the Depression and the degree to which those views reflected, diverged from, or helped shape public opinion. Chapters 6 and 7 look at expulsion, a previously unacknowledged function of the welfare state. Chapter 6 examines variation in the extent to which relief officials cooperated with the Immigration Service to expel dependent aliens, and chapter 7 details variation in relief officials' efforts to use their own funds to expel destitute individuals from the nation. Chapters 8 through 10 focus on the New Deal and how federal intervention affected each group's access to relief. Chapter 8 is centered on the first New Deal and access to Federal Emergency Relief, as well as the Civilian Conservation Corps, the Public Works Administration, and the Civil Works Administration. The subsequent battle over citizenship and legal status restrictions in the Works Progress Administration, and the local implementation of those restrictions, is the subject of chapter 9. Chapter 10 focuses on the Social Security Act and the disparate treatment of blacks, Mexicans, and European immigrants in the administration of Social Security, Unemployment Insurance, Aid to Dependent Children, and Old Age Assistance. The conclusion summarizes the principal findings and offers some reflections on the boundaries of social citizenship and the role of race and immigration in American social welfare provision.

CHAPTER 2

Three Worlds of Race, Labor, and Politics

BLACKS, EUROPEAN IMMIGRANTS, and Mexicans each suffered from significant discrimination at the hands of native-born whites in the early part of the twentieth century. But their treatment in the American welfare system during this period could not have been more different. European immigrants were largely included in the social welfare system, blacks were largely excluded, while Mexicans were often expelled from the nation simply for requesting assistance. How can we best make sense of these different trajectories of inclusion, exclusion, and expulsion? The existing scholarship in the fields of race, labor, and politics offers us important clues. We have excellent studies that focus on one or two groups or on a single location. Yet there has been no systematic, national comparison of these three groups in this period. Regional segregation might explain the dearth of this sort of comparative scholarship. On the eve of the Great Depression, the vast majority of European immigrants lived in the Northeast and Midwest, Mexicans lived overwhelmingly in the Southwest, while most blacks still lived in the South. So different were their experiences with the racial, political, and labor market systems in these regions that these groups could be said to be living in separate worlds.

Blacks typically lived in rural areas and often worked as tenant farmers, laboring under a system of paternalism and debt peonage. Subject to the one-drop rule and increasingly stringent Jim Crow laws, they were also disenfranchised by poll taxes, literacy tests, and white primaries. The result was one-party rule and the domination of the South by racially conservative Democrats. Southern and eastern European immigrants, by contrast, typically lived in large northern cities, toiling in the manufacturing sector. The cities in which they lived were often ruled by machine politics. Though they were subject to discrimination and stereotypes about their alleged racial inferiority, they were nevertheless treated by most major institutions as white. As a result, public schools, unions, politicians, churches, and settlement houses often encouraged their assimilation and political incorporation. Lastly, Mexicans lived mostly in rural areas of the Southwest. Unlike blacks, they were often migrant laborers, unattached to any single employer and therefore outside the system of paternalism and debt peonage. Cities in the Southwest were run by Anglo municipal

TABLE 2.1
Three Worlds Snapshot

	Regional concentration	Labor market context	Political context	Racial/color status
Blacks	69% South	agricultural workers, debt-peonage/ paternalistic system	low political power, white Democratic rule	racially inferior, black, unassimilable
Foreign-born whites	90% North	industrial workers, urbanized setting	moderate/high political power, machine politics	SEEs racially inferior, white, assimilable
Mexicans	87% Southwest	agricultural workers, migratory wage system	low political power, Anglo municipal reform system	racially inferior, white by law/ non-white in practice, liminal

reformers intent on decreasing the power of the immigrant vote. Institutions like the church and the public schools were ambivalent and sometimes downright hostile to their assimilation and political incorporation. While Mexicans were white by law, unlike European immigrants, they were increasingly treated as non-white in practice (see Table 2.1).

There was, of course, much internal variation and heterogeneity within these three worlds, and blacks, Mexicans, and European immigrants were never wholly confined to nor defined by these spaces. The labor historian Lizabeth Cohen, for example, studied black, Mexican, and European immigrant industrial workers in Chicago. And Neil Foley compared the experiences of black, Mexican, and poor white sharecroppers in central Texas. But life in Chicago or central Texas was not typical of life where most of these groups lived. And relatively few Mexicans were sharecroppers or industrial workers. Furthermore, since race, labor, and politics were so closely interconnected, we are better served by examining racial, political, and labor market contexts as whole systems—or worlds—rather than separate, mutually exclusive variables. This chapter explores these three worlds in greater detail. Like Evelyn Nakano Glenn, who compared blacks in the South to Mexicans in the Southwest to the Japanese in Hawaii, it takes a broad, comparative view, across groups and regions, and focuses on the factors—race, labor, and politics—that will best explain their differential incorporation into the American welfare state.[1]

AFRICAN AMERICANS

Labor

By the eve of the Great Depression, there were just under 12 million African Americans in the country, representing almost 10 percent of the population. Nearly 70 percent still lived in the South, typically in rural areas. A disproportionately high share of black men—four out of ten in 1930—worked in agriculture, and more than half of these (53 percent) were classified as farm operators. Very few of these farm operators were landowners; rather, most were either sharecroppers (45 percent) or cash or share tenants (35 percent). Planters had significantly more control over sharecroppers than cash tenants, but the difference was one of degree rather than kind, and the umbrella term "tenant" is often used to speak of all of these types of renting arrangements. Contracts between tenants and planters ran the calendar year, but most of the work on cotton plantations was concentrated during the "planting and hoeing season in the spring and early summer . . . and the picking season in late summer and autumn" and required the labor of the entire household. "Men, women, and children worked from 'can to cain't,'" wrote Leon Litwack, "stooping before the cotton plants, picking the white seedy cotton from the bolls, and placing their harvest in long white sacks strapped over a shoulder."[2]

Black women were an integral part of the home and paid labor force. Forty-five percent of black women labored outside the home compared to only a quarter of other women. The majority (62 percent) worked in domestic and personal service, usually in private homes as maids, cooks, or child nurses. Domestic work was one of the least desirable jobs. It put black women under the constant surveillance of white women, and at risk of sexual advances of white men. Another quarter worked in agriculture, often laboring alongside husbands or other relatives.[3]

During a good year, when cotton prices were at their peak, yearly earnings of tenants might rival those of northern industrial workers. When cotton prices dropped, however, tenants would be lucky if they ended the year with fifty dollars. "Season after season," wrote Neil McMillen, "whatever the fluctuations of the market, croppers with the rarest exceptions remained croppers . . . ending their agricultural year, when they were lucky, with enough cash to retire their debts, buy shoes for their families, and carry them through until the credit season began with spring plowing." Many fared far worse, however, ending the year in debt. Planters supplied their tenants with seed, fertilizer, tools, and other goods on credit—often at exorbitant interest rates. Contracts were often made verbally—not in writing—and all the accounting was handled by the planter, leaving the door open to all manner of "chicanery, larceny . . . and other forms of dishonesty." Since the legal system offered blacks no justice, tenant farmers had no means through which to safely challenge false accounting and so were often forced to stay all the longer. Only at the end of the year, after their debts were settled, could tenants move in search of better terms. If they tried to leave before "settlin' time," they could be arrested, jailed, and forced to work off their debts.[4]

Peonage was prohibited under federal law in 1867, but "enforcement proved exceedingly difficult." One federal investigator estimated that a third of the larger plantations in Alabama, Georgia, and Mississippi were "holding their negro employees to a condition of peonage." Debt, however, was not the only way that planters tried to compel black labor or limit their mobility. Some planters hired "riders" who monitored and meted out "physical punishment on recalcitrant tenants." Vagrancy laws forced "negro loafers to the field." Misdemeanor crimes might be upgraded to felonies with longer jail sentences, and the prisoners were then leased out to private employers. While the "convict lease" system was formally abolished in 1908, it continued to operate through the Great Depression. Minor offenses, such as swearing, were subject to exorbitant fines. Those unable to pay the fines were forced to work them off under guard. Though landowners often went to great lengths to keep black labor immobile, blacks still found ways to move "from plantation to plantation, from state to state and, after World War I, from South to North" in search of better opportunities.[5]

While landlords would provide seed, tools, work animals, and sometimes food and other supplies to sharecroppers on credit, they also sometimes provided paternalistic benefits to their tenants, including housing, garden plots, medical care, assistance in old age, and intercession with legal authorities to loyal and productive workers who displayed the appropriate amount of deference. Employers provided these perquisites as another way to "limit the departure of their own workers from the South." Paternalism was particularly useful in retaining black labor because, according to Lee Alston and Joseph Ferrie, the "rise in virulent racism in the post-Reconstruction period presented planters an opportunity to offer their workers protection from racist violence and the capricious judgments of a racist legal system, in exchange for continued dependable service in the planters' fields." Blacks in the South, for example, often needed to have a character reference from a white man simply to walk through an unknown community without fear of arrest.[6]

While the term "paternalism" might evoke images of noblesse oblige, it was likely often the result of calculated profit considerations. "From the standpoint of the planter, the optimum strategy" was to keep tenants "economically dependent enough to ensure that they would be ready to work whenever labor was needed without creating a sense of hopelessness and frustration great enough to cause them to seek employment elsewhere." Even where paternalism was "guided by . . . their sense of noblesse oblige," the offer of protection was ultimately necessary because of the increasingly hostile environment of the Jim Crow South—"a hostility, which over several decades, the white rural elite was instrumental in creating."[7]

On the face of things, the paternalistic ethos appears to have been widespread among planters. Harold Hoffsommer studied landlords and tenants in Alabama and found that "the conventional attitude of the landlord was that the tenant, and particularly the share-cropper, was dependent on him for direction and aid. More than nine out of every ten landlords interviewed stated that it was one of the functions of the landlord to maintain his tenants, if possible, in times of distress." Though 90 percent of the landlords *said* it was their responsibility to assist their tenants, the same survey showed that just over half the tenants stated that the "landlords [had] always taken care of" them prior to 1933, indicating some lack of correspondence between what employers thought or said they should be doing and what they actually provided. In order to get by, therefore, many tenant families had to find other employment during the "slack season."[8]

Whatever paternalistic benefits black tenants in the South may have received, their living conditions were nothing short of abysmal. Less than a quarter of black households in the South owned their own home, half the rate of whites. Prior to World War I, many tenant houses consisted of no more than one-room unpainted cabins. Overcrowding surpassed that of the "worst tenement districts of New York." The cabins, many once inhabited by slaves, were "always old and bare, built of rough boards, and neither plastered nor ceiled." Houses had few "amenities" beyond the most basic furniture. Many had no sanitary facilities at all, and most had only "unimproved outhouses." Dietary deficiencies were common, contributing to serious health problems. Deaths from typhoid, pellagra, and malaria were especially high. In 1900 infant mortality rates, generally regarded as "one of the most sensitive indicators of the health and well-being of a population," were twice as high among blacks (297 per 1,000 live births) as among native whites (142).[9]

Blacks were not the only ones to work as tenants in the South. Whites made up just under half of all sharecroppers and 70 percent of all non-sharecropper tenants. Still, a majority of sharecroppers in the South were black, and white landlords often evinced a preference for black labor. Stereotypes of blacks as "the workhorse or mule of the South, easily adaptable to the climate and every demand of labor, 'naturally cheerful and contented,'" dominated. Blacks were also thought to be more docile and tractable than whites. According to one Alabama planter, "Give me Negroes every time. I wouldn't have a low-down white tenant on my place. You can get work out of any Negro if you know how to handle him; but there are some white men who won't work and can't be driven, because they are white."[10]

Racial and Color Status

White planters could more easily "handle" and abuse black tenants because of the rigid color line that increasingly divided the Jim Crow South. Jim Crow was a system of state laws and local ordinances and regulations "designed to institutionalize the already familiar customary subordination of black men and women." Before the first laws were put on the books, during Reconstruction and even the first decade of Redemption, segregation was not as systematic and pervasive. Starting in the 1890s, however, any indeterminacy in race relations quickly began to disappear. Growing fears about racial amalgamation and increasing black political and economic power led southern state legislatures and city councils to pass Jim Crow laws and ordinances. Soon "whites only" and "colored" signs littered the southern landscape. Jim Crow came to regulate social interactions in all realms of public and sometimes even private life. There were segregated hospitals, schools, libraries, lavatories, theaters, restaurants, swimming pools, hotels, trains, prisons, and even cemeteries. No situation with potential for contact between the races was immune. In the Mississippi Delta, it was against the law for black motorists to pass whites because "the black man might stir up dust that would get on the white folks." Whites tolerated sex between white men and black women, and rape in such circumstances was virtually never prosecuted. But black men who slept or even flirted with white women risked being castrated or lynched. And all of the states south of the Mason-Dixon Line (plus fourteen others) had miscegenation laws barring blacks and whites from marrying. "There was no apparent tendency toward abatement or relaxation of the Jim Crow code of discrimination and segregation in the 1920s," wrote C. Vann Woodward, "and none in the thirties until well along in the depression years."[11]

Violations of these codes as well as unwritten rules of etiquette were met by insults and humiliation, jail sentences, threats, and brutal violence. Between 1889 and 1931, more than 3,200 individuals, by one estimate, were lynched in the South. Blacks were not the only victims of lynching, but they were the overwhelming target. The mob members who participated in lynchings did not fear reprisals for their actions since southern courts upheld Jim Crow, too. Even federal courts provided little relief. Northerners had proved their reluctance to interfere in the southern race question when the federal government pulled out of the South in 1877. And the Supreme Court explicitly sanctioned Jim Crow laws in their 7–1 decision in *Plessy v. Ferguson* (1896), which upheld the principle of "separate but equal."[12]

Jim Crow laws and customs made no distinctions between blacks. Whether educated or illiterate, dark or light skinned, all those classified as "black" were subject to the same strictures. According to the historian J. Douglas Smith, "custom and belief dictated to all white southerners that 'one drop' defined a black person," even if state law at times "said otherwise." In 1930 the one-drop rule was formally adopted by the U.S. Census, which for the first time clarified that "A person of mixed white and Negro blood should be returned as a Negro, no matter how small the percentage of Negro blood."[13]

Jim Crow practices were not limited to the South. In the North and the West, many public accommodations excluded or segregated black patrons. And across the country, blacks were often the last hired and first fired. When they could find employment, it was usually at lower pay and in the least skilled jobs regardless of their actual skill level.[14] Residential segregation was a growing problem, too. Racially restrictive housing covenants "spread widely throughout the United States" after 1910, "and they were employed frequently and with considerable effectiveness to maintain the color line until 1948, when the U.S. Supreme Court declared them unenforceable." Other methods used to enforce housing segregation included violence, deed restrictions, and discriminatory real estate practices. "Crowding black people into a separate section of the city was a tremendous civic project," wrote Thomas Philpott. "It involved every form of social action, from naked terrorism to economic discrimination to the might of the law. It was done by countless individuals, but also by banks and realty firms, neighborhood organizations, and government officials. Churches, hospitals, charity societies, and social agencies down to the Boy Scouts and Girl Scouts all took part in it." They all helped draw "the color line."[15]

Politics

Though "the problem of the color line" was a national phenomenon, the exceptionally rigid line of the South was built thanks in part to the unique political context there, marked by the wholesale exclusion of blacks from electoral politics and by one-party rule of racially conservative southern Democrats. The move to restrict access to the franchise was led in part by fear of "Negro domination" of party politics in the wake of Reconstruction and the Fifteenth Amendment, which prohibited denying the right to vote on the "grounds of race, color, or previous condition of servitude."

Granted access to the franchise, blacks declared their allegiance to the party of Lincoln, voted in large numbers, and were appointed and elected to local, state, and national offices, a situation that threatened the foundations of white supremacy. When the federal government withdrew its troops from the South in 1877, white southerners sought to "redeem" the region from Republican rule, and they used the threat of black domination to help enact suffrage restrictions. Led by Mississippi, the year 1890 "marked the beginning of systematic efforts by southern states to disfranchise black voters legally." By 1910 almost every southern state had adopted some combination of cumulative poll taxes, residency tests, registration requirements, and literacy tests, all with a mind to eliminate blacks from politics without running afoul of the Fifteenth Amendment.[16]

Most of these restrictions on the franchise also had the power to disqualify many poor and illiterate whites. To allay their fears, those who advocated a limited franchise promised that their intent was to disenfranchise every Negro "and as few white people as possible." Toward that end, states adopted "grandfather," "understanding," or "character" clauses that allowed local voting registrars discretion to ensure that whites could still participate in the political process. Voting registrars had so much discretion under these laws that even "an i not dotted or a t not crossed" was enough for a registrar to "disqualify 'em." Despite the public reassurances, poor and illiterate whites were still sometimes disenfranchised. But the primary aim and effect of these laws was the thorough disenfranchisement of African Americans.[17]

When blacks were barred from voting by literacy tests and poll taxes, these exclusions had to at least give the appearance of complying with the Fifteenth Amendment. But while the state could not enact laws disenfranchising blacks simply because they were black, the Democratic Party, as a private organization, it was reasoned, was not similarly prohibited. As a result, the "white primary" was born through which the Democratic Party prohibited the participation of blacks in primary elections. Since only whites could choose the Democratic candidate in the primary and since the South was essentially a one-party system, the white primary served to exclude blacks almost entirely from the political process.[18]

These suffrage restrictions were extremely effective. "In the South as a whole," according to Alexander Keyssar, "post-Reconstruction turnout levels of 60 to 85 percent fell to 50 percent for whites and single digits for blacks." With the black electorate decimated and the Republican Party "rendered virtually insignificant," the Democrats were the only party left standing in the South. And throughout the first third of the twentieth century, the South voted consistently for the Democrats in every presidential election (see Figure 2.1). In South Carolina, Mississippi, and Louisiana—

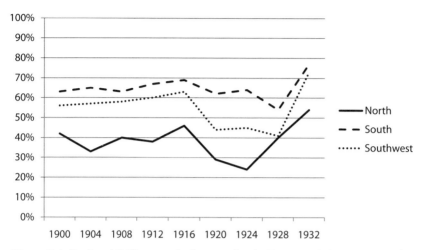

Figure 2.1: Regional Differences in Support for the Democratic Party in Presidential Elections, 1900–1932

Source: Historical Statistics of the United States, Colonial Times to 1970 (Washington, DC: GPO, 1975).

states with the largest black populations—the fraction of voters who supported the Democratic candidate averaged over 80 percent. "By 1920," noted Gunnar Myrdal, "in recognition of its lack of significance in the South, the Republican party practically abandoned primaries and often did not even put up candidates in the general election." As a result, the only real political competition was in the Democratic primary, from which blacks were barred from voting. The lack of political competition gave southerners tremendous power at the federal level. Southern whites displayed a united front in national politics, reelecting racially conservative Democrats to Congress, thereby gaining leadership positions in key congressional committees and wielding disproportionate influence in national affairs.[19]

Without access to the franchise, blacks had little hope of being elected or appointed to local and state offices. Between 1900 and 1965 "only whites held elective office in Mississippi, and blacks were denied state appointments even as notaries public." In Virginia, a nominee for governor in 1921 could reassure white voters in his state that no black man had held office in Virginia for the past thirty years. Indeed, when Chicago's Oscar De Priest was elected to Congress in 1928, he was the only black man to hold that office since 1901. And it was not until 1945 that another African American was elected to Congress.[20]

EUROPEAN IMMIGRANTS

Mirroring the size of the black community, by 1930 there were nearly twelve million European immigrants in America, representing almost 10 percent of the population, a little over half (54 percent) of whom were southern and eastern European. Most of these immigrants came through Ellis Island. Some took to the rails and headed west, but most "new immigrants"—as southern and eastern Europeans were often called— arrived between 1890 and 1920, a time when "opportunities to settle agricultural areas" had already declined, and there was little industry to draw them west of the Mississippi. The new immigrants were also reluctant to cross the Mason-Dixon Line. In the South, they found few opportunities for upward mobility, "relatively undeveloped transportation, communication, and education infrastructures," and high levels of nativism and an uncertain—and worrisome—position in the region's racial hierarchy. For these reasons, almost nine out of ten southern and eastern European immigrants lived in the Northeast and Midwest in 1930, the overwhelming majority (83 percent) in urban areas.[21]

Labor

As an urban labor force, many European immigrants worked in garment factories, meatpacking houses, and iron, steel, rubber, and automobiles factories. By the eve of the Great Depression, nearly half of all foreign-born white males worked in manufacturing and mechanical industries, compared to only a quarter of black men. Only 10 percent worked in agriculture. The new immigrants typically started off in unskilled or semi-skilled jobs. Workdays were often long and working conditions could be abysmal. Factory workers typically toiled amid extreme heat or cold, stench, deafening noise, or dust. They suffered from skin ulcers and infections, burns, rheumatism, and lung diseases and were always on guard against accidents that might take life or limb. In 1907 there were nearly three hundred industrial fatalities in the state of Illinois alone.[22]

In the decades after 1900, there were dramatic improvements in working conditions in many factories, shorter hours, and a considerable amount of socioeconomic mobility among the new immigrants. With greater time in the United States, southern and eastern European immigrants, but especially the second generation, were able to move out of the mostly unskilled jobs that they held at the turn of the century and into the semi-skilled and skilled positions and professional occupations. Where two-thirds of European immigrant workers in the steel industry held unskilled jobs in 1910, that proportion was down to less than half by 1930. The new immigrants were also soon placed in positions of some authority, getting jobs as foremen and work supervisors in the Midwest's packinghouses and steel plants, where they could help their countrymen get jobs. Despite important labor victories—a shorter workday chief among them—workers continued to agitate against the seven-day work weeks during peak periods, layoffs during slow periods, dangerous and unhealthy working conditions, and low pay.[23]

Largely in response to labor militancy during World War I, some larger employers began providing corporate welfare benefits to their employees. Benefits included sickness pay, free medical care, life insurance, pensions, paid vacations, assistance in buying homes, and employee stock owner-ship plans. With these benefits, employers hoped to encourage the "faith-ful service" of their employees and decrease labor turnover and militancy. Corporate welfare benefits were not widely adopted, however, and even where they were they did not prove to be the panacea employers antici-pated. Many workers stayed with a company for a year or two and then moved to find better conditions.[24]

While there were virtually no differences in labor force participation among black and European immigrant men—virtually all those of work-ing age were in the labor force—there were big differences in the labor force participation rates of women. While 45 percent of black women worked outside the home, only 21 percent of foreign-born white women did the same. Part of the difference can be explained by marriage rates, but even among those who were married, foreign-born white women were far less likely than black women to work outside the home (8 per-cent versus 29 percent, respectively). Immigrant women in the paid labor force typically worked as machine operatives (26 percent) or in the do-mestic (23 percent) or commercial service sector (15 percent). Chicago's Italian working women found work in the garment industry or in the "candy, paper, or tobacco factories. Others worked at home making ar-tificial flowers, knitting lace, or picking and cracking nuts. Whether la-boring at home or in a factory, these women worked long hours, under sweatshop conditions, with little pay."[25]

Most industrial workers lived with their families near their jobs, mak-ing "their homes in the shadow of the steel mills, behind the stockyards, or a walk away from the garment factory." They often lived in immigrant enclaves, centered around a national parish or synagogue, which were replenished—at least until immigration restriction in the 1920s—by new migration. None of these neighborhoods were homogeneous. Even neigh-borhoods identified with a national origin group, like "Little Italy," were often less than 50 percent Italian. In fact, many of these neighborhoods were quite diverse, with an average of twenty or more different national origin groups all living in the same community.[26]

Jacob Riis is famous for chronicling the lives of New York's "other half," the "twelve hundred thousand" tenement dwellers living in slums. The tenements he photographed were typically brick buildings, four to six stories high: "Four families occupy each floor, and a set of rooms consist of one or two dark closets, used as bedrooms, with a living room twelve feet by ten." There was little light, ventilation, or privacy. Tenement houses in Chicago also tended to be dark, stuffy, and cramped. Outdoor privies, open sewers, factory pollution, and trash-strewn streets made for unsanitary conditions and a stench that was unbearable, particularly in the stiflingly hot summer months. Settlement house workers documented high rates of tuberculosis and intestinal disorders and typhoid outbreaks, and described Chicago's tenement dwellers as "noticeably undersized and unhealthy" and their babies as "starved and wan." But social workers may have exaggerated the extent of morbidity. When federal officials surveyed tenement residents, asking if they were suffering from disease, "the people overwhelmingly replied no." Infant mortality rates varied by immigrant group: in 1900, the rate was 142 deaths per 1,000 live births for native whites, compared to 112 for Poles, 113 for Hungarians, 159 for Germans, 170 for the Irish, and 189 for Italians—all significantly lower than the rate among blacks (297).[27]

On the whole, the working and living conditions of European immigrants improved in the first three decades of the twentieth century, and these immigrants made important socioeconomic gains. By 1930 a slightly larger proportion of foreign-born white households (52 percent) owned their own homes than did their native-born white counterparts (49 percent). By the eve of the Great Depression, the infant mortality rate among European immigrants had fallen dramatically and converged with that of native-born whites. Life was not easy for these immigrants, especially those too poor to leave the tenements. But before the stock market crashed in 1929, European immigrants had reason to hope that living conditions would continue to improve and that through toil and sacrifice, they—or certainly their children—might one day leave the slum.[28]

Racial and Color Status

One reason they could leave the slums is that European immigrants did not face a rigid color line. Poverty may have temporarily trapped many European immigrants in the slums, but it was color that locked blacks in the ghetto. Indeed, for all of the discussion among historians about whether the new immigrants had to "work toward whiteness," a wide range of evidence suggests that southern and eastern European immigrants were, in fact, "white on arrival." The new immigrants were consistently classified as "white" by the census. They were also considered "white" for the purposes of naturalization law and therefore racially eligible for citizenship.[29]

To be sure, there were challenges to southern and eastern European immigrants' status as whites. The new immigrants were sometimes portrayed in popular discourse or popular culture as a little less than white, or at least a few shades off: "swarthy," "dark white," or "dark-complected." Some were directly equated with blacks. Southern and eastern Europeans were "refused admission to a movie theater or restaurant on occasion," but they were not systematically excluded by "whites only" signs on public accommodations; nor were they placed in segregated hospitals, jails, military units, or cemeteries as were blacks. In 1903 the Democratic Party in Louisiana "attempted to exclude Italians . . . from voting in their 'white primaries' since they did not qualify on color grounds." But the attempt was unsuccessful. On the whole, the new immigrants, according to Thomas Guglielmo, were "largely accepted as white by the widest variety of people and institutions—naturalization laws and courts, the U.S. census, race science, anti-immigrant racialisms, newspapers, unions, employers, neighbors, realtors, settlement houses, politicians, and political parties."[30]

That southern and eastern Europeans were largely treated as white does not mean that they were not perceived to be racially inferior and subject to sometimes virulent discrimination based on race (as well as religion, citizenship status, and nativity). Race and color were not perfectly synonymous terms in the first third of the twentieth century. "Color" was typically used to designate groups like "whites" or "blacks" or what some called "natural races." Race was used to designate groups like Italians, Mexicans, Hebrews, the French, Negroes, or Americans, terms that might sound to our contemporary ear as different nationalities or ethnicities. Yet the concept of race was distinct from nationality and ethnicity as we now understand it, in that the traits associated with the "English" or "Italian" race were seen as biologically based and heritable. As a result, one could be categorized as both "white" and, because a member of the southern Italian race, racially inferior to other whites. Naturalization applications through much of the early twentieth century, in fact, had lines for both the applicant's "race" and "color." Therefore, when Guglielmo examined these forms, he found that "while Italians were defined *racially*" as northern or southern Italians, "their *color* status was always 'white.'"[31]

There is, of course, ample evidence that the new immigrants were widely perceived to be *racially* inferior and undesirable immigrants. Eugenicists, popular in the early twentieth century, declared that southern and eastern Europeans were members of inferior races and fanned fears of "race suicide." The census consistently categorized all European immigrants as

white, but the superintendent of the 1870 and 1880 censuses also famously described southern and eastern European immigrants as "beaten
men from beaten races; representing the worst failures in the struggle for
existence." The census devoted many pages to detailed analyses of these
groups, broken down by nativity, foreign parentage, and mother tongue,
reflecting some of the anxiety that surrounded the large-scale migration
of the new immigrants. Congress even considered whether to insert a
category called "race or peoples" in the 1910 census, which would sepa-
rately enumerate, for example, members of the Polish or German races.
The proposed census distinction between "race or peoples" on the one
hand and nationality on the other was supposed to help with such "problems" of identifying whether an individual from Russia, for example, was
"a Finn or a Pole or a Jew"—a distinction that some thought indicated
something important about the individual's "moral, mental, and physical
characteristics." The Dillingham Commission, charged with investigating
the conditions of migrants from southern and eastern Europe, justified
the term in the *Dictionary of Races and Peoples* (1911) as a popular—not
scientific—designation largely synonymous with language and geogra-
phy. "Race or peoples" distinctions among whites, where they were used,
were generally dropped after the first or second generation. And this proposed "race or peoples" category, which was never adopted, would not
have supplanted southern and eastern European immigrants' color designation as "white." Indeed, Joel Perlmann noted that in the congressional
discussions over the 1910 census, "the peoples of southern and eastern
Europe are not 'in between' in the sense of being situated outside the
white race"; "there seems to be no doubt as to where Poles, Magyars,
Jews and others fit with regard to color divisions." They were white.[32]

Popular opinion, meanwhile, clearly placed southern and eastern Europeans below northern and western Europeans in terms of all measures
of desirability. In 1924 more than 1,700 college students were questioned
about their views on forty different racial groups. Where 60 percent of
respondents were comfortable with a close kinship by marriage with
northern and western Europeans, only 11 percent felt the same about
southern and eastern Europeans. And while 84 percent were happy to
have the old immigrants as neighbors, only 27 percent felt the same about
southern and eastern Europeans. But these attitudes were not institutionalized in laws or firm or enduring social practices, prohibiting marriage
or prescribing segregated residential neighborhoods. While it may have
briefly been a taboo for European immigrants to marry outside of their
racial, religious, or national origin group, it was not a crime, and intermarriage rates gradually increased. Similarly, there were few serious
attempts to bar European immigrants from native white neighborhoods.
Except for Jews, who due to anti-Semitism were sometimes singled out

alongside blacks in certain housing covenants, the new immigrants were, for all intents and purposes, "welcomed as 'white' and as fit neighbors in the grassroots campaigns to blanket whole urban areas with (racial) covenants."[33]

There is some evidence of discrimination in the labor market, but it was nowhere near as extensive as for blacks. At times because they were deemed to be racially inferior, or because they were not citizens, or due to religious bigotry, and occasionally because they were not seen to be white, employers paid southern and eastern Europeans lower wages than native-born whites, placed them in dirtier and more dangerous jobs, and occasionally barred them altogether. Southern and eastern European immigrants were also sometimes the subject of violence and even, at times, lynching. As John Higham explained, the period from 1920 through 1924 saw a resurgence of "racial nativism," with increasing focus on eugenic thinking, and the emergence of the Ku Klux Klan, a group that targeted not only blacks but Catholics, Jews, and the new immigrants more generally. But Klan activity was strongest in places where European immigrants were more sparsely settled: in small towns and rural areas, and in the South. These were areas where blacks predominated. Ultimately, growing nativism and racism directed against the new immigrants led Congress to pass the 1921 and 1924 Immigration Acts, which placed quotas on the number of southern and eastern Europeans allowed to enter the country. As a result, migration from those parts of the world was reduced to a trickle. This was probably the most important legacy of nativist and racist sentiment during this period. But for immigrants who had arrived prior to 1924 or for the few who managed to enter after, there was no rigid color line to straddle, and the racial discrimination to which they were subject did not lead to the same kind of social and political exclusion that blacks experienced.[34]

Politics

The difference in the political contexts in the North and South could indeed scarcely have been greater. Perhaps nowhere is this more evident than in a comparison of the levels of electoral participation in these regions. During the first third of the twentieth century, electoral participation in the North was roughly double that of the South (see Figure 2.2). Voter participation was higher in the North because there were fewer suffrage restrictions and greater political competition. Far fewer states in the North had literacy tests, poll taxes, or onerous registration requirements, and there were no white primaries.[35]

The North was, of course, not without voting restrictions. A few northern states and towns had poll taxes or property requirements for state or

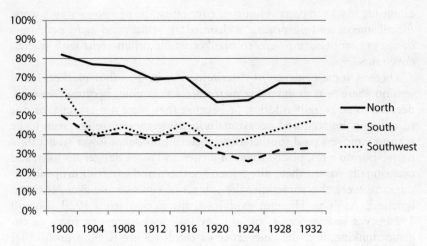

Figure 2.2: Regional Differences in Voter Participation in Presidential Elections, 1900–1932

Source: Historical Statistics of the United States, Colonial Times to 1970 (Washington, DC: GPO, 1975).

municipal elections, but these were not common. Far more common were pre-election day registration laws, which were "spearheaded by middle-class reformers" "to limit corruption and reduce the electoral strength of immigrants, blacks and political machines." Some northern states barred paupers from voting, while others had literacy requirements, which often required prospective voters to read the state or federal constitution. According to the 1930 census, virtually all native-born whites and naturalized northwestern Europeans old enough to vote were literate and English speaking. Though direct evidence is not available, English literacy tests would have likely disadvantaged southern and eastern Europeans. Among naturalized citizens old enough to vote, 4 percent of those born in southern and eastern Europe could not speak English (nearly all of whom were women granted derivative citizenship) and 10 percent were illiterate. While literacy tests and registration laws were sometimes inspired by anti-immigrant sentiment, there were also restrictions that specifically targeted naturalized citizens or religious minorities. This included a requirement to present one's naturalization papers to election officials before registering or voting—the law in Connecticut, Massachusetts, New York, Ohio, Pennsylvania, and Rhode Island, among others. A few states required immigrants to wait thirty to ninety days after naturalizing before they could cast their ballot. And in an effort to disenfranchise Jewish residents, many of whom were Socialist, New York City tried to hold registration on the Sabbath and on Yom Kippur. Such restrictions were typically passed in states with large non-citizen populations, mostly with the support of Republicans, rural legislators, and middle-class independent reformers.[36]

But even though some northern states had suffrage restrictions, they did not compare to those found in the South. In some places, political machines prevented the adoption of suffrage restrictions. Where the laws were in place, "party allegiance protected immigrant voters from strict enforcement." Moreover, prospective voters who failed New York's literacy test could make use of the free adult education programs and retake the exam the following year. Many scholars have argued, in fact, that suffrage restrictions had little effect on voter turnout in the North. "What transpired in the southern states was far more draconian, sweeping, and violent," wrote Alexander Keyssar: "The disenfranchisement was massive rather than segmented, the laws were enforced brutally, and they were always administered with overtly discriminatory intent. In New York and Massachusetts, an illiterate immigrant could gain the franchise by learning to read; for a black man in Alabama, education was beside the point whatever the law said."[37]

In fact, at the same time that states in the South were working to deny blacks the franchise, some states still allowed non-citizens to vote. In 1875 twenty-two states granted the franchise to non-citizen declarants—individuals who had filed their "first papers" declaring their intention to naturalize. While these states had repealed their alien suffrage laws by the eve of the Great Depression, 56 percent of southern and eastern European and 73 percent of northern and western European immigrants had already naturalized by that time. Differences in naturalization rates between the new and old immigrants were partly a function of the length of time these immigrants had lived in the United States. Lack of literacy or English-language skills also played a significant role.[38]

Political machines in the Northeast and Midwest also encouraged naturalization and political participation relative to other regions. Dominant or entrenched political machines could be found in cities like Cincinnati, Dayton, Kansas City, Jersey City, New York, Rochester, Albany, Philadelphia, Pittsburgh, and Pawtucket. But many more northern cities were home instead to competing ward-level machines that vied for political control. Chicago, for example, was rife with ward-level party politics up until the Democratic machine finally became dominant in 1932. The strength of ward-level machine politics can be measured indirectly by looking at the adoption of municipal reforms like commission or council manager style government, and non-partisan or at-large elections, reforms specifically designed to "erode the ties of party" and decrease the power of machine politicians. Cities with the largest numbers of white immigrants were those least likely to adopt these municipal reforms and therefore most influenced by party politics.[39]

These regional differences in the penetration of machine politics are an important feature of the political landscape across these three worlds. In many cities, political machines provided important services for immigrants, assisting them in navigating the complex maze of institutions. Politicians might serve as an interpreter, "fix" a property tax, assist a sick resident in obtaining medical care, secure a needed birth certificate, find legal aid, or procure an exemption from city ordinances. For the immigrant, the biggest prize was the patronage job. In return for it, ward residents were expected to vote for the machine candidate. Politicians also provided direct assistance in helping immigrants naturalize. This was a service that one Chicago precinct worker felt "particularly impressed the voters in his locality." Party workers could fill out naturalization papers, act as witnesses, teach immigrants English, and coach them for the naturalization test. In addition, the party worker might speak "to the naturalization examiner in behalf of the declarant, [and] pays his fees." In fact, more than 70 percent of Chicago's "Democratic precinct captains in 1928 reported assisting their constituents with naturalization." Party workers in other cities often did the same.[40]

Political machines did not attempt to bring every ward member to the polls, however. Especially once political machines were entrenched and faced little competitive pressure, they had no need to expend scarce resources on naturalizing new voters; they needed only to focus on those whom they could count on voting the right way. Furthermore, political machines were often controlled by the Irish, who were not always keen to provide patronage to new immigrants. Nevertheless, political machines did make efforts to incorporate new immigrants, especially when one immigrant group came to dominate a ward, where party competition was strongest, and the local boss found it necessary to court the group in order to keep his grip on the reins of power. In Chicago, machine politicians at times "lavished" Italians with political appointments, "especially just before an election." In 1894 there were so many Italians on the city payroll that they hired a full-time interpreter.[41]

Municipal reformers feared that "ignorant foreigners" voted in large numbers and wielded disproportionate political influence. But it was not until the late 1920s and the Depression years that their political power really took hold. A study of the 1923 Chicago mayoral election, for example, showed that while new immigrants made up about 10 percent of the city's eligible voting population, they made up 20 percent of the non-voters. Turnout among first- and second-generation immigrants—new immigrants included—increased significantly in

1928 with the candidacy of Al Smith and remained high throughout the 1930s as southern and eastern Europeans flocked to the polls to support FDR.[42]

Especially where there was strong party competition and concerted efforts to elect their own to public office, new immigrants gained descriptive representation in state and local government. They were appointed to the Board of Public Education and County Department of Public Works, and elected to the City Council, County Commissioners, and state legislature. Some served as aldermen in their wards. A few even managed to gain significant political power, including Anton Cermak, the Bohemian immigrant who became mayor of Chicago in 1931, and Fiorello La Guardia, the son of Italian immigrants who was elected mayor of New York in 1933 in an election in which four of the five candidates were sons of immigrants and the fifth was the Communist candidate. The new immigrants were less successful at the national level. Aside from German Jews, who were well represented in Congress and appointive office, relatively few southern and eastern Europeans were elected to Congress or served in the president's cabinet or on the federal judiciary.[43]

Even if machines did not everywhere work to incorporate immigrants, there were other forces in the North, especially during and after World War I, that worked to accomplish similar ends. John Higham traced the Americanization movement's origins to settlement houses and patriotic organizations near the turn of the century. Settlement houses not only provided immigrants with English and naturalization classes, they served as a clearinghouse of information for immigrants and helped them navigate city agencies. By 1917 the YMCA was providing English and civic classes and reaching tens of thousands of immigrants each year. In 1911 the International Institute was founded in New York as a division of the YWCA to assist immigrant women. By 1925 there were International Institutes in forty-seven cities.[44]

The workplace was another important site of political education and incorporation. When the United States entered World War I, immigration abruptly slowed and businesses looked for ways to deal with the labor shortage. To promote morale and increase efficiency, some employers started factory classes on English and naturalization and subsidized public evening schools. In Detroit the chief naturalization examiner visited several plants, and afterward, the employers took "the applicants for citizenship papers down to the government offices . . . at the expense of the company, and on the company's time." All of Chicago's large manufacturers, according to Lizabeth Cohen, "turned corners of their factory floors into classrooms and substituted English primers for machine tools several hours a week." The National Association of Manufacturers and the U.S. Chamber of Commerce urged their members to sponsor Americanization classes, and by 1919 they could be found in more than eight hundred plants. Coworkers and foremen also taught the new immigrants English and provided lessons in political socialization. Some labor unions even provided their members with optional English and naturalization classes.[45]

Between 1855 and 1922, an alien woman who was racially qualified for naturalization automatically gained citizenship if she married a U.S. citizen. But various organizations, like settlement houses, churches, and women's clubs, helped in the political incorporation of women, especially after women won the right to vote in 1920. The Catholic Church, for example, provided immigrant women with space to gather and discuss common problems, learn about the American political system, and gain leadership skills. Catholic women's clubs lobbied against immigration restriction, conducted voter registration drives, and got coreligionists to the polls.[46]

Compulsory education, enforced by truant officers, also helped in the political incorporation of immigrant children. Unlike blacks, who were taught in segregated and vastly inferior schools if they were provided schools at all, European immigrants were encouraged by white reformers to send their children to public schools. These schools, in turn, brought first- and second-generation children into contact with American culture and taught them—at times painful—lessons in American citizenship. Cultural assimilation was sometimes force-fed. Teachers in New York City sent their students home with loyalty pledges for their parents to sign. By 1923 thirty-nine states required public schools to teach "citizenship" and thirty-five states required English-only instruction. Where racism against blacks led to segregation and political expulsion, racism and anti-immigrant sentiment against the new immigrants required the stripping of their cultural heritage and, at times, coerced social and political incorporation.[47]

The coercive elements of these Americanization efforts increased during World War I. The "100 percent Americanism" movement mostly targeted Germans, who were forced to abandon their language, their German schools, and their newspapers. But after the war, the targets of nativism broadened. The immediate postwar period saw an increase in citizenship requirements for certain professions or union membership. Some businesses would only promote employees who were citizens or declared their intention to become citizens. Naturalization requirements grew more restrictive. In 1918 Congress passed the Revenue Act, which doubled the income tax rate on non-resident aliens. Congress also threatened to deport all immigrants who refused to naturalize. While the proposal did not pass, deportations of European immigrants increased significantly, fueled in part by the Red Scare. At the same time, however, there were also more benign methods of encouraging naturalization. The federal Bureau of Education established the Division of Immigrant Education, which funded English-language, literacy, and civics instruction. The Bureau of Naturalization also encouraged civic education among immigrants and cooperated with local school officials in two thousand communities to ensure they had lists of immigrant children coming under the compulsory school attendance law as well as adults eligible for citizenship classes.[48]

The forces at work in encouraging the political incorporation of European immigrants were many. Political machines, churches, unions, public officials, schools, and settlement houses used a range of methods, including the payment of naturalization fees, persuasion, paternalistic admonitions, material and symbolic incentives, and even threats and compulsion. European immigrants at times resisted efforts at Americanization by refusing to enroll in such programs or protesting the calls to renounce their citizenship or abandon their culture.[49] This process of Americanization and civic and political incorporation was by no means always very pleasant. But the naturalization of more than 1.2 million southern and eastern European immigrants between 1923 and 1931 alone helped set the stage for the dramatic increase in their political engagement by the 1930s.[50] More important, it stood in sharp contrast to the treatment afforded blacks. At a time when white Americans in the South were working to achieve the wholesale exclusion of blacks from American political and civic life, many of their counterparts in the North were virtually pushing and dragging European immigrants to jump into the American melting pot.

MEXICANS

According to the U.S. Census, by 1930 there were roughly 1.4 million Mexicans and Mexican Americans living in the United States, representing 1.2 percent of the total population. While significant Mexican colonies developed in parts of the Midwest, the vast majority of Mexicans (87 percent) still lived in the Southwest in 1930. Most of these were first- or second-generation immigrants who had arrived since World War I, pulled by a seemingly insatiable demand for their labor and pushed by economic and political conditions in Mexico. But Mexicans had lived in what is now the American Southwest since before the United States acquired the territory in the Mexican-American War.[51]

Labor

Like blacks, more than half (52 percent) of Mexicans living in the United States lived in rural areas, and 40 percent of Mexican males in the labor force in 1930 worked in agriculture. However, the structure of farm-labor relations in the Southwest was very different than in the South. Though peonage and paternalistic relations could be found in some sections of Texas and New Mexico, much of the West either never developed such relations or had long abandoned them. Mexicans were more likely to be migrant laborers, unattached to any single employer, and therefore largely outside the system of debt peonage and paternalistic relations. Thus while the majority of black male agricultural workers were classified by the census as farm operators—usually tenants or sharecroppers—only 21 percent of Mexicans were so classified. Instead, Mexican agricultural workers were far more likely than their black counterparts to work for wages (69 percent versus 28 percent, respectively).[52]

The production process in the Southwest was different than in the South. The rapid irrigation of the arid Southwest and the development of large-scale, labor-intensive agriculture required "an abundant, mobile, and cheap farm labor force." While western growers might employ a few farmhands year-round, they needed large numbers of temporary farm laborers for periodic labor-intensive tasks. Sugar beet farmers in Colorado needed laborers in the spring to block and thin the beets and again in the fall to harvest them. But during this six-month period, migrants might work for just fifty days. According to Mark Reisler, "No large, indigenous labor supply was present in the sparsely populated Southwest" and so growers "looked toward Mexico for workers to perform back-breaking tasks in desert heat." Mexicans were deemed necessary to fill this role because they represented a virtually unlimited labor supply, they worked for low wages, and they were reputed to be a tractable labor force. Growers also argued that there was something deep inside Mexicans that made them "want" to roam from farm to farm in search of work. "White and Negro labor," by contrast, seemed to be "less nomadic."[53]

Work conditions for Mexican migrants were difficult, characterized by long hours, monotonous tasks, low pay, underemployment, and hard labor. Blocking and thinning beets, for example, required either "working in a stooped position" or "moving through the rows on . . . hands and knees." Anglo growers described Mexican bodies as perfectly adapted to the rigors of field work, and their darker skin was seen as a distinct advantage for laboring in the scorching sun. The more Mexicans dominated an occupation the more those occupations came to be seen as "Mexican jobs." As a result, the farm-labor market in the Southwest was stratified: "almost all field labor was done by Mexicans, while most agricultural foremen were Anglos." Mexicans repeatedly frustrated their employers when they defied stereotypes and demanded better pay and working conditions. Employers sometimes retaliated by calling the Immigration Service. A Los Angeles Chamber of Commerce official, in fact, explained that Mexicans were a superior choice to southern blacks, Puerto Ricans, and Filipinos because, should any of these groups come to present a severe problem for relief agencies, "the Mexican may be deported; the Filipino, the American, and Porto Rican negroes are American citizens and could not be deported."[54]

Unlike southern planters who often espoused an ethos of paternalism, western growers did not believe it was their responsibility to care for their laborers year-round. Comparing his region to the situation in the Southwest, Congressman Samuel Rutherford (D-GA) noted that southerners would have a shortage of labor too "if we undertook to employ a man a month or two and then let him go. . . . That is what makes expensive farming in my part of the country. We try to take care of those colored people 12 months of the year." That is not to say that Mexican laborers did not receive any perquisites from their employers—they did. Mexican laborers sometimes received housing, credit, or assistance in times of emergency. However, Mexicans rarely received these benefits year-round, and, at least in the twentieth century, the character of the relationship between Mexican laborers and their employers was rarely called paternalistic. A grower in California described the limits of his obligation to his Mexican migratory workers: "They have finished harvesting my crops. I will kick them out on the country road. My obligation is ended." The social critic Carey McWilliams, who exposed the harsh labor conditions endured by the Southwest's migrant farm laborers during the Depression, overheard a ranch foreman tell a Mexican worker: "When we want you, we'll call you; when we don't—git."[55]

A good measure of paternalism, according to Alston and Ferrie, is the fraction of farm wages paid in perquisites—or non-cash benefits—including board, shelter, food, the privilege of keeping livestock, garden space, use of the employer's horses or mules, use of the employer's farm tools and vehicles, garage space, and other miscellaneous items. According to a 1925 Department of Agriculture survey, nearly half of average wages for non-casual workers in Alabama, Georgia, Mississippi, and South Carolina consisted of perquisites as opposed to cash, compared to only 28 percent in California. Even in Colorado, where perquisites made up 36 percent of non-casual farm wages and where offers of cheap housing and extensions of credit encouraged beet workers to stay year-round, the relationship between worker and employer was not like that in the South. Paul Taylor, an economist who performed an influential study of Mexicans in the United States in the late 1920s, clearly distinguished the treatment of migratory laborers in Colorado from that of tenants: "Peonage means debt servitude. It usually arises out of a landlord-tenant relationship, the tenant being kept continually in debt to the landlord and compelled to remain to work off the debt. In this sense the practice of advances to beet laborers is not peonage." Southern landlords wanted their tenants to be dependent upon them for assistance. But according to Taylor, "growers and company men alike [in Colorado] either oppose advances altogether or accept them as an unwelcome necessity, to be held strictly within the limits of the Mexicans' ability to repay. Some growers object altogether to making advances not only because they may lose through failure to repay, but also because it makes for an unsatisfactory employer-employee relationship." One grower told Taylor, "I don't want the men on my farm to be under obligations to me, so I have quit making advances to Mexicans."[56]

Mexicans were not the only group to work as migrant laborers. Even in California, only a third of the migratory labor force in 1929 consisted of Mexicans. Department of Labor officials, however, estimated that in particular sub-industries such as vegetable, fruit, and beet farming, Mexicans made up three-quarters of the labor force. Large growers in particular showed a clear preference for this type of labor. Mexicans, moreover, were more likely than all other groups to be migrant laborers. More than two-thirds of Mexicans employed in agriculture in 1930 were wage workers, compared to less than a third for all other groups.[57]

Like European women, few Mexican women (18 percent) were in the labor force. Many accompanied their husbands when they migrated from farm to farm. But among those in the labor force, nearly half (44 percent) worked in domestic or personal service, often doing child care along with "washing, cleaning and maid services for Anglo households." Mexican women (14 percent) were also more likely than white immigrant women (2 percent) to work in agriculture.[58]

The living conditions of migrant laborers were different from those of tenant farmers or industrial workers. Traveling in old jalopies, in standing-room-only trucks, by freight, or by foot, it was not unusual for Mexican migratory laborers and their families to journey nearly two thousand miles in search of work over the course of a year. Many of those who made the trek from Texas to Michigan's sugar beet fields traveled under cover of darkness, taking back roads whenever possible, trying to evade the Texas Rangers, who, during labor shortages, would try to force them back to the fields. According to McWilliams, though southern planters generally provided tenants with a shack or cabin, "with migratory labor this touch of paternalism has been eliminated." Migrants generally had to "provide their own camps; and to camp wherever they can find a site." As a result, the "ditch-bank camp" was the "typical temporary camp for the seasonal labor forces," according to Taylor. "This type of camp is usually located among the trees that line the irrigation ditches. Its shelters are commonly tents . . . or pieces of canvas stretched across a pole, with boxes, brush, burlap, or what-not across the end." Others lived in sheds or other structures, often with no ready access to water or toilet facilities.[59]

During the winter months, many Mexican migratory workers moved to nearby cities where they hoped to find some work. In San Antonio, migratory workers shelled pecans. Los Angeles had a large year-round Mexican population, but it swelled in the winter with the arrival of migrant laborers. Jacob Riis declared that he had seen slum conditions "of greater area, but never any which were worse than those in Los Angeles." Under such living conditions, Mexicans suffered from high rates of smallpox, diarrhea, pellagra, typhoid, typhus, scarlet fever, and tuberculosis. National data for 1931 show that while the infant mortality rate was 57 per 1,000 live births for the children of native-born white mothers and 58 for foreign-born white mothers, it was 93 for black mothers, and 118 for "other colored," a category that included Mexicans, Indians, Chinese, and Japanese. In Los Angeles in 1929, the infant mortality rate was 40 for "white" babies but 105 among "Mexican" babies.[60]

Racial and Color Status

When social scientists and reformers distinguished Mexicans from whites in infant mortality or other social data, they were mirroring broader trends in the "racialization" of Mexicans. Scholars have long noted that the degree to which Mexicans have been viewed and accepted as white has varied significantly across time and place, as well as by class and skin color. During the last half of the nineteenth century, Mexicans who were light skinned or elite were accorded relatively high status. Social mingling and intermarriage were common, and there were no widespread barriers to the use of public accommodations. The Treaty of Guadalupe Hidalgo in 1849 guaranteed to Mexicans who remained after the conquest "all the rights of citizens of the U.S." In theory, then, this treaty afforded Mexicans all the rights of free white persons. As a result, the U.S. Census Bureau generally categorized Mexicans as white. Poor and dark-skinned Mexicans, however, were generally perceived and afforded the treatment of other non-whites. Over time, however, the status of all Mexicans in the United States began to deteriorate. Certainly by the 1920s and 1930s, the notion that Mexicans on the whole were white and entitled to the rights of white persons was under significant assault. Anthropologists and race scientists increasingly contended that Mexicans were either primarily Indian or of mixed blood. One scholar argued that "If a color designation is used it is plainly a mistake to continue the common practice of speaking of the stock as white, for its basis is more copper than white."[61]

Facing pressure from Congress, in 1930 the Census Bureau distinguished Mexicans from whites, enumerating them as a separate color/racial group alongside Negroes, Indians, Chinese, and Japanese. However, this "Mexican" racial and color classification was only supposed to apply to the first and second generations, distinguishing it from the one-drop rule applied to blacks. Moreover, within a decade, the Census Bureau resumed classifying Mexicans as white. But this was not the result of any change in scientific or popular thinking about their color status. Rather, the reclassification was the product of years of pressure from Mexican American activists. Deeply concerned about the social and political implications of a Census Bureau report classifying Mexicans as "colored," the League of United Latin American Citizens enlisted the help of Mexican government officials, the U.S. State Department, and U.S. congressmen, who took the issue up with federal census officials. They asked the Census Bureau to reclassify Mexicans as "white." In response, the Census Bureau issued a new directive that Mexicans should be counted as white. But Mexicans also had to lobby other federal agencies, including the Treasury Department, the Social Security Board, and the Internal Revenue Service, to discontinue their practice of categorizing Mexicans as non-white.[62]

Census classifications had no direct implications for Mexicans' status as white persons under the law. But Mexicans were right to be concerned. In 1935 a judge denied the naturalization petitions of three Mexicans because they were not "free white persons" but individuals "of Indian and Spanish blood." Had it been sustained on appeal, this decision could have made most Mexicans ineligible for admission to the United States and would have further threatened a host of civil and political rights for those already in the United States. Concerned about how such a decision would affect relations with Mexico, the State Department tried to "quiet the controversy." Among other strategies, they convinced the judge not to sign the decision, which would have made the opinion an official ruling. A lawyer working on behalf of one of the petitioners convinced the judge to reconsider the naturalization petition. The petitioner revised his earlier estimate that he was 75 percent Indian down to 2 percent, and the judge agreed to grant him citizenship since the issue of racial eligibility was now moot. Because he was granted citizenship, the case could not be appealed or serve as a precedent. The larger issue of Mexicans' color status was not firmly settled, and so federal officials warned naturalization officers "to withdraw all appeals based on race" and ordered that "in all future cases, [Mexican] immigrants be classified as 'white.'" While the federal government upheld Mexicans' right to naturalize, the outcome was not always certain. And in some cases, the courts and federal officials believed these rights derived not from any scientific or popular understanding of Mexicans' "actual" color or race but from international treaty.[63]

As the color classification battles played out in federal agencies, the verdict was in in many communities. While state racial statutes about miscegenation or segregation in schools and public accommodations rarely singled Mexicans out for discrimination as they did blacks, Mexicans still experienced de facto segregation and discrimination. In many parts of the Southwest and in parts of the Midwest, Mexicans were prohibited by "white only" signs from jobs, restaurants, and other public accommodations. A sign on a Texas courthouse in the early 1940s announced separate visiting days for "colored & Mexicans" and "white only." Segregation of Mexicans in public accommodations was far more common than sporadic efforts to bar southeastern European immigrants but not as far-reaching as those erected against blacks. Indeed, because of the ambiguity of their color status, when Mexicans saw signs on company doors, as they did in Minnesota, marked "Only White Labor Employed," it was not always clear whether that meant Mexicans, too. One lunch counter proprietor in California said his white-only sign was directed at blacks only: "Mexicans are white people, just a little darker." At a drugstore fountain, the proprietor had three tiers of service: "We serve Mexicans at the fountain but not at the tables. We have got to make some distinction between them and the white people. The Negroes we serve only cones." Other establishments made exceptions based on class or skin color.[64]

Like black children, many Mexican children were forced to attend segregated schools or sit in segregated classrooms. Roughly 80 percent of school districts in Southern California were segregated. In Texas, segregation was especially severe. "We segregate [Mexicans] for the same reason that the southerners segregate the Negro," admitted one Nueces County official. "They are an inferior race, that is all." But even in Texas, exceptions were made for some students whom school officials deemed sufficiently "white" or "clean," or for students who made it to advanced grades.[65] Even where school segregation was outlawed it was sometimes achieved in practice because Mexicans often lived in segregated neighborhoods. While racially restrictive housing covenants primarily targeted blacks, they sometimes included Mexicans. Restrictive covenants in East Los Angeles and San Diego, for instance, forbade the sale or rental of housing to Mexicans. In neighborhoods without racial covenants, deed restrictions, violence, or intimidation often accomplished the same thing. But while the courts consistently upheld covenants targeting blacks, the same was not always true for Mexicans.[66]

Unlike with blacks, no miscegenation law explicitly barred the marriages of whites and Mexicans. In practice, however, it was heavily circumscribed. "The line against intermarriage is held," Taylor wrote, "although legal, it rarely occurs." But if Mexicans were legally eligible to marry whites, they were not always barred from marrying blacks either. One Texas official told Taylor that Mexicans seemed to fit in between: "We permit whites and Mexicans to intermarry, and Mexicans and Negroes. There is no law against Negro and Mexican intermarriage. We don't class Mexicans as white here." This liminal color status distinguished the Mexican experience from the experiences of blacks and European immigrants.[67]

Politics

Where cities in the North were often run by political machines and southern cities by Bourbon coalitions, cities in the Southwest were heavily influenced by the municipal reform movement. According to Amy Bridges, this movement arose out of middle-class Anglos' frustration with machine politics. Progressive structural reformers saw that machines drew their strength from "working class, especially immigrant, voters bought with the dispensation of favors and patronage." Instead, municipal reformers advocated non-partisanship to "erode the ties of party"; government by the city's leading experts, not party politicians; businesslike efficiency; and civil service instead of patronage. The result of the reforms was low overall voter participation, little competition, and the disenfranchisement of much of the naturalized immigrant community. The reach of municipal reformers in the Southwest is shown by an index of government reforms. Cities in the Southwest passed an average of 2.5 out of 3 structural reforms, compared to 2.1 in the South and just 1.6 in the North.[68]

Southwestern cities were especially receptive to the municipal reform message because the party system was not as well established there and "the issues dividing the Democrats and the Republicans" at the national level "did not have much salience for western voters." As a result, "the electorate was more easily drawn to voting for the Progressives and to supporting" these reforms. Reformers succeeded best where they could disenfranchise their opponents. Municipal reformers were often allied with nativists or eugenicists, sharing with these groups an "antipathy to immigrants and people of color" and "a desire to tighten the controls of voting." Consequently, among the measures championed by municipal reformers were literacy testing, poll taxes, early registration, and an extension of the residency period required for voting. Texas and Arizona had poll taxes while Arizona and California had both registration and literacy requirements. In addition, state and county residency requirements in Arizona, California, Colorado, New Mexico, Texas, and elsewhere, which required residence for as long as a year in the state, were especially hard on Mexican migrants. In 1918 Texas passed legislation that elimi-nated interpreters at the voting booth and stipulated "that no naturalized citizens could receive assistance from the election judge unless they had been citizens for twenty-one years." California required that naturalized immigrants present their naturalization papers in order to vote and im-posed a ninety-day waiting period on them.[69]

Like blacks, Mexicans in Texas were also at times excluded by white primaries and voter intimidation. In Hidalgo County in 1928, thousands of white residents—guarded by men with shotguns—showed up at the polls, "calling out, 'Don't let those Mexicans in to vote. Throw them out.'" V. O. Key argued that in many counties, especially where there were no political machines, "Mexican-Americans meet a barrier to the ballot similar in character if not in degree to that which discourages Negro voting in most of the South." But where most southern states adopted white primaries to exclude blacks, only a few Texas counties excluded Mexicans from primary voting.[70]

Little systematic research has been done to gauge how suffrage restric-tions affected Mexican Americans. There were reports of low political engagement in some areas, but we lack direct evidence about Mexican American political participation. Literacy tests would have certainly ex-cluded a significant proportion of Mexican Americans from the franchise. Only 70 percent of voting-aged Mexican Americans were literate in 1930 compared to 90 percent of naturalized southern and eastern Europeans. Similarly, only 69 percent of voting-aged Mexican Americans spoke En-glish compared to 96 percent of naturalized southern and eastern Euro-peans. And unlike with European immigrants, Mexican Americans were less likely to have a strong party organization to defend them against strict enforcement of suffrage restrictions. Voting rates were low in the Southwest (see Figure 2.2). During the 1928 presidential election, only 43 percent of eligible voters in the Southwest cast a ballot, compared to 67 percent in the North. Within the Southwest, turnout was lowest in cities with more Mexicans.[71]

The disenfranchisement of Mexicans was not as complete as it was for blacks, however. In New Mexico, Mexican Americans succeeded in pro-tecting their voting rights during the state's Constitutional Convention, and they remained active in local and state politics. Even in Texas, home to white primaries that excluded some Mexican Americans, alien suffrage persisted longer than in almost any other state. There was "considerable variety" in the "political role of the Mexican vote in south Texas." In some cities, like the border town of Laredo, Mexicans dominated poli-tics. In others, their political role was negligible. But even in San Antonio, where there was a machine that encouraged Mexicans to vote, their needs were still ignored.[72]

Not counted in the data on eligible voters were non-citizens, who by 1928 were ineligible to vote anywhere in the United States. But there were large differences across groups and regions in the proportion of adult immigrants who had naturalized and therefore were allowed to participate in the political process. In 1930, 29 percent of all Mexicans of voting age were American citizens by birth. But among foreign-born Mexicans, only 8 percent had naturalized, compared to 56 percent of southern and eastern Europeans and 73 percent of northern and western Europeans. As a result, cities in the Southwest had a much higher proportion of immigrants who had failed to naturalize (59 percent) compared to cities elsewhere (40 percent). Part of the reason for the difference in naturalization rates lies in the timing of immigration. Mexican immigration increased significantly only during World War I, more than two decades after the beginning of mass immigration from southeastern Europe. But even controlling for timing of migration, Mexicans were still far less likely to naturalize.[73]

A number of factors contributed to the low rate of naturalization. In order to naturalize, immigrants had to be able to speak English and show knowledge of the Constitution, and Mexicans had lower literacy rates and English-language proficiency than European immigrants. In addition, some Mexicans migrated to the United States with the intent of returning to Mexico after they had accumulated some savings, making the acquisition of American citizenship a lower priority. Also important, however, was the fact that Mexicans faced greater discrimination than European immigrants and therefore saw fewer benefits to naturalization. According to the Mexican anthropologist Manuel Gamio, European immigrants were eager to naturalize because they were more socially accepted. "There is no racial prejudice to keep him from intermarriage with Americans," and white immigrants were "more often able to reach a position of economic parity with native-born Americans." The situation was different for Mexicans. Even after naturalization, "the racial and other prejudice against him continues, and his social and economic conditions are scarcely changed." "What is the use?" said one Mexican. "They will call me a dirty greaser anyway." The historian Mae Ngai aptly described Mexican Americans as *alien citizens*, individuals with "formal U.S. citizenship but who remained alien in the eyes of the nation." There were also benefits for Mexicans in resisting naturalization. By retaining their citizenship, Mexicans could appeal to the Mexican consul when faced with discrimination.[74]

Whites were also ambivalent about encouraging the political incorporation of Mexicans, and there were few institutions in the Southwest dedicated to the task. There was little interest on the part of most southwestern politicians. As the political scientist Raphael Sonenshein explained, while political machines in New York and Chicago "were incorporating immigrant groups through the Democratic Party, the leadership of Los Angeles was hostile to immigrants and the political organizations and unions that would advance their influence." As a result, they ignored the concerns of Mexicans and Mexican Americans during this period. While other institutions, including the church, settlement houses, employers, and public schools, in the Midwest and Northeast worked to incorporate European immigrants, these organizations did less to Americanize Mexicans. The Americanization program that developed in California is a case in point. Established in 1913, California's Commission of Immigration and Housing (CCIH) was one of the earliest and at least initially most effective state-level boards in the country for the promotion of immigrant welfare. Among other aims, the CCIH was to "aid in the assimilation of immigrants, to protect them from exploitation, [and] to educate them in the duties of citizenship." Under its progressive early leadership, the CCIH devoted much attention to immigrants in the state. Though originally developed to help "digest" the southern and eastern Europeans that reformers anticipated would "flood" the state with the opening of the Panama Canal, California's Americanization programs soon targeted the growing number of Mexican immigrants when the anticipated flood of Europeans never materialized. By the mid-1920s, however, social reformers were starting to believe that their efforts at Americanization had failed. One reformer said that "the Mexican does not assimilate as other Nationals do; the second and third generation[s] do not profit by anything that is done for them in this country, and seldom do the older ones ever learn our language." Perhaps the most glaring piece of evidence of failure was the low (and declining) naturalization rate among foreign-born Mexicans. While social reformers initially wondered whether these low rates might be an indictment of their own failures, by the late 1920s all such questioning had disappeared. At the urging of agricultural interests who resented the commission's efforts to improve the living and working conditions of immigrant workers, Governor Friend Richardson purged the CCIH of its more liberal leaders in 1923, and appointed the conservative Catholic Archbishop Edward Hanna to head the department. Under Hanna's reign, the CCIH actively lobbied to restrict immigration from Mexico, noting that these immigrants had become great burdens to California communities.[75]

While the factory was an important site of political incorporation in the North, growers in the Southwest had less interest in Americanization. In fact, southwestern growers repeatedly assured restrictionists that Mexicans had no plans to stay in the country. If Mexicans returned to Mexico after the harvest, it should not matter whether they were incapable of assimilation or racially inferior as restrictionists contended. (That few

Mexicans actually returned to Mexico between harvests did not deter growers from making such claims.) Americanization was therefore not seen as desirable even if possible. Some employers, in fact, preferred an unassimilated workforce. If Mexicans failed to naturalize, they could function as a reserve labor army: a labor force available in large supply whenever needed, gone when they were not.[76]

There were also fewer social service agencies in the Southwest, and many of those that did exist refused to serve Mexicans. Even the Catholic Church was not everywhere a welcoming or assimilating institution. Efforts to Americanize Mexicans must have certainly felt insincere given that Mexicans were so often segregated from white Americans. While public schools in the North were working to assimilate European immigrants, public schools in the Southwest were less committed to those aims. Like their counterparts in the South, southwestern school officials were reluctant to enforce compulsory education laws. Over a quarter (26 percent) of Mexican children were not in school in 1930, five times the rate of European immigrants. Grinding poverty, fear of deportation, and frequent moves all contributed to low attendance rates. But school boards were also frequently dominated by growers, who had little interest in enforcing compulsory attendance laws. Even when in school, Mexican children, unlike European immigrants, were often taught in separate classrooms. Ironically, some schools claimed that one purpose "of segregation was to Americanize" Mexican children. But Americanization efforts were so weak in the Southwest that second- and third- generation Mexican Americans were less likely than *first*-generation southern and eastern European immigrants to speak English (73 percent versus 89 percent, respectively). Of course the desirability of Americanization, especially where it was coerced, is highly debatable. Nevertheless, the differences in efforts to Americanize Mexicans and European immigrants reflected differences in the ways in which these groups were viewed by white Americans, and they had important implications for each group's political incorporation.[77]

Low political participation meant that there were few Mexican Americans elected to local office or appointed to city bureaucracies. Near the end of World War II, Los Angeles still had "no Mexican Americans on the mayor's two dozen commissions" relating to "police, fire protection, civil service, public works, and health and social services. The Los Angeles City and County Civil Services Commission reported in 1944 that only 2.5 percent of Mexican Americans held civil service jobs" even though they made up 10 percent of the population. According to one observer, Mexicans were "singularly ineffectual in Texas politics": "Except in the city of Laredo, and in certain South Texas counties, where many elective city, county, and school officials are of Mexican descent, Latin Americans are without due representation on school boards, city councils, and other governmental or quasi governmental units." Unlike blacks, however, Mexicans appeared to have greater political power where they were more numerous.[78]

CONCLUSION

These three worlds that bound the experiences of most blacks, Mexicans, and European immigrants living in the United States in the first third of the twentieth century did much to shape the development of the early social welfare system. In the next chapter, I show how these three worlds helped determine not only how much cities in different parts of the country spent on relief but also the fraction of relief funds that came from public or private sources. Later, I show how they helped influence the ways in which social workers came to see and understand their charges and how they influenced each group's access to social services in their communities. The stereotypes that social workers adopted in turn influenced the extent to which relief providers would see fit to cooperate with the Immigration Service to deport public charges or find ways to expel certain relief recipients themselves when the Depression taxed local coffers. Even when the federal government stepped in and our modern welfare state emerged, these three worlds shaped the federal policies that were adopted, as well as the ways in which those federal programs were implemented at the local level.

Three Worlds of Relief

REVIEWING RECENT DEVELOPMENTS in the field of social work for President Hoover's Committee on Social Trends, Sydnor Walker noted that "No true idea of trends of social work in the United States can be given without noting the different stages of development in urban and in rural areas, in the east and in the south." In New Orleans in 1929, she explained, 100 percent of relief work was carried out by private agencies that spent just $0.12 per resident on social welfare assistance. In Detroit, on the other hand, 97 percent of relief work was funded by public monies, and the city spent nearly fifteen times as much per resident as in New Orleans, or $1.74. While New York City had more than 4,500 full-time paid social workers—or one social worker for every 1,700 residents—the state of Arizona had none.[1]

Despite Walker's admonition, social welfare scholars have paid little systematic attention to such regional variation in social welfare provision in the three decades leading up to the Great Depression. We have a large and vibrant social welfare literature for this period, but much of it is based on studies of relief systems in large northeastern or midwestern cities like Chicago, Boston, or New York; far less attention has been paid to rural areas, and to the South and West. Northeastern and midwestern cities have received disproportionate attention because they were leaders in the development of social welfare practices. But as Walker suggested, the welfare services available to poor and dependent individuals differed substantially whether one lived in Louisiana, Arizona, or Michigan.[2]

On the eve of the Great Depression, the southern and much of the southwestern relief system was stunted by comparison with the social welfare system that had begun to flourish in the North. To be sure, there were similarities across regions. The historian Michael Katz has noted that "the continuities in institutional patterns across a sprawling, decentralized, and diverse nation" are remarkable. Poor laws, almshouses, municipal lodges, Charity Organization Societies, state public welfare departments, schools of social work, state conferences of social work, and Mothers' Pension legislation were adopted by cities and states across the nation. Nonetheless, the South and much of the Southwest tended to spend considerably less on relief and depend far more heavily on private donations, while the North spent considerably more on relief and relied more heavily on public funding. These regional variations are important because they suggest that blacks, Mexicans, and European immigrants would have had significantly different access to relief services based solely on their region of residence, let alone whether they were granted access to the services provided where they lived. What is more, private agencies were more likely than their public counterparts to distinguish between the "deserving" and "undeserving," supervise relief recipients, and try to reform the "deviant" behaviors that allegedly made them poor in the first place, likely significantly shaping poor individuals' experience with their local relief system.[3]

Musing about the possible reasons the South had become such a welfare state laggard, a social worker in New Orleans rhetorically asked an audience of his peers in 1920 whether "the fact that there is little public outdoor relief in our part of the South" was any "indication of a lack of interest in relieving suffering? . . . One wonders too whether the fear of large demands on the part of the sick, aged, and destitute negroes has had anything to do with this situation." What the audience made of his comments, we do not know. But the idea that racial divisions could influence the development and size of the welfare state has now long been recognized.[4] In fact, though these regional differences were quite stark, disparities in the amount and type of relief available across cities with different racial and immigrant concentrations were even greater. Even aside from region, cities with more blacks and Mexicans spent less on relief and relied more heavily on private funds. Meanwhile, cities with more European immigrants spent more on relief and relied more heavily on public funding—even more, as it turns out, than cities with more native-born white residents.

Variations in urbanization, need, or fiscal capacity do little to clarify why cities with more European immigrants spent so much and cities with more blacks and Mexicans spent so little. Rather, differences in the structure of farm-labor relations across regions helps explain much of the racial patterning of relief spending, while differences in the political context—including differences in political party preference and political culture—help explain most of the racial patterning in the source of relief funding. In addition, however, whites' resentment of Mexicans' alleged overuse of the dole also significantly decreased spending and public funding of relief.

SCOPE AND REGIONAL VARIATION IN RELIEF PROVISION

Aside from the rapidly dwindling Civil War Pension program, which provided pensions to Civil War veterans and their dependents, the federal government was not much involved in the provision of relief in the three decades leading up to the Great Depression.[5] Instead, social welfare assistance, or relief as it was commonly called, was organized almost entirely at the local level. Local provision of relief was a legacy of the British poor laws, which made local authorities—counties, townships, or cities—responsible for granting relief to their dependent residents, provided the poor had no immediate family members on whom they could rely.

Most people in need of assistance had two broad options: "indoor" or "outdoor" relief. Poorhouses and almshouses were considered indoor relief because destitute individuals had to live in an institution in order to receive assistance. Though very popular in the nineteenth century, by the 1920s most cities and counties had moved away from the use of almshouses to serve the dependent poor. In 1923 only 78,090 people lived in almshouses, and many of the inhabitants of these institutions were older—eight out of ten were over fifty—part of a move by progressive reformers to remove children from poorhouses. There were big regional differences in the use of almshouses. States in the Northeast and Midwest served a larger fraction of their population through almshouses (90 per 100,000) than did states in the Southwest (76 per 100,000) and especially the South (42 per 100,000).[6]

More popular than indoor relief by the 1920s was outdoor relief, which typically consisted of in-kind benefits such as food, clothing, shoes, coal, rent vouchers, burial services, medical care, or cash for poor individuals who lived in their own homes as opposed to an almshouse. Especially in larger cities, relief agencies were staffed by caseworkers whose job it was to investigate all applicants for aid and supervise all open cases. Included as a subset of outdoor relief were Mothers' Pensions, which were more generous cash grants designed to allow destitute single mothers—usually widows—to stay home and care for their children. Illinois passed the first Mothers' Pension Law in 1911, and two years later twenty states had similar legislation. Despite reformers' success at passing state legislation, the program was quite limited in its reach, the result of monetary constraints and an ideological commitment to reserve the grants for mothers the reformers deemed morally exemplary. By 1926 more than forty states had laws authorizing the provision of Mothers' Pensions, but only "37 percent of children in need of aid actually received it," or probably no more than 200,000 children at any given time. Benefit levels were lowest in the South and Southwest and highest in the Northeast, ranging from a low of $4 per family in Arkansas to a high of $69 in Massachusetts. Alabama, Georgia, New Mexico, and South Carolina had no program at all. Many poor mothers with children, therefore, continued to rely on general outdoor relief.[7]

In addition to Mothers' Pensions, there were a few other special outdoor relief programs for groups considered especially deserving. While the first mandatory statewide Old Age Pension program was not passed until 1929, a few states had passed county optional programs as early as 1915. Local authorities also reserved some of their outdoor relief funds for the blind or for veterans. Homeless men—widely considered the least deserving of all—could sometimes find shelter and a meal in municipal lodging houses, in certain police departments, or from a private organization, often in exchange for hard labor. In general, local governments or private charities funded most of the programs for the poor, but states sometimes ran their own institutions or subsidized local efforts.[8]

Until now, scholars have provided little systematic evidence about the scope of outdoor relief spending in the United States prior to the Depression or how that spending varied across communities. This is most likely because relief expenditure data during this period were, according to one knowledgeable observer, "fragmentary, generally incomparable and always incomplete." Moreover, most of the early attempts at collecting relief spending data for large numbers of cities focused exclusively on public relief. But since many communities provided the bulk of their relief with private funds, these data are of rather limited value. Fortunately, the U.S. Census Bureau collected data on public and private outdoor relief efforts in American cities in the first quarter of 1929. Though scholars have not yet made much use of this obscure report, it was thought to represent the most carefully collected data on the subject at the time.[9]

The variety of organizations and programs included in this census report is extensive. Public relief expenditures in the report include city and county public outdoor relief, Mothers' Pensions, Old Age Aid, Blind Aid, local Veterans' Aid, and state grants to local relief officials. Private relief expenditures include agencies associated with nonsectarian community-wide agencies (e.g., United Charities or Associated Charities); religious or race-based organizations (e.g., Catholic Charities or Jewish Charities); the Volunteers of America; the Red Cross; the American Legion; settlement houses that dispensed outdoor relief; and various emergency committees. Also included are organizations—whether public or private—that aided homeless men, including emergency shelters, municipal lodging houses, police departments that sheltered homeless men, the Seamen's Institute, Traveler's Aid, and union missions.

According to this report, the nation's largest 295 cities—which included nearly all cities with a population of 30,000 or more—spent an estimated $61.5 million on public and private outdoor relief in 1929. This figure, which includes administrative costs, represents 72 percent of the total spending on outdoor relief for the entire nation. Nearly two-thirds (65 percent) of these funds came from public sources; the rest came from private funds. The number of families receiving relief in any given month in these large cities was estimated at 201,269, for a total of 812,837 individuals. In addition to the relief given to families, public and private agencies in these cities provided, per month, an average of 612,588 meals and 384,779 nights of shelter to homeless men.[10]

American cities varied greatly in their outdoor relief spending before the stock market crashed. The bottom 10 percent of cities spent less than $0.34 per capita on public and private relief while the top 10 percent spent upward of $2.95 per resident. Cities also differed significantly in the way in which they chose to fund relief. Thirty-two of the 295 cities used only private funds, twelve relied only on public sources, while the majority chose some mix of the two.

Cities in the Northeast and Midwest spent more per capita on outdoor relief to families and homeless men ($1.65) than did cities in the Southwest ($1.12) and especially the South ($0.58). Even after adjusting for differences in the cost of living across states, per capita spending on outdoor relief in the Northeast and Midwest was more than twice as high as in the South ($1.65 versus $0.65) and nearly 50 percent higher than in the Southwest ($1.13). Cities in the South and Southwest not only spent less on relief, a larger proportion of the funds came from private sources. In the Northeast and Midwest, nearly 70 percent of all city spending on relief came from public sources, as opposed to 43 percent for the Southwest and only 25 percent in the South. On the eve of the Great Depression, at least six southwestern and eighteen southern cities had no public relief system whatsoever.[11]

A city's choice to rely on relatively more public or private relief funds likely produced somewhat different experiences for the destitute individuals who sought aid. Despite some cooperation, private and public charity officials had historically seen the purpose of their work in starkly different terms and were often at odds, a rift that dates back to the mid-nineteenth century. During the 1870s, many middle-class social reformers grew alarmed at the rising class consciousness and militancy of the urban working class. The Depression that started in 1873 led to massive unemployment, militant strikes, an explosion in the public outdoor relief rolls, and the growth of a class of homeless men who traveled the country on the rails. Public relief officials and private social reformers began to feel that a vast chasm between the rich and poor had developed and that the dole, or indiscriminate relief giving, was partly to blame. Reformers began a campaign to end public outdoor relief and to replace it with indoor relief or private charity, scientifically administered.[12]

Scientific charity proponents had several goals, according to Michael Katz. First, they wanted to disabuse the poor of the idea that relief was an entitlement. Charity was to be voluntary, and private relief was to be subject to a labor test for able-bodied men—chopping wood or breaking stone—to help distinguish between the deserving and undeserving poor. Second, scientific charity proponents wanted to abolish public outdoor relief. Public outdoor relief, they complained, was impersonal. Relief administrators did not know the circumstances of the recipients' lives, and therefore could not properly gauge the best means to lift them out of their pauper condition. The dependent poor should instead receive either indoor relief—institutionalization in an almshouse where their behavior could be scrutinized and regulated—or private outdoor charity, administered under the watchful eye of "friendly visitors." Third, scientific charity proponents wanted to organize private philanthropy to avoid waste, fraud, and the duplication of services. Toward that end, they adopted the Charity Organization Society model, first developed in London. Charity Organization Societies served as a central clearinghouse for referring the poor to the proper relief agencies. In theory, the societies would not disburse relief directly except in cases of emergency. Instead, Charity Organization Societies were to investigate applicants; if necessary, send them to the appropriate charity; assign recipients of charity "friendly visitors" to help the family move toward self-sufficiency; provide an employment bureau; serve as a clearinghouse of information on the aid each recipient received; and collect data on the causes and consequences of dependency. The private charity organization model, then, was built on the notion that the causes of poverty were the result of individual failure, not larger economic or structural forces. The first Charity Organization Society in the United States was established in Buffalo in 1877, but the movement spread rapidly across the country in the first decade of the twentieth century.[13]

Not all private charities were members of Charity Organization Societies, however, and some were downright hostile to the movement's goals. In the end, the Charity Organization movement failed in its attempt to eliminate outdoor relief and privatize relief provision. Indeed, by the eve of the Depression, the majority of relief funds were once again coming from public sources. However, spurred by the efforts of progressive reformers who saw an enlarged role for the public realm in social welfare provision, many public relief departments by the 1920s actually adopted some of the principles of scientific case management, employing their own caseworkers or contracting with nonsectarian charity organizations for that purpose.[14] Despite these new trends toward the adoption of scientific charity principles in some public relief agencies, variation in funding practices still likely produced important regional differences in relief giving.

Another important difference between regions was the extent of urbanization. Almost 70 percent of the population in the Northeast and Midwest lived in urban areas, compared with 54 percent in the Southwest and only 31 percent in the South. Scholars have paid little attention to rural relief in the Progressive Era. What is clear, however, is that rural areas offered less specialized services, if they offered anything at all.[15]

Big cities often had a range of relief options. There were over 700 social service agencies listed, for example, in Chicago's *Social Service Directory* in 1926. Among these public and private agencies were 46 homes for the aged, 27 emergency shelters, 70 neighborhood centers and settlement houses, 65 homes for dependent children, and 48 day nurseries. In scores of rural communities, however, the only social welfare institutions were the church and the school. One expert on rural social welfare estimated that "not more than one-third" of the rural counties "have one or more forms of organized rural social work." Indeed, of the more than 30,000 social and welfare workers in the United States in 1930, nearly three-fourths worked in cities with a population of 25,000 or more.[16]

In New Mexico, for instance, only 18 percent of the population lived in urban areas—towns with over 2,500 residents—and the state's largest city, Albuquerque, had fewer than 27,000 residents. It was the only state without a single almshouse, and at the end of World War I it was the only state without a statewide public health system. It also failed to pass Mothers' Pension legislation over the course of the next decade. Charitable organizations and Women's Clubs did provide some relief, but the vast majority of destitute individuals probably survived through the help of extended kinship networks and the assistance of friends and neighbors.[17]

The relative lack of services in the countryside does not appear to have reflected any lack of need. One study of rural poverty in Virginia found that "five hundred thousand families lived below a subsistence level" in the state's rural areas in 1926. According to the executive director of Georgia's Children's Aid Society: "There is no suffering experienced by unfortunates in the city that is not as great in the more sparsely settled communities" and that "much suffering of a permanently handicapping nature is experienced by many rural children." Because rural areas lacked specialized services and failed to adopt modern social work methods, reformers often labeled their relief efforts as backward. At the National Conference of Social Work in 1918, one speaker listed among the "evils" of rural poor relief in Missouri a "lack of adequate or intelligible records," inadequate benefit levels, the "neglect of the most needy and important cases," lack of investigation or friendly visiting, patronage, the "passing on of transients from one community to another," and the "renting of poor unfortunates to the lowest bidder with no investigation ever made, and no questions asked as to how the poor people were cared for or treated." Georgia's Department of Public Welfare even complained that rural Georgians paid greater attention to their animals than to their destitute neighbors. It also described many of the state's sixty almshouses in 1926, housing more than eight hundred people, as "tumble-down shacks often vermin ridden" with no "proper toilet facilities, bathing facilities, nor any other minimum requirements for sanitation and health." Eighteen of these almshouses were managed by prison wardens, and in two cases pauper inmates and prisoners were integrated.[18]

California probably did more than many states for rural dwellers. Most rural counties had some form of outdoor or indoor relief, however inadequate. In fact, most counties had at least a few children supported by Mothers' Pensions. And the state's Commission of Immigration and Housing was entrusted with supervising the housing conditions of migrant workers and "educating the employers and the business interests regarding the necessity of providing adequate housing and sanitary conveniences for all agricultural laborers," a program that the U.S. Children's Bureau noted would greatly benefit other states such as Texas.[19]

But there were practical difficulties in setting up rural relief programs. In New Mexico, some counties were bigger than the entire state of Massachusetts. Roads were not always well maintained or even passable throughout the year. In some cases, rural social workers were responsible for 120 to 300 cases scattered across these vast expanses. One social worker found it "necessary to do most of her traveling on horseback." In wet weather, the roads were so bad that she had to ride "along the railroad track."[20]

Rural areas, however, began to receive greater attention from social reformers during the 1920s, much to the credit of the efforts of the American Red Cross. Answering the call by President Wilson during World War I to take on civilian relief work, 30,000 home service workers for the American Red Cross—over 90 percent of them volunteers—served 700,000 soldiers' and sailors' families in every region of the country with the dual "purpose of maintaining the morale of our fighting forces and of contributing to the welfare of their families." According to one official, Red Cross branches reached into "fifteen thousand communities, only three hundred of which, prior to the coming of home service, had any general family social work agency." At the end of the war, the Red Cross decided to continue its home service, extending its social work services to the general public. Because it was committed to not duplicating existing services, it focused on "fostering the development of social work in the small town and the open country." In 1922 there were 744 American Red Cross chapters providing home relief work to the civilian population, but by 1929 that number had dropped by more than half. Despite the declining number of chapters, a Red Cross official in Atlanta credited the organization with a change of heart in many southern communities from a belief that "there was nothing to do, to one in which the demand for trained social workers far exceeds the supply."[21]

Along the U.S. side of the border with Mexico, many rural Mexicans and Mexican Americans were served not by the American Red Cross but by the Mexican Cruz Azul or Blue Cross. In Calexico, a border town located in California's Imperial Valley, the Cruz Azul had four hundred members in 1927: "They maintain clinics in their hospital in Calexico and 6 or 8 beds are filled there at all times with their own Mexican people." Most rural communities in Texas failed to develop any real public or private relief system prior to the Great Depression. "In the rural districts and among the Negroes and the Mexicans," observed one reporter, "social work has never been far advanced or particularly progress[ive] in Texas." Rural Dimmit County had no "organized American charity in the county." It did, however, have a few "fraternal and charitable societies which play the double role of social club and relief agency," including some branches of the Cruz Azul. Their membership, however, was "rarely large, although their influence and benefactions extend to the entire colony."[22]

In addition to the Red Cross, federal initiatives such as the Sheppard Towner maternal education program as well as efforts of national social service organizations to extend relief services to rural areas also helped stimulate some southern states to do more. In 1924 the Georgia Department of Public Welfare "set up a Division of County Organization devoted primarily to assisting the rural sections of the State and to helping such communities develop sound programs for social service." In 1920 they had only eight social workers in rural counties, but six years later that number had doubled. The Department of Public Welfare's goal was to have a trained social worker in every rural county.[23]

While southern progressive reformers were moving toward providing more services to rural areas prior to the Depression, one should certainly not overstate their success. Interviews with more than 1,000 Alabama farm households in 1933 found that 99 percent had not used relief prior to 1930, "the chief reason being that few of them had had access to any agency before that time." "For many rural southerners," according to the historian Elna Green, "there simply was no such thing as public welfare, as no county boards existed in many places. State legislatures authorized, but did not mandate county almshouses, so many areas remained without them. Rural counties often had few private charities either, since the populations were scattered and insufficient to create the necessary organizations to offer private assistance."[24]

Regional differences in the provision of relief by the eve of the Depression, then, were stark. States in the South and Southwest spent significantly less on relief and were more likely to fund their relief system with private funds. That much of the South and Southwest was rural and made few provisions for social welfare only exacerbated regional disparities. A focus on these regional differences, however, obscures some very important differences in spending within regions, and nowhere is this better exemplified than in the Southwest. The state of Texas, where over 50 percent of Mexicans lived, had virtually no public relief system. Per capita spending across Texas's thirteen largest cities averaged only $0.49. However, in California, where 30 percent of Mexicans lived, a far more generous relief system emerged. Average per capita relief spending across California's twelve largest cities was $1.80, well over triple the average in Texas. Furthermore, California passed its Mothers' Pension legislation only two years after Illinois passed the pioneering legislation in 1911. Not only did it spend a considerable amount of money on outdoor relief and Mothers' Pensions, California also spent lavishly on almshouses. The proportion of people served by its almshouses lagged behind that of only four states. Nevertheless, within California and the Southwest more broadly, cities with a larger proportion of Mexicans generally spent a lot less on relief.[25]

RACE, IMMIGRATION, AND LOCAL RELIEF PROVISION

As stark as these regional differences were, an especially striking feature of the American social welfare system in 1929 was, in fact, the racial patterning of local relief provision. Even after controlling for region of residence, cities with more blacks or Mexicans spent *less* on relief, while cities with more foreign-born whites spent *more*. To put this in context, for each ten-percentage-point increase in the black or Mexican population, cities spent roughly $0.17 *less* per resident on their total relief spending. But for each ten-percentage-point increase in the European immigrant population, cities spent $0.22 *more* per resident in their public and private relief spending. Native-born whites are the reference point for these comparisons, meaning that cities with more foreign-born than native-born whites spent the most on relief. Since cities were spending an average of just $1.39 per resident, these spending differences are significant. Indeed a city's racial and immigrant demographics alone explain almost a quarter of all of the variation we observe in spending across cities. While some scholars have argued that immigration decreases social welfare spending, these results suggest that there is no universal tradeoff between diversity and redistributive spending.[26]

Relief systems in cities with more blacks and Mexicans were also more likely to rely on private as opposed to public funds. For each ten-percentage-point increase in the black or Mexican population, cities decreased the fraction of relief funds coming from public sources by thirteen and seven percentage points, respectively. But a ten-percentage-point increase in the European immigrant population increased the share of relief funding coming from public funds by six percentage points. Racial and immigrant demographics explain 42 percent of the variation we observe in the source of relief funding across cities.

Controlling for Urbanization, Need, and Fiscal Capacity

How much of these spending and funding differences are simply a function of differences across cities in urbanization, need, or fiscal capacity? We might imagine that the growth of cities created a surge in demand for public programs to help individuals who could no longer rely on the land for sustenance. There might also be returns to scale in the development of public relief systems. Larger cities then might spend proportionately more on relief but might also be more likely to fund relief systems with more public as opposed to private funds. Since European immigrants tended to live in larger cities, this might explain why cities with large shares of European immigrants spent more on relief and relied on more public funding. We might also think that cities with greater need invested more in relief. Congested cities might produce more illness and want, or destitute individuals in the North might need more coal to get through the especially harsh winters. In Cook County, Illinois, in 1927, about 22 percent of relief funds were spent on "coal for free delivery." In fact, historically some outdoor relief departments provided nothing but coal to their most destitute residents and even then only during especially harsh winters. Therefore the differences in spending across cities we observe might simply be a product of differences in need or climate. Finally, we might think that differences in a city's ability to pay for relief services—its fiscal capacity—might really be driving the results. The Civil War decimated the southern economy and there may have been less wealth or income there to distribute. Perhaps, then, what was actually driving the relationship between racial or immigrant context and relief provision is the greater ability of cities with large numbers of European immigrants to fund public relief programs.[27]

If we account for these differences, however, we actually do little to explain the racial and ethnic patterning in relief spending or funding. Figures 3.1 and 3.2 show the size of the "effect" of racial and immigrant context on per capita relief spending (see Figure 3.1) and the fraction of relief funds that came from public as opposed to private funds (see Figure 3.2). The first set of bars on both figures shows the strength of black, Mexican, and white immigrant context after controlling for differences across cities in urbanization, need, and fiscal capacity. They show that even after controlling for these differences, cities with more blacks and Mexicans still spent less on relief and were more privately oriented. Cities

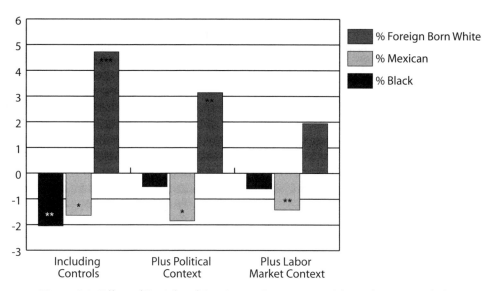

Figure 3.1: Effect of Racial and Immigrant Context on Public and Private Relief Spending in American Cities, 1929

* p < .1   ** p < .05   *** p < .01

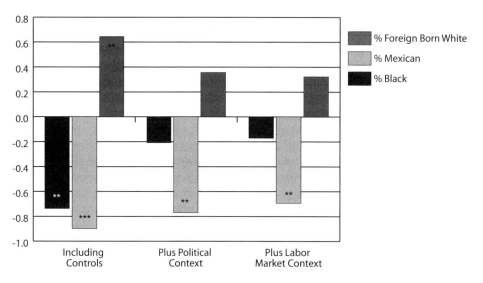

Figure 3.2: Effect of Racial and Immigrant Context on Fraction of Relief Funds Coming from Public Sources in American Cities, 1929

* p < .1   ** p < .05   *** p < .01

with more foreign-born whites spent more on relief and were more publicly oriented. (The stars on the bars denote that these differences were still quite significant.) Differences in urbanization, need, and fiscal capacity, therefore, do not explain the racial patterning in relief provision.[28]

Political Context

Scholars have long noted that politics can influence policy outcomes. And there is good reason to believe that some of the differences in political context outlined in chapter 2 should explain some of these differences in relief spending and funding. Voter turnout was low in the Southwest and especially the South. Scholars have found that "greater democracy in political processes promotes redistributive social spending policies" because those most in need get a greater voice in the political process when they have the vote. Naturalization rates also varied tremendously across regions, with immigrants in the Southwest much less likely than immigrants elsewhere to have naturalized. If lack of access to the franchise depresses social spending then we would expect that cities with lower voter turnout or more non-citizens would spend less on relief. On the other hand, one of the purposes of the relief system was to facilitate the Americanization of recent immigrants. As a result, cities with proportionately more recent immigrants might spend more on relief in their efforts to promote assimilation.[29]

Party preferences or ideology may also help explain some of the differences in welfare provision. One southern social worker argued that southern legislators were conservative and simply uninterested in passing welfare legislation: "Very few of our legislators care for the methods of charities and corrections; they believe in letting well enough alone." While the southern one-party system had a significant effect on the structure of local race and labor market relations, studies have actually found few differences in the social welfare spending preferences of Democrats and Republicans during this period. Progressives like presidential candidate Robert La Follette, however, were more supportive of social welfare spending. So we should expect that cities with more Progressives—a party more popular in the North—would spend more on relief and rely more on public funds to pay for their programs.[30]

Whether a city was governed by a political machine (as was often the case in the Northeast and Midwest) or municipal reformers (as was frequently the case in the Southwest) could also influence the size and form of relief provision, although there are conflicting theories in the existing literature about exactly how. For example, there is ample evidence of patronage in the distribution of public relief. Sonya Forthal, a political scientist, interviewed six hundred Chicago precinct captains in the late

1920s and found that 60 percent provided their constituents with medical care, 50 percent provided food, more than two out of five gave coal, and 38 percent supplied rent money. While some of the funds were provided directly by the precinct captain, in many instances the captain secured relief through public agencies. According to Forthal, in one case "a physician in a public institution who owed his appointment to politics was expected to arrange hospitalization for the constituents of his benefactors." In another, "the assistant superintendent of the Cook County Bureau of Public Welfare had formerly been a captain and was at the time of the interview a ward committeeman in the Democratic Party." In still other cases, the precinct captain would refer applicants to the Cook County Bureau of Public Welfare or help them with the application process. According to Steven Erie, while political machines were sometimes reluctant to share patronage jobs with the new immigrants, they made other efforts to gain the support of these voters: "In New York, Tammany was responsible for securing the passage of important state labor and social welfare legislation," including a slew of laws designed to improve the wages and working conditions of the state's women and children. They also helped pass legislation for workmen's compensation, tenement housing reform, Mothers' Pensions, and scholarships for the poor: "In Jersey City, Frank Hague converted the city's public hospital into the nation's second largest medical center, providing free health care for the city's residents."[31]

Given such anecdotes, we might think that cities with more European immigrants spent more on relief because they were more likely to be run by a political machine. However, little is actually known about exactly who received these spoils or whether machine cities spent more or less on the whole than non-machine cities. There is in fact remarkably little systematic evidence that "political organizations either wanted or had the resources to be uncritical respondents to the needs of the urban masses" and little evidence of significant differences in citywide social welfare spending across machine and non-machine cities. Jessica Trounstine has made sense of these seemingly contradictory findings by showing that during their rise to power, before they achieved monopoly status, political bosses lavished benefits on the new immigrants. But once political machines achieved a monopoly in city government, electoral turnout declined and benefits were directed to "governing coalition elites and core coalition members, [and] away from the broader community." During monopoly periods, spending on health and welfare in machine cities declined.[32]

There is also some evidence that on the whole reformed cities actually spent more than machine cities on health and welfare services. That is because municipal reformers—sometimes called progressive structural reformers—occasionally teamed up with progressive social reformers, who were most concerned with the social welfare of the urban poor. In addition, machine politicians often provided benefits directly to the poor, bypassing the public or private relief systems entirely. For years Albany political boss Dan O'Connell "had the habit of walking home over a long route through poor areas of the city. Each day he would begin with several hundred dollars in small bills, and reach home with next to nothing." A settlement house worker told of "a United States congressman who hails from a ward of foreign-born citizens in a Middle West city" who "seems to have a private key to the mint, so full are his pockets always of half-dollars available for friends in need." One Chicago ward leader in a Polish neighborhood said that the "dispensation of charity is one of the important functions of the organization. . . . if someone comes there in need, they have one of their men investigate the case, and if necessary give relief until the proper social agency takes over the case. . . . 'If we can help these people,' he said, 'it means we can get their votes.'" Indeed, social reformers argued that machine politics "would disappear once the city itself provided the services currently offered by the boss." Moreover, since relief benefits were quite meager, machines preferred to control the disbursement of jobs over relief. During the Depression, one federal relief official commented that "Politicians did not especially mind turning relief over to a group of citizens for they felt there was nothing but grief in that job. However, it drove the politicians wild to find themselves without anything to say about who was going to get a job on public work." Because political bosses sometimes provided benefits directly to the poor and because jobs were a far more important source of patronage than relief, the effect of political machines or machine politics on relief spending is not entirely straightforward.[33]

A final important difference to consider is the political culture. Daniel Elazar famously categorized the political culture of the fifty states and various subregions as *Moralist*, *Individualist*, *Traditionalist*, or some combination thereof. Political culture, he argued, was partly the product of the particular ethnic and religious backgrounds of the individuals who migrated to and settled in different communities. Southern states were more likely to have a traditionalist political culture whereas northern states were often either moralistic, individualistic, or some combination of these two. Southwestern states, meanwhile, were rarely characterized by a single political culture but rather by a blend of individualistic and traditionalist as in Texas or moralist and traditionalist as in Arizona, New Mexico, and Southern and central California. Each political culture held different views on government, bureaucracy, and politics in general, and these cultures could in turn explain much about state politics: the level of political participation; the size and perquisites of government bureaucracy; and the scope, magnitude, and cost of government programs. Importantly, each political culture also had different outlooks on the desirability and purpose of government intervention in the community. The Moralist welcomed "intervention for the good of the commonwealth; the Individualist would minimize intervention to permit a balance of satisfactions from activities in the private and the public sector; and the Traditionalist would oppose all government interventions except those necessary to maintain the existing power structure." Given these differences, we should expect that cities in areas that were more traditionalist would fund relief programs primarily through private means while more moralistic areas would favor more government-funded relief provision.[34]

After accounting for all of these differences in political context across cities, I found that the political context explains much of the association between black racial context and relief spending but little else. White immigrant and Mexican contexts are still significantly related to spending (see Figure 3.1). But political context appears to explain more of the funding choices of individual cities (see Figure 3.2). Cities with more Progressive voters and more unnaturalized immigrants were more likely to finance their relief system with public rather than private dollars. Cities run by dominant political machines or located in more traditionalist states were more privately oriented. Political context, therefore, helps explain a significant amount of the racial patterning evident in the source of funding of relief systems across cities but not the relationship between Mexican context and source of relief funding, which so far remains unexplained.

Labor Market Context

In addition to political context, there are good reasons to believe that the structure of farm-labor relations across regions could have a substantial impact on the scope of relief provision in various cities. As part of their ethos of paternalism, southern planters believed it was in their interest to provide perquisites year-round to their tenants and saw the provision of relief as a threat to the control of their labor supply. Harold Hoffsommer, who interviewed landlords and tenants in Alabama, found that "Many landlords were fearful of any governmental program, whether relief or rehabilitation, that promised to bring independence to share-croppers. The general opinion (90 percent) was that the landlord should take care of his tenants if possible." Even during the depths of the economic crisis in 1933, many continued to view relief "with suspicion," fearing that with access to relief, the tenant would "escape from under his influence." Tenants, for example, might leave the farm or grow discontented with traditional customs and labor arrangements. They might also grow too accustomed to the cash economy. According to Hoffsommer, the entire sharecropping system was predicated on "the subordination of the tenant group. If the cropper were to become selfdirecting and take over his own affairs, the system would necessarily crumble."[35]

Unlike southern planters, growers in the Southwest had more incentives to support—or at least not oppose—the development and extension of relief. In contrast to southern planters, they did not rely on paternalism or debt peonage to control their labor, and western growers were generally content to let their migrant laborers use relief between harvests, at least prior to the Great Depression, because it functioned to keep a large agricultural labor supply in nearby cities. Relief could help tide Mexicans over during spells of seasonal unemployment and keep them at hand for future harvests. Commenting on a grower who did not provide assistance to his migratory laborers between harvests, the CCIH noted that while the grower might have thought his obligation had ended, in fact, "the obligation of the community at large, of which he is an integral part, has just commenced." Some farmers were well aware of this fact. Addressing the charge that Mexicans were overly dependent on relief, a representative of the California Cattle Raiser's Association testified at a 1928 Senate hearing on immigration that Mexicans did become public charges "to quite an extent, though not any more than any other kind of people." "Why should they not become public charges?" he asked the Senate committee. "I just as soon send a bunch of Mexicans to the county hospital or county tuberculosis farm . . . as a bunch of white men." Despite farmers' protests to the contrary, the relief system served as a subsidy to the agricultural industry in the Southwest. And it served as a threat to the system of farm-labor relations in the South that was governed by debt peonage and a paternalistic ethos.[36]

Even if *rural* elites had reasons to resist or support the development of a strong relief system, why would they try to influence the provision of relief in *cities*? Mexican agricultural laborers typically migrated to cities between harvests, and it was there that they were thought to rely on relief. While blacks were generally not migrant laborers, by the 1920s they were resettling away from rural areas and into more urban locales within the South (and from South to North). Aware of these shifts, southern planters looked for ways to keep black sharecroppers tethered to the land or induce those who migrated to the city to return. Any alternative means of subsistence available to them in cities posed a threat to southern planters' labor supply. Rural elites not only had incentives to influence the provision of relief in cities, they also had the means to do so. Much public welfare provision actually took place at the county level. For smaller cities, counties might include substantial rural areas and may therefore have been controlled directly by rural interests. In larger cities, planters had indirect influence through familial and business ties to urban industrial elites. State legislatures, dominated by rural interests, also supplemented local relief spending in many areas and any state or county funds are reflected in the city spending data. There is ample evidence, moreover, that southern states were often less willing to provide such funds. The South was slow to adopt statewide boards of charities. By World War I, Alabama, Georgia, Mississippi, South Carolina, and Texas were still without statewide welfare boards. When they did create them, they generally had "limited supervising powers over state institutions and agencies . . . [and] little or no influence on the administration of local relief and almshouse care." The Georgia legislature gave its Department of Public Welfare, established in 1921, "strictly visitorial and advisory powers." It had no funds to distribute. Similarly, Louisiana's constitution prohibited the state from contributing funds to local public or private charities.[37]

We should see lower spending on relief where farmers relied more heavily on paternalism—measured here as the fraction of farm wages paid in perquisites—than where they did not. And in fact, though paternalism has little effect on funding choices (see Figure 3.2), it proves to be a powerful predictor of spending on total relief assistance (see Figure 3.1). Cities in states with the lowest levels of paternalism spent nearly two dollars more per capita on total relief than did cities in areas with the highest levels of paternalism. And the relationship between black and white immigrant context and relief spending appears to have disappeared once we take into account this measure. Taken as a whole, these results suggest that the political and labor market contexts help explain much of the reason that cities with more European immigrants spent so much public money while cities with more blacks spent so little.

Racial Resentment

We have yet to fully explain why cities with more Mexicans spent less and were more privately oriented, however. The effect of Mexican racial context is still significant even after accounting for differences in political economies. This unexplained gap in spending and funding is best explained, I argue, by racial resentment. In the same way that whites today are resentful about blacks' use of welfare and support less overall welfare spending as a result, in the 1920s, white social workers and the general public were resentful about Mexicans' alleged overuse of relief, and public spending on relief dropped in response. Racial resentment does not help explain why cities with large numbers of blacks spent less on relief, however, because, as chapter 5 shows, there was no association between blacks and dependence prior to the Depression.[38]

Indeed, while western growers were more than happy to let Mexican migratory workers receive relief between harvests, sharing the cost of relief for seasonal laborers was not something that other white taxpayers and social workers favored. James Batten, a Claremont College professor, made the point forcefully. "When no work is available they [Mexican migrants] congest in such centers as Los Angeles, El Paso, and San Antonio, presenting social problems and becoming a liability upon the taxpayers. In a certain sense," Batten argued, "the large centers of the Southwest" where Mexicans congregate during the winter season "are subsidizing the agricultural sections through this indirect payment of 'charity wages' to the Mexican laborers during their period of unemployment." Many charity officials thought this whole situation was unfair. "Why the citizens at large, the Community Chest, the churches, the tax-payers, should have to care for the employees of the sugar companies, the railroads, and mines, between seasons of labor, is not clear to the students of economics and justice" argued the director of Colorado Catholic Charities. Similarly, Robert McLean, a Presbyterian minister, explained that "The ugliest charge laid at the door of the employers of cheap labor is that they are annually receiving large subsidies out of the funds of churches, settlement houses, associated charities and community chests. It is insisted that the employers, in bringing unskilled labor from Mexico, assume a moral responsibility for them, and that when society through doles ekes out an insufficient wage during periods of unemployment, the charity fund is in reality being paid out to maintain the labor reservoir of the industries interested."[39]

Exactly how Mexicans came to be seen as overly dependent on relief is the subject of the next chapter. But it is important to note here that there is evidence of communities abandoning efforts to serve Mexicans as a result of this resentment. In response to anger over rising relief costs among Mexican migratory beet laborers in Colorado, the state legislature passed a law in 1927 prohibiting the use of local public relief funds for burial services for the poor. As a result, the bodies of paupers were removed "to one of the medical colleges for dissection." Social welfare workers in Calexico, California, feeling "very much burdened with Mexican charity," asked the local Mexican consul—also head of the Cruz Azul—to care for their own compatriots. "As a result of it," according to one local grower, "the Mexican Blue Cross became very active, and at the present time they are taking care of their own people." There is also some evidence that growers sometimes felt compelled to donate funds to private charities to reduce the burden on the taxpayers. In Colorado, where a local news headline during the depression of 1920–21 read, "Denver's Safety Is Menaced by 3,500 Starving Mexicans," the Sunshine Mission, a private charity supported in part by funds from the Great Western Sugar

Company, provided the majority of assistance furnished to the Mexican community. These reports suggest that cities with more Mexicans spent less on relief and were more privately funded, at least in part because residents and welfare providers in those areas were resentful that Mexicans were receiving relief.[40]

CONCLUSION

By the eve of the Great Depression, there were three separate worlds of relief. The relief systems in the South and much of the Southwest were stunted by comparison to the relief systems that had developed in the Northeast and Midwest. This was partly a function of urbanization. The North was more urbanized, and there were few relief services in rural areas, despite the obvious need. But even in large urban areas, disparities persisted. Cities with large proportions of European immigrants were characterized by high spending, most of which came from public funds. Cities with more blacks or Mexicans, meanwhile, typically invested significantly less, and most of the funding in those cities came from private sources. But even though cities with more blacks and Mexicans both spent less and relied more heavily on private funds, they did so for different reasons. Particularly important in explaining the racial patterning of outdoor relief spending across cities was the extent of paternalism in the areas surrounding these communities. Extending perquisites to laborers was an important part of the paternalistic system of labor relations in the South, and southern landlords viewed relief as a threat to their control over black laborers. Southwestern growers, in contrast, relied more heavily on migrant laborers, did not view relief as a threat to their labor supply, and were content to let Mexican laborers get relief between harvests because it served to keep a large labor force in the area with minimal costs to the growers. However, relief workers and the public grew resentful that Mexicans were granted relief and that taxpayers were forced to subsidize the agricultural industry. This resentment led cities with more Mexicans to spend less on relief net of other factors.

While paternalism was a powerful determinant of the level of total relief spending, it was less important in determining how relief systems were funded. To understand why cities with more Mexicans and blacks relied on more private funds, while cities with more European immigrants relied on more public funds, we must consider the political context. Cities run by a single dominant political machine tended to be more privately oriented, while cities in more Progressive communities with more unnaturalized immigrants and more moralistic political cultures relied more on public funds. But even net of these factors, cities with more Mexicans were likely to rely more on private funds to finance relief. Faced with growing resentment from taxpayers about Mexicans' use of relief, growers subsidized local private charities, and social workers asked private Mexican charities to take over the responsibility of providing assistance. As the next two chapters will show, the stereotype of Mexicans as especially dependent on relief was, as it turns out, not based in any social fact; Mexicans were less likely than European immigrants to make use of relief. But the stereotype nonetheless became widespread, and it affected not only the size and scope of relief provision in communities with large Mexican populations but, as chapter 6 will show, the degree to which relief agencies cooperated with immigration officials to deport those who sought assistance.

CHAPTER 4

The Mexican Dependency Problem

ON THE EVE OF THE GREAT DEPRESSION, the Los Angeles Municipal
League asked R. R. Miller, the superintendent of outdoor relief for the
County Department of Charities, to answer "a criticism on the alleged
excessive amount of relief that goes to Mexicans." Miller responded in
an article for the *Municipal League Bulletin* entitled "The Mexican Dependency Problem." According to Miller, the "best population statistics"
indicated that Mexicans made up 11 percent of the county but furnished
24 percent of the outdoor relief caseload, "showing that proportionally
the dependency problem is very large." The burden on the "taxpayers"
was perceived to be so great that the Department of Charities had abandoned all efforts at "intensive, constructive case work," offering instead
only "the most temporary assistance" and "stressing immediate employment at all times." Miller emphasized that unless the flow of immigration was "checked," the Mexican dependency situation might never be
"corrected."[1]

Social workers' views of their dependent charges from the Progressive
Era through the stock market crash in 1929 are the subject of this chapter
and the next. In these chapters, I argue that social workers had very different perceptions of Mexicans, European immigrants, and blacks prior
to the Depression and the subsequent widespread federal intervention in
relief provision. By the 1920s, social workers had come to believe that
Mexicans were an especially dependent and undeserving group, and they
did what they could to convince others of their views. Nativists often
saw European immigrants as welfare dependent, too, but social workers firmly rejected these characterizations and tried to forge a competing
perspective—of a group that was, by their account, thrifty, hardworking,
and worthy of assistance. Blacks, meanwhile, were often simply ignored
by white welfare workers or portrayed as the least dependent group of
all. Social workers' disparate views of their charges were shaped by their
perceptions about each group's potential for racial assimilation, as well as
the political and labor market context in which they lived. These views, in
turn, profoundly influenced the treatment each group received.

In this chapter, I document the emergence of the perception of a "Mexican dependency problem," which gained early traction in Los Angeles. By
1930 Los Angeles County was home to more than 167,000 Mexicans—

the largest concentration of Mexicans outside Mexico City. But the population fluctuated with the seasons, swelling in the winter months when migrant workers came to look for work between harvests. And it was in Los Angeles and cities like it that migrant workers sometimes turned to relief when no work could be found.

Prior to the 1920s, social workers in the city were cautiously optimistic that Mexicans could be assimilated, and they saw relief as one step in that process. As Mexicans made greater use of relief, however, social workers' initial optimism waned. By the mid-1920s, they became convinced that Mexicans were a dependent and diseased population, lacking in thrift and ambition. They decided that their efforts at Americanizing this group had failed. Migrant workers did not stick around long enough for Americanization efforts to bear fruit. Naturalization rates among Mexicans were low and declining, and there was little evidence of socioeconomic mobility. Concerned that charity funds were essentially subsidizing the agricultural industry, they came to believe that Mexicans represented an illegitimate economic and social burden to "American taxpayers." Mexicans, they concluded, were racially inassimilable after all.

These social workers played a critical role in constructing Mexicans as an undeserving population. To make their case, they collected data on the Mexican "dependency problem" and selectively cited statistics that exaggerated their reliance on relief. They disseminated these findings widely and used them to lobby for restriction on immigration from Mexico. From their perspective, restriction was needed in order to "check" the flow of a people they now saw as undesirable, who drained municipal coffers and spread disease. But restriction also provided the best hope they had to incorporate those already here. Over time, the stereotypes associated with the "dependent Mexican" spread throughout much of the country, especially during the debates over immigration restriction. Though Mexicans protested these unfair characterizations, their lack of political power prevented them from dispelling such stereotypes. Ironically, it was often the Americanization teachers who went door to door through Mexican neighborhoods who had referred them to these charities. After telling Mexicans to apply for relief, these social workers criticized them for following through on their suggestions.

THE MEXICAN DEPENDENCY STEREOTYPE

The first references to Mexicans as welfare dependent date to the late nineteenth century, but it was not until the 1920s that the stereotype became widespread. Between 1890 and 1920, the stereotype appeared only sporadically in academic and popular writings. In 1911 the Dillingham

Commission noted that "because of a lack of thrift and a tendency to regard public relief as a 'pension,' many Mexican families in Los Angeles were becoming 'public charges.'" Similarly, at the National Conference of Charities and Correction in 1913, a YMCA official presented a report on immigration to the Pacific Coast. While he focused on European immigration and the likely effects of the opening of the Panama Canal the following year, he called for more stringent examination of Mexicans attempting to enter the country. "This need is felt the more keenly when we realize the amount of dependency and delinquency cases among the Mexicans in the southern part of California," he said. Occasionally such stereotypes were challenged, but on the whole, social workers during this period expended little effort promulgating a dependency stereotype.[2]

In the early 1920s, however, social workers started to pay greater attention to Mexicans. The foreign-born Mexican population in California had increased tenfold between 1900 and 1920. And in 1921, the University of Southern California opened a School of Social Work under the direction of Emory Bogardus. Bogardus had been a student of the noted sociologist Robert Park and, according to the historian George Sánchez, "saw his mission in Los Angeles to be much like the more famous studies of social conditions of Chicago's ethnic working classes." Following the Chicago School model in which he was trained, Bogardus sent his students into various neighborhoods to document the social and economic conditions they observed. But he took a more "heavily moralistic" approach to studying Mexicans than did sociologists studying European immigrants in Chicago. According to Sánchez, Bogardus and his students saw their role "as awakening the growing Anglo American population of Los Angeles to the social realities and dangers represented by the poorer, ethnic newcomers to the region." The school produced many local teachers, principals, and settlement house workers, as well as several leading social reformers and public officials. It also provided training to caseworkers from the Los Angeles Department of Charities.[3]

By the mid-1920s, the idea that Mexicans constituted a "dependency problem" had become a constant refrain among social workers in Los Angeles. Bogardus led the charge, remarking that "A situation is clearly abnormal when a race [Mexicans] representing seven or eight percent of the population . . . furnished 28 to 30 percent of the charity cases." According to another "student of the problem," "social workers are almost a unit in testifying that of sick, dependents, delinquents and criminals, the Mexican furnishes a number quite out of proportion to the relative size of his group." Though Los Angeles was nearly always held out as an acute case, "In almost all cities and counties in which there is a large Mexican population," argued an anthropologist without data to support his claim, "the Mexicans receive most of the charitable assistance."[4]

Social workers in Los Angeles, as in much of the rest of the Southwest, were overwhelmingly native-born whites. These men and women believed a number of factors led Mexicans to become dependent. Some advanced racial arguments, suggesting that biology or culture made Mexicans prone to overuse relief. Archbishop Edward Hanna, head of the CCIH, argued that "Mexicans as a general rule become a public charge under slight provocation." He attributed this and other supposed liabilities to the fact that Mexicans "are for the most part Indians." A supervisor in the Department of Compulsory Education concurred that genetics were to blame: "The mixture of the two races (Spanish and Indian), is fundamentally responsible for the carefree, if not indolent characteristic of the race." Charles Goethe, a local businessman who was a member of a eugenics organization and of the national council of Survey Graphic—the leading national publication for social workers—spoke out against the fiscal costs of Mexican dependency. In one anti-Mexican screed, he declared that "The Mexican, with his low living standards, is a tremendous burden to our relief agencies. Our border cities are becoming surrounded with Mexican slum belts, and our relief costs are mounting because the peon requires relief out of all proportion to his numbers." Tying stereotypes of excessive fecundity with those of dependence, Goethe provided an anecdote about a Mexican man who had applied for charity to pay for haircuts for his thirty-three children. Invoking eugenic themes of "race suicide," he suggested that "at the same rate" this one Mexican, who "evidently does not hesitate to beg for charity," would become the "progenitor of 1,185,921 descendents in but four generations."[5]

Eugenic arguments were widely accepted among the white elite in the state, and its precepts were incorporated into state policies regarding mental health, public health, corrections, and educational institutions. Emory Bogardus, in fact, became a member of the Advisory Council of the American Eugenics Society in 1927 and served in this capacity for almost a decade. According to the historian Alexandra Stern, California was a leader in the national eugenics movement; one-third of all involuntary sterilizations carried out in the United States between 1909 and 1979 were performed in California. These eugenic themes were reflected in public health officials' belief that Mexicans were biologically susceptible to diseases such as tuberculosis. A public health official argued that "Mexicans are possessed of an extremely low racial immunity [to tuberculosis], which is probably due to the large admixture of Indian blood." Indeed, Mexicans "less contaminated by Indian blood" were said to show "more resistance to the disease." Because tuberculosis sometimes led to the death of a breadwinner and because it often disabled its victims for years, the disease led some sufferers and their family members to rely on relief. The Department of Charities observed that nearly a quarter of all Mexican outdoor relief cases could be traced, ultimately, to tuberculosis.[6]

Many social workers rejected biological explanations for dependency in favor of cultural ones. "Americans who understand the Mexican best have confidence in his ability," observed Bogardus. "They consider his backwardness a matter of heritage, rather than of heredity." These social workers believed that Mexicans were prone to dependency at least in part because they were, as a people, lazy. A social worker who conducted a study of fifty Mexican homes in the city traced this indolence to conditions in Mexico: "We seldom think of the Mexican at all, and when we do, it is to picture him a heavy lipped, sleepy eyed Latin reclining in the sun, too lazy to seek the shade. . . . Few persons stop to consider that behind those dull eyes lies the tragedy of a nation, that his idleness is due to lack of mental development—the result of years of oppression—and that his contentment with so little is but the heritage of generations who have been forced to adapt themselves to bitter poverty and insupportable tyranny." Similarly, Alfred White, who wrote his thesis on the Americanization prospects of Mexicans, described them as "procrastinators," a quality he believed was derived from the climate of Mexico, apparently sapping their "vitality" and making Mexicans "indolent and shiftless." According to White, the Mexican only works "when he feels like it or when hunger and shelter drive him to it. Among the masses the standard of living is so low that the Mexican has to work but little to exist, hence the apparent laziness." Still, when "treated like human beings," he added patronizingly, "a great deal can be accomplished."[7]

Mexicans' supposed lack of thrift was also said to contribute to the "dependency problem." Seasonal laborers were excoriated for their perceived failure to plan for long spells of unemployment. "The Mexican peon," White argued, "spends his money as fast as he earns it and when it is all gone he appeals to charity. From the Creole to the Peon the Mexican lives as if he were going to die tomorrow, and works as if he were going to live a thousand years. 'Mañana' is the squeak at every squeeze." Even sympathetic white reformers were nearly unanimous in their appraisal of Mexicans as "spenders not savers." Referring to the fictional "Juan García," the Mexican everyman, Robert McLean noted that: "Partial and incomplete statistics show that Mexican casuals participate in the budgets of relief organizations, to a degree far out of proportion to their share in the total population of the communities where they live. Always Juan García has been a poor man; never has he known what it means to have something laid by for a rainy day."[8]

In addition to these racial arguments, social workers' views of Mexicans were profoundly shaped by the labor market context. The National Conference of Catholic Charities explained that the Mexican was overrepresented on the relief rolls because "His labor is seasonal, when his job is finished he is out of employment; his wages are insufficient to carry him and his family . . . and he becomes a public charge." Charles Thomson, a Presbyterian minister, argued that Mexicans' dependence on relief was largely an "industrial problem," the result of "cheap labor . . . which loads upon our agencies the greater part of the burden of our social ills." McLean agreed: "We must remember that it is the laborer, the man who lives and works closest to the margin of existence, who needs the most charity. In Los Angeles . . . it is the Mexicans who do the common labor. In fact, we have imported them for that very purpose. We should not be surprised, then, if they should present what seems a disproportionate demand for charity." As a result, many came to blame the agricultural industry for the alleged social costs of Mexican immigration. "The employer pays for cheap labor but he does not pay for the Mexican," wrote Wilson Wallis. "The citizenry of the county, of the state and of the United States, pays the real expense of Mexican immigration. . . . They pay for it in the form of public hospitals, nurses, physicians, charity assistance, jails, retarded children—to say nothing of the community's inheritance of poor material for citizenship."[9]

There were a few social reformers in California who believed that Mexicans were not particularly dependent or an intolerable burden, but their numbers were small. Paul Taylor provided some of the more balanced accounts. Nevertheless, Taylor admitted that in and around Los Angeles "accounts of the pauperization of Mexicans were freely told to me in 1927 by both charity workers combating it, and by outsiders."[10]

AMERICANIZING THE MEXICAN

Despite the fact that many social workers had long believed that Mexicans were indolent, thriftless, and used to having others care for their needs, most had hope, especially in the early 1920s and before, that Americanization programs could help assimilate Mexicans and instill in them the Protestant work ethic. "The experience of those who have a right to speak," noted the Los Angeles United Charities in 1915, "seems to prove that efforts made in behalf of the Mexican bring results which carry infinite promise for the future." According to Sánchez, curing Mexican families of their indolent ways was a critical aim of the Americanization programs. "Because the Southwest lagged behind the rest of the nation in industrialization, local reformers were anxious to introduce Mexican[s] . . . as rapidly as possible to the temperament of industrial society and inculcate Mexican families with the 'Protestant work ethic.'" Mexican women, it was thought, needed to be taught the value of hard work, not only because it would keep the family off the dole but because it would fill the labor shortage in traditionally female industries—garment work, laundering, domestic service, and food preparation—which emerged with the restriction of immigration from Asia and Europe.[11]

Ironically, though keeping the family off charity was an important goal of the Americanization program, the entire project facilitated—even encouraged—Mexicans' use of relief. One of the primary functions of the Americanization program's home visitors was to connect immigrants to social services. The CCIH believed that one of the best ways to help immigrants assimilate was to provide the proper environment. If they lived in un-American conditions, social workers wondered, how could they expect them to become loyal Americans? Since home visitors encouraged their use of relief, some Mexicans were especially frustrated by the "dependent" stereotype that was emerging. "Mexicans are ashamed to ask for charity, and will not do it till they just can't help themselves," averred one man. But social workers "often send people around to visit and tell us that we need aid." These visits—sometimes as many as five to one household in a single day—were not always welcome. "Very frequently great resentment is felt by the Mexicans against the 'intrusions' of American social workers, nurses, etc.," wrote one Orange County resident. "'Why don't they leave us alone,' they say and frequently there is some measure of justice in their complaints." Seemingly oblivious to how they were perceived, social workers were confident Americanization programs were directly responsible for any "progress" made. "When the Mexican first arrives, he is, according to our standards, dirty, shiftless and lazy," explained one social worker. "His children go to school, to improvement clubs, to the mission, and it is to these institutions that the improvement in the home is due."[12]

By the mid-1920s, at the same time that the color status of Mexicans was increasingly being questioned, social workers started to believe that Americanization had failed. Compared to the Northeast and Midwest, Americanization efforts in the Southwest had been rather half-hearted. Municipal reformers did little outreach to incorporate immigrants, and other institutions like the church, schools, or employers were not committed to the task either. But social workers were not thinking about how these factors—or the severe racism Mexicans faced—shaped assimilation. They simply noted that naturalization rates were low, and they saw little evidence that Mexicans would ever become self-sufficient. Growers, who had a strong incentive to temper hostility toward Mexicans—lest it lead to immigration restriction—claimed that after Mexicans "are here a while they are perfectly able to earn enough money to take care of themselves." But social workers disagreed, noting that many could not support themselves even after they had lived in the United States ten years or more. According to one public health official, such data showed "very conclusively" that migrant labor work did "not promote the economic independence" of Mexicans. It was also difficult to conduct effective Americanization programs on a migrant population. "Obviously," argued McLean, "if we as Americans are interested in the post-war idea of 'Americanization,' our system of casual labor is the very worst that could be designed to accomplish such a result."[13]

Another part of the problem, according to social workers, was that Mexicans were coming in too quickly and in numbers too large to be assimilated. According to outdoor relief superintendent R. R. Miller, the problem of Mexican dependency would only come under control if the flow of Mexicans were "checked." And some social workers were concerned that "charity aid" was keeping Mexicans "from assuming full economic initiative." Mexicans, according to Bogardus, were not "accustomed to ask for public aid" in Mexico. But in the United States, they had "often been pauperized" and had "learned to look for more charity as a result of ill-advised charity methods." Bogardus suggested that social workers were learning from their past mistakes and that "Less emphasis on groceries and rent and more emphasis on personal rehabilitation is the newer attitude of the public relief agencies."[14]

But many social workers simply failed to see Mexicans as legitimate claimants on the public or private purse, especially since they were seen as not only foreign but temporary visitors. After providing statistics purportedly showing how "dependent" Mexicans had become, McLean ended by noting that more than 55 percent of the Bureau of Catholic Charities' funds "are absorbed by these visitors." Making the point even more directly, McLean wrote: "I think of him [the fictional Juan García] as a visitor in our commonwealth, and I want to say, 'Mr. García, please sit down!'" Because whites like McLean saw Mexicans as visitors—not community members—Mexicans were seen as less entitled to the community's charity. Rather, industry should provide for them if and when they required assistance. Reformers thought of Mexicans' use of relief not as aid to a struggling member of the community who was a current or future U.S. citizen; they grew to see relief as an illegitimate subsidy to the agricultural industry.[15]

MAKING THE CASE FOR RESTRICTION

Because Americanization was viewed as such a failure and because the social costs of Mexican immigration were thought to be so great, by the mid-1920s nearly all social workers in Southern California started to favor restrictions on Mexican immigration. Restriction was seen as necessary to exclude people they viewed as undesirable but also to give social workers a chance to assimilate those already here. Consequently, they marshaled data to support their claims that Mexicans were dependent, diseased, and inassimilable, and they actively lobbied for restriction. In 1925 the California Conference of Social Work released a study on the issue that was widely quoted in subsequent years by the press, in congressional hearings, and in scholarly journals. Mexicans, it said, represented 10 percent of Los Angeles County but 27 percent of the cases in the outdoor relief department, 52 percent of the cases at the Bureau of Catholic Charities, 43 percent of the cases at the General Hospital, and 62 percent of the cases of the city maternity service. Social workers and other city leaders subsequently visited women's organizations to talk about the charitable needs of the Mexican community and about the costs of Mexican immigration.[16]

Religious organizations also played a role in the construction of the dependency stereotype. Protestant churches were particularly interested in the welfare of the Mexican community, hoping that its charitable work would invite converts. Bromley Oxnam, pastor at the Church of All Nations, conducted a study of Mexicans in Los Angeles in 1920, the results of which were published in a variety of venues. In each, Mexicans' reliance on relief was highlighted: "The result of bad housing, illiteracy, and disease is seen clearly in the records of the Los Angeles County Charities. The Mexican, representing but one-twentieth of the population, contributes nearly one-quarter of the poverty cases handled by the county." The church boasted using the "pulpit and the press" to help educate the public about the causes of dependency among Mexicans, especially the role of sickness. While Oxnam believed his efforts would ultimately benefit Mexicans, they also helped spread the stereotype of Mexican dependency.[17]

Compared to Protestant churches, the Catholic Church in Los Angeles was slow to respond to the needs of the Mexican community, prompted to extend services only when Protestant denominations made concerted efforts to convert Mexicans. In 1920 the Church established the Catholic Welfare Bureau, which distributed outdoor relief, and ran health clinics and settlement houses. Through the *Associated Catholic Charities Report*, the Church disseminated data on Mexican charity cases. But out of concern that white parishioners would not appreciate that such a substantial portion of their donations were benefiting Mexicans, the Church stopped publicizing the work done to assist this community in the late 1920s. No such concern was evinced by the National Conference of Catholic Charities, which released a study in 1929 claiming that "In many cities with a large Mexican population, the Mexican is a great burden on the charities and social agencies of the city and state."[18]

Data on the social costs of Mexicans were also furnished by various public welfare agencies. In their 1927 annual report, the Los Angeles Department of Charities observed that Mexicans "come to the United States in destitute condition. . . . Their families are large in number and many of the members syphilitic or tuberculous. . . . Although they have no intention of becoming citizens and cannot be persuaded to return to Mexico, they early learn to demand aid from the public funds. Desertion, jail sentences, illness, illegitimacy and unemployment are the sources of poor citizenship among these immigrants." Public health departments were among some of the most vocal participants in the construction of Mexicans as an undue financial burden. A California State Board of Health report indicated that there were more than three hundred Mexican families in Los Angeles receiving county or state relief because a member of the family had tuberculosis. The Los Angeles County Health Department director argued that while the costs of treating the disease itself were high, the costs of supporting the victims and their families on public relief were truly "staggering": "Probably no other organization is as cognizant of the seriousness of the Mexican problem as is the county health department." The director then urged that employers reconsider their addiction to "cheap labor."[19]

Carey McWilliams decried the social workers' role in the construction of Mexicans as a "problem." The "Mexican Problem," McWilliams argued, was defined as "the sum total of the voluminous statistics on Mexican delinquency, poor housing, low wages, illiteracy and rates of disease." "Once assembled and classified," he wrote, "this depressing mass of social data was consistently interpreted in terms of what it revealed about the inadequacies and the weaknesses of the Mexican character."

> The data "proved" that Mexicans lacked leadership, discipline, and organization; . . . that they were lacking in thrift and enterprise. . . . Most of this theorizing was heavily weighted with gratuitous assumptions about Mexicans and Indians. Paradoxically, the more sympathetic the writer, the greater seems to have been the implied condescension.[20]

Looking at all the available evidence, however, it is clear that social workers exaggerated the extent of Mexican dependency, selectively citing statistics to make their case for restriction. The most comprehensive account of Mexican relief use came from Governor C. C. Young's Mexican Fact-Finding Committee, which was charged with investigating the "industrial, social and agricultural aspects of the problem of Mexican immigration into California." The report corroborated some of the findings put forth by social workers: while Mexicans represented 11 percent of the population in the county, they made up somewhere between a quarter and a third of all cases in the Los Angeles Outdoor Relief Department. And Mexicans made up between 46 and 73 percent of all children cared for by the Catholic Welfare Bureau.[21]

The data social workers reported, however, did not represent the entire story. Though Mexicans made up more than half of all children cared for by the Catholic Welfare Bureau, they only made up between 13 and 25 percent of family cases. More important, the vast majority of private charities in Los Angeles did not serve any Mexicans at all. Of the more than one hundred charities in Los Angeles's Community Chest, only seventeen served Mexicans. These were facts that social workers conveniently omitted, however. They also failed to mention that Mexicans were underrepresented among residents of the Los Angeles County Farm, where they made up only 4 percent of almshouse residents. Finally, social workers said nothing about Mexicans' use of Mothers' Pensions. According to the State Department of Social Welfare, Mexicans were only slightly overrepresented on the Mothers' Pension rolls. In 1928 about 10 percent of families on state aid (Mothers' Pensions) were Mexican, while they made up 7 to 9 percent of the population of the state. Any overrepresentation in the Mothers' Pension program was slight and certainly indicated that Mexicans were underrepresented relative to need. In fact, the State Department of Social Welfare acknowledged that many Mexicans who were eligible for state aid were denied it, forced onto the outdoor relief rolls instead. Los Angeles County had a policy of carrying Mexican families on outdoor relief who were eligible for state aid because they believed "that the feudal background of the Mexican makes it difficult, if not well nigh impossible, for him to understand and not abuse the principle of a regular grant of money to the state. For this reason the county gives relief in most cases on an emergency basis, and carries families on county aid who are legally eligible to state aid."[22]

Though social workers exaggerated the extent to which they were dependent, Mexicans in Los Angeles did have generous access to relief compared to Mexicans outside the state (or compared to blacks living in the South). And Los Angeles was not alone. Indeed in most Southern California counties, Mexicans appear to have been overrepresented in the outdoor relief rolls relative to their numbers in the population. Relative to their need, however, it seems unlikely that Mexicans were overusing relief. Bogardus estimated that the poverty rate among Mexicans was five times the rate of whites. A Los Angeles Health Department official noted that "There is more poverty and squalor among the Mexicans than among all the other foreign populations (43) combined." Describing the conditions of the residents of Maravilla Park—home to an estimated forty-five thousand Mexican residents—the Los Angeles Department of Charities claimed that "There are possibly not ten homes in Maravilla where the income is really adequate for the family needs."[23]

Once the data were culled and the reports written, social workers educated the public and legislators about the burdens of Mexican immigration and lobbied for immigration restriction. In 1926 the president of the CCIH sent a letter to every U.S. congressman and senator from California, urging restriction. "The Mexicans," the letter read, "as a general rule become a public charge under slight provocation and have become a great burden to our communities." The letter went on to state that Mexicans "are Indians," "know little of sanitation, are very low mentally and are generally unhealthy." The following year CCIH's annual report asserted that Mexicans were "causing an immense social problem for our charities, schools and health departments" and recommended that "unrestricted immigration from Mexico should be stopped."[24] The Los Angeles Department of Charities contended that Mexicans would never become self-supporting and urged restriction. A State Board of Health official also urged restriction and sent copies of her reports on the burdens of Mexicans with tuberculosis to the chair of the House Immigration Committee for him to circulate among his peers. These data were subsequently cited by advocates of restriction at congressional hearings on immigration in 1926 and 1928. She also spoke to various civic organizations, urging that a quota be placed on Mexico. Doctors and public health nurses in Los Angeles, citing the "unity and safety of our country" as well as the "intolerable" burden on the American taxpayers, also wrote to the House Immigration Committee in support of a quota on Mexican immigration. Politicians got into the act as well. The California legislature passed a joint resolution in 1929 calling on Congress to restrict immigration from Mexico. And the governor of California gave congressmen statistics on Mexicans' use of relief in his state.[25]

At the annual Friends of the Mexicans conference in 1927, an event sponsored by Pomona College to deal "with the problems growing out of the large Mexican population in the Southwest," an informal poll was taken on the question of whether the quota should be applied to Mexico: "All the representatives of the industries and of the Chambers of Commerce were opposed to any restriction upon Mexican immigration; all the teachers, ministers and social workers unitedly favored it." According to one observer, social workers favored restriction because they recognized "the social menace and economic burden of a mass of undigested Mexican population in the large centers of the Southwest." But he also argued that advocates of restriction were similarly concerned about the "best interests of the Mexican himself, recognizing that the Mexican labor supply now here is large enough to meet the demand if properly distributed. Restriction would force this distribution and bring about better living conditions, better wages, and a better understanding of the Mexicans now here." Bogardus likewise explained that social and public health workers "do not want more Mexicans to come until those who are here are better able to take care of themselves than they are now." Bogardus added, however, that "the danger of contagious diseases originating in and spreading from unsanitary Mexican quarters to the better-class American districts is great."[26] Charles Thomson questioned the wisdom of unrestricted immigration given the racial composition of Mexican migrants:

> [T]he Mexican laborer who comes to us is largely and in many cases wholly Indian in blood. He need not apologize for his race, and he does not; it has had a mysterious and romantic history, and he may well be proud of it. Yet the fact remains (whatever its implications) that his is a different race from the dominant strains which now people the United States. . . . At this juncture we may ask if the continuance of Mexican immigration means the creation of another racial problem with which our democracy must wrestle.[27]

While some social workers may have been concerned about the well-being of Mexicans already in the country, most rationales were heavily laden with stereotypes of the dependent, diseased, and unassimilated Mexican.

CURTAILING THE MEXICAN DEPENDENCY PROBLEM

Over time, charity officials made concerted efforts to trim the relief rolls of Mexicans. In Los Angeles the fraction of Mexicans on public outdoor relief declined from a high of 36 percent in 1926 to less than a quarter three years later. In 1929 Miller, the outdoor relief superintendent credited with tackling the "Mexican dependency problem," explained that it was now the policy of his department to restrict the length of time Mexicans could access relief. Though scientific casework principles called for intensive supervision of cases, Miller argued that it was too expensive to carry out the kind of casework necessary to make a difference.

> We do not presume to carry on an intensive, constructive case work program among these people [Mexicans]. If such should be our policy we could spend several millions of dollars in Maravilla Park alone . . . and see very little result for the amount of money spent. Wretched housing conditions, undernourishment, acute and chronic illness, etc., are prevalent in this community, and to adequately correct conditions it would demand an extremely large expenditure of funds.

Miller explained that in a recent study of the "Mexican Problem," it was found that one-third of the men cared for by relief were seasonal laborers, many of whom found it difficult to find work between harvests. These men, according to Miller, should be put to work for their groceries: "In order to protect the taxpayers from the constant requests for assistance . . . we arranged in Belvedere district [a Mexican community] to provide each man applying for help with a hose, spade, rake, paint brush, etc. and gave groceries to the families if the man would dig up the yards of other clients, repair out-buildings, plant gardens, etc." The "work test"—granting relief only to able-bodied individuals who were willing to labor for their bread—was a time-honored tradition among early relief providers. But in Los Angeles, the work test was reserved for Mexicans.[28]

Not only did local practices ensure Mexicans would be trimmed from the rolls, the state Pauper Act was amended in 1927, providing that "no one who has not resided in the State for one year will receive County aid." According to the County Board of Supervisors, "Heretofore anyone in need, even if they had just arrived in the State, was legally entitled to aid. This [new] law is bound to cause much suffering at first, but the responsibility of the County for the care of these people is at an end." This amendment disproportionately burdened migratory workers. Los Angeles also had a formal policy of giving Mexicans food and rent budgets that were 20 percent lower than those of other residents. Los Angeles's relatively generous treatment of Mexicans appears somewhat less generous upon further investigation. Nevertheless, nowhere else did Mexicans have so much access to relief.[29]

THE STEREOTYPE OF MEXICAN "DEPENDENCY" GAINS
A NATIONAL AUDIENCE

While the stereotype of Mexican dependency took root most firmly in Southern California, Mexican immigration also started to draw greater attention beyond the state in the early 1920s. Just as immigration from Mexico was increasing, the United States experienced a brief, yet severe, depression in 1920 and 1921. Hundreds of banks failed, nearly half a million farmers lost their land, and more than one hundred thousand businesses went under. Six million people were out of work by October 1921. Mexican immigrants were particularly hard hit. More than 20 percent were unemployed, while many of those who kept their jobs experienced wage cuts.[30]

As relief rolls rose, news articles called attention to the charitable work being done on behalf of destitute Mexicans. White residents in Denver were in a state of near hysteria over the mounting relief needs. One article described Denver as "crowded with Mexicans who are near starving." The city was "faced with the necessity of building new jails or chartering a railroad train for the deportation of hundreds of destitute Mexicans who are flocking into the city." Officials estimated that 70 percent of the five thousand Mexicans in Denver were "without means of support and must be fed by charity." Rather than holding the depression responsible, the deputy city attorney blamed Mexicans' poor work ethic and lack of thrift. "The idle foreigners," he argued, were responsible for "many of the holdups that have occurred in the city recently. 'They have squandered their summer earnings,' he said, 'and are a menace to the peace of the community.'" A year later, the situation had not abated. According to city officials, "between 3,000 and 3,500 unemployed Mexican men are roaming the streets of Denver, destitute." During the month of December, "Mexicans became so numerous at the [municipal] lodging house that unemployed white people had to sleep on the floor."[31]

While the Mexican population was heavily concentrated in the Southwest, they were also beginning to move north and east in search of work in the beet fields and especially in the factories, which promised better wages and more stable employment. They formed colonies all over the Midwest and even as far as the East Coast. The 1920–21 depression hit Mexicans living in the Midwest hard as well. Almost all of the Mexicans employed at the Ford Motor Company plant in Detroit lost their jobs. Sixty-five percent of Mexicans in Chicago were unemployed. According to the historian Zaragosa Vargas, "Officials in cities gripped by the fiscal crisis demanded that the federal government not feed the immigrants but promptly deport them to Mexico." In response, the Commissioner General of Immigration conducted a special investigation of Mexican immigrants who became public charges during the depression. The focus of the inquiry was on Mexican contract laborers who came into the United States under special exemptions during and immediately after World War I. The 1917 Immigration Act barred contract workers, illiterates, and those unable to pay the $8 head tax from entering the country. But growers complained of a labor shortage and received special exemptions for temporary Mexican labor. The contracting companies were liable for returning those workers to Mexico at the end of employment, but investigators found that most of the Mexicans on relief were not contract workers. And due to inadequate funds, the federal government engaged in only limited deportation efforts. Consequently, local officials, often at the urging of the Mexican Consulate and local charities, undertook efforts to repatriate the destitute Mexicans. By the end of this depression, more than 150,000 Mexicans had returned to Mexico.[32]

With not so distant memories of this brief depression already etched in the minds of these social workers, the growing presence of Mexicans outside the Southwest appeared all the more noteworthy when immigration from Europe was restricted in the mid-1920s. "With the passage of the 1924 Immigration Act," remarked Carey McWilliams, "the immigrant social agencies and Americanization institutes simply had to discover a new 'problem' and it was the Mexican's misfortune to appear on the scene, sombrero and all, concurrently with the impending liquidation of these agencies. As a consequence, he was promptly adopted as America's No. 1 immigrant problem." Western hemisphere immigrants—including Mexicans—were not included in the 1924 Immigration Act largely to appease agribusiness's desire for an unlimited supply of cheap labor. McWilliams noted that the number of articles on the "Mexican Problem" more than doubled in the decade after 1920. In danger of losing their jobs, he argued cynically, social workers refocused their energies toward better understanding the social and economic consequences of Mexican immigration.[33]

Indeed in 1925, only one year after the quota was applied to restrict southern and eastern European immigration, "the topic which above all others seemed to arouse the intense interest of a large number" of participants at the National Conference of Social Work "was that of Mexican migration to the United States and the community problems that are caused by it." Over the next few years, social workers made numerous presentations on the burdens of Mexican immigration at this annual conference. In 1926 a Red Cross official gave a talk titled "Social Problems of Our Mexican Population," noting that "Mexican people get into all kinds of difficulties and make big demands upon the staff and resources of the social agencies" in Los Angeles, El Paso, Chicago, and Denver. The following year, one speaker observed that "Scattered data which has come to my hands suggests that in Texas, California, and Arizona the Mexicans produce more than their share of pauperism and crime." The speaker acknowledged that plenty of other immigrants also had high rates of dependency in their early years of adapting to American society. Dependency and other social problems, he thought, were "solvable by proper environmental influences, provided that the cause of the conditions is not inherent in the blood of the Mexican immigrant," a theory he was not yet ready to discount. Some of the talks at these conferences were sympathetic toward Mexicans, noting their burden on local relief rolls but underscoring that such was the "price of cheap labor." Whether sympathetic or not, these presentations to a geographically diverse audience of social workers helped spread the stereotype of the Mexican dependency problem.[34]

Social workers outside California, however, were not as united in their assessment of Mexicans' propensity to rely on relief. In fact, in many areas charity officials provided anecdotal accounts claiming that Mexicans were hesitant to ask for charity. According to Paul Taylor, prior to the Great Depression concern about Mexican dependency was very strong in some places, like Los Angeles and northern Colorado, and weak in others, especially Chicago, Bethlehem, Pennsylvania, and Nueces County, Texas. A charity official in Nueces County, for example, told Taylor that Mexicans were generally reluctant to seek public relief. A crippled

Mexican man lived for more than a decade "on nickels and dimes from friends; he had no relatives." Charity officials did not "know he existed" until "Mexican friends called on us eleven days before he died, and the county buried him." According to this official, "Mexicans take more care of their own peoples, as individuals, than do whites. When the Mexicans get sick with tuberculosis . . . they wait [before seeking aid] until it's too late to be accepted in the State Sanitarium. Then we supply them with milk and eggs until they die." A social worker in Gary, Indiana, concurred that Mexicans tended not to seek charity on their own: "The Mexicans for us are not such a problem. They take care of themselves pretty well. Most of our cases on the Mexicans are cases that have been reported to us either by social workers, settlement houses [or] landlords. . . . They [Mexicans] are very shy and not on to the ways of this country." These newcomers were apparently unaware of the various resources available and did not ask for help. Taylor explained that Mexicans used less relief because they relied on the mutual aid of their fellow co-nationals but also because of their "low standards, to acceptance of whatever happens, and to timidity or pride."[35]

When Taylor investigated the situation in Chicago, he found few people who felt Mexicans represented a burden. Robert Jones, who studied Chicago's Mexican colony, similarly concluded that "Mexicans have not frequent[ed] charity institutions to marked degree," though "poverty and unemployment are a very real problem to them." The data bear out this assessment. There were few Mexicans on public outdoor relief or Mothers' Pensions, in part because residency requirements made accessing these programs difficult. Most Mexicans who needed assistance relied on the United Charities instead.[36]

According to the historian David Weber, most social workers in Chicago remained convinced "of the ultimate assimilability of the Mexicans." While social workers in California spread popular stereotypes of Mexicans as a dependent population, with a few exceptions "social workers and settlement house residents in Chicago rarely played upon Mexican poverty." Nevertheless, some privately resented their presence. A man who referred Mexicans to social agencies averred that "The United Charities and Cook County charities think that there are too many Mexicans in Chicago." And a United Charities employee told Taylor that Mexicans were "wretched house-keepers," formed households without the sacrament of marriage and failed to use the birth control information offered them: "We find that Mexicans do get on even if we don't help them. We don't know how they do it. The nurses marvel at how the Mexicans get on living on tortillas and tomatoes."[37]

Though it was challenged or less prevalent in some places, the stereotype of the dependent Mexican was certainly not confined to California and Colorado. Many reformers argued that Mexicans became overly dependent in most urban areas where they were found. In a broad (but hardly representative) study of Mexicans outside the Southwest, McLean argued that Mexicans comprised 2 percent of the population in which his survey was conducted but 7 percent of the relief budget. Elsewhere he argued that "In Detroit, Michigan, over a period of three years, one Mexican out of every eight has been given relief through the Public Welfare Bureau."[38]

Mexicans were not as well-known for relying on relief in Texas, but there was little organized relief there to rely upon. Still, signs of growing resentment could be found. The director of San Antonio's Social Welfare Bureau carped that Mexicans were the biggest beneficiaries of charity yet contributed little to the charity purse. He estimated that "75 per cent of the public-welfare work" performed in the city benefited "the Mexican people." But "Speaking for my own organization, in the past 10 years which I have been associated with it, there has only been $1 donated by Mexican people to help Mexican charity." Reflecting on this statement, the state commissioner of labor exclaimed, "One dollar in 10 years contributed by the large Mexican population of Texas's largest city to the important and necessary work of charity; that is the measure of interest taken by these alien people in supporting public welfare organization[s] of which their own kind are chief beneficiaries. . . . Very clearly the city of San Antonio has about all the Mexicans it can take care of. . . . there can be no shadow of doubt that the Mexican population of the city of San Antonio, of the State of Texas, and of the nation, constitutes a heavy liability upon our civilization." Reports of the Associated Charities in San Antonio contradict any claim that Mexicans were disproportionately dependent on relief. In fact, in San Antonio, Mexicans made up 35 percent of Associated Charities cases but represented 36 percent of the population. The story was largely similar elsewhere in the state. In most cities, Mexicans used relief in proportion to their numbers in the population.[39]

The issue of Mexican dependency became a central concern in the national hearings on immigration restriction in the late 1920s. In general, supporters of restriction—including social workers, labor unions, nativist organizations, and small growers who did not employ Mexican labor—tended to portray Mexicans as social and economic burdens. However, opponents of restriction—including large growers, the Chamber of Commerce, and politicians who represented these interests—were not uniform in their response to these charges. Some argued that the Mexican dependency problem had been exaggerated. The secretary of the United States Beet Sugar Association sent out questionnaires to all local sugar beet producers, asking them to report on Mexican relief use in their communities. The results, they told Congress, suggested Mexicans were actually underrepresented on relief. Local Chambers of Commerce also solicited data from charitable organizations to be used toward the same ends. Citing the variation in welfare use among Mexicans across different communities, other growers argued that high rates of dependency, where they existed, were the result of overly generous social workers, not anything inherent in the Mexican. Claiming that Los Angeles charities were pauperizing Mexicans, a Los Angeles Chamber of Commerce official asserted that it was "our social-service organizations, both governmental and civic, which [need] investigation and regulation rather than the Mexican population." Finally, other growers conceded that relief usage was high but argued that cutting off Mexican immigration would entail greater economic costs and that any other source of labor would lead to similar problems. While growers benefited from the extension of relief to Mexicans, they were primarily motivated to avoid restriction and ensure a steady supply of labor. Challenging the dependency stereotype was not necessary to achieve those ends.[40]

The most vigorous challenge to the dependency stereotype came from Mexicans themselves. Many Mexican Americans favored a quota on Mexican immigration. They rightly believed that whites failed to differentiate between Mexican Americans and Mexican immigrants and worried that the high rate of immigration was increasing racism toward both groups. But Mexicans resented accusations that they were too quick to rely on relief. Ernesto Galarza, a Mexican American activist, spoke at the National Conference of Social Work in 1929. Claiming to speak "for those who cannot speak for themselves," "I flatly disagree," Galarza told the audience, "with those who maintain" that Mexicans "refuse to work, preferring to live on charity." Mexicans were responsible for the rapid growth and development of the Southwest and because of this, he believed that social workers had a duty to assist Mexicans as they would anyone else. "If it is true that the Mexican has brought to you arms that have fastened a civilization on the Pacific slope," Galarza argued, "then give him his due. If you give him his earned wage and he proves improvident, teach him otherwise; if he is tuberculous, cure him; if he falls into indigence, raise him. He has built you an empire!" In response to Archbishop Hanna's diatribe against Mexicans, one woman wrote to him, incensed that a fellow Catholic would spread such vile stereotypes.

> You say that the Mexicans exhaust the supplies of our charitable institutions. Please consider that, per contra, more than one half of our nationality are catholics [sic]. From our prosperous people you derive more profits than the Mexican Government itself and from the poor crowd you squeeze out whatever you can in the churches.

Paul Taylor interviewed a Mexican man in Clovis, California, who acknowledged that there had "been a great deal of comment in the American press and in our own papers about the conditions of the Mexicans in Southern California. It seems that . . . state, county and city authorities have had to aid these Mexicans because they are sick, diseased, without work or money." But it was Mexicans, Mr. Martinez explained, who performed the "hardest, the dirtiest, the meanest and the lowest paying work. . . . under unsanitary, unhealthy conditions that no man, no white man would allow any other white man to tolerate." "But it is all right!" he added sarcastically. "We are Mexicans. We can stand it. If one of us becomes sick, dies or gets tuberculosis there will be more Mexicans to take our places." Mexicans, Martinez explained, were "ashamed to ask for charity" and would only ask for it as a last resort. "I would like to have you think," Mr. Martinez continued, "that most of the Mexicans . . . are not the . . . paupers as the papers say there are. We like to work, not for low wages, but for the highest we can get. We are not loafers. . . . We never beg and if we must ask for a id [sic] from charity it is only a small part of our people and they cannot do more. They are down to their last resort because of no work and because of the hard working conditions."[41]

Though Mexicans vigorously protested the dependency stereotype, those who did were usually not in positions of power that would allow them to successfully combat it. Social workers were seen as experts on the dependent population, and their attitudes toward their charges carried weight. These experts were cited in newspapers, in magazines, and at the congressional hearings on immigration. But few social workers were Mexican. There were no more than seventy—and perhaps only half as many—Mexican social workers nationwide, representing less than 0.2 percent of all social workers. Since they had little political power, Los Angeles city leaders were not inclined to give Mexicans a voice in city services. Like other immigrant groups, Mexicans ran their own mutual aid associations and a few private charities. In Los Angeles, organizations such as Las Ligas Mexicanas de Los Angeles, La Liga Cultural Mexicana, La Liga Latina Americana, and La Alianza Hispano Americana established cultural centers and provided after-school programs, adult education, health clinics, old-age homes, and libraries. Some of these *mutualistas* granted limited unemployment insurance, sickness and death benefits, and, less frequently, direct relief. But these mutual aid associations had limited resources and the mobility of the population made sustaining such organizations difficult. All of these factors contributed to limiting the effectiveness and reach of mutual aid organizations as sources of charity and economic support. Consequently, prior to the Depression, most destitute Mexicans in Los Angeles turned to the County Department of

Charities or to the Catholic Welfare Bureau when in need of support. And these agencies, in turn, were staffed by whites.[42]

The debate over Mexican restriction was widely covered by national magazines and journals, as well as in newspapers across the country. The *Saturday Evening Post*, "America's foremost" national weekly magazine, perhaps best remembered for its Norman Rockwell covers and with a circulation of almost three million, published five articles in 1928 on Mexicans and the quota. Three of the articles were part of a series written by *Post* correspondent and future Pulitzer Prize winner Kenneth Roberts. Roberts argued that the social problems attendant with Mexican immigration were too great a burden for the American taxpayer to bear. In both San Antonio and Los Angeles, Mexicans were said to require a disproportionate percentage of the charitable funds, primarily in the form of free medical services. "It is the contention of Californians who work among the Mexicans of Los Angeles County," argued Roberts, "that if those who clamor for more Mexican labor could travel with them through the Belvedere and the Maravilla Park sections of Los Angeles . . . and see the endless streets crowded with the shacks of illiterate, diseased, pauperized Mexicans, taking no interest whatever in the community, living constantly on the ragged edge of starvation, bringing countless numbers of American citizens into the world with the reckless prodigality of rabbits, they would realize the social problems brought into the United States by an unrestricted flow of Mexican peon labor are far in excess of any labor problems with which the state may be confronted." Because of its wide circulation, the *Post* "served as the chief vehicle for anti-Mexican propaganda," but articles in various periodicals across the country offered a similar message. Though partly a reflection of the racist and nativist sentiment of the public at large, the coverage of the quota question helped spread the stereotype of the "dependent Mexican."[43]

CONCLUSION

In the middle of the ravages of the Depression, a perceptive social worker in St. Paul, Minnesota, acknowledged that the failure to imagine Mexicans as a group capable of assimilation was itself creating a barrier to their acceptance and incorporation: "If we can permit the Mexicans to feel that they can become a normal part of our community by first believing it ourselves, and if we make a special effort to help them help themselves, they need not become a permanently disadvantaged and delinquent group. The solution of their problems rests with the white group more than within the Mexican community."[44] In many ways, this realization came too late.

Mexicans had greater access to relief in California than anywhere else in the nation. Access, however, came at a steep price. Once social workers started to feel as though Mexicans were not capable of racial assimilation they worked to convince the public and legislators that Mexicans were a social and economic burden and therefore should be excluded from the nation. To do so, they selectively cited statistics that made Mexicans appear more reliant on relief than they actually were. The political and labor market context of the Southwest helped shape social workers' attitudes. The low rate of naturalization, for example, was used as evidence that Mexicans would not assimilate, but this was in part the legacy of the municipal reform movement's failure to politically incorporate immigrants and the racism that made them resistant to the idea. The fact that many Mexicans were seasonal agricultural laborers helped fuel the perception that they would never become self-sufficient but also that they were not *worthy* of assistance. Their use of relief was not characterized as assistance to a community member in need. Rather, it was portrayed as a subsidy to the agricultural industry, which was only too happy to have their laborers use relief between harvests as long as that relief use did not endanger support for liberal immigration laws. Unfortunately, the stereotype of Mexican dependency was reaching its peak on the eve of the Great Depression. After the crash in October 1929, the critique against Mexicans' use of relief intensified and spread, becoming more truly national in scope. Driven by the belief that Mexicans were not entitled to the community's beneficence, social workers and relief officials from California to Detroit would soon help launch aggressive campaigns to expel destitute Mexicans from the country.

CHAPTER 5

No Beggar Spirit

IN 1917 THE FAMED SETTLEMENT HOUSE LEADER GRACE ABBOTT wrote that "Untrustworthy generalizations as to the extent of dependency among the foreign born, especially those from southern and eastern Europe, are frequently made." Mexicans indeed were not the only group stereotyped as charity prone prior to the Great Depression. Nativists and eugenicists had long tried to build a case that southern and eastern European immigrants were hereditary paupers and represented an enormous social and economic burden to the country. Unlike with Mexicans, however, social workers firmly rejected this characterization of European immigrants. Abbott concluded, based on "the evidence"—here, a single survey of paupers in public institutions—"that such dependency as exists among the foreign-born is not due to race or nationality." Southern and eastern European immigrants, she argued, had "by far the lowest ratio of almshouse pauperism." It was the older immigrants—the Irish, the Swiss, and the French—who represented the greatest burden on the nation's poorhouses. And if foreign-born whites needed more relief than native-born whites, it was because they were "at the bottom of the scale industrially." Immigrants were more likely than natives to have "industrial accidents and industrial disease" and poor English-language skills, to lack training, and to face discrimination. Abbott continued: "For these reasons his wages are more frequently inadequate, and he is, therefore, unable to provide for sickness and old age. As a larger per cent. of the newly arrived immigrants live on the margin, so a larger per cent. are pushed over for one reason or another into that unhappy group of public dependents."[1]

Immigration scholars have long noted that European immigrants were once perceived to be especially prone to rely on relief. Welfare scholars, on the other hand, have paid little attention to these stereotypes, focusing instead on how social workers viewed their charges. These reformers, they argue, saw European immigrants as culturally inept but nonetheless imagined them as "objects of reform" and so included them in their early social welfare efforts.[2] Social workers did more than simply imagine European immigrants as objects of reform; they became their defenders before a sometimes hostile public. They refuted assertions that southeastern European immigrants were paupers and worked to forge a competing construction, marshaling "evidence"—at times even selectively citing statistics—to prove that the new immigrants were hardworking, thrifty, sober, and self-sufficient. Part of their confidence in these immigrants rested on their firm conviction that southern and eastern Europeans were capable of economic and racial assimilation. Indeed, looking around, they would have found much evidence confirming these beliefs: from high naturalization rates to growing socioeconomic mobility, all facilitated by the racial, labor, and political context in which these immigrants lived. Social workers then lobbied against national origins quotas and tried to protect European immigrants from harsh immigration and deportation laws. All the while, they believed it was their duty to temper public opinion toward the group to help reduce prejudice and discrimination. Given the starkly different treatment afforded to Mexicans, it is ironic that European immigrants were more likely than Mexicans to benefit from relief.

The stereotype of dependency in America is typically associated with blacks. Contemporary scholarship has convincingly showed that white Americans now hate welfare in large part because they think most people on welfare are black and that blacks are undeserving of assistance.[3] But during the first third of the twentieth century, blacks were often thought to be the group *least* likely to depend on the dole. Indeed, most social workers and relief officials—whether black or white, in the North or in the South—described blacks as extremely hesitant to apply to the poorhouse. This was not because social workers had particularly positive views of blacks—they did not. But most studies of dependency showed that blacks were underrepresented in the relief rolls. Unlike western growers, southern planters were opposed to their tenants receiving relief. And because white reformers never believed that blacks were capable of achieving middle-class Anglo norms or transcending the color line, they had little desire to include blacks in their reform efforts. Rather than acknowledge that underrepresentation was due to lack of access (their greater poverty, after all, should have led them to be overrepresented), many social workers came up with cultural or biological reasons to justify low rates of dependency. On the whole, however, white social workers in the North and the South generally ignored blacks and black poverty prior to the Depression, preferring to spend most of their time and money on European immigrants. Despite demands for access, without any political power, blacks were unable to make significant or consistent gains against discrimination in relief provision. More thoroughly excluded than Mexicans, blacks responded by developing a parallel system of charitable institutions. By doing so, black elites were able to gain some measure of control over how the black poor would be treated and portrayed. Exclusion and segregation, then, allowed blacks to escape the stereotype of dependency, at least prior to the Depression.

EUROPEAN IMMIGRANTS AND THE DEPENDENCY STEREOTYPE

The idea that European immigrants—especially the new immigrants—were a dependent population was promoted by American eugenicists and was quite popular among nativists prior to the Depression. In the 1920s Kenneth Roberts wrote a series of *Saturday Evening Post* articles condemning southern and eastern European immigrants for the social costs they allegedly imposed on native-born whites. In one unsparing critique, he described southern and eastern Europeans as "the defeated, incompetent and unsuccessful—the very lowest layer of European Society. They are usually paupers by circumstance and too often parasites by training and inclination. They are expedited out of their countries by governments that do not want them, and they usually travel on money they have begged or demanded from America." Roberts found support for his assessments from the work of immigration restrictionists and eugenicists such as Prescott Hall, Edward Ross, and Harry Laughlin. Drawing on Darwin's theory of natural selection, American eugenicists in the early twentieth century tried to prove the heredibility of characteristics like mental illness, criminal behavior, feeblemindedness, and pauperism.[4]

The notion that a person could carry a heritable trait that would lead to dependency dates back to the first of the "family studies" of cacogenic (or "bad gened") families: Richard Dugdale's investigation of the "Jukes" in Ulster County, New York, in 1874. Dugdale and the authors of similar studies of the Ishmael or the Kallikak families "conceptualized cacogeneity as a kind of core rot, a degeneration of the germ plasm which might manifest itself in any one of a number of forms" including pauperism, crime, or disease. Dugdale's study originally began as a survey of inmates in New York State Prison where he worked. There, he found four inmates who were related and was able to trace the family line back to six sisters, born sometime between 1740 and 1770. Dugdale's survey of the family, which included 540 direct descendants of the original six sisters, revealed that the Jukes had been "breeding" generations of criminals, prostitutes, paupers, illegitimate children, and other "degenerates" ridden with mental illness and disease. While none of the most prominent works that came out of this family studies tradition targeted immigrants, they still reflect the concerns social reformers had with intermarriage and immigrants, as some of the "degeneracy" was directly attributed to marriages between native whites and "mixed breeds" or immigrants. A variety of solutions to the problem naturally followed, including laws that prohibited miscegenation, condoned involuntary sterilization, and excluded "defective" immigrants.[5]

The case of the Jukes and other similar family studies were "aired widely in the 1910s and 1920s" and were influential in the way many

people thought about dependency and immigration policy. Harry Laughlin, a prominent eugenicist, made an explicit link between the family studies and immigration restriction. "[Y]ou have to recognize the fact that
although we give opportunities in this country, everybody is not educa-
ble," Laughlin wrote. "This backwardness is not all due to environment,
because our field studies show that there is such a thing as bad stock . . .
while these three families [the Jukes, Ishmaels, and Kallikaks] have been
famous in magazines and newspapers, our field workers every month
send in case histories that deal with the same human types and conditions. The lesson is that immigrants should be examined, and the family
stock should be investigated, lest we admit more 'degenerate' blood."[6]

Eugenicists had two primary arguments about immigrants and dependency. First, they argued that the foreign born were overrepresented in
the nation's institutions for the insane, the feebleminded, the sick, and the
poor and therefore represented a tremendous fiscal burden to "American
taxpayers." Second, the fiscal costs of unregulated immigration were just
as important as the biological costs of the more recent immigration. Eugenics experts argued that immigrants from southeastern Europe were
biologically inferior to the native stock from northwestern Europe and
that southern and eastern European immigrants carried hereditary traits
that led to dependency and pauperism. Proving the link between dependency, degeneracy more broadly, and the new immigration became one
of Laughlin's primary aims. In 1922 he testified before the House Committee on Immigration and Naturalization about the social desirability
of America's new immigrants. He presented the committee with a report
on the prevalence of "socially inadequate" people—including the "feebleminded, insane, criminalistic, epileptic, inebriate, diseased, blind, deaf,
deformed and dependent"—in various racial and nationality groups. Not
surprisingly, Laughlin's study "proved" that southeastern Europeans were
more likely than northwestern Europeans to be "socially inadequate." Of
special interest here is his analysis of the dependent population, including
"orphans, ne'er-do-wells, the homeless, tramps, and paupers." He looked
at fifty-two state and federal institutions where dependent people were
housed, excluding municipal and private institutions as well as organizations that provided outdoor relief. His findings on pauperism, however,
ran counter to his hypotheses. His data showed that the white foreign
born were indeed overrepresented among institutionalized paupers relative to their numbers in the general population, but the new immigrants
were hardly to blame. Rather, it was the Irish, French, and British who
were most likely to rely on institutionalized relief.[7]

Laughlin tried his best to explain away this unexpected finding. First,
he argued that dependency was usually a condition for the very young
and the very old: "If very young, [the newer immigrants] would not be

admitted as immigrants if they were dependent on the state; that is, if they had no family to care for them. The same rule applies to old persons." Second, immigrants who became public charges within five years after entry could be deported, thereby lowering the representation of new immigrants on the relief rolls. Third, some immigrants were cared for by sectarian and ethnic organizations and therefore would not be found in public institutions. Fourth, state-supported institutions might give preference to the native born. All of these factors would artificially depress the number of new immigrants in institutions for dependents. In other words, the data did not reflect the true proportion of dependents that the newer immigrants would in time produce. In a convoluted deduction characteristic of much of his work, Laughlin concluded that since dependency, "besides being a sign of misfortune, is highly correlated with the lack of thrift and energy, allowing for all of these (four) factors, it seems clear that in the matter of family thrift, if not of personal industry, the immigrants of former generations were superior to those of the present time." Though southern and eastern Europeans were underrepresented among the dependents he surveyed, the data still, conveniently, failed to disprove that the new immigrants were hereditary paupers.[8]

Indeed for Laughlin as for other eugenicists, it was never solely about the high costs of dealing with defective immigrants; it was also about their biology. If the newer immigrants possessed this "dependent" character trait—which he firmly believed they did—then "The matter of soundness of family stock should be added to the balance when this Nation evaluates the worth of its immigrants, because many immigrants become parents and, by transmitting their own hereditary traits to their offspring, influence in the direction of their own inborn qualities, the character of the American future." It did not matter, then, that southern and eastern Europeans did not place an undue financial burden on state and federal institutions; in time they would as the "hereditary dependents" among them produced offspring who themselves would make their way into such institutions. To prove his point, he showed that the second generation was the group most likely to require relief in Massachusetts. Among nativists, Laughlin's analysis appeared, for the most part, rigorous and convincing. The chairman of the Committee on Immigration, Congressman Albert Johnson (R-WA), a fervent restrictionist and active member of the American Eugenics Society, found Laughlin's findings to be "biologically and statistically thorough and apparently sound."[9]

Despite the circular reasoning and questionable statistics, Laughlin's conclusions regarding the social inadequacy of the new immigrants made their way into the popular press, including Roberts's articles for the *Saturday Evening Post*. Roberts claimed that the financial cost of supporting dependent aliens was so great that "nearly 8 per cent of the total expenditures of all the states must be devoted to their upkeep in state custodial institutions," not including funds expended by private organizations. Quoting Laughlin directly, Roberts continued: "The present cash outlay for maintaining social inadequates is from the broader point of view, only one of the relatively minor costs of degeneracy. We found in several types of the inadequates that the children of immigrants fulfilled their quota to an extent several times greater than that fulfilled by their immigrant parents."[10]

Challenging the Dependency Stereotype

While both Mexicans and European immigrants were stereotyped as dependent, many more groups defended European immigrants against these charges. Business interests dependent on foreign-born white laborers immediately tried to poke holes in Laughlin's claims. The National Industrial Conference Board critiqued Laughlin's study for being unrepresentative. Laughlin had sampled only fifty-two institutions in thirty-five states but compared the racial composition of his sample with the racial composition of the country as a whole. The board criticized Laughlin further for comparing the rates of institutionalization in 1921 to the 1910 census data rather than the 1920 census. What is more, his analyses were based on small sample sizes, and the statistics were highly unreliable.[11]

By far the biggest defenders of European immigrants against charges of pauperism, however, were social workers and other social reformers; this is a key site of difference between Mexican and European immigrants. As early as 1912, the members of the Committee on Immigration of the National Conference of Charities and Correction argued that statistics showing immigrants "supply an undue proportion of criminals and paupers" were based on unfair comparisons. Though they did not provide alternative figures on the relative proportion of foreign-born paupers, they unanimously agreed that "the statement made by ill-informed persons regarding the undue proportion of criminals and paupers among immigrants is a mistake and has aroused unwarranted hostility." At the same conference the following year, Graham Taylor, founder of the Chicago Commons Settlement and incoming president of the National Conference of Charities and Correction, presented a report on the distribution and assimilation of immigrants. "It is claimed," Taylor told his audience, "that the physical, industrial and moral qualities of the southeastern immigrants are so inferior to those of the northwestern Europeans and British as to threaten to deteriorate American life and to increase our burdens in caring for dependents, defectives and delinquents." This, according to Taylor, was patently untrue: "As a matter of fact . . . the earlier immigrants are shown . . . to have had a larger proportion of pauper, mentally unsound, and criminally inclined people among them than the later immigrants have had." Taylor did not suggest that the new immigrants were culturally or biologically better or worse than the old; rather, he credited selective immigration laws with weeding out hereditary paupers and other "defectives." Nonetheless, Taylor argued, "By no demonstrable test has it yet been conclusively shown that the economic and social welfare of the United States has been impaired by the present immigration, in lowering wages, or the standards of living, in the increase of pauperism or delinquency." He called for a "halt in forming hasty judgments" until more data could be brought to bear on the question.[12]

Using census data on paupers in almshouses, Raymond Pearl, a professor of public health, also found that southern and eastern Europeans were less likely than older immigrant groups to rely on almshouses. "Immigration from five countries in particular, Austria, Mexico, Poland, Russia and Italy, has been subjected to much criticism," Pearl wrote. But "immigrants from each of these five countries contributed proportionately less to our almshouse pauperism in 1923 than any other group of foreign-born people in the country." The Irish and the Germans were, in fact, the groups who were substantially overrepresented in the almshouse population, while Russians and Italians were substantially underrepresented. The data, furthermore, indicated that the proportion of the foreign born in almshouses was declining more quickly than the native-born population. Pearl acknowledged that the almshouse data did not include paupers in private institutions or recipients of outdoor relief. In spite of these important data limitations, he maintained that the results had "a good deal of significance."[13]

The Foreign Language Information Service (FLIS), an immigrant advocacy organization, explicitly rejected the idea that European immigrants, as a group, relied heavily on relief. "One might think that aliens are prone to seek charity, that they fill more than their quota on the relief rolls" wrote the FLIS. "There seems to be no justification for such a charge nowadays and except in the early days of immigration, there probably never has been." In the eighteenth and first half of the nineteenth centuries, according to the FLIS, "this country was rightfully indignant at the dumping of paupers on its shores by certain foreign governments." But this problem had been solved by the beginning of the twentieth century. The FLIS based its conclusion in part on the data used by Pearl as well as data from the Dillingham Commission report.[14]

The Immigration Act of 1907 established the Commission of Immigration—popularly known as the Dillingham Commission—and charged it with making "an exhaustive investigation of the impact of immigration on the nation." The commission issued a forty-two-volume report in 1911 on the new "immigration problem." Two of the volumes concerned "immigrants as charity seekers." The commission examined data compiled by the Census Bureau and the Bureaus of Immigration and Naturalization for the period 1850–1908 and commissioned a study of "federated charity organizations in 43 cities during the winter of 1908–1909." They produced hundreds of tables detailing the race and nationality of charity recipients in these cities. The commission concluded that southern and eastern Europeans were not disproportionately likely to become paupers: "The number of those admitted who receive assistance from organized charity in cities is relatively small." Interestingly, the commission did not compare the fraction of immigrants in these forty-three cities with the fraction of the relief recipients who were immigrants—the 1910 census data were not available when the report went to press. Rather, it came to that conclusion because there was a small fraction of immigrants on relief who had recently entered the country, "while nearly half of all the foreign-born cases were those who had been in the United States twenty years or more." The commission concluded that the public charge doctrine (which excluded immigrants likely to become a public charge and provided for the deportation of those who became public charges within three years of arrival from causes existing prior to entry) had obviously been effective.[15]

Had the commission actually compared the fraction of southeastern European immigrants on relief in these cities with their distribution in the population, they may have been somewhat less optimistic. There were only nine cities where the foreign born were underrepresented among relief cases (Cincinnati, Dayton, Des Moines, Evansville, Indianapolis, Louisville, St. Louis, Springfield, and Washington, D.C.). While in some cities their overrepresentation was slight (Atlanta: 2.9 percent of the population and 3.1 percent of the relief recipients), in many it was quite large (Buffalo: 28 percent of the population but 68.5 percent of the charity recipients). Aggregating across all forty-three cities, the foreign born made up 27 percent of the population but represented 42 percent of the charity recipients. Southeastern Europeans, meanwhile, made up 11 percent of the population but 20 percent of all charity recipients. In some cities, the disparity was much larger. In Chicago the new immigrants were 16 percent of the population and 38 percent of recipients. In Cleveland they were 20 percent of the population and 38 percent of recipients. And in Buffalo, southern and eastern Europeans made up less than 10 percent of the population but almost half the relief recipients. The Dillingham Commission was excoriating Mexicans for becoming a public charge based solely on their representation on the relief rolls of Los Angeles, and they could have made a similar complaint about southern and eastern Europeans in the cities of Buffalo, Chicago, and Cleveland. But they did not. And given that the Dillingham Commission's verdict was favorable toward the new immigrants, social workers certainly were not going to be the ones to do it.[16]

While many social workers rejected assertions that European immigrants were paupers, most of the time social workers simply ignored or downplayed data on white foreigners' use of relief. In some cities, charity officials drew attention to the fact that the largest single group of relief recipients were native born, ignoring whether foreign-born whites were overrepresented. The Family Society of Philadelphia emphasized that "The American born white still leads in the number of applications with 40.2%," without dwelling on who made up the remaining 60 percent. Prior to World War I, Chicago public relief officials commented frequently on the "inferior physical make-up" of the new immigrants from southeastern Europe and the burden that this "lowest type" of immigrant was causing for their department. But through the efforts of the Immigrants' Protective League and other social workers, the attitudes of public relief officials softened considerably. During the 1920s, the annual reports of the Cook County Bureau of Public Welfare had numerous tables showing the race or nationality of its relief recipients, but they did not comment on the results of those analyses, nor did they provide information that would allow for a comparison with the population as a whole. When compared against data from the U.S. Census, however, Cook County's own relief statistics show that the new immigrants made up 16 percent of Cook County residents in 1920 but 49 percent of outdoor relief recipients and 56 percent of Mothers' Pension recipients. And yet Chicago's relief officials no longer made anything of this fact and often publicly defended southern and eastern Europeans from charges that they were a charitable burden.[17]

In 1921 the U.S. Children's Bureau undertook a comparative study of Mothers' Pension recipients in eight counties scattered across several states. The study showed that foreign-born whites were overrepresented in the generous Mothers' Pension rolls. For example, while they made up 13 percent of St. Louis's population, the foreign born represented 40 percent of the city's Mothers' Pension recipients. Southeastern Europeans in particular benefited from the program. While they made up roughly 6 percent of St. Louis's population, they represented 31 percent of the Mothers' Pension recipients. Northwestern Europeans, by contrast, made up 7 percent of the city but 10 percent of the Mothers' Pension recipients. This discrepancy probably reflects differences in the age structure and socioeconomic status of the two groups, as northwestern European immigrants were older, on average, than the "new immigrants" and were relatively advantaged socioeconomically. The report made little of the fact that foreign-born whites were overrepresented on the pension rolls, however, and even portrayed immigrant pensioners sympathetically as

good mothers who kept their houses "clean and neat." Had social workers wanted to make an indictment against southern and eastern Europeans, the data were certainly available. Just as social workers did with
Mexicans, they could have easily cherry-picked data from cities where
southern and eastern Europeans' reliance on relief was particularly heavy.
But they generally chose not to do so.[18]

While most social workers simply sidestepped the debate about dependency, a few tackled the issue head-on. But rather than focus on the
over- or underrepresentation of groups on relief, they suggested that
southeastern Europeans had cultural traits that would lead them away
from the poorhouse in the long run. Kate Claghorn, who worked in New
York's Tenement House Department, argued in 1904 that "in view of the
present uneasiness with regard to the changed racial character of immigration and its great and increasing volume," it was important to know
whether the newer immigrants "will follow their Irish, English and German predecessors to the poorhouse." Claghorn was fairly sanguine about
the prospects of the new immigrants. "On the whole," she concluded,
"there seems to be no reason why the second generation of Italian, Slavic
and Hebrew immigrants, as a body, should furnish more paupers than
did the Irish, Germans and English."[19]

Claghorn came to her conclusion using evidence from local studies, her
experience with the groups in question, and an analysis of the causes of
dependency among southern and eastern Europeans in a four-city study
of over seven thousand charity recipients. She argued that though Italians
generally came to the United States illiterate, with very little capital, and
with few skills, they were still unlikely to become public charges. There
was a high demand for Italian labor, and they had an ethnic network
of sorts—the *padrone* system—which connected new Italian immigrants
with employers as soon as they disembarked at port. In addition, Italians
displayed a tendency to return to Italy "at the close of the busy season
for unskilled work" or during an economic depression. To the extent that
Italians became dependent, Claghorn noted that it was the professional
immigrants—those who had been teachers, lawyers, or musicians—rather
than the unskilled laborers who needed relief sooner and were the hardest cases to resolve because they could not use their professional skills
immediately upon arrival. Italian families were more likely to need relief
than were single individuals, she noted. Still, "in cases where family relations were unbroken, the causes of need were mainly sickness and lack of
work" rather than misconduct. Indeed, she argued that "an encouraging
feature of the situation is that few cases were shown where the cause of
need was shiftlessness or laziness, or the 'beggar spirit,' and almost none
in which drunkenness appeared as a factor." Furthermore, in many cases,
Italians only needed relief for a brief period, and when the "head of the

family finds work, or the sickness comes to an end . . . the family is on its feet again." On balance, Claghorn was quite sanguine that Italians would not contribute an undue proportion of paupers to American charitable institutions, and her analysis of the cultural traits of Slavs and Hebrews led her to be similarly hopeful about those groups. Indeed, Claghorn concluded that relative to the old immigrants, the new immigrants were more likely to need relief due to misfortune (no male support, lack of employment, sickness, or death) rather than misconduct (drink, shiftlessness, inefficiency, crime, or dishonesty): "The main source of danger as to pauperism from our immigrants of to-day is the severe economic pressure they are subjected to." Low wages, unsanitary dwellings, poor health, and lack of social insurance led immigrants to require temporary relief. But over time, these immigrants were managing to save and their standards of living were rising, and as long as cities did their part to improve housing conditions, she saw no reason why they would not prosper.[20]

Lee Frankel of New York's United Hebrew Charities was similarly optimistic. He argued that Jews became dependent on relief mainly due to "economic and industrial causes." They stayed away from alcohol and were known, in fact, for many virtues including "love of home," "the inherent desire to preserve the purity of the family," a proclivity for education, and a strong desire for self-advancement. Most of those who applied for relief, moreover, needed only very temporary assistance. Long-term cases generally involved "respectable aged and infirm couples" or families where the wage earner had died or become incapacitated through illness. Even those in the latter category did not often remain on relief. According to Frankel, "The brightest and most hopeful chapter in the history of Jewish charity is the avidity and eagerness with which its beneficiaries, bereft of the main wage-earner, become self supporting and independent as soon as the children are old enough to contribute to the family income." Furthermore, since only 2 percent of the families who applied for assistance through Hebrew Charities were native born, he inferred that dependency ended with the first generation. Without considering whether the second generation sought assistance elsewhere, he claimed that "Roughly speaking, it may be said that there are no American born Jewish poor."[21]

Not all social reformers agreed, certainly, that immigration from southern and eastern Europe had little effect on pauperism. Robert Hunter, a settlement house worker and the author of the classic treatise *Poverty*, argued that the new immigrants contributed to relief costs indirectly by flooding the low-wage labor market, increasing unemployment, decreasing wages, increasing poverty, and thereby causing the native born to have to rely on relief. Though Hunter blamed the new immigrants for this state of affairs, he did not argue that they were more likely to depend on relief. He concurred that it was the older immigrants who were flooding the poorhouses.[22]

Whether or not they agreed that southeastern Europeans represented a "dependency problem," some social workers conceded that the foreign born—usually referring to European immigrants in general—were disproportionately dependent on relief. "The thing which most strikes one in a visit to the public institutions of the state," wrote Hunter, "is the great number of foreigners of all nationalities which one finds there. . . . the burden of the dependent foreign born is shown to be a very heavy one." Even Claghorn concurred: "It is plain enough that foreign immigration has some connection with the problem of pauperism since common observation and all the statistics available unite in showing that the majority of recipients of our charity, public and private, are of foreign birth." But when social workers acknowledged that foreign-born whites were more likely than native-born whites to rely on relief, they usually described it as an inevitable outcome of migration. And they stressed that the social benefits of immigration outweighed any costs associated with their greater dependency. A speaker at the National Conference of Charities and Correction in 1912 reflected that it would of course be desirable "that the immigrants coming to this country should be all educated, all moral, all immune from disease."

> In that event none of them would become public charges and the cost of maintenance for those that fall either physically or morally, would be spared us. This, however, cannot reasonably be expected. The people who come to us are average human beings with the average virtues and the average vices. What it may cost us to maintain in public institutions those who must be so maintained, is but an infinitesimal fraction of what they bring us in material wealth.[23]

Because social workers were confident that the new immigrants would eventually rise out of poverty, characterizations of individual European immigrant families on relief were often sympathetic. White foreign-born women in particular were often portrayed sentimentally, as the long-suffering "Madonna" whose culture and current degraded living conditions made the attainment of the motherhood ideal difficult but not impossible. In 1911 the Philadelphia Society for Organizing Charity described one Polish widow as "A beggar against her will."

> Six small children and a mortgage on his home was the legacy which Franczisck Wisnewsky left his widow. His lingering illness, before he died, had exhausted the savings of a thrifty life. . . . It is not strange that Mrs. Wisnewsky soon adopted the only-income producing course she could think of; she took one of the children and started out to beg.

Her poverty, in other words, was not her fault.

> We have been working with Mrs. Wisnewsky and her problems for a year. She has regular work and a friendly visitor who helps her to learn English and to understand the American point of view of her own children, who are now regular at school. Nor was it very hard to find someone to assume the mortgage payments until the children are old enough to work, when Mrs. Wisnewsky looks forward to entire independence.

The Wisnewskys were portrayed as thrifty and capable of independence, especially with a little guidance and a mortgage subsidy from the caseworker.[24]

Unlike Mexicans, southern and eastern Europeans like the Wisnewskys tended to be stereotyped by social workers as thrifty and hardworking, which only reinforced the view that they were less likely than Mexicans to be culturally dependent. The Department of Public Welfare in Chicago praised Italians for their thrift and work ethic: "Their steady, sober, sensible thrift and industry has helped to make us the richest nation in the world." The executive secretary of the Council of Social Agencies in Boston described Polish farmers living in rural Massachusetts as "hardworking" and upwardly mobile. Grace Abbott in Chicago described Greeks as "industrious" and "willing to do any kind of hard physical work," who also "thriftily take advantage of every opportunity for advancement." The secretary of the Buffalo Charity Organization Society asserted that while "the proportion of Poles exceeds all others in . . . the city poor office," all they needed was the attention of the social service community that had heretofore ignored them. "They are thrifty, they are clean, they are willing, and they are neglected. They are raw material of the first value, undeveloped and wasting."[25]

Whenever and generally wherever direct comparisons were made, Mexicans were ranked below Europeans in terms of thrift and ambition. Victor Clark described Mexicans as improvident, ranking them below Russians where thrift was concerned. Similarly, when comparing Mexicans against "German-Russians," Paul Taylor argued that "as a group," Mexicans "possess less foresight, ambition and initiative," and suggested that Mexicans' need for relief "may be heavier than with workers of a more provident race." Writing on Mexicans living in Denver, Theodore Rice argued that the earlier Russian and German immigrants to northern Colorado "were from the section of Europe where it is necessary to work exceedingly hard, and to be very frugal in order to exist. So as they went to the beet fields, through frugality and thrift, they soon began to acquire land of their own." "The Mexicans and the Spanish Americans," meanwhile, "were not of the frugal type who became property owners, as did the Germans, Japanese and the Chinese. They came from districts of America and Mexico where the standard of living is low, and where the domestic system has been largely untouched by the industrial revolution." An article in the *Detroit News* noted that before World War I, "Russians and others prospered. They established bank accounts and hundreds bought little farms, which they still hold. The Mexicans got the money but made different use of it. They spent it for silk shorts and silk stockings, jewelry and perfumery and canned beans." Mexicans may well have been more improvident than other groups, but accepting these stereotypes at face value is exceedingly problematic, especially since the stereotypes of dependency had very little basis in fact. Indeed, European immigrants were far more dependent on relief than were Mexicans. Furthermore, other work suggests that the volume of remittances to Mexico prior to World War II was high and perhaps underappreciated prior to the Depression, belying claims of Mexican thriftlessness. Whatever the truth of the matter, the perception that Mexicans were spenders, not savers—and that this trait was either culturally or biologically ingrained rather than the result of low wages and seasonal employment—contributed to the idea that Mexicans would always be forced to rely on others to get by.[26]

Right around the time that Claghorn, Frankel, and Hunter were writing, social workers, especially in the Northeast and Midwest, were starting to prefer environmental over hereditary or cultural explanations for poverty and dependence. Immigrants, they argued, were more likely to need relief than natives because their social networks were smaller. The Poor Laws required that individuals rely on family in times of need; relief was a last resort. Because the "alien laborer has frequently been alone, without relatives or friends to help him during a period of distress," explained Edith Abbott, "he has therefore been more likely than the native-born laborer to become a public charge." Immigrants, it was also argued, generally came as laborers, at the bottom of the socioeconomic ladder, and therefore had a greater need for relief. "Immigrants have constituted our unskilled labor supply," wrote Abbott, "and, as workers on the lowest economic level, have suffered disproportionately from the hazards of industrial accident and disease, unemployment and low wages." Hunter, too, argued that while Irish Americans were overrepresented in the relief rolls in Massachusetts, he did not believe that there were any "qualities inherent in the Irish to which may be attributed the cause of this degeneration. It seems difficult to explain it except on the ground of excessive competition among workers. In the rural communities, where the competition of the recent immigrants has not been felt, the Irish, on the whole, have developed into very excellent Americans." Low wages led to crowded living conditions in tenements or "the unsanitary dwellings of the mill or mining town," breeding tuberculosis and engendering poor health and ultimately leading immigrants to the poorhouse. A professor at Johns Hopkins argued that ten million Americans lived in poverty in 1914 but "neither race qualities nor national characteristics account for the presence of such poverty. It persists as an accompaniment of modern economic life. . . . It cannot be identified with alien elements in native race stocks." The stress of living conditions in their new home might also lead one to relief. "The difficulties of adjustment," argued Edith Abbott, "may prove too great for the new arrivals, even when they are desirable classes, and may lead to physical, mental or moral breakdown." For many social workers, then, the idea that the foreign born would be more dependent on charity was an inevitable byproduct of the process of mass migration. Immigrants did not have to have inborn traits that made them more likely to need relief; the difficulties of adjustment to a new land were sufficient. "Pauperism is not something that the immigrant brings with him," argued Claghorn, "but is the result of a considerable period of life and experiences here."[27]

A Boston social worker even portrayed immigrants' greater use of social services as a virtue. While immigrants may be more likely than natives to see a caseworker, she argued, they were not looking for a handout: "The immigrant gets into trouble and needs assistance most often because of a failure to understand American requirements or because of imperfect adaptation to our conditions." She estimated that 90 percent of immigrant cases involved simply giving advice on, for example, where to find work, get medical care, or apply for naturalization. "The immigrant comes to us strong, eager, ambitious," she concluded. "Give him a chance and he will do the rest."[28]

Over time social workers grew increasingly confident that social reforms and intensive casework could reduce dependency among the new European immigrants. It was in part because they always believed that southeastern Europeans were capable of racial assimilation; they were hopeful of their eventual economic integration in the mainstream. Lamenting the passage of the quota laws, Edith Abbott told an audience of social workers in 1924 that "Croatian and Slovenian, Ruthenian, Slovak, and Lithuanian, these names sound strange and foreign and 'unassimilable' to the ordinary citizen, but to those of us who have been meeting these people day by day, week by week, and year by year as neighbors in our settlements and as people in trouble in our charity offices, they are like the rest of us except that opportunities which have always been ours are new to them." Lee Frankel concurred, writing that "The history of the Jewish charities . . . demonstrates nothing more forcibly than that the Jewish immigrant readily adapts himself to his American environment, easily assimilates the customs and language of his adopted country, and even though he may temporarily require assistance, rapidly becomes independent of charitable interference."

The immigrant Jew is frequently poverty stricken. He is rarely a pauper. . . . He is not found in the besotted, degenerate, hopeless mass of humanity constituting the flotsam and jetsam of society. . . . Given the opportunity and the proper surroundings, the immigrant Jew will become an addition to the body politic and not a menace.

Relief, in fact, could speed that assimilation. Scholars have shown that one of the primary purposes of Mothers' Pensions was to facilitate the cultural assimilation of southern and eastern European immigrants. In return for a pension, reformers insisted on assimilation through literacy and language instruction, vocational training, civics lessons, and health services.[29]

By insisting on cultural assimilation in return for assistance, caseworkers were exercising an incredible amount of social control. They expected immigrant families to "improve" their housework habits, learn English, alter their family's diets, and save and spend as the caseworker dictated. In Minnesota, Mothers' Pension recipients were required to speak English at home. Immigrants, in turn, often felt that caseworkers were intrusive, controlling, patronizing, and condescending. Complaining about snooping social workers, one immigrant from New York's Lower East Side exclaimed: "soon they'll look into my teeth or pump my stomach to find out what foods I've been eating." Many immigrants resisted this control and tried to use the services offered without fully giving in to the assimilationist designs. The reward for even partial conformity was near full social inclusion for the immigrant parents and full social inclusion for their American children. Inclusion came at a heavy price, but not everyone was given the option.[30]

Wherever social workers made direct comparisons during the late 1920s about the assimilative potential of Mexican versus European immigrants, Mexicans came up short. In 1916 the CCIH compared "the Italian with his love of industry and frugality, whose adaptability makes him quickly assimilated," to "the Mexican with his lack of initiative, whose roving temper increases the difficulty of adjusting him." Noting that they were not "Americanizing [Mexicans] or doing half of what we might," a County Charities worker in Mason City, Iowa, questioned the logic of restricting immigration from Europe and not Mexico: "Why should we prevent good German or Greek women from coming to this country? They are better than the miserable, dirty, nasty Mexicans as they are many times." A charity worker in Gary, Indiana, was, in fact, one of the few Anglos to rate Mexicans favorably against other groups on issues of dependency: "Charity does not pauperize the Mexicans. They get away from it as soon as they can. But the other nationalities around here. Some of them are just beggars. The Mexican as soon as he gets well, or as soon as he get[s] work is gone. We hear no more of him." This perspective was more common outside the Southwest, but even in Gary it was hardly universal. The head of Gary's Catholic settlement house, Reverend De Ville, protested that "we have shut out European immigrants and have accepted the uncivilized Mexican in his place. . . . You can Americanize the man from southeastern and southern Europe, but [you] can't Americanize a Mexican."[31]

The fact that De Ville was Austrian born may have influenced his views of southern and eastern Europeans. Indeed, while the vast majority of social workers in the Southwest were native-born whites, social agencies in the Northeast and Midwest increasingly employed caseworkers who were first- or second-generation European—a group they called "nationality workers." In 1930 there were more than 3,100 foreign-born white social workers nationwide, representing 10 percent of all social workers. The vast majority worked in the North, where they represented roughly 18 percent of all social workers. Another 20 percent were second generation. Most of the nationality workers were of northern and western European or Canadian stock, but some were of southeastern European heritage. In some places, political patronage may have been responsible for the diversified relief force. But social workers in the Northeast and Midwest also made it a point to hire nationality workers because they believed that they had foreign-language skills and cultural knowledge that gave them unique insights into the lives of the foreign-born poor.[32]

Despite their growing presence in the field, nationality workers certainly did not dominate the profession. The vast majority of reform leaders were still Anglo, Protestant, American-born women.[33] Yet most social workers—whether first, second, or third-plus generation—believed that their efforts to assimilate European immigrants would ultimately prove successful. They were simply not as sanguine about their ability to assimilate Mexicans. Social workers, of course, had ample reason to believe that European immigrants would assimilate more quickly than Mexicans. European immigrants were largely treated as white, while Mexicans were increasingly perceived to be non-white. And the local context of the Northeast and Midwest encouraged naturalization and a certain degree of socioeconomic mobility. Mexicans, on the other hand, were trapped in a vicious circle. Great racism and a less hospitable political context led Mexicans to resist naturalization, which in turn led to more racism.

Advocating on Behalf of European Immigrants

Social workers and relief providers became strong advocates for European immigrants. They actively constructed European immigrants as deserving, wielded data to prove their preconceptions, and made sustained efforts to convince legislators and the broader public of their "expert" opinions. Social workers believed they had a duty to help shape public opinion toward European immigrants. According to the *Social Work Year Book* "'Interpreting the foreign born to America is regarded by both public and private social agencies as an important part of their activities." Social workers did this by staging cultural events and conferences, giving talks at women's clubs, and refuting nativists' biased claims by providing accurate (or at least more sympathetic) information to the press. The FLIS was one of the principal vehicles through which immigrant advocates could get information not only to the foreign-language press but also to the English-language press. In its public education work, it endeavored to give "the native born accurate information on the foreign born groups, and the conditions affecting them in the effort to break through the wall of prejudice."[34]

Sometimes in concert with academics, social workers conducted research in order to dispel myths or better understand the impact of various policies on the lives of European immigrants. When Mothers' Pension legislation was first passed in Illinois in 1911, there was no citizenship requirement. However, by 1913 the policy came under attack by nativist and economizing legislators, and a law was passed limiting the pensions to U.S. citizens. Soon thereafter, the School of Civics and Philanthropy, which trained Chicago's social workers, conducted a study on the effects of the new legislation. They found over 1,100 families who had had their pensions cut as a result of the new law. The survey showed that the restriction "hit children hardest, eliminating 79 percent of them from the rolls because their mothers no longer met the qualifications." They noted that some of the families who were cut off did not get assistance from any other source and that "families were broken up and children institutionalized" in some cases. Ultimately, the Mothers' Pension law was liberalized somewhat and American-born children of non-citizens were given access to the pensions. Where Los Angeles social workers were crafting studies to show how dependent Mexicans were, social workers in Chicago were trying to demonstrate how citizenship requirements hurt immigrant well-being.[35]

Unlike social workers in the Southwest who lobbied for restriction on immigration from Mexico, social welfare workers in the Northeast and Midwest lobbied for immigration, deportation, and naturalization reform. Many settlement leaders, for example, tried to "block or modify the restrictive immigration laws of 1921 and 1924." Once the laws went into effect social workers were almost a unit in decrying the hardships the new law imposed on the foreign born. They coordinated their efforts to tackle the problem of separated families or the hardships related to deportation laws and procedures.[36]

None of this is to say that social workers in the Northeast and Midwest were against *any* immigration laws that might affect European immigrants. While they opposed national origins quotas, some were open to numerical restriction especially if it helped the assimilation of those already in the United States. Moreover, historically, charity officials had lobbied to pass selective immigration restrictions. In the late nineteenth century many charity officials believed that European governments—especially England and Ireland—were dumping their paupers on U.S. soil. When state efforts to deal with the situation were ruled unconstitutional, various states lobbied the federal government for some sort of federal legislation. It came soon thereafter in public charge legislation, which excluded individuals who were likely to become a public charge and provided funds to deport individuals who became paupers. While some social workers complained about the application of the exclusionary clause of the public charge law, the principle of selective immigration was never seriously challenged. Excluding public charges was important, Edith Abbott argued, because "every country should take care of its dependent members." While social service workers did not oppose the principle of *excluding* public charges, deportation of immigrants who became public charges after landing was often seen as an entirely different matter (a topic discussed in chapter 6). On the whole, however, social workers did not advocate for repressive immigration laws. Indeed the immigration scholar John Higham averred that "After 1910 very few social workers who had intimate contact with foreign groups favored a further restriction of immigration."[37]

While social workers in Los Angeles were abandoning the idea that Mexicans could assimilate, withholding casework services, and lobbying for restriction on Mexican immigration, social workers were behaving quite differently toward their European clients. That social workers saw a distinction between European and Mexican immigrants was not lost on *Saturday Evening Post* writer Kenneth Roberts.

> Relief workers and representatives of charitable organizations that have to do with aliens—with Italians, let us say, or Greeks or Armenians—are almost invariably devoted to them and deeply resentful of all efforts to prevent them from entering the United States in large numbers. They are, they say, so sweet and so gentle and so appreciative, and America will be better for their presence. There is a quite different attitude on the part of relief and charitable workers who devote their time and energies to Mexicans. There is the same sentimental appreciation of the individual, but there is widespread aversion for the mass.

A charity worker who worked with Mexicans explained to Roberts that Mexicans were "not like our people and they never will be like our people!" In short, while social workers no longer perceived Mexicans to be capable of assimilation, European immigrants, or at least their children, were a part of their imagined community.[38]

"THE LAST TO APPLY FOR RELIEF": BLACKS AND THE STEREOTYPE OF DEPENDENCY

Between the turn of the century and the first New Deal the general perception among social workers was that blacks were not particularly welfare dependent. The Chelsea District Committee of the New York Charity Organization Society argued in 1906 that while blacks were coming to the city in large numbers, few applied for relief. This view was widespread. Whites in the South during the first third of the twentieth century, according to the historian Elna Green, "were convinced that Blacks feared the poorhouse." One southern newspaper explained that "in fact, anything which smacks of charity—the ambulance, physicians of the poor, free dispensaries, or what not—galls them to the quick and they avoid such blessings as if they carried pestilence, When a darky goes to the 'po'-house' you can set him down as lost to hope and socially dead." Similarly, a chronicler of the Charity Organization Movement argued that in "but few places" in the South "were [Negroes] found to apply to the local charity organization society, and those who did usually needed hospital treatment." As late as 1933 there was a "widespread impression among relief workers and in the general population [in Alabama] that the Negro was better adjusted to the open country environment than the poor white and was consequently better able to shift for himself and less in need of relief." A National Charity Society official argued that "At the south as at the north, the colored race is not a begging race. They seldom apply to strangers for alms except in case of death in the family." Pearl's study of paupers in public almshouses in 1923 also found that "the negro certainly made no worse showing in respect of almshouse pauperism than the white, and in fact a somewhat though not greatly better one." In 1928 the executive secretary of the National Urban League informed an audience of social workers that family service societies "quite uniformly report that the Negro families are the last to apply for relief and the first to become independent again." "High as is the Negro dependency rate," wrote the White House Conference on Child Health and Protection in 1930, "it is lower than might be expected for other races or nationalities in similar economic circumstances. The independence of the Negro family and the tendency of relatives and neighbors to help in any need are notable characteristics of the race."[39]

In contrast to their work on behalf of European immigrants, social workers were not trying to counter claims by eugenicists or others that blacks were dependent. In fact, even eugenicists found little evidence that blacks were dependent on relief. Harry Laughlin's research showed that American blacks showed a very "low quota fulfillment" in regards to dependency, a fact he quickly attributed to low standards of living among blacks, such that "dependency does not show itself." If 100 represents an equal proportion of blacks among the dependent population as among the population as a whole, then the "quota fulfillment" for blacks was only 25 as opposed to 103 for native whites (and 138 for foreign-born whites).[40]

One could certainly find scattered reports to the contrary. A white professor at Paine College in Augusta, Georgia, for instance, suggested that southern whites believed blacks were more dependent than whites: "We say, here in the South, that the mass of the Negroes are thriftless and unreliable; that their homes are a menace to the health of the community; and that they largely furnish our supply of criminals and paupers. And most of us believe that all this is the natural result, not of the Negro's economic status, but of the Negro's being Negro. There is truth in the indictment; yet it is by no means so largely true as many of us believe." If some whites believed that blacks furnished more than their share of paupers, it was certainly not a widespread stereotype during the first three decades of the twentieth century. Any such view, moreover, would have found little support from social workers and reformers.[41]

Outside the South, white social workers typically paid little attention to whether blacks were a dependent population or not. In charity reports, social workers often broke down the relief population by nationality, often including "Colored," "Negro," or "Afro-American" only as one of several "nationalities," rarely highlighting their unique contribution to the relief rolls. While the Los Angeles Department of Charities wrote about the Mexican "dependency problem" in their annual reports, it made no mention of blacks. Cook County's Bureau of Public Welfare also did not comment on the black presence on the poor relief rolls.[42] This overall lack of concern likely partly reflected the fact that in many studies of the dependent population, blacks often appeared to be underrepresented in the charity rolls. Blacks were slightly underrepresented in the almshouse population in 1923. While they made up almost 10 percent of the population, African Americans were only 7 percent of institutionalized paupers. Blacks were also underrepresented in the Mothers' Pension rolls. The 1921 U.S. Children's Bureau report on Mothers' Pension recipients showed only one black family receiving Mothers' Pensions across the eight areas studied. While 10 percent of St. Louis's population in 1920 was black, only one "negress" was to be found on the Mothers' Pension rolls out of a total ninety-four mothers. In 1931 the U.S. Children's Bureau released the results of a second nationwide study of

Mothers' Pension recipients. Of the more than 46,500 families receiving Mothers' Pensions in areas that responded to the survey, 96 percent were white, 3 percent were "Negro," and 1 percent were of "other racial extraction." The data revealed that in only twelve of the thirty-nine reporting states were blacks overrepresented in the Mothers' Pension rolls. In some states, like Pennsylvania, that overrepresentation was slight: blacks made up 5 percent of the population of the areas reporting and 6 percent of the Mothers' Pension recipients. In other states, the discrepancy was quite large. In Kansas, blacks made up 3 percent of the population in the areas reporting but 13 percent of Mothers' Pension recipients. Overall, and especially in the South, however, blacks had extremely limited access to Mothers' Pensions. In North Carolina, where blacks made up 29 percent of the population, there were only four black families on Mothers' Pensions, representing 1 percent of recipients.[43]

Blacks had a little more access to private charities. Across the forty-three cities in the study of federated charities for the Dillingham Commission, African Americans made up 4 percent of the population but 9 percent of the individuals on the charity rolls, indicating they were overrepresented relative to their population numbers. To the extent that blacks were overrepresented in the relief rolls, this appears to have been more of a northern phenomenon. Blacks in the South had little access to relief, even when it was offered. For example, though blacks in Atlanta represented a third of the community, they made up only 11 percent of the federated charity relief rolls. Southerners, wrote the chronicler for the Charity Organization Society, felt that "it was wiser to concentrate on the problem of poverty among the whites, leaving that among the colored for the future." In fact, Linda Gordon has argued that so strong was the association between social work and immigrants that even in the South, where immigrants made up a trivial proportion of the population, "white women's reform activism was nevertheless primarily directed at recent immigrants, not African Americans." Because most blacks still lived in the South, exclusion from relief was by far the most common experience among African Americans.[44]

White social workers in the North also ignored the needs and concerns of blacks prior to the Great Depression. "For white northern reformers early in the century," wrote Gordon, "the primary fact was that they did not notice these minorities—did not imagine them as indicated objects of reform." While California social workers *eventually* came to see Mexicans as inassimilable, northern reformers never imagined that blacks could ever be "reformed" and "integrated." As a result, white charity workers often refused to serve blacks, or did so only on a segregated basis. Black conference attendees protested, for example, that the National Conference of Social Work spent too little time addressing the

needs and concerns of the black community. The executive secretary of
the New York Urban League charged that "some welfare agencies are . . .
exploiting the Negro for furtherance of other projects. There have been
instances where the Negro district with its high death-rate and its slum
areas was played up as the sore spot—used as a sob story to secure funds
only to be forgotten when those funds were administered." White social
workers were not completely unconcerned with the economic conditions
of the black community. Some of the more left-wing reformers such as
Jane Addams, Edith Abbott, Sophonisba Breckinridge, Florence Kelley,
Frances Kellor, and Louise de Koven Bowen were racial liberals who
"understood how blacks had been exploited and denied opportunity." A
number of white women reformers were even founding members of the
NAACP, and Abbott and Breckinridge were "deeply involved in efforts
to improve the care of dependent black children in Chicago" prior to the
Depression. Still, white social workers rarely insisted on social equality
and almost always accepted and sometimes even promoted segregated
relief and social service programs.[45]

Responding in part to their exclusion from relief services, blacks in
the South and in the North developed their own system of private relief
agencies. Black women reformers, in fact, began to organize nationally
in the 1890s, creating a wide network of private orphanages, homes for
the aged, nurseries, clinics, settlements, and reformatory institutions. By
1930 there were over one thousand black men and women social workers.
Because white reformers largely ignored blacks and because elite African
Americans had built up their own parallel system of philanthropy and social work, they had some control over the way the black poor were treated
and portrayed to other social workers and to the wider public. Indeed,
starting in World War I with the black migration north, many of those
who spoke about the needs of blacks at the National Conference of Social
Work were themselves African Americans representing institutions such
as the Urban League and the NAACP. They focused very little time on
dependency rates and sometimes explicitly rejected any notion that blacks
were paupers or lacked ambition. The executive secretary of Nashville's
Urban League, George Haynes, told social workers that "The Negro is
really feeling his way toward a better and larger life. He is seeking larger
opportunities—'Not alms, but opportunity!' is his cry." Two years later, in
his new position as an assistant to the secretary of labor, Haynes made a
similar point, arguing that "the old charge of laziness and shiftlessness"
can no longer "be upheld," and he cited statistics showing blacks were far
more likely than their white counterparts to be gainfully employed.[46]

Black social workers and reformers understood that whites saw few
class differences within black society, and many were keen to both dis-
tance themselves from the poor and work among them to "uplift" the

race. In their welfare work, black reformers emphasized education, health care and prevention, vocational training and placement, and homes for the aged. They emphasized social services over charity and direct relief. To ward off the stereotypes that many whites attributed to all African Americans, these social workers emphasized that thrift, dependability, and a strong work ethic were values that were being instilled in the black poor. The Emmanuel Settlement, a black Chicago-based agency established in 1908, tried "to inspire higher ideals of manhood and womanhood, to purify the social condition, and to encourage thrift and neighborhood pride and good citizenship." Similarly, the director of Detroit's Urban League told an audience of social workers in 1917 that "In the adjustment of the negro a definite place must be given to the development of industrial efficiency. The welfare of the negro in his new environment depends upon the opinion that the community has of him." The Urban League, therefore, "uses every opportunity to develop individual efficiency by calling the attention of every negro employee to the fact that he must be punctual, zealous and ambitious in his work." The secretary of the New York Urban League told an audience of social workers that "If we create for our people the reputation for thrift, reliability, dependability and soberness, we will be in demand" for industrial jobs. Racial uplift work often went hand in hand with efforts to secure civil rights and social justice. At the same time that black reformers insisted on self-help for the black poor, they also campaigned vigorously against lynching, rape, and discrimination, and they saw these efforts as intimately connected to their social welfare work.[47]

A few black social workers acknowledged that in certain areas blacks were disproportionately represented on relief rolls, but they blamed this fact on environmental factors. At a speech at the National Conference of Social Work, James Robinson, the head of a black social welfare agency, spoke of a survey his organization had conducted of the black population in Cincinnati. Robinson noted that "the colored population contributes more than its quota of dependents found in the alms houses of the city and county." But he attributed this state of affairs to discrimination, poor working conditions, and the lack of opportunity for advancement: "It is well to remember the mass of colored people do their work fairly well, pay their debts, serve their God more or less faithfully and try to love their neighbor. The problems of their race arise from the weaker elements— the poor, the delinquent, the ignorant, the incompetent, the diseased and dying. These classes are unduly large, and the public knows so much of ill and so little of good about them that an unsavory reputation tends to cling to the race like a body of death." Robinson was hopeful that with better and more constructive social work and greater coordination across agencies, the problems of the black poor would be addressed. W.E.B.

Du Bois similarly tackled the issue of pauperism head-on in *The Philadelphia Negro*. He argued that blacks in Philadelphia were more likely than whites to be paupers, but he concluded that this should be anticipated: "This is what we would naturally expect: we have here the record of a low social class, and as the condition of a lower class is by its very definition worse than that of a higher, so the situation of the Negroes is worse as respects crime and poverty than that of the mass of whites." Class differences were not the sole cause, Du Bois claimed. Also important "are the problems which can rightly be called Negro problems: they arise from the peculiar history and condition of the American Negro," which included the long-term effects of slavery and emancipation, immigration and its attendant job competition, and the social environment in which blacks found themselves.[48]

Segregation and exclusion gave elite black reformers some measure of control over how poor blacks would be portrayed. But this control was by no means complete. Helen Pendleton, a Charity Organization Society agent, published a piece titled "Negro Dependence in Baltimore" in 1905. Pendleton did not argue that blacks were more dependent than whites, but she nonetheless portrayed black dependents in a very negative light: "Forty years ago the Negro . . . turned to the city as toward a door of golden opportunity. . . . Very soon the more ignorant, incompetent and defective among the newcomers fell into temptations and degradations of city life, and the Negro pauper became a factor in the problem of dependence." She complained that blacks begged for food and coal, and said that this "'basket habit' among the Negro women is the direct cause of the great excess of idleness and viciousness among the Negro men in this city." Pendleton suggested that poor blacks cheated welfare workers and that black women's alleged sexual promiscuity contributed to their problems.[49]

Precisely because most whites held such stereotypes of blacks as thriftless, lazy, unreliable, sexually amoral, and intellectually inferior, it was particularly challenging for some to explain why so many studies showed that blacks were the group least likely to use relief. As a result, some whites felt that they needed to explain this "peculiar" result. Harry Laughlin quickly attributed blacks' underrepresentation in state and federal pauper institutions to low standards of living among blacks, such that "dependency does not show itself."[50] Similarly, trying to make sense of why blacks were more likely than other groups to need assistance due to "lack of employment" or "sickness" and slightly less likely than all other groups to need assistance because of "drink, shiftlessness and inefficiency," Amos Warner wrote in 1894 that "Those who know the Colored people only casually, or by hearsay may be surprised to find the misconduct causes running so low among them, while the sickness as a cause is of greater relative importance than in any other nationality. But to one who has worked with blacks it seems a natural result, and, indeed, a confirmation of the reliability of the statistics." "The Colored people," he explained,

> are weak physically, become sick easily, and often die almost without visible resistance to disease. At the same time they have a dread of taking relief, especially when they think an institution will be recommended, and this, together with a certain apathy, will often induce them to endure great privations rather than ask for help. Besides this there are many associations among them for mutual help, and the criminal and semi-criminal men have a brutal way of making their women support them.[51]

Any suggestion that low rates of relief use implied that blacks were not inferior—and perhaps even superior to whites—was immediately challenged. For instance, after concluding that blacks were somewhat less likely than whites to live in poorhouses in 1923, Raymond Pearl wrote that "it would appear that any social indictment of the negro race, as a race, in respect of pauperism would probably be difficult to maintain." Finding such a statement a little hard to swallow, one scholar submitted a response to Pearl's article, saying Pearl had failed to consider the fact that the vast majority of blacks lived in the South, where the milder climate and lower levels of wealth made the poorhouse a relatively rare institution, underestimating the "true" extent of pauperism in the black population.[52]

A few years after Pearl's article was published, Niles Carpenter, a professor of sociology at the University of Buffalo, wrote an article titled "Feebleminded and Pauper Negroes in Public Institutions." Using the same data as Pearl, Carpenter argued that on the face of things, "Negroes are less numerous than the whites, both in almshouses and in institutions for the feebleminded." This did not mean, however, that blacks were "coping more successfully with their environment than the whites." Most blacks lived in the South, where there were few almshouses. In other words, using almshouse data to get at blacks' innate proclivity to use welfare was not particularly effective if they had no opportunity to get relief in the first place. Furthermore, there were wide variations in the extent to which blacks could be found in institutions. By looking at the data state by state, Carpenter showed that "in a preponderating number of states the Negro group has a larger quota of its total population institutionalized than had the white, for both pauper and feebleminded." Carpenter argued that to truly gauge the "relative capacities of Negroes and whites," one should look at states that made the most use of the almshouse as a means of alleviating destitution. Here the data still revealed that blacks' use of the almshouse varied significantly. In some states they were highly overrepresented relative to their numbers in the population (though some of these were based on exceedingly small sample sizes), and in others they were quite well underrepresented. Noting that blacks entered the almshouse at an earlier age than whites and that they were more likely to be deemed incapacitated, Carpenter speculated that "the Negro is particularly susceptible to certain types of disease which result in blindness and crippledness, chief among them tuberculosis and venereal disease. It is possible, therefore that these and other pathologies are playing such havoc among the Negro group as definitely to disable a significant proportion of them, and as to render unfit for self-support an even larger population." Ultimately, Carpenter concluded that the data on the institutionalized pauper population were "inconclusive and unsatisfactory." The data did not allow for a true test of the dependent characteristic of the institutionalized pauper population. In other words, a "social indictment of the Negro race, as a race, in respect of pauperism" could not be refuted. Though whites were generally unanimously reluctant to suggest that blacks were superior to whites along any dimension, on the whole, there was no strong association between blacks and pauperism among social workers—whether white or black—in the years leading up to the Great Depression. Most would have concurred with the charity worker in Louisville, Kentucky, in 1909 who said that "As a rule the Negroes of this community accept charity with reluctance. A large number may be improvident, but by some means they manage to make both ends meet and only accept assistance in this connection in the last extremity."[53]

CONCLUSION

Social workers constructed very different images of European immigrants', blacks', and Mexicans' use of relief. They marshaled "evidence" to prove, contrary to popular opinion, that southern and eastern European immigrants were not, in fact, welfare dependent. To the degree that they acknowledged that foreign-born whites were more likely than native-born whites to rely on relief, they explained these differences as the result of structural or environmental causes, not cultural or biological differences between groups. So protective were they of European immigrants that social workers not only worked to improve public opinion of the group but lobbied to ease the effects of harsh immigration and deportation laws. This approach stood in sharp contrast to how social workers portrayed Mexicans—as a social and economic liability, a charity-prone population whose dependence was rooted in culture, biology, and the environment. White social workers collected data to document Mexicans' use of relief, exaggerated their findings, and spread the stereotype of

Mexican dependency, all with an eye toward securing a quota on immigration from Mexico. Blacks, meanwhile, were largely ignored by white social workers, but to the extent that they came to their attention, they were seen and portrayed as the group least likely to ask for relief.

Much of the difference in perceptions stems, ultimately, from divergent views about each group's racial assimilability. Social workers were convinced that all European immigrants—new and old alike—were capable of racial assimilation. Their use of relief was seen as temporary, deserved, even necessary for their ultimate assimilation. Social workers were equally convinced, however, that blacks were incapable of assimilation. As such they barred blacks from many relief programs or relegated them to segregated charities. Ignored by white social workers, black elites developed their own philanthropic agencies, and they gained some measure of control over how the black poor would be portrayed to other social workers and to the wider public. European immigrants were fully embraced by white social workers, and blacks were largely overlooked, but in neither case did white social workers label the group as dependent. The comparison suggests that the racially liminal position of Mexicans—neither clearly white nor non-white—may have helped spawn the stereotype of the "dependent Mexican." Because Mexicans were initially seen as capable of assimilation, they were included on relatively generous terms in Los Angeles's relief system. Explicitly encouraged to apply for assistance, their numbers on relief increased. And since they had access to some measure of relief, they were not forced to develop their own relief system. Once these white reformers decided that Mexicans were not capable of assimilation, their presence on the charity rolls became proof that they would never assimilate and would forever remain a burden on "American taxpayers." This was all happening at the same moment that many government officials, schools, realtors, and others were coming to the conclusion that Mexicans were not really white, whatever the law implied.

The political and labor market context also helped fuel these differing perceptions. Because Mexicans were more likely to be migrant laborers, social workers saw them—whether U.S.- or Mexico-born—as mere temporary visitors, individuals who should come when work was plenty and disappear when it was scarce. Since wages in agriculture were so low, and labor seasonal, social workers had little confidence that Mexicans would ever escape their dependent condition. They were not imagined to be future citizens, and other local institutions were doing little to encourage their political incorporation. European immigrants, by contrast, generally settled in cities and worked in industrial jobs that held out a promise of opportunities for advancement and a life beyond the tenements. Even at its worst—when motivated by nativism and racism—the political context in the Northeast and Midwest encouraged the Americanization and naturalization of the European immigrants already in the country. As a result, social workers saw the extension of relief to European immigrants as temporary assistance to a struggling new member of the community. This was not how they perceived the extension of assistance to Mexicans. Rather, they came to see the distribution of relief to Mexicans as an illegitimate and possibly permanent subsidy to the agricultural industry.

The fact that Mexicans were concentrated in the Southwest, blacks in the South, and European immigrants in the Northeast and Midwest no doubt facilitated these different perceptions and portrayals. But these stereotypes were not simply confined to these regions. They spread, in part through professional networks, journals, and national conferences, and they had powerful effects on the subsequent treatment of these groups. When the stock market crashed in 1929, the stereotype of Mexican dependency was at its height. And as social workers tried to tackle the mounting burden of relief, they allowed their stereotypes of Mexicans to determine their solutions to the problem of unemployment. Social workers who worked primarily with European immigrants, meanwhile, chose a different path.

CHAPTER 6

Deporting the Unwelcome Visitors

IN OCTOBER 1935, the *Los Angeles Times* reported on a group of mostly Mexican individuals deported from Southern California during the Depression. The article, which labeled those deported "unwelcome visitors," played off the all too common stereotypes of Mexicans as "breeders," "lazy," and "dependent." Below a picture of one family, the caption read in part, "Among those sent out was Simon Alvarado and his family. . . . He and his wife acquired eight children in the eleven years they have been here and the county has spent more than $7,000 on them." How did immigration authorities know the Alvarado family had become public charges or how much relief funds they had "used up"? They knew because local relief officials told them. "This is just part of the work that the Immigration Bureau is doing in co-operation with the County Department of Charities to relieve taxpayers of the burden of supporting persons not entitled to relief," an immigration inspector explained. "We are working with the county authorities to rid this section of all cases like this."[1]

Welfare scholars have paid little attention to this sort of cooperation between welfare and immigration officials. But as this chapter and the next show, in certain times and places, the welfare state may best be viewed as an extension of the Immigration Service, where one of its functions becomes not the provision of assistance but rather the expulsion of individuals or even segments of an entire population from the nation. In addition to simply excluding from benefits those they saw as unworthy, during the first third of the twentieth century local relief officials attempted to expel some groups from the nation permanently. This was accomplished through a combination of deportation, threats of deportation, and, as the next chapter will show, forced and "voluntary" repatriation. In the most extreme cases, the welfare office quite literally turned into an immigration bureau or became an extralegal arm of the Immigration Service, expelling those immigration laws could not touch.

While the public at large favored the expulsion of all aliens on relief, and federal immigration officials in cities across the country attempted to expel or facilitate the expulsion of all dependent aliens during the Hoover years, southwestern relief agencies were most likely to cooperate with immigration officials. Cooperation was highest in the Southwest for two reasons: the distinct political context and the attitudes and actions of public and private relief officials.

Frustrated by the inability and sometimes unwillingness of immigration authorities to deport Mexicans en masse, relief and other public officials in Los Angeles took matters into their own hands. They asked the Immigration Service to conduct raids in their communities to round up deportable aliens, and they invited the Immigration Service to set up shop in their welfare bureaus to interrogate all aliens applying for relief. Aside from the protests of the Mexican community and some business leaders, there was little dissent to this course of action. Elected officials approved of these measures, as did local private relief officials. A similar situation unfolded in cities across the Southwest.

The situation was very different in northeastern and midwestern cities, however. When federal immigration and a few elected officials tried to find ways to expel dependent aliens in Chicago, for example, public and private relief officials came to their defense. They sometimes refused to give immigration officers access to their welfare rolls or, as the next chapter will show, refused to implement exceptionally harsh laws. Moreover, elected officials in the Northeast and Midwest were less likely than their southwestern counterparts to advocate the deportation of alien dependents. Chicago's mayor and other city Democrats joined social workers in opposing immigration officials' efforts to investigate the relief rolls.

THE CRASH AND NATIVIST RESPONSE

The stock market crashed at the end of October 1929. In less than a month, the securities in the New York Stock Exchange had lost 40 percent of their value. That year more than 650 banks failed, taking with them the life savings of thousands of individuals. By 1931 the bank failure rate had more than tripled. It is hard to overestimate the sense of shock and desperation so many were facing, even in the early months of the Depression. By March 1930 Chicago's United Charities noted that "The lack of jobs, the breakdown of public finances, the inability of homes and other agencies to take more cases—all the aftermath of this severe winter have combined to make" this "The worst year to be poor in . . . the history of Chicago." The United Charities, they went on, "finds itself besieged with desperate men and women who had held the wolf from the door for three months—four, five, even nine—but can hold him off no longer. They do not want charity; they want work. But there is no work."[2]

Amid this rising wave of despair, journalists, politicians, and members of the public began to pin the blame for the mounting crisis on immigrants. In June 1930 the *Saturday Evening Post* ran an article titled

"The Alien and Unemployment": "The United States, in the face of unemployment estimated as high as 4,000,000 . . . tolerates the admission every year of 450,000 or more aliens, most of them compelled to accept employment on any terms and conditions offered. American citizens are forced, thereby, out of employment, and a dangerous menace is created to the maintenance of high wages and living conditions." The article called on Congress to register aliens and place a quota on the western hemisphere. While the federal government did not immediately heed these suggestions, it was already using administrative means to achieve similar results.[3]

Cutting off immigration was not enough, however. There were concerns that aliens already in the United States were taking jobs away from "deserving" Americans—a proposition that was deemed doubly unfair when those aliens entered the country illegally. Removing illegal aliens, or at least preventing their employment, became the focus of some local and national efforts. In December 1930 President Hoover appointed William Doak as head of the Department of Labor. The Bureau of Immigration—a subunit of the Department of Labor—was under his command. Doak immediately got to work designing a campaign to rid the country of illegal and other "undesirable" aliens. He estimated that there were four hundred thousand illegal aliens in the country, only a quarter of whom could actually be deported. The methods his service employed, including raids of private homes and public places, arbitrary and warrant-less arrests, and various other "unconstitutional tyrannic and oppressive methods," came under heavy fire from liberal reformers. The U.S. Chamber of Commerce also viewed these measures with alarm, concerned that the raids violated the rights of both citizens and non-citizens.[4]

The general public, however, was far more sympathetic toward Doak's aims, and letters poured in from individuals across the country in support of those efforts. One North Carolinian wrote Doak: "Glory be! More power to you! Send all of them back where they came from. Just these few lines so you'll know at least one native-born North Carolinian is backing up your work." Telling Doak to "keep up the good work" in his efforts to deport large numbers of "undesirable" aliens, a woman from Rochester, New York, suggested that "while you are about it make a law that any foreigner in this country two years who won't become a citizen and learn to speak English be deported." "Every industry in this country," she explained, "is over loaded with these people who take work away from our American born taxpaying men and women." Describing Italians as "colored aliens," another writer decried the fact that he was "refused a job on the parkway" in New York, which he blamed on Italians without citizenship papers. Few groups were spared in the often vitriolic letters that flowed into the Department of Labor, as writers complained that

Canadians, the English, Germans, Greeks, Italians, Latins, Mexicans, and Slavics were taking American jobs or clogging the relief rolls.[5]

A few groups protested Doak's actions. The Liga Obrera Mexicana sent a resolution of protest against the persecution of foreign-born workers. Letters of protest also came from the Federation of the Slovenian National Benefit Society in Pittsburgh, the Finnish Working Women's Club in Seattle, and the Workmen's Sick and Death Benefit Fund in Aurora, Illinois. Demonstrations took place in Chicago, organized by the Communist Party, to protest anti-immigrant legislation pending in Congress and the Doak deportations. Fearing deportation was being used to divide workers they called on the native born to "move into the front ranks in the struggle for the protection of the foreign born workers." The Chicago Federation of Settlements, an umbrella organization representing twenty-five neighborhood centers, also complained about the Department of Labor's tactics. The settlements, "in direct and daily touch with the foreign-born and their problems," noted that they saw "at close range the unfortunate results in family life, which often follow the operation of these laws in their present form, and look to you for leadership in bringing about amelioration of the hardships so needlessly suffered." But these protests had little effect on Doak's actions. Under his watch, the total number of deportations increased from less than 12,000 in 1928 to more than 19,000 in 1932. Between 1930 and 1932, 54,000 individuals were deported, of whom 44 percent were Mexican and 20 percent were southern or eastern European. An additional 44,000 deportable aliens were allowed to leave voluntarily to avoid formal deportation proceedings, most of whom went to Mexico.[6]

AN IMMIGRATION RAID IN LOS ANGELES

One reason that Mexicans were targeted in Doak's deportation campaign was due to the efforts of local officials whose duty it was to relieve unemployment and care for the poor. Relief officials in the Southwest—especially Los Angeles—were more likely than relief officials elsewhere in the country to cooperate with immigration officials. In 1930 President Hoover created the President's Emergency Committee for Employment (PECE) to help advise local agencies on coping with the unemployment problem. PECE urged municipalities to develop committees made up of local social welfare agencies, city officials, and other leading members of the community to marshal resources in order to ease the burden of unemployment. Toward that end, on Christmas Eve 1930 the city of Los Angeles founded the Citizens' Committee on Coordination of Unemployment Relief, a body made up of the city's most distinguished residents, including Mayor John Porter, Supervisor Frank Shaw (who chaired the County Board's Public Welfare Committee), the president of the Los Angeles Chamber of Commerce, the publisher of the *Los Angeles Times*, and Charles Visel, a local businessman, who was appointed head of the committee.[7]

Less than two weeks after it was inaugurated, the Committee on Coordination of Unemployment Relief had already settled on a solution to the unemployment crisis: ridding Los Angeles of Mexicans. On January 6 Visel sent a telegram to Colonel Woods, the national coordinator of PECE, proposing a plan to help ease the twin burdens of a high unemployment rate and a rising relief load. Noting Doak's estimate that there were likely a hundred thousand deportable aliens in the country, Visel speculated that twenty thousand of those were located in Los Angeles County alone, a contention that immigration authorities denied. Because the local immigration office was understaffed and ill-equipped to handle the problem, Visel pledged the support of the local police and sheriff's office to round up deportable aliens in the county. Pleading for Woods's advice on the best method of dealing with the situation, he wrote: "We need their jobs for needy citizens."[8]

Woods was eager to assist Visel, adding that "there is every willingness at this end of the line to act thoroughly and promptly." He urged Visel to contact Secretary Doak directly to formalize a plan. Over the next few days, Visel and other local and federal officials hatched a scheme to bring additional immigration officers from San Francisco, San Diego, and Nogales to Los Angeles to conduct a series of well-publicized raids. Visel was under no illusion that these raids would result in a large number of deportations; indeed, he believed that deportations were too time-consuming and expensive. Rather he saw the publicity surrounding the raids and a few arrests as a "psychological gesture," an attempt to create "a general scare campaign" that would "start large numbers moving south to the line." At the same time that Visel was coordinating with federal officials, William Holland, superintendent of the Los Angeles County Department of Charities, was commenting publicly on the growing relief rolls "and the possibility of lightening that load by removing aliens from the rolls."[9]

To generate publicity for the actions, Visel sent a press release to all the local newspapers in Los Angeles, including the foreign-language press. In the release, Visel noted that immigration officers from the surrounding districts would be in Los Angeles in ten days and, with the cooperation of local law enforcement officials, would help "clean up Los Angeles County." He argued that while deportable aliens in Los Angeles included individuals of "all races and nationalities," "it so happens that many of the deportable aliens in this district are Mexicans." While perhaps factually accurate, Visel's statement generated concerns that the Mexican community would be singled out in the raids—a fear that was given voice in Los Angeles's leading Spanish-language newspaper, *La Opinión*.[10]

While the press release noted that the Mexican government was eager to have its citizens return to Mexico, the Mexican consul in Los Angeles was furious that Visel's press release insinuated—even when it explicitly denied—that the deportation raids would target the Mexican community. Indeed, papers in Mexico soon carried stories describing the targeting of Mexicans for deportation as a "national calamity," and the Director of Immigration in Los Angeles, Walter Carr, was eventually called upon by higher-ups in Washington to account for all the negative publicity. Federal officials were worried about the effects on diplomatic relations with Mexico and on relations with southwestern farmers. Carr blamed local welfare officials and the Chamber of Commerce for bringing "pressure to bear upon the Immigration Service to immediately deport any and all aliens who happened to be out of employment." He said that he vehemently opposed Visel's plan to publicize the raids in advance and acknowledged that the net effect of the publicity, and the insinuation that Mexicans would be targeted, had led the Mexican community "to believe, in many instances, that Mexicans were not wanted in California and that all would be deported whether they were legally here or not." According to the historian Abraham Hoffman, the federal government was so displeased with the negative publicity that resulted from the Los Angeles campaign that it intimated that in the future, local authorities should cooperate with the federal government but not initiate such action.[11]

Over the course of a three-week period authorities rounded up three to four thousand people. The total number of aliens deported (or allowed to leave voluntarily) was under four hundred, 70 percent of whom were Mexican. More important than the total number of Mexicans deported, however, was the fear this campaign engendered in the Mexican community more generally and the exodus it helped spark, a movement that became so large that it was described as "the greatest exodus since the Huguenot hegira in the sixteenth century."[12]

Protests against the raids came from a number of sources, including members of the business community who worried about the effects of the raids on the local labor supply and on local businesses, the press in Mexico, as well as the Spanish-language press and the Mexican consulate in Los Angeles. The Los Angeles Bar Association organized a committee to investigate illegal raid practices, and James Batten, organizer of the annual Friends of the Mexicans conference, criticized the raids in the local press. Even famed Chicago settlement house worker Jane Addams, in town for a conference of social workers, denounced the targeted deportations. Most social workers and local reformers, however, were conspicuously silent. There was little attention given to the deportations at the annual meeting of the California Conference of Social Work in May of that year. The section on "Racial and Citizenship Problems" had decided to "limit the discussion to the general field of racial relationships in the State" and therefore "it did not seem possible to include the topics of immigration laws and deportation" in the conference schedule. Section members did receive a mimeographed summary of the "history and existing status of the immigration laws of the United States," and Batten held an afternoon session—outside the regular section format—on the "problem of deportation," the contents of which were not covered in the published conference proceedings. Agencies specifically devoted to the problems of immigrants—the CCIH and the International Institute—also remained silent.[13]

Los Angeles was not the only city in which raids took place. Across the country, immigration officers raided dance halls, missions, hospitals, and prisons in an attempt to provide jobs for "worthy citizens in need of employment." Early in 1931, immigration authorities in New York City raided the Finnish Workers' Education Association dance. Twenty immigration agents and ten policemen blocked hall entrance doors, lined up the thousand revelers, and demanded identification. Federal authorities also sent fifty immigration agents to Chicago in October and November 1931 in search of aliens who had been smuggled into the country. The first action was a raid on Chinatown, where five hundred Chinese residents were questioned and forty-two were held for further "search and examination." The next drive occurred in the Mexican Colony of South Chicago, where more than one hundred men were picked up "from the streets and the pool-rooms" and taken in for questioning. Of these, only three were held overnight for further questioning. "When taken to task by the press" about the Finnish dance hall and other raids, Hoover described the "handful of deportables found" in the raids by saying, "well we struck pay dirt, didn't we?"[14]

Cooperation between Relief and Immigration Officials

What was distinctive about Los Angeles was not that such raids occurred but that relief officials encouraged and even helped plan the raids. As we will soon see, this sort of interagency cooperation was not common in the Northeast and Midwest. Furthermore, the 1931 raids were not the first time that relief officials in Los Angeles had called on immigration officials to help deport "dependent" Mexicans. For at least five years prior to the Depression, the Los Angeles Department of Charities had an unusually high degree of cooperation with the local Immigration Service.[15]

A certain degree of contact between charitable institutions and the Immigration Service was written into the law. Section 23 of the Immigration Act of 1917 provided that the Commissioner General of Immigration send its officers "from time to time as may be necessary" to "penal, reformatory and charitable institutions (public and private)" in order to "secure information as to the number of aliens detained" therein, as well as "inform the officers of such institutions of the provisions" of the public charge laws. Public charge laws, of course, have a long history in the United States. First enacted in Massachusetts in 1639, they were used to exclude and sometimes remove England's "tired, poor, wretched refuse." Municipalities derived the authority to remove foreign paupers to their native land from their state poor laws, which also allowed for the removal of non-resident paupers to their county of settlement. Relief officials did not frequently remove paupers across the ocean, however. Rather, much of the early legislation was focused on preventing the landing of paupers and defraying the costs of assistance by imposing a head tax on all alien passengers or requiring that vessels pay bonds on passengers deemed likely to become a public charge. For example, New York State passed a law in 1847 that placed the responsibility for the care of the alien poor with six Commissioners of Emigration, a body appointed by the governor that included the mayors of New York and Brooklyn as well as the heads of the German and Irish societies. The state collected commutation taxes on all "healthy, self supporting passengers" and bonds on all infirm passengers. The funds—over $5 million in the first fourteen years—"supported a vast network of services" for immigrants, including medical care, temporary board and shelter, cash relief, and job placement services.[16]

In 1876 the Supreme Court ruled that New York's bond and commutation tax on immigrants entering Ellis Island was unconstitutional because it represented state regulation of foreign commerce, a power reserved for the federal government. If states could not tax immigrants entering the United States, New York and other states maintained, the federal government had to take some sort of action. The first federal legislation came soon after in 1882, imposing a fifty-cent head tax on immigrants and barring the entry of "any persons unable to take care of himself or herself without becoming a public charge." It was not until the Immigration Act of 1891 that funds were provided to deport immigrants who became public charges within one year of arrival from causes existing prior to landing. Over time, the deportation clause of the public charge doctrine came to allow for the removal of individuals who became public charges within five years of entry to the United States or were deemed to have been liable to become a public charge at last entry. On average, fewer than 1,500 individuals per year were deported nationwide due to the public charge doctrine between 1906 and 1932. More than ten times that many were *excluded* from the country as likely to become a public charge. Given that on average more than half a million people were admitted to the United States each year, public charge deportations affected less than a third of a percent of all legal entrants.[17]

While federal law required that immigration agents visit charitable institutions, it also expected that these institutions would report suspicious aliens to the Immigration Service. It was, after all, in these institutions' financial interests to do so. The federal law did not mandate cooperation, however, and in practice the extent of cooperation varied greatly, a conclusion reached by three different studies of administrative policies and practices relating to deportation. "State institutions where aliens are patients are supposed to report all cases of possible deportability to the immigration service," wrote Jane Clark, an immigration law expert, "but the procedure and frequency with which the states do this [vary] widely from state to state, and even sometimes within the same state."[18]

Concerned about the variability in reporting and inspection across districts, the Commissioner of Immigration sent memorandums to each District Director of Immigration in 1923 (and again in 1934) to try to ascertain the extent of cooperation between immigration offices and state and local penal, mental, and charitable institutions. The results of these inquiries confirmed Clark's assertions. In Michigan and Maine, for example, the heads of institutions were required by state law to report all alien public charges. Other states, such as New York, reported alien public charges in asylums and hospitals eagerly, even though not required by state law. In some areas, immigration inspectors made very frequent visits to these institutions, and in other areas immigration inspectors made none, citing lack of funds and personnel.[19]

District directors were asked to describe their cooperation with charitable *institutions*—almshouses, homes, sanitariums, orphanages, and asylums for the "deaf, dumb, blind and feebleminded"—not with charitable organizations that provided outdoor relief. Aliens detained in institutions were deemed the most "undesirable" since they placed the greatest financial burden on society because they generally needed more expensive treatment over an extended—even indefinite—period of time. They were also less likely than aliens receiving outdoor relief to "disappear" if they found out deportation proceedings had been initiated.[20]

The "Closest Possible Cooperation" in Los Angeles

In 1923 the Los Angeles immigration inspector, Alfred Burnett, reported "the closest possible cooperation" between the Immigration Service and local charitable institutions. California's Department of Institutions employed a "State Deportation Agent," whose job it was to "keep track of aliens in State institutions who may be subject to deportation and to call such cases to the attention of the Immigration Service." In addition to cooperating with institutions, however, Los Angeles was the only immigration district to report on cooperation with outdoor relief agencies. Burnett wrote that he had "satisfactory" cooperation from the County Department of Charities and the City Social Service Commission, organizations in charge of both indoor and outdoor relief in Los Angeles. "These organizations understand the possibility of relieving themselves of alien public charges through reports to the Immigration Service in proper cases," he wrote. "Much attention is devoted to such reports by the Bureau's officers in this District." While Burnett found that the "spirit of cooperation is satisfactory as a whole," he felt that "in Los Angeles in particular the available Immigration force is insufficient to give all cases that prompt attention to public charge cases so much desired."[21]

Burnett was not the only one frustrated by the lack of resources for deporting public charges. In 1923 the California state legislature passed a law requiring that the Department of Institutions cooperate with the Immigration Service "in arranging for the deportation of all alien public charges who are now confined in or may be hereafter admitted or committed to any State hospital, Whittier State School, Preston School of Industry, or California School for Girls." The deportation agent of the California Department of Institutions wrote a series of letters to the Commissioner General of Immigration in the early 1920s, objecting to the delay in deporting Mexican alien inmates from institutions in Southern California. The commissioner general responded to these complaints by increasing the personnel of the Los Angeles immigration office, "particularly with a view to keeping in closer touch with the cases of aliens confined in institutions."[22]

The Los Angeles County Department of Charities also complained in 1925 that "Our alien dependents present a problem which is still unsolved." "In previous years . . . Immigration Service was able to assist the ODR [Outdoor Relief] but little due to their inadequate staff and insufficient funds. Because of this, it has been almost impossible to deport those dependents who rightly were the responsibility of other countries." The Department of Charities quickly seized on a solution: "An arrangement was made in May 1925, whereby an Inspector from the United States Immigration Service worked in the Outdoor Relief Office four days a week interviewing aliens who were eligible for deportation." This arrangement was evidently successful and the following year, the Department of Charities noted that "We report to the local immigration office all deportable cases who receive more than the minimum emergency aid." Over the years, the cooperation between the Department of Charities and the

Immigration Service became institutionalized. A relief worker was given the responsibility of "handling all questions relative to deportation . . . in order to facilitate the work of deporting alien dependents to Mexico," and the Department of Charities proudly reported in 1931 that it had "centralized its deportation of alien dependents work" in the Deportation Division. In 1937 the staff in the deportation division was increased on orders of County Supervisor Leland Ford, and "the augmented staff interviewed 700 alien Mexicans during September," resulting in the closing of "16 percent of these cases."[23]

Over time, the Department of Charities also appeared to take on more and more of the functions of the Immigration Service. "Our Deportation Division is responsible for co-operation with the United States Immigration Service and for the arrangements incident thereto," the department wrote in 1931.

> After a case has been thoroughly investigated it is necessary to secure necessary deportation evidence which may consist of immigration papers, verification of landing, medical certificates, proof of immorality or criminal conduct, previous records either in this country or abroad, securing an interview with the Immigration Service, and finally the delivery of the family to the deportation train with the necessary attention given to their baggage and their welfare enroute.[24]

The Department of Charities even provided the immigration inspector with "desk space, two stenographers to record and transcribe preliminary and warrant hearings and an automobile to convey him to the various places where he is required to go to complete his investigations."[25]

The total number of individuals deported as a result of the immigration inspectors' work inside the Department of Charities over the years was never particularly high. Each year it succeeded in deporting fewer than fifty families. The reasons for this were numerous. The entire process from investigation to successful deportation was expensive, bureaucratic, and time-consuming. Many more families were investigated than were ever deported, and some individuals "disappeared" as soon as they learned that deportation hearings had been initiated. Some others were allowed to leave voluntarily. Furthermore, the deportation figures underestimate the full impact of the new procedures, as they appear to have deterred some families from asking for assistance. One official from the U.S. Children's Bureau found just such an effect, noting in 1933 that "Fear of deportation because of acceptance of relief . . . was deeply rooted in several Mexican communities. This may have been due partly to their experience in 1931, when 1,240 Mexican aliens were deported on this charge, but usually it was the result of unsocial attitudes on the part of some local public officials."[26]

Such close cooperation between outdoor relief departments and the Immigration Service, however, was fairly uncommon. Gudrun Rom, a social worker at United Charities in Chicago, sent out a questionnaire to "family welfare societies in the largest cities and those 15 cities with the highest ratio of foreign-born to native born," asking about their experience with deportation. To Rom's surprise, she found that there were actually few problems related to deportation. Many social welfare agencies and settlement houses worked to acquaint the new immigrants with U.S. immigration laws: "To be sure, all experience in the past has gone to show that the newly arrived immigrant did not go to a family agency any more than he appealed for public poor relief. He was aware that he must avoid dependency." One group of cities had virtually no cases of deportation to report, including Boston (none), Chicago (one), and Philadelphia (two). Another group of cities did not initiate deportations, but revealed that they were not opposed to such an outcome. These cities were not named. There were three, however, that took the initiative in reporting families for deportation—El Paso, Los Angeles, and Cleveland—two of which (El Paso and Los Angeles) had large Mexican populations. Los Angeles reported thirty-seven cases of deportation—a list they admitted was incomplete. A caseworker told Rom that during the "deportation drive in the spring of 1925," an immigration officer was stationed in the relief office for weeks. While the Immigration Service paid the costs of deportation from Los Angeles to the border, a private agency, "usually Catholic," paid the "fare of the deportee from the border to the place of residence in Mexico." The caseworker explained that they "made every effort to diminish the hardships of travel." But they did nothing, it seems, to prevent deportation in the first place. "We all know," Rom noted, "that the law is mandatory in theory but discretionary in practice. Hence with such cases that come to the attention of family agencies there is abundant opportunity to mitigate unnecessary practice of severity." Not all relief agencies, it appears, were so inclined.[27]

A Lack of Cooperation in Chicago

If Los Angeles is an example of a city with extremely close cooperation with Immigration officials, Chicago is an example of a city on the other end of the cooperation spectrum. In its 1923 letter to the Commissioner General of Immigration, the local immigration inspector noted that he received little cooperation from Chicago charitable institutions: "The Cook County agent reports some cases from the county institutions at Oak Forest, Illinois. He reports practically none from the Cook County Hospital." Indeed, Cook County provided a graded hospital fee scale so that aliens who sought public medical care but did not want to risk deportation as a public charge "may pay their way if able."[28]

Despite the Department of Labor's efforts to educate the heads of institutions in Illinois about the deportation laws and supply them with the necessary forms to report aliens to the Immigration Service, they remained "reluctant to report cases on account of the work involved." When the new director of the Illinois State Department of Public Welfare pledged to support the secretary of labor and pursue a more vigorous deportation policy for aliens in the state's penal and mental institutions, the Immigrants' Protective League (IPL) arranged a meeting with the various social agencies in the city as well as the new director and tried to exact a promise to avoid any wholesale dumping of aliens and instead work on a case-by-case basis. Pressure was applied, too, from a room packed with social workers who attended the Illinois Conference of Public Welfare's session titled "Social Considerations in Deportability." And the state director, seeing "the temper of the audience," "promised that the State would not separate families, in its policy of reporting for deportation, inmates of the State Institutions, but that regard would be given to the alien's natural home."[29]

Eight years later, during the Depression, the issue came to the fore again. While Los Angeles relief officials were calling the Immigration Service in 1931 to initiate a deportation drive, when asked whether the Immigration Service was "getting cooperation from local and state authorities," Doak singled out Chicago, saying that the city "hasn't done much so far to help the deportation drive." But he added that "there are signs of better cooperation. After all, they have their own problems." Better cooperation was perhaps on Doak's mind when in January 1932 he reassigned Shirley Smith, the Chicago District Director of Immigration, to the Salt Lake City Bureau and replaced him with C. A. Palmer, a veteran of the service. A news story on the "shakeup" reported the transfers were the result of a reorganization designed to "tighten up the immigration service's border patrols."[30]

In September 1932, less than a year after Palmer took office, he "appealed to the [Cook County] welfare bureau for the names and addresses of aliens" who had entered the United States since 1924 and who were now receiving public charity, arguing that "the government had the power to deport many of these aliens and thereby, in some measure, relieve the taxpayer of the burden caused by the expenditure of $1,500,000 a week for relief in Cook County." According to one immigration inspector, "20 percent of the 105,000 families on the Cook County welfare rolls were aliens or had alien members." Palmer suggested "that if he had access to the Bureau's records . . . [they] might be used by the government in ordering deportations." However, the Cook County Bureau of Public Welfare, citing a 1926 confidentiality law, said that the county poor relief rolls could not be made available to the public and refused to comply with the request. Palmer challenged the notion that providing a federal agency with the list of names was tantamount to releasing the names to the public. "Aliens who entered this country illegally," Palmer continued, "have no right to be here, much less to be supported at public expense."[31]

The Cook County Bureau of Public Welfare denied allegations that 20 percent of the relief load was composed of aliens. While Cook County did collect data on the citizenship of its relief recipients, such data had never been compiled so they did not know how many aliens were actually receiving relief. A study of the nativity of over three thousand men over the age of sixty living in shelters had been performed, however, by the Council of Social Agencies. This study found that a little over 40 percent of these men were foreign born, and of these, less than 12 percent were, "by their own admission," unnaturalized. Palmer was unimpressed by the study, however. The *Tribune* reported that the experience of immigration inspectors had shown them "that most foreign born persons claim citizenship whether they have their first papers or none at all, and an investigation might disclose a greater percentage of unnaturalized aliens." Indeed, some local service providers agreed that self-reported figures on citizenship were unreliable. "These aliens think they will receive better treatment if they are thought to be citizens," said a director of homeless shelters in Chicago. "But we cannot make citizenship a requirement for admission. Many aliens have lived and worked in Chicago for years and are as much entitled to relief as anybody else."[32]

Joseph Moss, director of the Cook County Bureau of Public Welfare, also defended the right of non-citizens to get relief and keep the immigration officers from snooping on the rolls. "It was the unanimous opinion of the [Bureau of Public Welfare advisory] committee," said Moss, "that an examination of the people getting relief, to find out whether they are deportable aliens, would destroy faith in the community. If the government sent its agents around asking questions the people would become suspicious and frightened. . . . The immigration service, anyway, is held in ill repute, particularly among the foreign born, because of its methods in handling the immigrants." Moss was not saying that the Bureau of Public Welfare would never report a case to the local immigration bureau. "Of course, we want to cooperate with the government," Moss said, "and when we find questionable persons seeking relief we do. If there is some question about their legal status here, or for some reason they might be deported, we inform federal inspectors. We also inform the government about those who tell us they would like to go back to their native lands." He refused, however, to give immigration officers unqualified access: "[W]e do not believe that a general investigation by the government would accomplish enough from the economic standpoint to compensate for the harassment it would cause. Most of the aliens who could be deported for entering the country illegally since 1924 have married and have wives and children who are citizens. There would be no economic advantage in deporting them, for they would leave permanent dependents behind them."[33]

The Cook County Bureau of Public Welfare's refusal to cooperate with immigration authorities was met with heavy criticism from some circles. At a subcommittee meeting of the State Committee on Taxation and Expenditures, Moss's actions came under fire by some of the committee's members. At a meeting of the Cook County Board of Commissioners there was a "brief and stormy exchange of views" between Commissioners Peter Kelly and Amelia Sears on the issue. Commissioner Kelly, a Democrat from the city's west side, was in favor of greater cooperation, and the Board's welfare committee appointed him to investigate the idea that the Immigration Service should be allowed to search the relief rolls. Commissioner Sears, a Democrat and prominent social worker in the city who was also chairman of the board's welfare committee, backed Moss and suggested that Palmer's request was a ploy by the government to give work to idle inspectors. Like Moss, she argued that most of the illegal immigrants had American wives and children, noting further that "the distrust raised by snooping immigration agents would be very detrimental to the welfare relief service." She said that "foreign dependents would become frightened and the agents probably would disrupt the system which is working smoothly."[34]

Kelly's investigation found that 15 to 20 percent of those on the relief rolls might be deportable, resulting in a savings of nearly half a million dollars to the county, financial relief that was sorely needed. Chicago's fiscal situation in 1932 was nothing short of a disaster. The city had entered the Depression with an enormous deficit, many property owners were on a tax strike, and as a result the city had long stopped paying municipal employees—including the city's teachers—their salaries. Running desperately low on funds, the county had cut all relief recipients' benefits in half on October 1. On October 30 Kelly told the *Tribune* that he favored the plan to deport "alien reliefers" and proposed "to present it in detail to the county board at the meeting next Wednesday."[35]

The following day, tens of thousands of unemployed workers, chanting "We want bread," marched on city hall in the cold rain, protesting the recent cut in relief budgets. Alongside demands to restore benefit levels, end foreclosures, and provide free medical care to the indigent, the unemployed workers demanded that there be "no discrimination against Negroes and foreign born unemployed" and that "deportations of foreign unemployed be halted." Though the parade was peaceful, the marchers were flanked by a thousand policemen. Men and women, school children and the elderly, white, black, Mexican and European foreign born all marched together, snarling traffic and carrying banners that read: "Don't starve: fight," "Free hot lunches for schoolchildren—with milk," "Less cops, more bread," "We want work, not charity," "Stop evictions," and "Down with Doak and his deportations." The protest made the newspapers from Los Angeles to Washington, D.C., and many small towns in between.[36]

Fearful they might be deported for marching in what the press would likely brand a Communist parade, forty-three Mexicans from the University of Chicago Settlement House nonetheless risked the billy clubs and Immigration Service to participate in the protest. As the majority of the marchers moved on to listen to speeches in Grant Park, representatives of the Worker's League, the Chicago Workers' Committee, and the Unemployed Councils of Chicago met with Mayor Cermak and presented their list of eleven demands.[37] At the meeting, Cermak "assured the representatives he would do all in his power to improve the status of the unemployed," but the following day he issued a formal statement saying that while he "agreed that all the proposals should be carried out," he had no authority as mayor to carry them out. "I wish I really had the power, which you seem to imagine I possess, to bring about change," Mayor Cermak's statement read:

> If I had one hundredth part of the influence that you attribute to me, conditions would be very materially improved. Unfortunately I have no such power or influence as you credit me with, but to the extent that it is humanly possible for me to help, you can count on every ounce of power that I do possess in aid of every legitimate effort to ameliorate the want and the suffering that you have described. As an individual I shall answer your questions, and as a mayor I shall aid wherever it shall lie in my power to do so.[38]

The mayor's claims of powerlessness in this situation stemmed from two sources. First, the city was broke, and he simply did not have the funds available to restore benefit levels. Second, he had no formal authority over the Bureau of Public Welfare, which was under the jurisdiction of Cook County officials. Within days, however, the city announced the full restoration of relief benefits, a feat made possible through a loan from the federal government's Reconstruction Finance Corporation. The issue of deportations was still unsettled, however. As a former president of the Cook County Board of Commissioners and the city's political boss, Cermak may have tried to influence members of the Board of Commissioners who were set to meet in a few days to discuss the results of Commissioner Kelly's investigation. On November 4, representatives of Chicago's unemployed workers were invited to present their demands to the Illinois Emergency Relief Commission. The representatives objected again to any deportation of foreign-born unemployed but acknowledged that the Cook County Bureau of Public Welfare had already refused to cooperate with immigration authorities.[39]

At the same time that Commissioner Kelly was making his investigation of the relief rolls, Republican state senator James Barbour suggested that if a confidentiality law was preventing the county welfare office from divulging the names of welfare recipients, then the law could be amended. "I shudder to think," said Barbour, "what will become of us if we have to feed and house all these people for another fall and winter after this one, and if some of them can be taken back to their homelands, the county authorities owe a duty to the taxpayers to see that it is done." In mid-November Barbour tried to fulfill his promise, introducing Senate Bill 47 "calling upon the Cook County Bureau of Public Welfare to turn over to the immigration authorities the names of all aliens on its charity relief rolls." The bill made failure to cooperate a misdemeanor, subject to a fine of "not less than twenty-five dollars nor more than three hundred dollars," a significant sum of money during the Depression. Though relief authorities did not believe that Barbour would try to push the bill, immigrant advocates nonetheless believed it represented a significant threat. Pressured by the IPL to take a stand on the issue, the Illinois Committee on Social Legislation voted to oppose the bill. It did not pass, and there is no evidence that Cook County ever granted such access.[40]

The contrast with what transpired in Los Angeles could not have been greater. Where Los Angeles relief officials invited the Immigration Service to conduct raids in the city and to set up shop in their relief offices, Chicago relief officials were pushing immigration officials away and publicly defending the rights of non-citizens to assistance.

The Politics of Relief

To what extent does political context help explain the different treatment of aliens in Chicago and Los Angeles? Los Angeles's Citizens' Committee on Coordination of Unemployment Relief—which pressured the Immigration Service to conduct raids in the city—included Mayor Porter and County Supervisor Shaw, among others. Local government officials in Los Angeles were also reported to be "thoroughly in accord with any steps" to deport indigent aliens and thereby "reduce the relief burden."[41]

In both cities, however, there were politicians who were keen on deporting dependent aliens. In addition to Senator Barbour and Commissioner Kelly, James Mooreland (R), in his campaign for Congress from Chicago's Seventh District, said that if aliens "subject to deportation were sent back to the countries from which they came, relief rolls undoubtedly would be lightened." And Congressman Leslie Arends (R) presented a bill in Congress to deport all aliens on welfare. With the exception of Kelly, however, it was Republicans who advocated for the deportation of dependent aliens in Illinois. But Democrats ruled Chicago, and Mayor Cermak—a Bohemian immigrant whose election to office was due to votes among many new immigrant communities—did not advocate the deportation of alien public charges. Had he been in favor of cooperating with the Immigration Service, things might have turned out very differently.[42]

Politics might also have entered into the situation indirectly through elected officials' influence over the hiring and administration of public relief workers. At the beginning of the Great Depression, both the Los Angeles Department of Charities and the Cook County Bureau of Public Welfare operated on a civil service system. Employees in both counties therefore were, at least in theory, chosen based on merit, not for political patronage. Patronage was certainly not absent from relief provision in Chicago, but elected officials seem to have intervened more heavily in the administration of relief in Los Angeles.

When Anton Cermak became president of the Cook County Board of Commissioners in 1925, he helped establish the Cook County Bureau of Public Welfare and made sure it operated on a civil service basis. Public relief workers were mostly college-educated and trained social workers. The bureau had an advisory board made up of the city's most respected social workers, which met regularly and kept "close watch on the bureau, particularly on the budget and personnel." Joseph Moss had a long career as a probation officer in Juvenile Court before he took charge of the welfare bureau, a post he would keep for twenty-eight years. His appointment was not political—he could not "even vote for Cermak for mayor" since he lived in Evanston. According to one news article, "The employees of this bureau, with the exception of a small fringe of 'special case workers' that come and go, are quite innocent of precinct politics, and have not even been asked to get pledge cards signed up for the candidacy of their chief for mayor. The picture of Cermak as a hard boiled political boss who demands votes for jobs gets something of a dent here." Indeed, the paper reported that "Cermak has kept politics out of this field to an astonishing degree." Why would Cermak voluntarily pass up political patronage? Observers speculated that "the boss of the party came to the conclusion that good service, and the respect of those high in social service work, was worth more politically than the bringing in of a few precinct votes." The director of the Chicago Council of Social Agencies, who oversaw the hiring of the welfare bureau staff, explained that Cermak told him: "I am a politician, but I want to keep public charity out of politics. Any politician who doesn't will suffer in the end." Because of his strong support of their profession, social workers in the city rallied behind Cermak when he ran for mayor. Of course, politics was not completely eliminated from relief provision. Sonya Forthal's interviews with Chicago precinct captains revealed the use of outdoor relief as a source of patronage even in the late 1920s. In addition, the work of the Bureau of Public Welfare was overseen by the County Board of Commissioners, who had control over the budget and over various policy matters. The County Commissioners, however, were divided over the deportation of dependent aliens.[43]

Los Angeles's relief system also operated on a civil service basis, and there was no machine as in Chicago. Still, the Department of Charities was overseen by the County Board of Supervisors, who not only set policy but interfered heavily both in personnel and administrative issues. Unlike Chicago, many of the public welfare workers, even some of those "in high level positions," were "unqualified, at least from a social work perspective." Los Angeles city officials, in fact, appeared to have significant disdain for professional social work. In the late 1920s, there was a grand jury investigation of the administration of outdoor relief that called the Department of Charities inefficient, "urged a complete revision in methods and principles in administering outdoor relief," and called for the replacement of the superintendent, William Holland, the assistant superintendent, R. R. Miller, and the chief case supervisor for outdoor relief, Emily Wooley. The grand jury charged Holland with having lost control over the work in his agency and complained about the scientific casework methods that Miller and Wooley had recently implemented. They urged Holland's replacement with a man who "would protect the taxpayers" and for the complete elimination of Miller and Wooley's positions, a move that County Supervisor Frank Shaw admitted allowed for the employees' removal "without the necessity of a civil service hearing."[44]

One issue that particularly troubled the grand jury was the county's alleged generous treatment of Mexican dependents in the late 1920s: "The immigration of mendicants into the county is . . . one of the gravest situations faced by the department. Foreigners, particularly Mexicans, it is declared, are being brought into the county in a 'wholesale' manner, thousands of them being sick and incapable of self-support. When asked why they come here, these persons frequently reply that it is because of the generous treatment this county accords its poor. Immediate investigation and vigorous action to reduce this class of immigration are recommended." In response, county officials subsequently lobbied the state legislature to raise the state residence requirement for relief from one to three years.[45]

Miller promised his office was doing what it could to correct the "Mexican dependency problem." The Municipal League of Los Angeles and private social workers defended Miller and Wooley's work, praising the "constructive methods of scientific social welfare work, the aim of which is rehabilitation and restoration to independence, rather than mere distribution of the doles." Ultimately, however, Miller and Wooley's positions "were abolished at a secret meeting of the Board of Supervisors." Superintendent Holland, who blamed the "enemies of county government" for the investigation, was initially spared, but the Board of Supervisors continued to meddle in the affairs of the Department of Charities, and he was pressured to resign within a few years. Despite the civil service system, elected officials played a strong role in nearly all aspects of the administration of public relief in Los Angeles.[46]

The Role of Social Workers

Politics clearly mattered in both cities. The IPL nonetheless claimed credit for the policies adopted by the Cook County Bureau of Public Welfare. "At every stage in the policy adopted in this County," the IPL's director told the Chicago Council of Social Agencies, "the League has furnished material and experience, upon which the County has based its position." Though the IPL privately claimed to have tried to play "as silent a role as possible, in order not to flaunt opposition to the District Director of Immigration," they noted that immigration inspectors nonetheless blamed the IPL for the Bureau of Public Welfare's failure to cooperate.[47]

Whatever other factors one might point to, there is no doubt that the IPL had a significant impact on how social agencies in Chicago and elsewhere treated non-citizens. Gudrun Rom attributed the low number of deportations from family welfare societies at Chicago's United Charities to the efforts of the IPL. For years the IPL had been working to educate social workers and public and private relief officials on the social problems around deportation. For example, the IPL's director gave six lectures each spring to the students at the University of Chicago's School of Social Service Administration on immigration, naturalization, and the social considerations involved in deportation and repatriation. The IPL also spoke at local and national social worker conferences and trained new staff members of the Cook County Bureau of Public Welfare on the problems of the foreign born, and fielded "constant calls from the offices of the Cook County Bureau of Public Welfare, the Unemployment Relief Service and other relief agencies to settle all kinds of questions as to deportability and other immigration matters."[48]

Sophonisba Breckinridge, a leading social reformer, described one successful intervention on behalf of an immigrant in a speech at a national conference in 1914.

There was in Chicago a very nice Polish woman who after her husband's death in the old country sold the little farm and came to America with her twoboys. She got a job in a pickle factory at $1.00 a day, and the boys went to school. When winter came, other widows in her tenement lightened their own burdens by getting "coal from the county," and so she got coal from the county. Getting county coal means, in the terms of the statute, "becoming a public charge."

Because the cause of her misfortune (her widowhood) preceded her entry into the United States, she was eligible for deportation under the public charge doctrine. As a result, she was "referred by the county authorities to the immigration office and a deportation warrant issued as a matter of routine." According to Breckinridge, "When the inspector came to serve the warrant she was so overcome with terror and despair at the thought of being sent back to the home in which all ties had been broken, where her small strip of land had been sold, that she ran away. Through the efforts of the Immigrants' Protective League, who knew that she was a hard-working woman, capable of self-support, the warrant was annulled."[49]

The IPL was not alone in this sort of advocacy and public education work, although it was among the most well-known. Private agencies in the Northeast and Midwest often intervened on behalf of immigrant public charges. The Bridgeport Family Welfare Society in Connecticut, for instance, sent letters and telegrams to various officials in Washington and at Ellis Island on behalf of a fourteen-year-old Italian girl who was to be deported—and separated from her family—because she was hospitalized for kidney trouble. Despite their efforts, the girl was deported to her aging grandparents in Italy, a move the welfare society decried: "A better example of stupid and heartless bureaucratic method could hardly be found." Similarly, the International Institute in St. Louis counseled social workers not to deport aliens solely because they were dependent on relief.[50]

Due to the efforts of the IPL and other private agencies, such deportations do not appear to have been common occurrences in Chicago, especially during and after World War I. Prior to the war, about sixty people were deported each year at the request of the Cook County relief officials. Even then, some private agencies agreed to place aliens subject to the public charge laws on their own rolls to prevent their deportation. Chicago's United Charities cared for 177 such cases in 1912. The Jewish Aid Society cared for an additional 144.[51]

During the war, deportation to Europe was virtually stopped because of the complications involved in travel across the Atlantic. But even after the end of hostilities, the Cook County Bureau of Public Welfare did not resume any large-scale deportation campaign. By the 1920s Cook

County made it a policy not to "deport when the necessity for public care is only temporary. It was only when the evidence points to the possibility of continued care being necessary that deportation proceeding are begun." In general, any anti-alien drives conducted by the Immigration Service in Chicago were met with the "vocal opposition of the Immigrants [sic] Protective League, which sent its own people into the field to determine the facts and to raise questions about official misconduct." The IPL also sent representatives to examine routine deportation proceedings, and they were often quite successful in their interventions.[52]

The IPL was not alone in its misgivings over the actions of the Immigration Service. Prior to FDR's administration, there was in general a sense of "distrust and antagonism . . . between the [Immigration] Service and social agencies." This distrust was bred because social workers who worked with immigrant—that is to say, European immigrant—populations would see firsthand the poor treatment they received at the hands of immigration authorities and the often arbitrary procedures and harmful consequences of the rigid deportation laws. Describing attitudes toward the outflow of immigrants in the early years of the Great Depression, George Warren, an official with the International Migration Service in New York, said that this movement was "perhaps satisfying to the economist, to the politician, and to the man in the street who visualize more elbow room here, more jobs for citizens, lighter relief burdens for our own communities, and a reduction in those elements of our population supposedly contributing to our more recent forms of criminal activity." Social workers, he argued, felt differently. Their vocation made them more "sensitive to the social considerations surrounding this migration, to the shattered hopes and the atmosphere of defeat and despair in which these returns are made," as well as the "intangible and immeasurable losses created by this disruption in family life."[53]

Another reason that some social workers were suspicious of immigration authorities was the seeming arbitrariness of the process. The vast majority of aliens who came to the attention of immigration inspectors were described by one immigration official as "spite cases," often anonymous reports from individuals who had a grudge against the alien. Immigration law also placed the burden of proof on the individual immigrant; he had to show that he had no inherent conditions that should have excluded him at time of entry. If an alien developed tuberculosis within five years of entering the country and was admitted to a hospital supported either in part or in whole by public funds, the immigrant had to prove that he had acquired the disease in the United States, a fact that even medical experts were usually unable to conclusively establish. If he could not offer such evidence, according to Jane Clark, "it is assumed by law to have arisen before" and the immigrant could be deported. Because of these onerous policies, Clark cautioned social workers that "Social agencies should make thorough investigation before reporting cases for deportation" and "they should, by their knowledge of social problems, work for the appointment of immigration inspectors who have had training in social work methods." Clark felt that deportation, like the settlement laws that merely passed the "socially inadequate" from town to town, offered "no real solution." "Deportation," she argued, was "merely 'passing the buck.'"

> The time must come when the desideratum on the part of all nations will be international social responsibility, so the problems will be met where they can best be treated. In that day the individual will be regarded internationally and will be thought of as the product of more than the country where he happens to have his legal citizenship, and nations themselves will cooperate in his care.[54]

Not all social workers, however, shared this view.

Given that elected officials had so much power over the administration of relief, especially in Los Angeles, how can we determine if constructions of deserving and undeserving groups were critical to the differences in treatment and not just differences in local political power? One approach is to look at how private relief officials behaved. In Los Angeles, not only was the County Department of Charities cooperating with immigration officials, but even the local private charities, including the Catholic Welfare Bureau (one of the only private charities serving Mexicans in Los Angeles), the Council of Jewish Women, and the British Benevolent Society, were reporting cases to the immigration inspector. In San Diego, too, private charities "from time to time" cooperated with the local immigration inspector in locating deportable aliens. This is notable because in other cities, private social welfare agencies were often accused of doing the opposite, of keeping "an alien in a private institution until five years have elapsed, so that it is then too late for deportation." The Wickersham Commission—appointed to investigate the deportation practices of the Hoover administration—made a similar observation. It found that private hospitals were less likely than public hospitals to report aliens to the Immigration Service: "Many of these private institutions are actively interested in rehabilitating the alien who has become a public charge or in keeping him from becoming one."[55]

That the British Benevolent Society and the Council of Jewish Women in Los Angeles also reported cases to the immigration inspector suggests that Los Angeles social agencies may have been hard on all aliens, not just Mexicans. Indeed, there is some evidence to support this assertion. The head of the Los Angeles County Department of Charities protested the action of immigration authorities who deported part of a Canadian-born family but left some American-born children behind. He wanted the

entire family deported instead. In a separate incident, two years after a
Canadian man entered the United States "he developed some sore throat
trouble and became a charity patient at the Los Angeles Hospital" where
deportation proceedings were initiated against him. Though he applied
for a writ of habeas corpus the court denied his request, citing that before his entry he had "suffered from an ailment of the throat and that he
required hospital treatment in Los Angeles for a similar diseased condition." He had also had a hernia operation when he lived in Canada, and,
when combined with the fact that he had no property, this provided "satisfactory evidence to the point that the man at the time of his entry was
not physically sound and strong" and thus should have been excluded
because he was liable to become a public charge. Marian Schibsby, an
immigrant advocate in New York, described the court decision as "severe
and alarming."

> If the immigration officials and the federal courts in other sections of the
> United States were to interpret the immigration provisions equally strictly and
> if a throat ailment and a hernia operation before entry were to be held to clas-
> sify an alien as "likely to become a public charge" then most aliens who receive
> free hospital care would most likely be held to have become public charges
> "for cause existing prior to entry." As a matter of fact there is evidence that in
> most sections of the country a more liberal attitude prevails than was shown in
> this instance. It is when an alien or an alien family appear generally undesirable
> that the full severity of the law is invoked.[56]

While Los Angeles courts may have been stricter in their interpretation of
the public charge law, it is also the case that social agencies in cities like
New York and Chicago would have been far more reluctant to report
such a case to the immigration authorities in the first place. Indeed, New
York public welfare officials only reported cases to the Immigration Service after the department had made a "full investigation in each case" and
where the aliens were found to be "incapacitated by disease or disability
and therefore likely to be permanently dependent."[57]
Another difference for immigrants living in the Southwest was the relative paucity of social service organizations devoted specifically to assisting the foreign born in proving such things as legal residency, citizenship,
or previous residence in cases of re-admission. When an official from the
U.S. Children's Bureau went to the Southwest to investigate the condition
of Mexicans in the early 1930s, she found that "In contrast to the seeming need, there are surprisingly few agencies along the border specializing
in services to foreign-born persons." Furthermore, most of the private
agencies were serving the "white population, only a small amount of service being given to the Mexican group." She did visit a few organizations,
often "under church auspices" that served the Mexican community and

had "been helpful in presenting their case to the Immigration and Naturalization Service when occasion arose." Part of the reason there were few social agencies was the fact that there were few large cities along the Mexican border. On the Canadian border, by contrast, there were large cities "well served by social agencies near or at the major ports of entrance to and from the United States."[58]

But Los Angeles was a large city, with at least one non-sectarian agency, the local branch of the CCIH, the state-level board charged with promoting immigrant welfare, which in theory might have worked like the IPL in Chicago to protect immigrants in Los Angeles from similarly harsh deportation practices. But by the Depression, Governor Richardson had long since purged the CCIH of its more liberal leaders and appointed the conservative Archbishop Edward Hanna to head the department, a man who made no effort to hide his antipathy toward Mexicans. When the liberal Carey McWilliams took over the CCIH in 1939, he confirmed that between the early 1920s and the late 1930s, very little work was actually conducted on behalf of immigrants.[59]

Mexican organizations in Los Angeles did intervene on behalf of immigrants on many occasions, but lack of finances or other barriers often got in the way of their advocacy efforts. According to the historian Francisco Balderrama, some Mexican merchants who lost business during the deportation raids in 1931 wrote letters to local and national officials protesting the Immigration Service's tactics. They even tried to raise money to hire attorneys to build cases around the indiscriminate arrest of Mexicans and Mexican Americans and illegal search and seizures. But they were unable to raise the needed funds. The Mexican consul, meanwhile, went to the District Director of Immigration to present the fears and complaints of the Mexican community, but he was cautious in his advocacy. "Official consular policy only authorized consuls to determine whether deportation was warranted under the host country's laws," and the consul did not have any solid evidence that illegal deportations had taken place. The Mexican government also refused to formally object to mass roundups and other "questionable tactics," leaving the local consul with little leverage to intervene. Some Mexican organizations even aided immigration authorities in the raids, "informing immigration authorities about illegal residents." And unlike in Chicago where radical labor leaders staged a dramatic protest, demanding—among other things—an end to deportations of unemployed aliens, labor unions in Los Angeles did little to protect Mexicans from these early raids. Without the vigorous support of Mexican and non-sectarian agencies and labor, and with virtually no political representation, Mexican immigrants in Los Angeles were placed in a very vulnerable position.[60]

Cooperation in the Greater Southwest

Los Angeles was not the only city where welfare officials were keen to have their charges deported. Rom's study showed that El Paso cooperated eagerly, too. In addition, Denver relief officials worked closely with the Immigration Service to deport destitute Mexicans in the winter of 1921–22. During those months, Denver was, according to the local immigration inspector, "over-run with Mexicans." A local newspaper ran a story with the inflammatory headline "Denver's Safety Is Menaced by 3,500 Starving Mexicans," which claimed that an estimated "two crimes daily" were being committed by these destitute Mexicans. Between 100 and 175 Mexican men were being housed in the Municipal Lodging House, but the number of Mexicans who applied for aid became so numerous that "the management there discontinued allowing them to come after they had been there three nights." Private charities assisted those who were unable to get assistance at the Lodging House, "until they issued orders also for their own people to be cared for first." A mildly sympathetic employee from Denver's Bureau of Charities said that Mexicans in the city were "utterly demoralized. . . . There is not a center for them. Their whole tone is low as possible. The community is not trying to do anything, and another thing, we cannot feed Mexicans. They come in hordes."[61]

In response to the situation, the local police conducted raids of popular Mexican establishments—soda fountains and pool halls—and on one day arrested almost three hundred Mexicans. The immigration inspector, W. R. Mansfield, questioned most of them but found only thirty-five whom he believed "were subject to deportation beyond all doubt." Mansfield claimed not to have encouraged the police raids or to endorse the idea of mass deportations. Deportations of Mexicans were somewhat futile, he believed, because Mexicans regarded deportation as a "free ticket to visit relatives," after which they could simply cross the border surreptitiously and make their way back up to Denver. He told officials in Washington that he had "endeavored to avoid committing the Immigration Service to any great expense in the deportation of aliens who are principally public charges owing to the present financial depression, and who in many cases would immediately return to the United States after deportation was effected." Though city officials and the Mexican consul approved of Mansfield's decision, "the charitable organizations," however, "seem 'peaved' [*sic*] because we do not take action against all aliens whom they report to us, notwithstanding what the merits of their individual cases may be." Though he did not want to commit department resources to the deportation of public charges, Mansfield did believe that the "raids by police, and the fear of deportation" had been "beneficial" as they seemed to pressure many Mexicans to leave town on their own initiative. Though he would continue to question the value of deporting Mexicans, Mansfield later assured Washington officials that "all aliens, Mexicans included," detained in charitable institutions who were brought to his attention were "investigated with a view to their deportation."[62]

Such scenes played out all over the Southwest. The American Red Cross and the Fort Worth Welfare Association in Texas complained in the early 1920s that Mexicans were depleting their resources and hoped immigration officials would do their part to deport illegal immigrants. In San Antonio, the secretary of the Associated Charities observed in 1928 that "It has been the custom of the associated charities of San Antonio to give the Mexican who has recently come to the State from Mexico and finds it necessary to appeal to us, one or two chances to adjust himself to his new environment. However, if we find this applicant continues to appeal to us and our investigation reveals the fact that he is an undesirable citizen, we immediately report him to the immigration authorities." During the Great Depression, immigration inspectors in San Antonio increased their cooperation with relief committees and interrogated "all Mexicans or other persons appearing to be of foreign nationality." While Mexicans made up 90 percent of the relief rolls, according to local estimates, and "probably more than fifty percent of these Mexicans are aliens," there were actually few aliens who were found to be deportable: "The immigration officers in San Antonio have gone to the various places where relief is being distributed and checked up on applicants for charity and the total results have been one or two aliens deported. . . . The last check was made about two weeks ago, no results being obtained." In 1935 Pueblo, Colorado, relief administrators told relief workers to cooperate with immigration officials. "The workers will investigate all aliens on relief and turn their findings over to the immigration bureau," reported a local newspaper.[63]

There is no evidence that immigration officers were stationed in San Diego welfare offices as they were in Los Angeles, but cooperation was close nonetheless. Unlike in Los Angeles, however, there were times when relief authorities had to be goaded into collaborating with immigration authorities. In 1934 an immigration inspector noted that "Long ago arrangements were made with the San Diego County Welfare Commission and the San Diego County General Hospital to report all charity cases to this Service. We frequently check to see that they live up to their agreement to report these cases and sometimes in the past when there has been reluctance or failure to report all cases, it has been necessary to contact County Supervisors and others to bring about the full co-operation desired." But he assured higher-ups that "the organizations mentioned are now, and have been for some time past, satisfactorily co-operating." In this case, county politicians were more eager than relief officials to deport dependent Mexicans and applied pressure on relief authorities to cooperate. But there is no evidence that relief officials resisted such pressures like they did in Chicago.[64]

In Phoenix relief officials working under the Federal Emergency Relief Administration (FERA) during the Depression were also initially hesitant to cooperate with immigration officials. According to local immigration officers, the reason for this hesitation was twofold: welfare workers had "sympathy for alien families who might be deported" and, more important, there was so much chaos and confusion in the first months of federal cooperation in the distribution of relief that they had failed to collect information that would divulge the status of alien relief recipients. In truth, while the head of the Arizona Board of Public Welfare had no objections to letting immigration officers have access to the personal histories of all aliens applying for relief, the county board's lawyer advised against it, "on the ground that many deserving aliens would be afraid to ask for help." Instead, the Board of Public Welfare appointed an official from the Spanish-American Society to conduct investigations of relief recipients and then report deportable aliens to the Immigration Service. Immigration officers later complained that the official, "who was a citizen of the United States," never reported a single relief recipient to the Immigration Service. Perhaps due to the continued pressure of immigration inspectors or demands by local whites, in May 1934 arrangements were made to increase cooperation between the local Immigration Service and the Maricopa County Board of Public Welfare. The board made its relief lists available to the Immigration Service, and an immigration inspector visited the welfare offices "daily when possible, and in any event not less than twice each week."

> During these visits the personal history records of all new applicants for relief are checked, and those heretofore on the relief rolls are being gone over as rapidly as possible. In all cases where foreign birth is shown, and the record does not indicate positively that residence in the United States has not been beyond the statutory limit, an investigation of the alien is made. Three applications for warrant of arrest have gone forward so far this month in which the aliens were on the relief rolls.

Despite reports from groups such as the United White Americans that large numbers of Mexican aliens who could be deported were receiving relief, the local immigration inspector did not believe this to be true. "It has been found from experience," the inspector concluded, "that as a rule an alien who is unlawfully in the United States does not apply for relief unless he finds it absolutely necessary, through fear that he will be found and deported." However, "every possible effort [was] being made to locate" the few who did.[65]

Data on public charge deportations corroborate that Mexicans were targeted for expulsion, though such data are not perfect for our purposes. Aliens could be reported by welfare agencies to immigration authorities for undocumented entry or for other offenses; the public charge data will not capture those instances. Furthermore, incarcerated aliens were sometimes deemed to be public charges, or immigration authorities could determine that their crimes were evidence that they were morally suspect, "proving" they should have been excluded at time of entry as liable to become a public charge. Because it was amenable to such circular logic, the "liable to become a public charge" category was sometimes liberally applied when immigration authorities wanted an excuse to deport an alien. Ideally, we would like to know the number of aliens reported to immigration authorities by welfare offices for any cause. No such data appear to exist. Instead, we have public charge data broken down by nationality. Still, the public charge data are the best available aggregate measure of the degree of coordination between relief officials and immigration authorities.[66]

In terms of sheer numbers of people deported for being a public charge or as liable to become a public charge at time of entry, Europeans as a group were most affected by this provision in the first third of the twen-

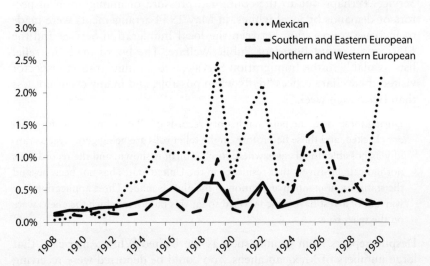

Figure 6.1: Public Charge Deportations as a Percent of All Documented Admissions, 1908–1930

Source: United States Bureau of Immigration, Annual Reports 1908–1930, Washington, DC.

tieth century. This is reasonable given that many millions more Europeans than Mexicans entered the United States during this period. A better comparison can be made by looking at public charge deportations relative to the number of co-nationals entering the United States each year. Using this metric, Mexicans were deported at a higher rate than any other group (see Figure 6.1). More important, especially given that the border was relatively unpoliced during this period, the sheer number of Mexicans deported for this cause between 1906 and 1932 was higher than any other *single* nationality group. That is, 6,310 Mexicans were deported due to the public charge provisions between 1906 and 1932 as compared to 4,106 people from England, 3,940 Italians, and 3,196 Germans (see Figure 6.2). Most of the Mexican public charge deportations occurred during the 1920s, but no other nationality group was ever deported due to the public charge doctrine in the same numbers, even during the years of relatively open migration from Europe.[67]

CONCLUSION

The local administration of relief allowed for wide disparities in cooperation with immigration officials, and welfare offices in the Southwest or in areas with more Mexicans tended to cooperate more. Cooperation could take many forms. In some areas, relief officials invited the Immigration Service to conduct raids in their communities to help solve their relief and unemployment problems. They also invited or simply allowed the Immigration Service to set up shop in their relief bureau, peruse case files, or interview clients at will, even furnishing immigration inspectors with administrative assistance to facilitate their task. Sometimes relief officials reported all relief clients who "were Mexican" or "appeared foreign." This was not the only course of action relief agencies might follow. They could resist Immigration Service demands to look at relief rolls, fail to report cases, or only report those cases that were most severe. They could also work actively in the immigrant community to ensure that immigrants understood immigration laws; they could even "hide" aliens in private charities until their probationary period was over. These were courses of action more commonly taken in areas where there were more European immigrants.[68]

The attitudes of social workers help explain much of the variation in treatment across regions. Both public and private social workers in the Southwest appeared eager to cooperate with immigration officials. In the Northeast and Midwest, private social workers and immigrant advocates were often credited with softening the attitudes of public relief officials. The political context mattered as well. While politicians in both Chicago

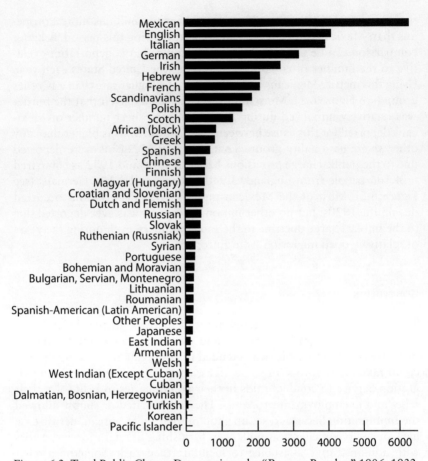

Figure 6.2: Total Public Charge Deportations, by "Race or Peoples," 1906–1932

Source: United States Bureau of Immigration, Annual Reports 1906–1932, Washington, DC.

and Los Angeles made serious attempts to deport dependent aliens, the political machine in Chicago—reliant as it was on immigrant voters—appears to have been wary of deporting European immigrants. Mayor Cermak, moreover, typically deferred to the judgment of the city's professional social workers in relief matters. Both agreed, however, that dependent aliens should not be deported. In Los Angeles, on the other hand, virtually all elected officials were eager to deport dependent Mexicans, and they interfered regularly in the administration of public relief.

Local politics mattered a great deal, but it would be a mistake to portray social workers as mere pawns of local politicians. The evidence indicates that they wielded a considerable amount of discretion. Social workers could choose to fight on behalf of their charges, acquiesce to local demands, or take the lead in urging the deportation of relief applicants. Los Angeles social workers—both public and private—often took the lead in deportation, while Chicago social workers fought to protect dependent aliens, and immigrant advocates in the city made efforts to help liberalize local policies toward non-citizens. Moreover, social workers believed that they had the power to affect the plight of their charges. Edith Terry Bremer, an immigrant rights advocate, challenged social workers at the start of the Depression to recognize that they were in a position to mitigate the effects of the public charge doctrine. "For all 'public-charge' cases . . . the decision as to who shall be reported to the Immigration Service for deportation and who shall not, rests squarely with the charitable institutions and agencies to determine. No federal law requires them to report," she argued. "Have people who have come here to make a home, who have passed the tests, and were regularly admitted, have these foreign-born no stake in this land regardless of the economic weather? . . . Are these, then, to be the forgotten folk of this great civil disaster? The answer rests not with the immigration service," she maintained, "but squarely with the social workers."[69]

CHAPTER 7

Repatriating the Unassimilable Aliens

WRITING IN THE *AMERICAN MERCURY* in the early 1930s, Carey McWil-liams pointedly described the origins of the great exodus of Mexicans and Mexican Americans streaming south across the Rio Grande.

> When it became apparent last year that the program for the relief of the un-employed would assume huge proportions in the Mexican quarter, the com-munity swung to a determination to oust the Mexican. . . . At this juncture, an ingenious social worker suggested the desirability of a wholesale depor-tation. But when the federal authorities were consulted, they could promise but slight assistance, since many of the younger Mexicans . . . were American citizens. . . . Moreover, the federal officials insisted on, in cases of illegal entry, a public hearing and a formal order of deportation. This procedure involved delay and expense, and, moreover, it could not be used to advantage in ousting any large number. A better scheme was soon devised.[1]

That "better scheme" was repatriation: the voluntary removal of aliens to their native country. Aliens can repatriate themselves or they may receive assistance in doing so from friends, relatives, local public or private agen-cies, the federal government, or their local consulate. It is distinct from deportation, which can only be carried out by the federal Immigration Service and does not require the alien's consent.

While welfare scholars have ignored the role that welfare agencies have played in the expulsion of individuals from the country, historians and Chicano studies scholars have produced rich and compelling accounts of the mass repatriation of Mexicans during the Great Depression.[2] What this literature has typically overlooked, however, is how European im-migrants were treated during this period. By comparing the treatment of Mexicans and European immigrants, we can better understand the distinctiveness of the Mexican experience.

The last chapter focused on cooperation between relief and immigra-tion authorities to deport dependent aliens in the Southwest. In this chap-ter, I argue that relief agencies across the country helped repatriate immi-grants during the Depression. But the scale, scope, and character of these efforts differed drastically depending on the *target* of repatriation. Relief officials both inside and outside the Southwest used their own funds to repatriate Mexicans who requested relief assistance. These officials conducted mass-removal programs, often using coercive practices, targeting Mexicans and Mexican Americans alike, and placing greater emphasis on the economic savings than on the effects on those repatriated. Where European immigrants were concerned, however, repatriation programs developed on a more limited "casework basis," where the needs and wishes of the individual were paramount.

The different treatment of Mexicans and European immigrants is not well explained by differences in levels of nativism in the general population. Individuals from all regions of the country wrote to their public officials saying that expelling destitute aliens was just and would help solve the economic crisis. And public opinion polls from the mid- to late 1930s showed only slightly higher support in the Southwest for expelling indigent aliens. Most American residents believed mass expulsion was a good idea. Nor are these differences well explained by the level of economic distress in different cities. Los Angeles, where the repatriation campaign was carried out with special vigor, was not in more dire straits than cities with more limited repatriation campaigns.

The role of politics in this chapter is also less straightforward than in the last. It is certainly true that elected officials in Los Angeles not only supported repatriation, they helped come up with the plan and authorized the funds to help carry it out. But the New York State legislature went a step further, authorizing a statewide forced repatriation plan. Yet social workers there refused to implement it. Furthermore, even many of the most ardent immigrant advocates supported repatriation as long as it was truly voluntary and as long as the immigrant would be better-off in his homeland. Federal relief officials in FDR's administration—sympathetic to the plight of destitute immigrants—were therefore ambivalent about using federal relief funds for repatriation. While they wanted to provide stranded immigrants opportunities for voluntary repatriation, they also worried that some local relief officials would pressure repatriates to leave. Social workers' discretion in the implementation of repatriation therefore proved especially important. As a result, the different attitudes social workers held about Mexicans and European immigrants produced much of the variation in treatment.

REPATRIATING MEXICANS IN LOS ANGELES

The Los Angeles County Department of Charities was not satisfied with efforts to deport or scare aliens, particularly Mexicans, out of the country. First of all, aliens who became public charges, even within five years of entry, could not be deported except "from causes not affirmatively shown to have arisen subsequent to entry," and the Bureau of Immigration made a decision early in the Depression not to deport those who had "fallen into distress through inability to obtain employment." Second, only non-citizens who were living in the United States in violation of the law could be deported. But many families in Los Angeles were composed of an alien head of household with American-born dependents. If immigration authorities were to deport only the head of household, the American-born dependents would surely become a burden on charity. Third, county relief officials complained that the "U.S. Immigration Service was handicapped by inadequate staff and insufficient funds," and as a result, "the procedure, which of itself is slow moving and requires considerable time in proving the evidence and securing deportation warrants, was slowed up much more."[3]

More to the point, though, illegal aliens were not the only "problem" that California had. Los Angeles relief authorities wanted to rid the county of as many Mexicans as possible, regardless of their citizenship or legal status. An immigration inspector explained that local officials there hoped "to rid this locality of a great financial burden through the voluntary return of such aliens."

> They anticipate not only that the departure of many deportable aliens as well as undeportable aliens will be accomplished in this way, but also that many who are not aliens but who are of Mexican extraction whom the Mexican Government is willing to receive, will take advantage of the opportunity to enter Mexico under the conditions outlined, it being borne in mind that all of these classes are now receiving charity in this community.[4]

Mexicans, whether born in Mexico or the United States, were seen as "unassimilable aliens"—a group that county relief officials did not feel obliged to support.[5]

Ironically, the fraction of Mexicans on the outdoor relief rolls had been steadily decreasing over the preceding years, from a high of 34 percent in 1924–25 to a low of 12.5 percent in 1930–31. The decline was due to the growing number of native-born whites applying for assistance but also to the concerted efforts of the Department of Charities to take Mexicans off of relief. Still, relief officials were eager to further reduce the number. According to McWilliams, social workers "reported that many of the Mexicans who were receiving charity had significant 'willingness' to return to Mexico." The county negotiated a charity rate with the Southern Pacific railroad, and a plan soon developed to ship Mexicans to Mexico "in wholesale lots" for the low price of $14.70 per person, "less than the cost of a week's board and lodging." The repatriation program was "regarded locally as a piece of consummate statescraft" because it achieved better results than deportation and at a lower cost. Best of all, because repatriation was "voluntary" it allowed relief officials to argue that it was "designed solely for the relief of the destitute—even in cases," McWilliams added sardonically, "where invalids are removed from the County Hospital . . . and carted across the line."[6]

Repatriating Mexicans, instead of continuing to provide them with relief or medical care, did indeed make economic sense, and the County Department of Charities never missed an opportunity to tout the estimated savings that accrued from the project. "In returning to their 'home land' numbers of Mexican citizens who were dependent here as a result of unemployment conditions in this County," the 1931 annual report read, "Los Angeles County with vision and far sightedness, wisely expended $2767.85 last year. While the immediate aggregate cost seems high, this repatriation has actually saved the taxpayers since by returning these persons, Los Angeles County has been relieved from long time relief in 254 cases effecting 1364 persons." The average cost of keeping a Mexican family on relief was estimated at $0.42 a day per case or $153 per year, while the one-time cost of repatriation averaged just under $15 per individual or approximately $72 per family. The County Department of Charities estimated that between March 1931 and June 1933 it had saved $326,784.[7]

The local District Director of Immigration claimed that repatriation was the brainchild of the Los Angeles Chamber of Commerce and local relief authorities. The business community, however, was not of one mind on either the deportations or the repatriation. Some merchants who catered to the foreign born complained about the loss of business. And growers were concerned that the exodus would endanger their labor supply. The head of the Los Angeles Chamber of Commerce even issued a press release "disclaiming any anti-Mexican sentiment on the part of the Los Angeles community" and advising Mexicans that they "should in no way be influenced in leaving this section because of idle rumors that the people of Los Angeles do not entertain for them the most cordial friendship." But businessmen did not help matters when they refused to hire Mexicans, and their concern over the exodus clearly emanated from self-interest. It was also much harder to make a credible case that they needed more labor when unemployment rates were rising so quickly. Furthermore, the Chamber of Commerce was on record as saying that one of the virtues of importing Mexican laborers over other sources of labor was that Mexicans could be deported should they present a problem for the relief agencies. "If we had been hiring Porto Ricans, Northern Negroes or Filipinos," testified one Chamber of Commerce official in 1932, "we would be feeding them now." Still, speaking of the large exodus of Mexicans from Los Angeles due to both repatriation and deportation, the head of the agricultural division of the Chamber of Commerce argued that the problem lay with "the County Charities group, the Social Service group and the radical labor group," and if pressure could be put on them to stop scaring the Mexicans "much trouble would be eliminated."[8]

The county-sponsored repatriation program was likely the brainchild of Supervisor Frank Shaw. Shaw was chairman of the Board of Supervisors' Charity and Public Welfare Committee, and, in 1933, he was elected the city's mayor. There is more than a bit of irony here since Shaw was a Canadian citizen by birth, whose own claim to U.S. citizenship via his father's naturalization was called into question during his mayoral campaign when no one could find the relevant documents. According to the historian Richard Lester, Shaw saw himself as an advocate for "homeowners" and "bona fide taxpayers" or what he considered "worthy residents" over "unworthy" welfare recipients. Shaw was not an advocate for the city's Mexican community, but he was not alone. Virtually no elected officials in the county were looking out for their interests. The Board of Supervisors also showed their support for the plan by authorizing the funds for the repatriation trains.[9]

The District Director of Immigration was concerned that the term "deportation" was being used as a synonym for "repatriation," leading many—the Mexican press included—to believe that the Immigration Service was actually behind the movement. The local office of the Immigration Service did not officially sponsor the repatriations, but they were kept abreast of the developments and participated in meetings to develop the plan, which included the Superintendent of Charities, the agricultural director of the Chamber of Commerce, and the Mexican consul. Though aliens who received relief would have normally been investigated by the Immigration Service, the Superintendent of Charities decided that "such volunteer groups should not be brought in contact with the immigration department." The Immigration Service, meanwhile, promised that they would "in no way interfer[e] with the voluntary return of Mexican aliens or others, even those who have through ignorance or design been caught up in the net as illegally in the United States."[10]

Though the local Mexican consul had been incensed at Visel's "scareheading" campaign, in so much as it targeted the Mexican community, he approved of the Department of Charities' repatriation plan. According to Balderrama, the consul believed that it was the obligation of the local government to assist in repatriating Mexican nationals who wanted to return since the United States had profited heavily from their labor. Furthermore, he believed that the impetus for the larger exodus was the discrimination Mexicans faced in Los Angeles. The Mexican government, meanwhile, had long worried about the large emigration of Mexican workers, fearing that it undermined the country's economic growth, and viewed it as an embarrassment, proving that post-revolutionary Mexico could "not take care of its own." Furthermore, Mexicans who had labored in the United States were an especially valuable resource to Mexico because they had learned essential skills that would help in Mexico's economic development. As a result, the Mexican government offered repatriates transportation from the border to the interior of Mexico, as well as land, hand tools, and other incentives to draw Mexicans "home."[11]

The first repatriation train left Los Angeles for the El Paso–Ciudad Juárez border crossing on March 23, 1931. The event was a solemn affair. Three hundred and fifty Mexicans and Mexican Americans were on the first train. "The majority of the men were very quiet and pensive," according to one witness, while "most of the women and children were crying." Mexican repatriates were, in general, a varied lot, comprising people of all ages and family situations. In August 1931 George Clements, accompanied by Robert McLean, a member of the County Department of Charities, and two other men went down to the Southern Pacific Depot to examine two trainloads of departing repatriates, estimated at between 1,000 and 1,400 individuals. Walking through the railcars, he observed that "there were about ten able bodied men to the car. These men were all artisans or workmen, none having any criminal stigma. . . . There were on an average twenty young females between the ages of 18 and 30; about 40 children to the car, the most of them American born; the balance aged people." Most of the men had lived in the United States for more than 11 years, and the vast majority spoke English. "None of them . . . knew what they were going to except that they were returning to their own country hopeful of finding something." All told, nearly three-fourths of the repatriates were families. Repatriates also included orphans, the mentally ill, and bedridden, even terminally ill patients, many of whom had to be accompanied by an orderly. Public health officials were only too eager to see infirm Mexicans go, as they had linked high rates of tuberculosis and other diseases to Mexicans' supposed biological and cultural inferiority.[12]

The plan, as originally designed, was a *Mexican* repatriation program. This was the case even though European immigrants were getting onto relief in larger numbers than Mexican immigrants at the start of the Depression. Among the nearly forty thousand new cases analyzed by the Department of Charities during the 1931 fiscal year, two-thirds of the new clients were native-born whites, 12.5 percent were Mexican, 4 percent were black, and the remaining 16 percent were mostly foreign-born whites, including large numbers of Norwegian, Russian, Italian, French, and German immigrants. Comparing these cases to the 1930 census for Los Angeles County, it is clear that Mexicans were hardly that dependent on relief. Southern and eastern Europeans made up less than 3 percent of the population but almost 6 percent of the new relief cases, while Mexicans made up nearly 8 (and perhaps closer to 11) percent of the county population and 12.5 percent of new relief cases. The "facts" were unimportant, however. Mexicans had been constructed as a dependent population and one that needed to be removed.[13]

In theory, as in the official discourse on the subject, the repatriation of Mexicans at county expense was a voluntary program. Any forced repatriation would be tantamount to deportation, a power reserved for the federal government and subject to various rules and procedures. Social workers were often quick to stress that the program was entirely voluntary, even humanitarian. The chairman of the Good-Will-To-Mexico Committee noted, for example, that a county welfare official had advised him "that 1500 Mexicans whom they have been caring for have virtually begged them to send them back to Mexico." However, it was not lost on county relief officials that many did not perceive the program to be humanitarian. Defending the repatriation program, an official with the Department of Charities said that "even though it may seem egotistical . . . to organize and send out Mexican citizens who have contributed so much to the development of the State, the reasons for this voluntary exodus are quite just and fundamentally economic. If our community cannot furnish employment to its own citizens, there is little possibility that it may be able to provide employment for foreigners." Though relief agencies argued publicly that economic concerns prompted them to initiate the repatriations, behind the scenes, officials admitted the cause was the unassimilability of Mexicans. Summarizing a discussion he had with a Los Angeles charity official, an American official in Mexico noted that one of the important benefits of the repatriation program would be "relief to . . . Los Angeles County from the almost unbearable burden of supporting thousands of unassimilable aliens."[14]

Many Mexicans probably did ask to be repatriated and wanted desperately to return to Mexico. In normal times, immigrants flowed back and forth across the border. The Mexican government's hints of some measure of self-support alone would have compelled many to return given their dire circumstances in Los Angeles. Some Mexican nationals, furthermore, had never naturalized in part because many imagined they would one day return to their native land. In practice, however, the repatriation of Mexicans occurred under the specter of duress and coercion, making any discussion of choice highly illusory. The environment in Los Angeles was incredibly hostile toward Mexicans. Even apart from the deportation raids, Mexicans faced discrimination in relief budgets as well as active campaigns to "hire American," which in practice meant only *whites*.[15]

Social workers were also pressuring, even coercing, Mexicans to leave. "Many Mexican Immigrants are returning to Mexico under a sense of pressure," wrote Emory Bogardus. "They fear that all welfare aid will be withdrawn if they do not accept the offer to help them out of our country.

In fact, some of them report that they are told by public officials that if they do not accept the offer to take them to the border, no further welfare aid will be given them and that their record will be closed with the notation 'failed to cooperate.'" George Clements concurred, noting that Mexicans had "been persuaded to leave Southern California either through coercion or actual starvation." Later in his life, John Anson Ford recalled that during his time as County Board Supervisor, which began in 1934, "welfare officials, though lacking the legal authority to do so, pressured Mexican nationals to return to Mexico, trying to convince them that they had to go back." Social workers were even instructed to offer incentives to get Mexicans to accept repatriation, including small amounts of cash and more liberal policies on the number of personal and household goods they could bring with them on the trains duty free.[16]

Clements also charged that local relief officials lied to prospective repatriates, telling them that they "could come back whenever they wanted to." "I think this is a grave mistake," Clements continued, "because it is not the truth. Each card being stamped on the back 'Los Angeles Department of Charities, Welfare Department' and signed by one of the department makes it impossible for any of the Mexican born to return, since it shows that they have been" charity recipients. Because they had been public charges, they would be barred from reentering the country. Furthermore, Clements cautioned that "No child could return, even though born in America, unless he had documentary evidence and his birth certificate." James Batten made similar allegations. He had heard that "county welfare workers in both Los Angeles and San Diego counties have taken advantage of the ignorance of our laws by Mexicans in order to induce them to cross the border voluntarily, giving them to understand they could return at will. When they sought return they were denied admittance, resulting in great hardships to them and to their families."[17]

Indeed, when Mexican repatriates discovered conditions in Mexico were not as rosy as they were led to believe and tried to return, they were refused entry. A U.S. Children's Bureau official explained that "a large number of the returned Mexicans" found themselves "unable to make a living" in Mexico. According to one federal relief official, hundreds of American-born children who were repatriated with their Mexican parents were living under the "most wretched conditions" a stone's throw from the border. One family in particular caught this official's attention. A repatriated widow with seven American-born children had "found her way back as far as Nogales, Mexico and then was not permitted to come into this country again. She lives in the most wretched hut with a dirt floor." Two of her children had just died—one from tuberculosis, the other from a scorpion bite. "All of the children bear marks of malnutrition. The youngest little boy had a pot belly that indicated very serious malnourishment." The situation was so critical that the local federal relief representative asked his superiors in Washington for funds to alleviate the plight of repatriated American-born children: "I certainly think that if anyone with a heart would visit as I did, these children existing and some of them dying, just a few hundred feet across our border, they would agree that the United States should take care of her citizens." While federal relief officials contemplated finding a way to get some funds across the border, none of the parties involved suggested that the affected families simply be let back in if they so desired, and it is unclear whether the families in Nogales or elsewhere were ever assisted.[18]

Because of these incredible hardships, many Mexican repatriates attempted to return to the United States, crossing the border illegally: "At one port of entry it was estimated that 90 per cent of the cases of illegal entry coming to the attention of immigration authorities were those of persons who had been repatriated."[19] A Hollywood resident wrote to FDR and suggested that "a very stringent law" be enacted "whereby any Mexican returning to the United States," after having been deported or repatriated, "should be placed in a prison detention camp for not less than five years nor more than ten, and whereby he will work for his board and clothing." The writer was under the illusion that half of all local county charitable funds were devoted to "people of Mexican blood." Such misperceptions had been nurtured by social workers in the years leading up to the Depression. Underscoring the notion that Mexicans were only valuable as laborers when there were labor shortages, the man gave voice to the views of many Anglos in his community when he wrote that unless something was done quickly, Mexicans would "become a very serious menace. . . . The tax payers here are getting TIRED of supporting this HORDE of lazy, shiftless, worthless human beings, so far as their value to this section is concerned at this time, they are worse than worthless" (all caps in the original). The Department of Labor evinced no sympathy for the plight of the repatriates, either. "On the southern border," they noted, "the utmost vigilance is now demanded to prevent the illegal reentry of those Mexicans who during the depression either returned to Mexico on their own initiative or were repatriated at the expense of American communities."[20]

Among those who returned to the United States illegally after being repatriated were Mr. and Mrs. Garcia. The pair was born and married in Mexico but came to the United States in 1915. By 1938 they had six children between the ages of five and twenty, all born north of the line. Mr. Garcia was a gardener and nurseryman and had full-time work until the Depression struck and the family first requested relief. In 1931 their family was repatriated by the Los Angeles County Department of Charities. It soon became apparent to the Garcias, however, that they could not be self-supporting in Mexico. Mr. Garcia "felt certain the family would never adjust itself there after having lived in the United States for twenty-four years." Furthermore, all of their relatives lived in the United States, save for an "aged mother, who lives in Mexicali." Because the family had been repatriated by the Department of Charities, however, they could not all reenter the United States legally, and so the parents crossed the line illegally, probably within less than a year or two after their initial departure. Mr. and Mrs. Garcia escaped detection by immigration authorities until 1936, when they were forced to ask for medical assistance when one of their children became ill and eventually died of meningitis, and again in 1938 when Mr. Garcia himself fell ill and received care at a local hospital. These were the only recorded instances in which the Garcias asked for assistance since their return to the United States. Because they reentered the United States illegally, however, the parents were considered for possible deportation.[21]

The response from even the more liberal elements of the Anglo social service community in Los Angeles was lackluster at best. The Good-Will-To-Mexico Committee, headed by Ernest Besig, provided departing Mexicans with food, clothing, money, as well as toys and candy for the children to ease the journey. "While in one sense we have been engaging in charitable work," noted Besig, "in a larger sense we are seeking to foster a feeling of good will and friendship toward our Mexican neighbors; we are seeking to show them that they are leaving American friends behind, and that if they have suffered from exploitation and discrimination, there are yet many who would treat them as brothers. We have no patience with the shelving of Mexicans until our convenience demands their return again."[22]

Some private and ethnic organizations resisted the repatriation by providing Mexicans alternative forms of relief. The Cooperative Society of Unemployed Mexican Ladies raised funds to relieve the suffering of their unemployed compatriots. The Confederación de Uniones Obreras Mexicanas advocated that Mexicans establish their own almshouses, hospitals, and asylums. The Catholic Welfare Bureau helped more than 9,000 individuals in 1931–32. But the organization discriminated against Mexicans when they began to feel fiscal strain, reducing the size of Mexican budgets by 25 percent against the 10 percent reduction applied to white cases.[23]

Conferences were held to discuss the conditions of the Mexican community and its exodus. Representatives of thirty-five organizations attended the annual Mexican Welfare Conference in September 1931, co-sponsored by Ernest Besig and Elsie Newton, executive secretary of the International Institute. Guests included Emory Bogardus, Robert McLean, Mexican consulate members, and other community organizations. The individuals present discussed a variety of means to ease the burden of Mexicans still living in the community, including an employment bureau, public jobs, "a clearing house for legal aid cases, and the need to educate the Mexicans as to their rights and duties under the law," but nothing ever came of their discussions. The following year Rex Thompson, an official for the Department of Charities, spoke at the event, drawing a crowd of more than 250. Thompson acknowledged that more than 100,000 Mexicans had returned to their homeland during the Depression, the vast majority of whom had been assisted in doing so. But he stressed that "no attempt had been made by the county to discriminate against Mexicans" and that it had "been necessary to encourage the emigration of all aliens." That the county targeted Mexicans for "emigration" was apparently not relevant.[24]

The CCIH made no mention of the exodus of Mexicans in its 1930–32 annual report. Similarly, the Los Angeles Archdiocese's newspaper *The Tidings* contained only one article on repatriation or deportation during the same period. It reported that at a meeting of the Social Workers' Club of San Diego, Catholic Welfare Bureau representatives were told that "great care should be taken that justice may be served and technicalities eliminated in decisions of officials handling deportation cases." At the 1931 meeting of the California Conference of Social Work there was very little discussion of deportation or repatriation. The following year there was a single session on the Mexican exodus, led by McLean. Describing the repatriation, McLean characterized it as a movement that included "voluntary returns," "semi-voluntary returns," and "direct deportation," and estimated the total number of repatriates at one hundred to two hundred thousand, but no other information on this session survives. It was only at the 1933 conference, after hundreds of thousands of Mexicans had already left the country, that issues of immigration and emigration finally took center stage. Paul Taylor acknowledged that Californians had always been on the vanguard of nativist sentiment and that "The verbal salvos have been punctuated by discriminatory legislation, threats of violence, and shootings and bombings until even now. The intensity of California feeling has been so great that the Federal Government frequently has taken exceptional notice of it in an endeavor to temper its effect upon international goodwill." In addition to discussing numerical restriction, social workers addressed the "*method* of restriction," a topic described as a "matter of heated concern" (italics in the original). But there is no evidence that California social workers took a stand against repatriation or deportation after this conference. Indeed, relief officials in California resorted to greater coercion and intimidation starting in 1934.[25]

All evidence indicates that Los Angeles mounted the single largest repatriation program in the country. Harry Hopkins and Frances Perkins alerted FDR about the repatriations being carried out by state and local relief agencies. "While detailed figures of this movement are not available," they wrote, "the total number of Mexican repatriates alone since 1930 is estimated as between thirty and forty thousand. Los Angeles County, which has carried on the single largest program of repatriation, sent back 13,332 Mexicans between March 23, 1931 and April 25, 1934." Had the Department of Charities had its way, that figure would have been above 50,000.[26]

The total Mexican population in Los Angeles County at the time was somewhere between 167,024 (the official 1930 census estimate) and 250,000 (the estimate of the Mexican population in 1928 made by the Department of Charities, the Mexican consul, and other agencies that dealt with Mexicans). In just three years, then, the Los Angeles Department of Charities succeeded in repatriating at county expense somewhere between 5 and 8 percent of the total Mexican-origin population. These figures do not include the tens of thousands of Mexicans who were deported or who repatriated themselves, sometimes with assistance from the Mexican consulate or from friends and relatives. Indeed George Sánchez estimated that a third of the Mexican-origin community left Los Angeles for Mexico during the Depression. In addition, more than 5,000 Mexicans and Mexican Americans were repatriated by relief authorities from San Bernardino, Riverside, and San Diego counties between 1931 and 1932.[27]

Not all relief agencies in the Southwest financed the repatriation of Mexican immigrants. While many Mexicans left Texas during the Depression, for example, few did so with the assistance of either public or private relief authorities. This was not because there was no interest in getting rid of Mexicans or aliens on relief; there was. Texas had not developed any significant welfare system prior to the New Deal. According to the historian Reynolds McKay, relief funds were limited, and relief agencies were "poorly organized and lacked the personnel to organize and implement repatriation programs." While the costs of repatriating Mexicans in Texas were quite low, relief funds were so limited that these agencies were largely unwilling to finance trips south. Still, some relief officials did participate in repatriation programs. Concerned that destitute Mexican miners from nearby Bridgeport—a city with no relief agency of its own—might flood into Fort Worth, Reverend G. A. Walls, who was a pastor at the Mexican Presbyterian Church and superintendent of the Fort Worth Mexican Mission, tried to raise funds to repatriate the miners, stating: "The deprivations will be as great in the city as they are in

Bridgeport and . . . their coming will put an additional burden on local [relief] agencies." According to McKay, "a local relief committee under the auspices of the Red Cross was . . . established at Bridgeport" and in other nearby communities to raise the necessary funds. While details of the repatriations that subsequently took place are sparse, it is clear that the best interests of Mexicans were not motivating factors. Walls admitted that "Those who go to Mexico will be no better off. . . . They have been away from Mexico for 15 or 20 years and are completely out of touch in that country. They will actually go there as foreigners." In addition to these scattered repatriations, some Texas relief agencies co-ordinated with immigration officials in deporting dependent aliens, and they did their part in encouraging repatriation by making it difficult for Mexicans, especially non-citizens, to receive relief. Those who did receive relief in El Paso had their immigration papers stamped "AC" for "Associated Charities," ensuring they would be unable to reenter the United States legally.[28]

As Donald Young, the future president of the American Sociological Association, wrote in 1937, the repatriation of tens of thousands of Mexicans by relief officials during the early years of the Depression, properly viewed, reveals "the power of nativistic forces to accomplish an extra-legal objective in time of national crisis." The deportation of many illegal Mexican aliens was too costly, bureaucratic, and time-consuming, and deporting legal Mexican immigrants and Mexican Americans was not permitted. But a large-scale expulsion of the Mexican-origin community is what local social workers, elected officials, and many city residents supported nonetheless.[29]

PUBLIC SUPPORT FOR MASS EXPULSION

While many residents of Southern California eagerly supported mass expulsion, they were certainly not the only ones who favored this idea. The chairman of the Superior Democrat Committee in Pinal County corresponded with various state and federal officials for years about aliens, especially Mexicans on relief in Arizona. In 1933 he sent a letter to the president, the secretaries of commerce and labor, the State Department and the governor of Arizona, asking that the government "repatriate all alien indigents in Arizona, who have become an insupportable [sic] on charity and public finances." Ominously, he wrote this was "a final and complete solution of mass alien indigency which our present methods perpetuate indefinitely." Even outside the Southwest there was considerable support for mass removal. A minister of a "foreign speaking church" in New York complained to the Department of Labor about his "unassimilated French" parishioners who worked in the "lowest paid trades, who do not learn to speak the English language, and who do not become naturalized." He argued that it would be "cheaper in the long run" to deport these aliens than to keep them on relief, and he urged the federal government to "do its share this way" to help solve the unemployment problem. A woman representing the Allegheny County Democratic War Veterans Auxilliary in Pittsburgh wrote to the president, asking that aliens who were employed or were receiving relief be "sent back to their native country, and thereby giv[e] the American Citizen a better opportunity to obtain employment." An "old lady" from Verona, Pennsylvania, asked the president why he didn't "make a law to see all foreigner born that are not naturalized [are sent] back to their own country. I think that will help more with the Depression than anything else[.] [O]ur place is a small town but the foreigners are most all on relief and we that have worked so hard to have a home have to help keep them." One New Yorker asked Harry Hopkins to investigate the local relief offices: "No wonder the cities are now on the verge of bankruptcy because we are feeding a lot of ignorant foreigners by giving them relief. . . . I would suggest to deport all foreigners and jews who are not citizens over [sic] the United States back to any land where they choose to go and who will admit them."[30]

In June 1935 the *Chicago Tribune* ran an editorial cartoon on page 1 titled "Round 'Em Up!" One strip of the cartoon warned that "Many idle aliens who entered this country illegally are on the dole . . . while American taxpayers must work to support them." The Junior Order United American Mechanics put out a pamphlet claiming that had the sixteen million foreign born currently in the United States been refused admission there would be no Depression, and they advocated the deportation of the more than one million aliens allegedly on relief. The pamphlet included a cartoon to vividly illustrate that aliens were illegitimate claimants on the public purse (see Figures 7.1 and 7.2).[31]

In fact, mass expulsion of dependent aliens was a popular idea. The practice of nationwide polling was still in its infancy in the early years of the Depression and there are few national polls before 1936. But in 1937 Gallup asked a sample of nearly three thousand American residents whether they thought the unemployment problem could be solved. Approximately two-thirds of those polled believed it could and among the top ten solutions suggested by these respondents was to "stop further foreign immigration and send unemployed aliens back to their own nations." Polls conducted in 1936 and 1938 specifically asked respondents whether "aliens on relief should be returned to their own countries." Less than a third of respondents in both polls opposed mass removal of indigent aliens. Individuals in the North were somewhat less likely to support removal, but the differences are not large (see Figure 7.3). The majority of residents wanted something done about the indigent aliens in their midst.[32]

Figure 7.1: Round 'Em Up!

Eliminate this Calf
Warren G. Harding Council

Figure 7.2: Eliminate This Calf

Source: Pamphlet by the Junior Order United American Mechanics, 74A-J12, RG 46, National Archives.

REPATRIATING EUROPEAN IMMIGRANTS

Despite strong support for expelling aliens across the country, social workers and reformers outside the Southwest were often uneasy about the concept of repatriation. In particular, they were suspicious of any plan that involved coercion and mass repatriation. Repatriation on an in-

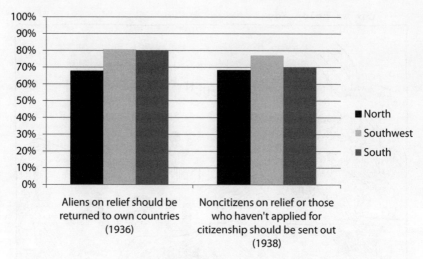

Figure 7.3: Percent of Public Who Supported Expelling Alien Dependents, by Region

Source: Author's calculation from American Institute of Public Opinion Polls, #1936-0062 and #1938-0141.

dividual casework basis, however, *was* an acceptable practice, especially for those who had lived in the United States for only a few years and still held strong ties or had immediate family members in their home countries but were too destitute to rejoin them. Many single migrants who had settled in the United States before World War I had always expected to bring their families over when they could but "found their plans delayed by the War, by the establishment of immigration quotas, and then by the depression. For many the hope of reunion in this country had faded out completely, so that reunion in the 'Old Country' appears to be the only possibility." In these cases in particular, repatriation was seen as the most humanitarian policy even if it also saved money for the relief agency.[33]

Ohio

Ohio presents an interesting case of contrast to Los Angeles. According to federal officials, "the Ohio Relief Administration embarked on a general program of repatriation" in 1934 and within eleven months had repatriated 220 families representing 382 persons "largely of European origin." The number of individuals Ohio officials repatriated pales in comparison to those repatriated by Los Angeles, and one of the most impressive differences in the two programs was the way in which each repatriation program was implemented. Ohio's State Relief Commission created a manual detailing the procedures to be followed in repatriation. According to the manual, "Repatriation must mean betterment of alien's welfare." To guard against coercion, the State Relief Commission had all applications for repatriation referred to the local International Institute, which would then interview the prospective repatriate. The International Institute would discuss with each applicant "the economic conditions in his native country, the means of support he will find there, his family situation, and many other matters. It is made clear to him that though repatriation is not deportation, he undoubtedly will never be able to re-enter the United States." If after this discussion the applicant was still interested in returning to his or her native land, the International Institute would refer the case to the International Migration Service, an agency devoted to international casework, which would investigate the conditions abroad. If the investigation revealed that "the alien's relatives wish him to return, that conditions in his native country are at least no worse than they are here and that he is sure of a livelihood, the Institute recommends repatriation, and soon the alien is started on his way." By contrast, relief officials in Los Angeles did not inquire about the prospective conditions in Mexico until more than a year after the repatriation had begun.[34]

The director of the International Institute in Cleveland proudly noted that there was "no evidence of coercion on the part of any welfare agency." Repatriation was "done on a purely case work basis and the International Institute and the Cuyahoga County Relief Administration work very closely together regarding policy and administration." Agreeing with this sentiment, the FLIS remarked that "this same lack of coercion is not found everywhere" and that "there is evidence that in certain communities aliens who need relief are more or less compelled to take it in the form of repatriation."[35]

The vast majority of individuals repatriated in Ohio were single men who had lived in the United States often only a few years, many with families living abroad to whom they could return. As of March 1935, 172 individuals had either been repatriated or were being investigated for repatriation in Cleveland. Of these, 73 percent were adults. While three-quarters of Los Angeles repatriate cases were families, in Cleveland "in only eight cases thus far have wives and children been repatriated and where they are concerned the social investigation abroad is especially thorough." These agencies were hesitant to repatriate families with either naturalized or American-born citizens because it was possible they would have no rights to work or social assistance in "the fatherland." The welfare department, furthermore, required that U.S.-born children of European—but not Mexican—immigrants have birth certificates before they departed, which would ensure the children the ability to return if they so desired. Many repatriates in Akron were older, homeless men. Although these men had lived in the United States many years, they had never become citizens and still had families living abroad. According to the International Institute there, "These men bring letters from relatives abroad who ask them to come home and they will give them a home, but they cannot send them money for transportation. Their chances for again becoming self-supporting are very meager, and their only prospect being the county home, they are now very eager to return to their relatives and the little piece of land where they can exist for the remainder of their lives." The small number of repatriates from Ohio did not reflect lack of interest in the program; it reflected a lack of funds. One Ohio man, interested in reuniting with his family, wrote the president for assistance:

> Just a few lines to see if I can find out anything about my return to Jugoslavia as I made application . . . at Dayton and cannot find out anything here about it. I complied with all of the requirements and was all ready to return to my family as I cannot get any work here and am on relief. I have children in the old country also a wife and can make a living there if I would only get there but am unable to go as I have not been working and have no money.

Many letters like these were sent to Washington or to immigrant aid agencies with the hope of receiving some assistance in returning home.[36]

Chicago

In Chicago the IPL helped sponsor a repatriation program similar to the one enacted in Ohio. It was not, according to the agency's director, Adena Miller Rich, a "mass movement but repatriation case by case of persons who left the United States with better prospects in view in other parts of the world." The IPL advised that "the well-grounded case-worker does not embark upon" a plan of repatriation for an individual or family until the agency was sure that the individual had a real "prospect of support or care in" his or her native country. "The agency that 'dumps' clients from one country to another merely because it is possible," Rich opined, "does not meet the test of sound family rehabilitation work." Rich cautioned against any organized repatriation plan: "It would be dangerous . . . to assume that repatriation should be generally applied, even as an individual case method and 'solution.' It would be far from socially desirable as a wholesale policy." Any Los Angeles–style repatriation program, in other words, was not socially desirable according to the IPL.[37]

Just as the International Institute in Ohio advised clients that repatriation would likely be permanent, the IPL also instructed caseworkers to tell their clients that any "return to the United States would probably be extremely difficult or entirely impossible." Repatriates from Chicago were individuals who had maintained important ties to their home country. The IPL described the repatriation of a nineteen-year-old woman who came to the United States from Germany in 1928. She met a man in New York, and they became engaged and soon moved to Chicago. When she became pregnant, her fiancé left her. Since her family was in Germany and she had no friends in Chicago, she wrote to the local German consul to ask for assistance in returning home to her mother. The consul, in turn, sent the woman to the IPL for "advice and assistance."

> All the considerations in her problem were carefully discussed. Some plan to locate the father of the coming baby was suggested, with a possible bastardy proceeding if necessary, and arrangement for her own care in a maternity home. But the attachment had faded. The girl wanted her mother more than such a future in Chicago.

The woman eventually miscarried, but as she still desired to return to Germany, she left on the steamship *Berlin* in June 1931, "happy to leave behind forever her experiences in the United States." Unlike in California where repatriation was "encouraged . . . on a rather wholesale basis," the IPL in Chicago gave applicants for repatriation alternatives to removal.[38]

The first repatriates from Chicago returned to India, Mexico, Czechoslovakia, and Greece. Over time the IPL helped immigrants return to more than thirty different countries, but soon most of the repatriates were headed for Bulgaria, Greece, and Scandinavia. "So many of the Greek immigrants must have remained in Chicago without succeeding in bringing their families to this country," the IPL opined. "There is now great eagerness on the part of many of them, to return to their little plots of land; their wives and grown children, rather than continue in the Shelters in Chicago, with no prospects of employment."

> Those immigrant men are older now. Many have always been single. Most of them have some claim to a little piece of land in the Aegean, and they seem to wish more than anything in the world, to return to it now. Some have wives still waiting there, and it is rare, in Greek investigations abroad, not to find that these wives wish their husbands back, even though they are empty of pocket.

Similarly, two Bulgarians, one blind and "placed in the care of the other," set sail for their homeland in December 1932. Each had left a little farm near the port of Varna on the Black Sea. When the IPL inquired whether the blind man's sons would be able to care for him, they told their father that while they were in hard circumstances as well, "if there is a piece of bread for us, there will be one for you too."[39]

Though the IPL assisted one hundred to two hundred foreign-born individuals a month in returning to their homeland, in general it did not pay for the removal of any repatriates; it used a grant from the Governor's Commission on Unemployment and Relief and coordinated with local relief agencies—including the Cook County Bureau of Public Welfare—for additional funds to secure charity rates for the train to New York or the steamship fare and to ensure that the repatriate arrived safely in his homeland. It noted, however, that the demand for repatriation far outweighed the funds available. While Los Angeles relief officials were practically begging Mexicans to leave, in Chicago relief officials had to turn away prospective repatriates.[40]

The Fate of European Repatriates

Certainly not all aliens were ultimately happy with their decision to repatriate; indeed most were probably saddened that their dreams of happiness and prosperity in America had been shattered. The FLIS reported, moreover, that reports from Europe indicated that "many of those who have gone back have bitterly regretted leaving the United States. European social workers warn that economic conditions are in most of the home countries fully as bad as here, that jobs are equally scarce and housing facilities much scarcer." Two Greek families who returned to the United States after having been repatriated were forced to apply for relief five months after their return. Though the parents in each family had originally migrated to the United States in 1909 and 1912 and had labored in America continuously until 1934, they were immediately deported for having been "liable to become a public charge" at *last* entry. Their American-born children were left behind. Still, a number of repatriates wrote letters to the IPL, thanking them for their assistance in returning home. The daughter of a Polish repatriate wrote on behalf of her father, who wanted to thank the IPL for their "deed of kindness": "I am so very grateful for the words of courage which you have given my father. He has spoken of you very frequently, how kindly you treated him when he would come to the office, how good you were to him and how encouragingly you always spoke of him. He remembers it all and has begged me to write to you these few lines."[41]

Not all organizations were as optimistic as the IPL as to the value of repatriation for destitute aliens. According to FLIS, "Some social workers maintain that in most cases repatriation is merely helping the alien from the frying pan into the fire and that even though his present state is very hard, an alien will find it to his ultimate advantage to remain in this country where some day opportunities will again abound." In fact, social workers in Europe felt that some American relief authorities underestimated the difficulties involved in the repatriation of American-born children. "The social adjustment, especially in Central Europe, for the child who has already been a part of the American School System, is almost impossible," one report said, and it was often difficult for these children to get work permits when they got older. "Repatriation is recommended therefore only for recent arrivals in the United States, for families without children or with grown children who can be left in America."[42]

Social Workers, Politics, or Economics: The Case of New York

Though social workers in the Northeast and Midwest were averse to organized mass expulsion, some politicians in these regions were not at all opposed to mass removal. Republican officials in Illinois, as the last chapter noted, tried to pass legislation to deport aliens on relief or require cooperation between relief and immigration officials. The Pennsylvania legislature also attempted to pass a law "which would make anyone dispensing relief from public funds liable to a fine if they did not report all cases of illegal entry which came to their attention. Fortunately," noted one Pittsburgh social worker, "the bill did not pass."[43]

One of the most alarming pieces of anti-alien legislation in the entire country came from New York State, which alone was home to almost a quarter of the foreign-born population. In April 1933 New York governor Herbert Lehman, a Democrat, signed into law a bill authorizing "the forcible removal to their native country of aliens who are inmates of public institutions or are otherwise a charge upon public funds of New York but who cannot be deported by the United States immigration service because of the length of their residence in this country." The bill passed through the state assembly and senate fairly rapidly and "was signed by the Governor before its foes could organize effective opposition." Federal immigration officials suggested the law reflected "public attitude on removal of aliens" but doubted the constitutionality of the law. Similarly, the FLIS argued that the law was likely to be found unconstitutional because it impinged on the exclusive power of the federal government over foreign affairs, "including the admission and expulsion of aliens." However, as late as 1940, the law—in slightly amended form—was still on the books.[44]

The forcible removal clause afforded the New York State Department of Social Welfare a great deal of discretion in the implementation of the law. Forced removal was only authorized when "in the judgment of the state department of social welfare, the interests of the state and the welfare of such person will be thereby promoted." And it appears that the Department of Social Welfare was not eager to abuse this discretionary power, admitting the power was "rarely invoked." In fact, both the New York State Department of Social Welfare and the New York City Department of Public Welfare agreed that they had no authority to remove aliens against their will. Aliens "not subject to deportation, who are unwilling to return to their native countries, cannot be forcibly repatriated," they repeatedly stated in the years after the law was passed. This is not to say that the Department of Social Welfare did not see the economic value of removal—it did. But they stressed that repatriation should be done on a "case work basis" and with the "greatest possible leniency." Still, it was the policy of the department to "encourage the removal of aliens who are unwilling to return to their native countries when it is found after due inquiry, that it is in their best interests to be returned, and that such action is desirable and expedient."[45] It is not clear what New York meant when it said it encouraged removal, but whatever encouragement they gave does not appear to have been that forceful or effective. The Department of Public Welfare referred only 63 cases (containing 106 people) to the Department of Social Welfare for possible repatriation or deportation in 1934, and of these, only 28 cases (including 53 people) were actually removed. Far from targeting aliens for repatriation, there were frequent charges that New York City caseworkers gave preference to aliens over citizens in the distribution of relief.[46]

Given that Ellis Island was the principal port of arrival for immigrants from Europe—welcoming hundreds of thousands of immigrants per year—it is astonishing, in fact, how few alien poor the New York State Department of Social Welfare removed over the years. Between 1880—when the then-named New York State Department of Charities was first authorized to remove indigent aliens—and 1941, the department deported with the assistance of the Immigration Service or repatriated at their own expense fewer than twenty thousand alien poor. In just three years, then, Southern California relief agencies removed nearly as many "alien poor" as the New York State Department of Social Welfare did in the course of over sixty years of work.[47]

Because New York had long felt it bore a disproportionate share of the burden of immigration that benefited the nation as a whole, it was probably more eager than other cities in the Northeast and Midwest to coordinate with the Immigration Service to help defray some of its enormous costs. But it did not have immigration officers stationed in relief offices; it referred cases it deemed appropriate to the Immigration Service. Its stated policy was to report individuals only when they were "incapacitated by disease or disability and therefore likely to be permanently dependent." Similarly, but for aliens who were a "menace to the health and safety of the public," the State Department of Social Welfare's official policy was to repatriate only individuals who had lived in the United States for a "comparatively brief length of time" and who had friends and relatives in their native country.[48]

In 1934 Edward Corsi, a New York City relief official who was the former Immigration Commissioner at Ellis Island, proposed a plan, which was never implemented, to voluntarily repatriate large numbers of indigent aliens. Corsi said he had received pleas from aliens, many in "pathetic situations," who had "relatives and friends, perhaps property in their home countries," who were asking to be returned. While he estimated that there were a million aliens on the relief rolls nationally, Corsi thought that many had not volunteered to be repatriated because the quota laws made their reentry too difficult. If such people were guaranteed readmission when the economy improved, he was "positive that many persons would take advantage of such a plan." Corsi argued that the cost of repatriation would average approximately $90, equal to four to six months' worth of aid, though other estimates suggested the cost of repatriation was significantly lower. Though the cost of repatriating European immigrants was considerably higher than repatriating Mexicans ($75–90 versus $15–20), Corsi still believed that it was cost-effective. He noted that even if only 100,000 aliens took advantage of this plan, it would result in a savings of $10 million—money that New York sorely needed at the time.[49]

Indeed, nearly all cities in the United States were bankrupt or near bankrupt, especially before federal intervention in 1933, and any city with a large alien population might have stood to benefit financially from mass repatriation. One might expect, then, that Los Angeles pursued such drastic measures as a last resort or because of an especially disastrous financial outlook. But in fact expulsion was not a last resort; it was one of the first courses of action considered and taken. Furthermore, Los Angeles was no worse off and on many measures better-off than New York and other large cities, particularly in the first few years of the Depression when most deportations and repatriations took place. Los Angeles had a smaller fraction of immigrants and aliens than New York did, and it had a somewhat lower unemployment rate in 1931 than that of most other large cities. Los Angeles's public and private charities spent less per capita than did New York and some other cities, and the rise in per capita expenditures over time was not as steep. In fact, Los Angeles spent a smaller fraction of city revenues on public relief than did many other cities. The large-scale expulsion in Los Angeles was not the result of more dire financial straits.[50]

THE FEDERAL GOVERNMENT'S REPATRIATION EFFORTS

A number of elected officials, especially from the South and Southwest, called on the federal government to join local efforts to expel aliens on relief. The California State Assembly sent memorials to Congress in 1935 asking the federal government to appropriate more funds to deport illegal immigrants and to deport aliens who were dependent on public relief. Similarly, Congressman Thomas Blanton (D-TX) stood on the House floor in 1935, blaming aliens for unemployment. "Is it not silly and nonsensical," Blanton asked, "to have 12,000,000 Americans out of jobs and cannot get jobs, and at the same time to have 20,000,000 aliens in the United States . . . ?" "I am reliably informed that if we could deport all of the aliens now in this country there would be a job for every American, and there would be no more suffering and shivering and hunger in our big cities." Calls to expel dependent aliens also came from Senator Robert Reynolds (D-NC), and Representatives Joe Starnes (D-AL) and Leslie Arends (R-IL).[51]

Though Hoover administration officials were only too eager to expel dependent aliens, federal officials in FDR's administration were ambivalent about getting involved in the business of repatriation. FDR came to office with the support of many first- and second-generation European immigrants, and the federal relief officials he appointed were quite sympathetic toward the needs and concerns of non-citizens, as upcoming chapters will show. Repatriation was complicated, however. While voluntary repatriation might be in the best interest of the immigrant, the policy was ripe for abuse. Harry Hopkins—the head of the Federal Emergency Relief Administration (FERA)—told the Commissioner of Immigration that FERA would cooperate in repatriating families who wanted to be reunited with alien family members who had been deported, but "In regard to the aliens who are not deportable but who are receiving relief and may wish to be sent to their native country," Hopkins wrote, "I have some reservations. The thing I am afraid of is that our local administrators would take arbitrary attitude toward this and really use compulsion by advising the families that relief would be refused here if they are unwilling to go." Because of his concerns, Hopkins decided to experiment in one city and see how such a program worked on the ground. He conducted such a test in Los Angeles. Hopkins had received a letter from Los Angeles's local Emergency Relief Administrator, R. C. Branion. Branion noted that California had a "problem . . . with the large number of Filipinos and the large number of orientals who are in need and dependent upon public support. There are reported to be some 2500 single Filipinos in Los Angeles County alone, who are anxious to return to their own country, if transportation can be provided for them. There are also in Los Angeles County about 65 Chinese who would be glad to return to China under the same conditions." Branion went on to say that Los Angeles County would like to ship the Filipinos and Chinese to their "homelands" and wanted to know whether they could use federal funds to do so. "Incidental to this general problem," Branion continued, "I would like to know what your attitude is with regard to the general program of repatriation of Mexican citizens which has been going on in the Southwest for many months. . . . Specifically, may we consider the cost of such repatriation a proper charge against federal funds?" Federal officials advised Branion that he could use FERA monies to repatriate Mexican, Filipino, and Chinese individuals from Los Angeles provided that "careful individual case work has been done and no attempt is made to force those affected to leave the country." According to one federal official, few of these people, it seems, were willing to "avail themselves of the privilege of repatriation" and local relief administrators were subsequently advised that they could not use FERA money to repatriate destitute aliens. Another federal official, however, conceded that the reason that FERA money could not be used toward those ends was that "it is so easily subject to abuse. It is always easy to claim that deportations are voluntary when the consent to the transportation has been secured under duress."[52]

The federal government, however, continued to receive requests from "welfare workers in many parts of the country . . . that some provision be made for such repatriations." The Department of Labor recommended that FERA reconsider using federal relief funds for the repatriation of destitute aliens and their families, and in 1935, Hopkins indicated he was reevaluating his stance. That same year, according to one historian, some FERA monies were made available for this purpose, "but it does not appear that large numbers of repatriates were served by this program." And when the governor of Colorado asked for help in deporting destitute aliens, federal relief officials "emphatically stated" that FERA would "take no part in a program to deport aliens." They refused again when Arizona relief officials asked whether they should cooperate with immigration authorities who wanted to root out and deport dependent "aliens who are members of the Communist Party."[53]

Though federal relief officials were reluctant to use relief funds for repatriation, the federal government did initiate a voluntary repatriation program through the U.S. Immigration Service instead. Citing provisions in the 1917 Immigration Act, the U.S. Bureau of Immigration—renamed the Immigration and Naturalization Service (INS) in 1933—offered to finance the voluntary repatriation of indigent aliens who had entered the country within the preceding three years. The INS sent circulars to charitable agencies throughout the country, advertising the service. Whenever possible, the charitable organizations were asked to pay the costs of transporting repatriates to the "port of embarkation," with the INS covering the costs from there on. But even if the charitable organizations were unable to pay these costs, the aliens could still "travel with the so-called deportation parties which every six weeks or so start on the Pacific Coast and proceed to the Atlantic coast, picking up deportees along the route." The federal government was willing to cover the entire tab if cost was an issue. However, only aliens who had entered the country in the previous three years could take advantage of the program, and their American dependents were not eligible for this federally sponsored repatriation. Relief agencies could, however, pay for the cost of repatriating American dependents themselves. Furthermore, aliens were strictly screened to ensure they were destitute and not simply looking to save money on the return fare. Partly as a result of these restrictions, few aliens took advantage of the free transportation. Between the 1931 and 1934 fiscal years, only 5,269 aliens nationwide were repatriated under this federally sponsored program, the vast majority of whom were men. Eighty percent came from six northeastern and midwestern states: Michigan (1,339); New York (1,322); Illinois (754); Pennsylvania (412); Ohio (298); and Wisconsin (168). The IPL's approval of these federal measures suggests that the INS program was truly voluntary. The IPL lobbied to extend the program to cover more immigrants and offered the federal government "its cooperation in social investigation and in execution of repatriation plans" in the larger Chicago immigration district.[54]

With the urging of the Department of Labor, in 1935 Representative Samuel Dickstein (D-NY), "a stalwart opponent of the discriminatory features of the quota system," sponsored legislation in Congress to increase the number of years to five in which aliens could be voluntarily repatriated by the INS. Dickstein told his colleagues that his bill would help "repatriate 100,000 or more of aliens who are stranded in the United States and have indicated a desire to return to their native land." Though the bill passed, the projected exodus of aliens did not materialize, and in 1937 Congress removed the five-year time limit entirely but added a stipulation that repatriated aliens would never be able to return. The federal program ended in 1940, and in its nine years of operation a total of only 9,549 aliens were removed. Most of those who were repatriated went to England, Scotland, Italy, Germany, Mexico, Sweden, Ireland, and Greece. Again, the contrast with California was stark. In nine years, the INS repatriated fewer than 10,000 aliens while relief agencies in Southern California repatriated roughly double that number in approximately a third of the time.[55]

REPATRIATING MEXICANS FROM THE MIDWEST

While tight cooperation between relief and immigration authorities was generally limited to the Southwest, targeted repatriation efforts were not. State and local relief agencies across the Midwest—including Gary, East Chicago, St. Paul, Detroit, and other cities—singled out Mexicans for special treatment. Just as in the Southwest, many social workers in the Midwest believed that Mexicans were an inassimilable population and an illegitimate relief burden. While allowing immigration authorities access to relief files risked ensnaring European immigrants in the deportation net, targeted repatriations carried no such risks. Because they financed and ran the operations themselves, local relief officials retained control over whom they would expel.[56]

In Gary, Indiana, the initial idea to repatriate Mexicans came from business elites who believed Mexicans to be criminally prone and unassimilable and who no longer needed their labor. But the effort garnered support from relief agencies as well. During the first phase of repatriations, most Mexicans left voluntarily and social workers assisted on a casework or humanitarian basis. Many Mexicans wanted to return during this phase of the repatriation, and the files of the International Institute in Gary were filled with letters from Mexicans requesting assistance in returning to Mexico. According to the institute, "In administering relief it has been the policy of the Township Trustee to refer aliens applying for relief to the Immigration Officer for deportation or voluntary removal," but Mexicans in particular were encouraged to leave. The International Institute's national office evinced concern that one of its branches was involved in the repatriation because they had heard of coercive methods being applied in other places. The local office responded, however, that they knew of no instances where Mexicans had been forced to leave. This soon changed. By September 1932, Gary's International Institute withdrew its initial support "unless it could be shown that emigration was purely voluntary and that a specific job awaited each repatriate." According to one International Institute worker:

> We did everything we could to secure individual treatment, but the Investigator for the Township Trustee, who was working on Mexican repatriation, said it was his job to send them back and he was not interested in what would happen to them after they got there. Free transportation was offered to the border to all Mexicans applying for relief, and relief refused to those who preferred remaining in the United States, regardless of the length of their residence and number of American born children.[57]

In addition to being cut off of relief for refusing to repatriate, some Mexicans were, according to one repatriate, "sort of fooled into it" because of language barriers, lack of information, and fear of government authorities. As one girl boarded a repatriation train, she said bitterly, "This is my country, but after the way we have been treated, I hope never to see it again. . . . As long as my father was working and spending his money in Gary stores, paying taxes and supporting us, it was all right, but now we have found we can't get justice here." Condemning the pressure Gary relief officials applied to Mexicans, the local Mexican consul reminded the welfare department that "regardless of their nationality [the repatriates] are members of your community."[58]

Unlike in Gary, Mexicans living in Chicago appear to have been treated like any other immigrant group and repatriated on a casework basis. The IPL assisted a Mexican widow and her baby to return to Mexico. She had entered the United States in 1924 with her husband, who subsequently became ill and died in the hospital. She did not have money for his burial or "even for the candles." Her rent was in arrears, and she was dependent on the United Charities for food. When her mother wrote that she could take care of her and the baby if only they returned to Mexico, the IPL agreed to help fund the trip. There were certainly isolated reports of Chicago relief officials pressuring Mexicans to repatriate as in other areas of the country. It is clear, however, that "more than in other Midwestern cities, organized opposition to abusive agency efforts to remove Mexicans developed." Among the organizations that opposed the discriminatory practices, according to the historian Dionicio Valdés, were the Spanish-language press, the IPL, Mexican organizations, the Communist Party, and local settlement houses. In addition, the political power that southern and eastern European immigrants had amassed in Chicago protected Mexicans as "local politicians generally refrained from assailing any alien group" for fear of retaliation at the voting booth. Gabriela Arredondo, who carefully studied Mexicans living in Chicago during this period, has argued that the IPL in particular "took some pains to look out for the welfare repatriates." And the IPL contacted Mexican officials in Mexico to try to ensure that repatriates would be cared for when they reached their destination. On the whole, scholars generally agree that no organized large-scale relief office–sponsored repatriation of Mexicans took place in Chicago.[59]

Detroit, on the other hand, engineered the largest county-sponsored Mexican repatriation program in the Midwest. The original idea for repatriation in Detroit can be traced to the local Mexican consul. Quickly, however, the Detroit Department of Public Welfare turned what was supposed to be a voluntary program into one that pressured, even coerced, Mexicans into leaving the country. The Department of Public Welfare created a special "Mexican Bureau" to which all Mexicans and Mexican Americans were sent when they applied for relief and where they were asked whether they would consider returning to Mexico. As in Los Angeles, Detroit welfare officials negotiated a special charity rate with the railroad, and the total cost of repatriation per person was less than twenty dollars, including food. According to Norman Humphrey, who investigated the situation there and interviewed the caseworkers responsible:

The view that repatriation was the most appropriate method of handling the problems of Mexicans on relief received considerable impetus . . . and various pressures in sundry forms were exerted to attain the goal. Stereotypes of the lazy, improvident work-hating Mexican were built up . . . The case workers themselves brought pressures to bear in the form of threats of deportation, stoppage of relief . . . or by means of trampling on customary procedures.[60]

In some cases, caseworkers continued to hound Mexican relief clients well after they had indicated a desire to stay. Even Mexicans who had lived in the United States for more than ten years or had U.S. citizenship were sometimes urged to repatriate. One social worker wrote in her case file that "Although Mr. M. had citizenship the worker demanded that he repatriate himself in view of the continuing dependency of his family." So hard was it for some relief workers to acknowledge that Mexican Americans were Americans, entitled to remain in their own country, that when one fifteen-year-old girl, born in Michigan, told the caseworker that she did not wish to go to Mexico, the caseworker wrote that she found this "odd, since she had never been there." As a U.S. citizen, the girl was understandably offended to be asked to "return" to a country she knew nothing about.[61]

The official policy of the Michigan State Department of Welfare was that "the State Welfare Department *will not* assist in the repatriation of a person whose best interests are not apparently so served, or who does not desire to be repatriated" (italics in the original), a view confirmed by the director of casework in Detroit at the time. Nonetheless, caseworkers came to believe, according to Humphrey, that "in view of their degree of assimilation, the extent of their skills, and their opportunities in Detroit, to inquire whether Mexican heads of families wished to avail themselves of transportation privileges was to open the door for them to a more favorable and hopeful situation. If seeming coercion occurred in actually carrying out departmental policy, it may be ascribed to the existence of personnel lacking a trained social-work perspective and not to departmental policy per se." "Repatriation as a voluntary measure," Humphrey wrote, "may well conform to the best standards of case work procedure, but actually, in the carrying-out of the program, untrained case workers exerted undue pressures in some instances, and in others actually violated clients' rights."[62]

Conclusion

There is probably no single reason why Mexicans were targeted for expulsion at the hands of relief authorities in the years leading up to and during the Great Depression or why European immigrants received such different treatment. It is clear, however, that expulsion was not a last resort or a response to an especially bleak financial outlook. Los Angeles did not fare worse than New York or Chicago or other cities in that regard. While it was certainly more expensive to repatriate Europeans than Mexicans, agencies often still saw the value of returning immigrants to Europe. And it cost social agencies very little—and in fact may have saved them quite a lot—to cooperate with the Immigration Service, and still many social service agencies in the East and Midwest, as the last chapter showed, chose not to do so.

To say that there was more nativism in Los Angeles or the Southwest oversimplifies the story. While nativist—and especially anti-Mexican—sentiment may well have been stronger in the Southwest, most American residents wanted *all* destitute aliens removed from the country. Mexicans were coercively repatriated from the Midwest, not just the Southwest. And if Southern California residents perceived Mexicans to be an especially welfare-dependent group, they had social workers to thank for this view, for it was these elites who had constructed and spread the stereotype of the dependent, inassimilable Mexican only a few years earlier.

Politics was certainly a factor in the disparate outcomes. Elected officials in California were not responsive to Mexican or Mexican American interests and demonstrated their fervor for expulsion. County Supervisor Frank Shaw came up with the idea for Los Angeles's repatriation campaign, and his board colleagues signaled their support for the plan by authorizing the funds for the repatriation trains. California's State Assembly, meanwhile, was eager to expel indigent aliens, too, and memorialized Congress in 1935 to deport them all. With more political power, Mexicans would likely not have faced such a fate. Meanwhile, Chicago's political machine, as the last chapter showed, did not support the Immigration Service's request to give them access to their local relief rolls. But this is not simply a story about the differential political power of immigrant groups. The most draconian repatriation law was passed by the New York State legislature, authorizing the forcible removal of alien dependents. But the law allowed the state's social workers considerable discretion, and they proved unwilling to abuse their authority.

Local social workers and relief officials were central actors in this story. They had considerable power to shape, interpret, and resist formal policies and practices related to repatriation. They did not target all non-citizens or all illegal immigrants for removal. Rather, guided by their stereotypes, social workers found creative ways to expel Mexicans and Mexican Americans. When deportation proved too costly, time-consuming, restrictive, or blunt an instrument, social workers in the Southwest and Midwest organized and financed their own repatriation programs, and they deceived, coerced, and cajoled Mexicans and Mexican Americans into leaving. Illegal or legal non-citizen Europeans were treated very differently by relief authorities. While European aliens were repatriated, too, steps were taken to avoid coercion, and the interests of prospective European repatriates were usually paramount.

For many Mexicans who were "removed," especially those who had lived in the United States sometimes for decades, who had raised their children here, and who had contributed so much to the development of the nation, deportation and coerced repatriation was not only a personal affront but tantamount to banishment. If they tried to return to the United States, they generally found their lawful reentry blocked. If they chose to cross the border undetected, sometimes to rejoin family and friends in the North, they did so with the recognition that they would no longer enjoy their former legal status, forced to live in the shadows of a country they had helped make prosperous. Considered at the group level, the welfare office–sponsored repatriation and deportation of so many Mexicans intensified the process of social exclusion. Knowing that immigration officers would be stationed at relief offices in their communities caused an untold number to refrain from seeking relief assistance.

While no exact figures exist, Frances Perkins and Harry Hopkins estimated that 30,000 to 40,000 Mexican repatriations were sponsored by relief agencies between 1930 and 1935. And historians estimate that 350,000 to 600,000 Mexicans and Mexican Americans—20 to 40 percent of the Mexican-origin population in 1930—ultimately left for Mexico during the Depression. The total number of Mexicans repatriated by county relief officials, then, represents a small fraction—5 to 11 percent—of the total number of Mexican repatriates.[63] But this figure does not include the unknown number of deportations that occurred as a result of coordination between immigration and relief officials. Nor does it include the number of individuals who left without the assistance of relief agencies—but nonetheless in response to agency actions—as when Los Angeles's Committee on Unemployment Relief invited the Immigration Service to conduct raids in their community or when agencies refused Mexicans access to relief. All of these practices should be considered when we think about how welfare agencies can serve as agents of expulsion.

CHAPTER 8

A Fair Deal or a Raw Deal?

UNLIKE MEXICANS, black Americans were not expelled from the nation for using relief, although the thought had certainly occurred to some. In the late 1930s, Mississippi senator Theodore Bilbo advocated the deportation of American blacks in order to solve the economic crisis. Using data that showed twelve million unemployed, Bilbo argued that the Depression would come to an end with the "firing [of] these 12,000,000 Negroes back to Africa." According to the *Chicago Defender*, the motion "fell flatter than a pancake," as few of Bilbo's colleagues would even listen to the senator's tirade. Southern blacks who used relief relatively soon after they migrated to northern cities were sometimes removed or "deported" to the South under the settlement laws, which allowed for the removal of non-resident paupers to their county of origin. But because charity officials did not publish data on such removals broken down by race, the scope and implications of this phenomenon are not well understood. Though black Americans could not be expelled from the nation for use of relief, they were largely excluded from most public relief and relegated to segregated private charities prior to the New Deal.[1]

The election of Franklin Delano Roosevelt at the end of 1932, however, promised a new beginning. The administration provided states and local governments with billions of dollars for emergency relief and public works, stipulating that there should be no discrimination on the basis of race or color in the distribution of relief. Given the large-scale exclusion of blacks from relief prior to the Depression, the federal pledge of non-discrimination—taken in the context of the times—was a radical promise indeed. It was also a promise left unfulfilled. Millions of blacks received federal assistance—for some, raising their standard of living above anything they had previously known. But greater access also led to greater white resentment. Furthermore, state and local administration of federal relief virtually guaranteed widespread discrimination in its distribution. Despite the New Deal's nationalizing reforms, intended largely to standardize relief policies across the country, local political economies and racial regimes continued to influence the administration of relief. Though committed to non-discrimination in theory, the federal government never fully enforced its mandate. Depending on one's perspective, the New Deal was either a "godsend to the Negro masses" or nothing but a "raw deal." There was truth in both perspectives.[2]

Though much has been written about how blacks fared under the New Deal, less is known about how the New Deal treated European immigrants or Mexicans. In addition to mandates against discrimination on the basis of race or color, federal officials also stipulated that there should be no discrimination in the administration of direct relief on the basis of citizenship. This was not, however, the radical promise that it was for racial minorities, as non-citizens—or at least those of European origin—had enjoyed roughly equal access to assistance prior to the New Deal. Because cities and counties had never made significant distinctions on the basis of citizenship, and because social workers did not believe they should, local control of federal relief did not present the same problem for European immigrants as for blacks. White non-citizens generally received the federal relief to which they were entitled.[3]

Early work relief programs (1933–35) were a slightly different matter, however, since some of these programs included citizenship requirements, or at the very least preferences for U.S. citizens and aliens with first papers. However, these early federal work relief programs generally provided the means to benefit white non-citizens indirectly, either by hiring their American-born children or by raising direct relief benefit levels for those who were disqualified from work relief because of citizenship status.

Like blacks, Mexicans gained significantly greater access to relief during the New Deal, although they continued to face racial discrimination at the local level. Citizenship barriers were also typically strongest for local public work programs out West, and Mexican Americans were sometimes wrongly denied work relief on the assumption that they were non-citizens. Social workers' views of Mexicans explain some of this disparate treatment, but growers deserved part of the blame as well. The advent of federal relief altered the incentives of agricultural elites, and for the first time, the views of southern planters and western growers converged. Prior to the New Deal, southwestern growers were content to let Mexicans get on relief because it served as a subsidy to the agricultural industry. But as relief benefits rose and wages fell, growers began to worry that federal relief would threaten their access to cheap, dependable labor. Southern planters, meanwhile, began to see that if they could control the distribution of relief, the flow of federal money could relieve them of some of the financial obligations of paternalism. During harvests, however, both southern planters and western growers called on relief officials to cut agricultural laborers from the relief rolls.

DIRECT RELIEF

By the time FDR came into office in 1933 the situation across the nation was dire. A quarter of the labor force was unemployed and local relief budgets were stretched beyond their limits. Between the start of the Depression and FDR's inauguration, a third of the private charities "disappeared for lack of funds." Relief spending in the nation's largest cities increased sevenfold, but it was still not enough to meet the demand. Meeting the crisis with what one social worker called "callous indifference," President Hoover's administration had done little to assist cities in their struggle, opposing any federal grants in aid. With despair spreading, in July 1932, Hoover finally signed the Emergency Relief and Construction Act, which offered state and local governments loans to pay for relief. Only a fraction of the funds appropriated were ever distributed, however, as some states simply refused the terms of the loans, while others did not have the administrative capacity to apply for or use them. Thousands of individuals in desperate need were therefore turned away without relief, and as the bread lines grew, social workers despaired at the extreme privations.[4]

Desperate times called for bold action. But no one could have predicted the great transformation in the federal government's economic role during FDR's first one hundred days. The largest relief program during the first New Deal was the Federal Emergency Relief Administration (FERA), passed by Congress in May 1933. The act appropriated $500 million to states as matching grants—not loans—which states could spend on either direct relief or work relief. Though the program was administered by the states, federal relief officials sent a memo to all state relief administrators dictating that in the administration of FERA funds, "There shall be no discrimination because of race, religion, color, non-citizenship, political affiliation or because of membership in any special or selected group." Furthermore, federal authorities assured black leaders that blacks would not be "'overlooked' in the administration's 'vast reconstruction plans . . . for employment and relief.'"[5]

By October 1933, roughly three million individuals were already receiving federal relief, and four out of five of these were white. Though blacks and Mexicans represented a small minority of beneficiaries, federal intervention nonetheless brought these groups unprecedented access to relief. Often previously underrepresented on the relief rolls, blacks (4.9 percent) and Mexicans (3.4 percent) were now more likely to receive relief than whites (2.3 percent). Given the large exodus of Mexicans still under way, these numbers probably underestimated Mexicans' share on the federal relief rolls.[6]

Resentment toward Blacks and Mexicans

That blacks gained unprecedented access to federal relief did not go unnoticed. In 1934 Forrester Washington, Director of Negro Work with FERA and a member of FDR's "Black Cabinet," noted that "The most striking fact in connection with the Negro and relief is that the Negro bulks on the rolls of the Federal Emergency Relief Administration all out of proportion to his numbers in the general population." Washington identified four principal causes for this state of affairs. First, blacks were first to be fired and therefore had the greatest need. Second, organized white labor insisted that only organized labor—and therefore only whites—be employed. Third, southern landlords took advantage of federal relief and deliberately placed black tenants on relief rolls, often to use the relief money for themselves. Lastly, black farmers experienced discrimination in the administration of federal farm relief programs like the Farm Credit Administration.[7]

Presciently, Washington worried that by limiting the employment opportunities of blacks, there was a "danger of developing racial friction through creating resentment on the part of the majority public against the presence of so many Negroes on the relief rolls."

> Already community-chest executives in certain cities have stated that they are averse to the publication of data touching on the number of Negroes on relief rolls because, in spite of the fact that community-chest agencies are not carrying Negroes on relief, nevertheless, certain of their large contributors have indicated an intention to discontinue their contributions if so many Negroes continue to be supported on relief.

Prior to the Depression, social workers and relief authorities had paid little attention to blacks and, if anything, judged them to be the group least likely to use relief. After federal intervention, their attitudes changed. "Even some employees of various local relief administrations," noted Washington, "are becoming emotional and 'jittery' on the subject, and in their exasperation are beginning to blame the Negroes themselves for their presence in large numbers on relief rolls." He worried that "social workers have become blinded" to the "underlying factors" that led blacks to relief. Instead, they were "predisposed to allow one or two examples of Negro 'chiseling' to convince them that the great mass of Negroes are 'chiselers.'" Social workers in turn used these beliefs to justify the arbitrary reduction of black caseloads.[8]

Relief officials were not the only ones who noticed blacks' new reliance on relief. Senator Millard Tydings (D-MD) told an investigative committee that "he could not understand why so many Negroes are on relief." Writing for the *Journal of Negro Education*, Edward Lewis related that one of the "major topics for private conversations at luncheon clubs throughout the country is, why is there such a disproportionate number of Negroes on relief?" The "off-the-record conclusions" as to why blacks "bulked" so much on the relief rolls, according to Lewis, were that blacks were "shiftless, lazy, indolent and irresponsible." Once blacks gained greater access to relief, whites' stereotypes of blacks started to look a lot more like their stereotypes of Mexicans.[9]

Anglos continued to resent Mexicans' use of relief just as they had prior to federal intervention. One federal relief official described the community attitude in San Antonio as "a mixture of indifference and resentment toward the Mexicans. 'They ought to be sent back to Mexico,' is a common remark," even though many were citizens or had American-born children. In Brighton, Colorado, many people felt strongly that in the distribution of relief, "the Mexicans should come second and that the native population should be cared for first." South Denver civic leaders complained to their governor that the local relief rolls were "over burdened with alien Mexicans who have no right . . . to receive relief." In El Paso, according to one observer, there were constant "worries about a heavy case load of alien Mexicans." Residents there charged that half of the Mexicans who came in before immigration restriction were on relief. Even more galling, "They also feel they are carrying a big load of Mexicans who actually live in Mexico!" Residents complained that Mexicans "come across the bridge from Juarez and rent rooms in El Paso . . . so they can get our relief." In response, the city "installed an immigration man in the relief office, and they are marking grocery packages so they can be detected on the bridge. It's all pretty much of a mess, hard to control, and, in the meantime, the American population of El Paso is resentful." Mexicans' use of relief was also sometimes ruthlessly exaggerated. Less than 4 percent of Mexicans nationwide—and less than 3 percent in California—were on federal relief in 1933. Yet when a member of the Los Angeles Board of Supervisors went to Mexico to discuss Mexican repatriation, he insinuated that the *majority* of Mexicans in Los Angeles were being supported by charity. According to Balderrama and Rodriguez, the accusation so infuriated the Mexican press, which was already incensed by the deportations and coerced repatriations, that the supervisor allegedly "had to be smuggled out of Mexico because American authorities feared for his personal safety."[10]

The Views of Agricultural Elites

The attitudes of southern planters and western growers toward relief also converged during the first New Deal. While agricultural employers in the West had been indifferent or even supportive of migratory laborers using relief prior to 1932, their attitudes changed after federal intervention. Federal relief levels, though barely enough to subsist on, were sometimes higher than prevailing local wage rates. As a result, western growers began to see relief as a potential threat to their labor supply, just like their southern counterparts. George Clements, agricultural director of the Los Angeles Chamber of Commerce, complained that there were 150,000 Mexicans in California, most of whom were on either state or county relief. Mexicans, he carped, were "willing to take either [county or state relief] and idleness rather than work for the farmer at $48 a month, or for that matter at any price." Highlighting the threat inherent in this situation, Clements charged that "The Mexican on relief is being unionized and is being used to foment strikes among the still few loyal Mexican workers. The Mexican casual labor is lost to the California farmer unless immediate action is taken to get him off relief."[11]

On the other hand, with the advent of the Great Depression and federal intervention in relief provision, southern planters learned to use the new system for their own gain. As long as they maintained control over the distribution of benefits, planters learned that they could make federal relief work to their advantage. Some even encouraged their tenants to get on relief between harvests to help defray the costs of paternalism. One Mississippi welfare worker predicted that "As soon as the cotton season is over you will find these . . . planters bringing pressure (and you know monied pressure is strong) on the members of the Board to apply for aid to help carry [black] 'hands' through the winter, as the crop was mortgaged and 'nothing was cleared.'"[12]

Discrimination against Blacks and Mexicans

Though blacks and Mexicans were overrepresented on the relief rolls, they were also likely underrepresented relative to need since there is ample evidence of discrimination in the distribution of assistance. The drive to discriminate came from three interrelated sources: social workers' own attitudes about their clients, white public opinion, and pressure by agricultural employers to purge the relief rolls during harvests.

In order to assess how the federal relief program was operating on the ground, Harry Hopkins sent Lorena Hickok, a reporter and friend of the president's wife, to travel the country and assess the situation. Hopkins told Hickok that he did not want "statistics" or the "social worker angle"; he wanted "her own reaction as an ordinary citizen." In the course of her travels, Hickok became deeply troubled by the thought that federal relief might upset local race relations. She wrote that in Texas about half to two-thirds of the relief recipients were unmotivated to get off relief: "They're Negroes and Mexicans, to whom relief however inadequate for whites . . . doesn't mean any lowering of their standards of living at all—in fact, in many, many cases, a BETTER standard of living. They're apparently coming on relief just as fast as they can get on. For them, it's 'just swell.'" "You'll probably think I'm getting to be a hard hearted old Bourbon," Hickok wrote Hopkins. "Well, I'm no more hard hearted than are the case workers and case supervisors who are handling this job. They—and I—are thinking about these white people, especially white collar people. And we are worried. Plenty worried."

> "If it's a choice between a white man and a Negro, we're taking the white man," the administrator told me. "We're taking the white applications first and turning away just as many Negroes as we can. We've got to, because of the mental attitude of the whites. We've been threatened with riots here."

Hickok feared that whites would revolt at the thought of blacks or Mexicans attaining the same standard of living as whites: "If we continue to take on in San Antonio as many Mexicans as we now are—and in other parts of the South as many Negroes—it seems to me that we are forcing white people, especially white collar people, who are very apt to give us trouble, down to Mexican and Negro standards of living." She was also concerned that blacks and Mexicans would never work if they could achieve a better standard of living on relief.

> An awful lot of the trouble here in Texas seems to be that Mexican and Negro farm labor won't work for the prevailing wages if they can get on relief. And they've come to town to get relief. If anyone told me that except social workers, I'd be inclined not to believe it. But they say it's true. Not the higher-ups, in Austin. But social workers out here in the field.

As a result, Hickok urged Hopkins to consider officially condoning the already prevalent local practice of giving lower benefits to blacks and Mexicans or excluding them from relief altogether. She averred that in an ideal world with limitless resources, forcing "Mexican and Negro standards of living up to white standards" might be "nice." But resources were scarce.

> The more I think about it, the more I'm convinced that something ought to be done to clean up those Mexican and Negro case loads by thorough reinvestigation and that, as far as possible, we force them to go back to work by withholding relief—even though it may be forcing them back in peonage. What else can we do? Why, in the name of common sense, SHOULD they work—chopping cotton and so on—if we make it possible for them to live without working?[13]

While the availability of a higher standard of living through relief did affect the decisions of some destitute whites, blacks, and Mexicans to work, few relief recipients probably preferred relief to employment. Many people felt great shame in receiving relief. A study of relief recipients in rural Alabama, for instance, found that "less than 20 percent [of tenant farmers] preferred relief rather than make their own way, and this despite the fact that nearly 95 percent of them stated that they could live better on relief than they had recently been in the habit of living." But residency laws often compelled migrant laborers to stay on relief rather than take seasonal labor for fear of losing their residency status in their home county. And relief recipients did use relief to help sustain them through strikes initiated to better their wages and working conditions.[14]

Fears that blacks and Mexicans would never work were used to justify denying them assistance, especially in rural areas of the South and Southwest, and to justify shutting down local relief offices and work relief projects during the harvest. One group of angry white women in Arizona decried the actions of relief authorities for "making it impossible to get domestic help and very bitterly criticize[d] the Administration and the Welfare Board in particular for paying $3.50 per day to Negro and Mexican help who heretofore have only received from one to two dollars per day." Much of the pressure, however, came from agricultural employers. In Weld County, Colorado, the "field man" for the Great Western Sugar Company had to approve all beet worker applications for federal relief. Thomas Mahony, chairman of the Mexican Welfare Committee of Colorado, complained that federal relief "was cut off by local and county committees at the time the beets were ready to thin and by hunger pressure methods the workers were forced to take drastic wage cuts. Some of the higher officials in the Federal Relief denied that this was done with their approval," he claimed, "but it was done and the sugar industry profited by it." He claimed that Hopkins sent a telegram to county federal relief administrators, telling them "that all beet field laborers are to be stricken from the relief rolls," as he understood, "permanently." "I don't think Mr. Hopkins realizes that he is confirming the action of subordinate administrators, state and county, in what they have been doing in cutting of relief to force destitute people to accept wage cuts."[15]

For blacks in the rural South it was "next to impossible" to "secure relief without white sponsorship and in the case of tenants, this sponsorship must be that of the landlords." Despite the fact that planters were now less able to provide paternalistic benefits, they were still sometimes wary to allow access, at least for able-bodied blacks, because access to relief made them less willing to work during the harvest. One Mississippi landlord complained: "folks on relief won't pick cotton when there's cotton to pick." Without sponsorship, there was little hope of getting relief. One black tenant noted that "If the white man wouldn't vouch for you you couldn't get anything and Mr. Stone did not want the government to give us anything. He said he wished the government never did give us anything." Objecting to the lack of federal oversight, another tenant noted that "[The government] sends things down here for us but they gives it to some responsible white man to distribute and he does all right long as they looking at him but when they go way he don't give none of it away—he sells it to his croppers and puts a lot of names on them papers and the government don't know no better." Summing up the situation, a tenant remarked: "We colored folks in the South are in a bad fix. We don't get nothing the government sends us." Black tenants could not complain to the government about this state of affairs because if they filed an official complaint, it was bound to get back to the landlord.[16]

Planters and growers sometimes complained about the effect of relief on white workers as well. And as a result, white workers were sometimes affected by policies to deny relief during the harvest. Migratory cotton pickers in Arizona, for example, were overwhelmingly white yet at the "beginning of the cotton season they eliminate from the rolls all persons who have agricultural background and refuse relief or WPA certification to unskilled applicants who have had any agricultural experience whatsoever." Planters in the Mississippi Delta also tried to "use their influence over New Deal relief agencies to rid the Delta of potentially troublesome white tenants. One official reported that planters regularly urged him not to put poor whites on relief but to 'starve them out. They are not worth feeding. We do not want them in our county.'" In fact, one welfare worker complained to the governor of Mississippi that planters were trying to "pressure the local welfare board to discontinue relief work in order to force unwanted white farm labor out of the county." Though poor white agricultural workers were clearly affected, these policies disproportionately hurt blacks and Mexicans. Blacks and Mexicans were more likely to work in agricultural jobs, and some agricultural employers preferred their services since growers viewed them as more tractable. Moreover, at times blacks and Mexicans were assumed to have agricultural experience simply because of their race. In Pima County, Arizona, rather than try to ascertain which relief recipients were former cotton pickers, relief officials decided to simply "keep off of relief every Alien-Mexican able bodied man."[17] Similarly, according to the Colorado WPA director, "Men were laid off on the assumption that they were beet laborers . . . because of their names—Spanish and Mexican." Spanish Americans protested these policies, arguing, "Why should only the Spanish Americans be set when they like the rest have been born and raised right here in the United States?"[18]

While growers were not much involved in the relief-sponsored deportation and repatriation programs prior to the first New Deal, the availability of federal relief altered their incentives. Angered that migrant laborers now made use of federal relief to ride out strikes, growers had local officials pressure federal officials to deport Mexican public charges. In October 1933, the Commissioner of Immigration received an urgent telegram from local officials in Tulare County, California, where a strike was unfolding. It read:

> WE APPEAL TO AND URGENTLY REQUEST YOU TO AT ONCE TAKE THE NECESSARY STEPS TO DEPORT ALL ALIENS THE MAJORITY OF WHOM ARE <u>MEXICANS</u> NOW IN THIS COUNTY WHO HAVE BECOME PUBLIC CHARGES WHO ARE A MENACE TO PUBLIC PEACE AND HEALTH WHO ARE NOW AND WILL CONTINUE TO BE A HEAVY AND IMPOSSIBLE CHARGE ON THE RESOURCES OF THE COUNTY.

The strike was eventually settled and the pickers returned to work, but only after several strikers had been shot and killed and twenty-three had been arrested. The local immigration official charged with investigating the situation assured all concerned that the County Welfare Department had the local INS office address "and have been referring to us any cases in which there was doubt as to their status under the immigration laws."[19]

Agricultural elites had some influence over the distribution of relief at least in part because of their political power. Rural interests were well represented in state legislatures, and growers had even more control over county government. One Los Angeles Chamber of Commerce official boasted that "if the farmer controls his politics in his agricultural counties, and he can if he wants to, then he should arrange" to have agricultural laborers on relief rolls "released to him during his peak crop seasons." During one peak crop season, the governor of Louisiana ordered that relief payments to blacks be cut by half. In other cases, southern planters were appointed to local administrative positions, allowing for more direct control of relief provision. Moreover, many state and county relief administrators charged with distributing federal funds were appointed by state and county elected officials. In California, FERA relief funds were "placed in the hands of a state emergency relief administrator, appointed by the governor and approved" by federal officials. Governor James Rolph, for example, appointed the conservative Archbishop Hanna—who advocated restriction on Mexican immigration—to head California's unemployment relief commission. Since blacks and Mexicans had virtually no political power, their interests were rarely represented. While social workers at times resented or resisted grower pressure, many relief officials were quite sympathetic to grower demands because, like Hickok, they believed that blacks and Mexicans should be forced off relief to work in the fields. Moreover, cutting the relief rolls, even temporarily, could help them conserve strained relief budgets for those they believed actually deserved assistance.[20]

Whether due to outside pressure or social workers' own biases, discrimination in relief administration was rampant. There is evidence that black work relief projects were stopped while white relief projects were allowed to continue, that black benefit levels were arbitrarily cut in half while white benefit levels were held constant, and that communities developed "professional projects" to justify giving higher wages to whites.[21] According to the Arizona Board of Public Welfare, there was the feeling that "Professional projects are decidedly necessary . . . for the reason that it has been bitter for the educated people to have to see the peon type of Mexican receiving the same relief as they."

> [M]any of these American-Mexicans are living fatter than they have for a good many years and their constant prayer is that the depression will never end. On the other hand we have a group of people whose morale is almost at the breaking point. This professional projects program will be a life saver for them.[22]

Some relief officials simply decided to serve whites only. In El Paso one relief worker allegedly "played like he was not in his office" in order to avoid interviewing a Mexican man who was requesting relief. A black man in South Carolina charged that "Government wouldn't give me and my boys any work, they gave it to the white folks." According to another black tenant: "You know if a white man comes in [to the relief office] they wait on him and let you wait. They wait on you when they feel like it." Another tenant experienced similar treatment: "You go up there [to the relief office] and they tell you they ain't got nothing and these old poor white folks come out with their arms full of stuff." In the face of such discrimination, some blacks abandoned their efforts to secure relief: "I quit going up there. Everytime [sic] I go up there they say come back tomorrow." A southern Red Cross official simply remarked, bluntly, "We ain't go [sic] nothing for niggers."[23]

In many communities, blacks and Mexicans received lower relief budgets than whites on the assumption that non-whites had lower standards of living than whites or that non-whites were indolent. California state relief officials said that substandard budgets were "used in budgeting Mexican, Spanish, and Spanish-Indian groups because their natural food habits are followed and the expenditure for supplying them with an adequate dietary allowance averages 10 percent less than for the normal . . . standard allowance." This happened elsewhere, too. The International Institute in St. Paul, Minnesota, claimed that Mexicans' "lower standard of living made it possible for them to eke out an existence on seasonal earnings which would not have been sufficient for other families."[24] Hickok argued that the "Latin and Indian. . . . don't 'want' things. They haven't any ambition. . . . They are easy-going, pleasure loving."

Your Mexican, or your Spanish-American is a simple fellow, with simple needs, to be obtained with the least effort. . . . Now if these people can live on $10 or $12 a month and be reasonably healthy and so contented that they won't even take work when it is offered them, let alone go out and look for it, why, in the name of common sense, raise them above that? Especially when we have a limited amount of money.

Black businessmen in Galveston, Texas, complained that a county relief administrator discriminated in the allocation of relief payments. It was charged that "the cost of packages given Negroes was 15% less than that given to white[s] and the cost of groceries to Mexicans was 15% less than to Negroes." The administrator accused of discrimination told the "committee of colored men" who made the charge that it was "the government's order not to give as much groceries to Negroes and Mexicans as to whites." The federal government certainly did not make any such order, but neither did it do much to enforce equality of treatment. Hopkins was often reluctant to investigate claims of discrimination or hold local communities to federal standards.[25]

A Different Story for European Immigrants

Though there is ample evidence that blacks and Mexicans (whether American or foreign born) were often denied assistance and routinely given lower benefit levels, European immigrants could more often count on equal treatment. A study by the Social Science Research Council compared the difficulties in accessing relief during the Depression across groups. The authors conceded that there was "considerable opinion to the effect that certain minority groups have been discriminated against by relief agencies. Negroes, Chinese, Japanese, Filipinos, Mexicans, foreign-born citizens and aliens generally are regarded in many communities as an inferior class in the population which is not entitled to the ordinary rights of the general population." Still, they argued that "Aliens and foreign born citizens of Europe in most localities probably found themselves receiving allowances similar to those of the majority group."[26]

This difference in treatment between blacks and Mexicans on the one hand and European immigrants on the other can partly be attributed to the regions in which each group lived. Where European immigrants were more numerous, social workers and relief administrators often had local and state policies prohibiting discrimination, and they were more likely to follow up on cases of discrimination when they did occur. In Chicago, this official local-level policy of non-discrimination even extended to blacks and Mexicans. The director of the Cook County Bureau of Public Welfare maintained that "the relief given to all applicants, whether white or colored, native born or foreign born, aliens or citizens, is on the identical basis." The state's attorney of Cook County noted in 1934 that "no discrimination on account of race or color can exist in the public institutions of this state with legal justification or excuse." The state even passed a law in 1935 that made discrimination in the hiring of individuals for work relief on the basis of race, color, or creed a misdemeanor, with a possible jail term of thirty days to six months for public officials (or their agents) who violated it. The Chicago Urban League confirmed that non-discrimination was the official policy of public and even most private social welfare agencies in the city. They noted in 1936 that while the public and private social agencies in Cook County twenty years before often refused to handle Negro clients or employ Negro caseworkers, since then there had been a complete change of heart. This coincided with a significant increase in black political power in the city during the 1920s, causing Ralph Bunche to describe Chicago as "the seventh heaven of Negro political activity."[27]

This is not to say that relief officials in Chicago never engaged in discrimination. The *Chicago Hunger Fighter* reported that "a large number of Negro working women . . . in the 42nd ward, have been sterilized through pressure from the Emergency Relief Station and the United Charity Station." Members of the Mexican Frente Popular, who met regularly at the University of Chicago Settlement House, "discussed the hardships and discriminations afforded by the Colony at the hands of the Relief Agencies in Chicago. The opinion was advanced that . . . Mexicans in this country were exploited by the . . . railroads and the steel mills after which adequate relief was begrudged them when work was no longer available." The Urban League and the Cook County Bureau of Public Welfare also received numerous complaints of rude and discriminatory treatment by relief officials. Workers demonstrated in front of relief offices in certain districts of the city, demanding the abolition of discrimination against Negroes and, less frequently, Mexicans and other foreign-born workers in the distribution of relief.[28] But even public relief officials acknowledged that almost everyone who received relief—regardless of the recipient's race or color—had a complaint about the treatment they received by the welfare agencies. And public welfare officials, though sometimes a little too quick to deny discriminatory treatment, generally followed up on reports of abuse when they occurred. The public welfare department also employed significant numbers of black caseworkers. There is no doubt that discrimination took place, but more often than not, such abuse was not the result of any official or unofficial policy but the result of actions of individual caseworkers. This was in stark contrast to how blacks were treated in the city at the time of the Chicago Riots of 1919, after which many social agencies began to heed the Chicago Commission

on Race Relations' recommendation that they extend their work to the
black community. It was also in stark contrast to much of the South and
Southwest, where discrimination against blacks and Mexicans was either
an official or unofficial mandate.[29]

Why No Citizenship Restrictions?

As the Social Science Research Council's report suggested, non-citizenship
proved to be of little consequence for European immigrants. FERA regulations prohibited discrimination on the basis of citizenship status. And
while southern and southwestern officials defied federal orders against
discrimination on the basis of race and color, northeastern and midwestern officials did not discriminate on the basis of citizenship. As a result,
European aliens generally had the same sort of access to relief as naturalized European immigrants or even native-born whites. Where the promise of equal treatment on the basis of race or color was radical in the
context of the times, FERA's promise of equal treatment regardless of
citizenship status was not. In fact, it was more or less in line with how
aliens had always been treated by relief officials.

Historically, indoor and outdoor relief had been open to anyone who
had a settlement in a particular locality, regardless of an individual's
formal citizenship status. In his study of poor laws in the United States
on the eve of the twentieth century, Charles Henderson explained that
settlement was usually gained "by birth in the district, or by residence
for a term of months or years." In 1914 a survey sent to state agencies
supervising charity work revealed that of the thirty-six states responding,
only Connecticut mentioned citizenship in its settlement laws. But even
in Connecticut, the law allowed non-citizens to establish a settlement "by
a vote of its inhabitants, or by consent of its justices of the peace and
selectmen." "Relief in the United States," wrote George Warren of the
International Migration Service, "is given on the basis of residence and
not that of citizenship."[30]

That said, citizenship restrictions for the receipt of relief assistance
were not entirely unknown. A few states passed citizenship requirements
for Mothers' Pensions. And Old Age Pension programs—largely adopted
between 1929 and 1934—rarely covered aliens. Both of these programs
were underfunded, however, and reached only a very small fraction of
those in need. Most destitute individuals relied on indoor and outdoor
relief to meet their basic needs, and these programs rarely barred aliens.
Indeed, immigrant advocates could rightfully claim in 1936 that "Most
social agencies, whether public or private, make no discrimination against
applicants because of non-citizenship."[31]

Social Workers

One reason that direct relief was open to citizens and non-citizens alike was that social workers—especially those in areas with large numbers of white non-citizens—did not believe in making such distinctions. The American Association of Social Workers, for instance, was described by the Russell Sage Foundation as "a consistent champion of equal treatment for aliens as of all other needy groups." Public welfare officials—including the National Council of State and Local Public Assistance and Welfare Administrators and the heads of the New York City and Detroit public welfare departments—also formally protested any distinctions based on citizenship. The national office of the YWCA also pledged to support legislative measures designed to "prevent unjust discrimination in employment and relief against alien residents." As a result, the local administration of relief did not endanger non-citizens' access to relief, at least in the Northeast and Midwest.[32]

Federal relief officials, Frances Perkins and Harry Hopkins chief among them, also worked tirelessly to include non-citizens in federal policies. Prior to becoming the head of FERA, Hopkins had been the president of the American Association of Social Workers. Perkins began her career as an advocate for laborers volunteering in settlement houses, including the famed Hull House in Chicago. Like other social workers, Perkins and Hopkins did not believe that aliens should be barred from relief. In a memo to the president, Hopkins and Perkins outlined why there should be no distinctions in the distribution of relief based on citizenship. Distinguishing between the rights of legal and illegal immigrants, they explained that "Aliens who have lawfully entered the United States are the responsibility of the nation and its subdivisions." "Most aliens," they continued, "have been attracted to this country, either directly or indirectly, by prospective employers in time of plenty; and there is, therefore, a moral responsibility to care for them in time of need." Hopkins and Perkins also stressed that many alien-headed families had American-born children who were U.S. citizens: "When an alien family is given relief it generally means that citizen children are also being fed and clothed." So when some local relief administrators discriminated on the basis of citizenship—a practice most prevalent in the Southwest—federal relief officials protested the policy and made efforts to remedy the situation. The governor of Colorado proposed placing Colorado's needy aliens in a concentration camp and asked FERA to pay for their sustenance while they awaited deportation, but FERA refused and reaffirmed their commitment to provide aid regardless of citizenship status: "Just as long as the aliens . . . are in need of aid, the FERA will provide the same . . . we cannot be a part of segregating aliens . . . FERA is not particularly concerned with who or what the person is—the big question is whether people are suffering from lack of food, shelter or clothing, and [if] such is the case, aid shall be given." While FERA officials acquiesced to local demands to purge agricultural laborers from the rolls during the harvest, they saw no need to bar non-citizens simply because they were non-citizens.[33]

Perkins's and Hopkins's views may have also been influenced by the practices of other nations. In 1931 the League of Nations invited the United States to join its Committee of Experts to consider the question of assistance to indigent foreigners. The Hoover administration refused to send a representative but FDR's administration was more responsive. Perkins noted that the Department of Labor was "greatly interested in the work of the Special Committee" and she sent two delegates and a "technical expert" to the next meeting in December 1933. At that meeting, the League of Nations' Committee of Experts on Assistance to Indigent Foreigners—made up of experts from the United Kingdom, Denmark, France, Hungary, Italy, Japan, Mexico, the Netherlands, Poland, Switzerland, and the United States—met and produced a draft multilateral convention on assistance to indigent foreigners for the consideration of member nations. Article 1 of the draft convention provided that any national of a contracting party "standing in need of relief, medical attention or any other assistance whatsoever . . . shall receive in such territory the same treatment as its own nationals and subject to the same conditions as the latter." While Perkins did not believe the United States should become a signatory to the treaty, it was not because she was unsympathetic with its aims. Indeed, Perkins noted that individual states were already acting in conformity with Article 1: "It is the understanding of this Department that the various State governments make no distinction between citizens and alien residents in granting relief." But because relief giving was a "matter of State control," the federal government was not in a position to sign a treaty "which would be satisfactory to all of the State governments and which could be put into practice under State legislation." In particular, relief laws in Europe established individual rights to assistance, while relief laws in American states were generally permissive, allowing local authorities to distribute relief, or where mandatory, provided no mechanism for the enforcement of the obligation. Since individuals in the United States had no individual right to relief, it would be difficult to enter into a treaty or sign a convention detailing the rights of foreigners to assistance.[34]

But Perkins and Hopkins used the practices of other nations to justify their own stance. In their memo to the president, they mentioned American participation on this League of Nations committee and summarized the policies of countries that included aliens in their relief systems. In Switzerland, for example, where 9 percent of the population was foreign born, foreigners received the same treatment as nationals, though Switzerland did have a policy of repatriating aliens in need of assistance when possible. In Hungary non-citizens received the same benefits as citizens after three years of residence. In Chile and Poland foreigners received the same treatment as nationals. And the Scandinavian countries had adopted a multilateral treaty in 1928, which dictated the terms under which foreign nationals would be assimilated into the host country's relief system. Perkins and Hopkins mentioned only countries with liberal policies toward non-citizens, however, choosing not to dwell on—or even mention—the countries that engaged in welfare chauvinism.[35]

Political Power of White Immigrants

Perkins and Hopkins made no mention in their internal memo or in any public statements of the fact that extending relief to non-citizens might satisfy the Democratic Party's white immigrant and second-generation base in urban areas. Nonetheless, it may have been on some top officials' minds. European immigrants had started to join the Democratic Party in large numbers with Al Smith's run for president in 1928. Like many other Americans, these new immigrants looked to FDR to help turn the tide of the Depression, and Roosevelt had strong support in urban areas and among Irish, Jewish, and Italian voters. While immigration did not play any role in the Democratic Party platform in 1932, FDR acknowledged in his first campaign that in Hoover's "enforcement of the immigration laws too many abuses against individual families have been revealed time and time again." FDR's campaign speeches also sometimes celebrated the efforts of recent immigrants to become American: "They [the new immigrants] have never been—they are not now—half-hearted Americans. In Americanization classes and at night schools they have burned the midnight oil in order to be worthy of their new allegiance." "I am inclined to think," he continued, "that in some cases the newer citizens have discharged their obligations to us better than we have discharged our obligations to them," and to rectify the imbalance, he pledged to propose housing legislation to "help families in the overcrowded sections of our cities to live as American citizens have a right to live."[36]

Still, there is no evidence that FDR himself tried to push for alien inclusion. FDR seems to have held ambivalent feelings toward aliens and many southeastern Europeans. He supported quotas on Jews at Harvard, and though he counted both Jews and Catholics among his "inner circle," his attitude toward both was that they should know and heed their place. Harold Ickes recalled that the president had sympathy for illegal immigrants and wanted to help those who had entered the country illegally but had been "good citizens." However, he had little sympathy for immigrants who had lived in the United States for many years but had failed to become citizens, requesting that a rule be "laid down that all aliens within a reasonable time either take out citizenship papers or go back to where they came from." Furthermore, much of the impetus to liberalize the immigration and deportation laws, according to Ickes, was "entirely Perkins' and MacCormack's; there was very little impetus for it in Congress or the White House. Roosevelt was always distressed by [Perkins's] reports of hardship cases, but . . . he had little interest in the concept of due process. He cared about votes, but aliens had no votes."[37]

While aliens had no votes, their American spouses and children often did, and some did their best to remind the president of this fact. Indeed, 21 percent of the voting-age population in 1932 had at least one foreign-born parent and a little over 11 percent were themselves naturalized citizens. And roughly 60 percent of alien-headed households contained at least one U.S. citizen over the age of eighteen by 1940. As the next chapter will show, congressmen who represented these communities often fought against the imposition of citizenship restrictions in welfare policy. As the Depression wore on, however, nativism increased, even among the president's supporters, a fact the administration was keenly aware of. FDR's administration, then, had to tread lightly on this issue in order to find a way to include non-citizens in relief projects without alienating its supporters. Indeed, in order to pass liberal reforms, federal administrators often coupled them with selectively repressive measures. In 1935 the administration endorsed the Kerr Bill (H.R. 8163), which, had it passed, would have increased the discretionary power of the INS to grant stays of deportation to aliens who had shown that they were of "good moral character and where deportation would result in separating families." The bill also reintroduced statutes of limitations for the deportation of immigrants who entered the country illegally. But it also gave the INS more power to deport criminal aliens and increase certain fees associated with the naturalization process. This apparent hedging led some to charge that the administration's efforts to protect non-citizens from persecution were half-hearted. "The Roosevelt Administration, which has offered some resistance to this discrimination and persecution" against non-citizens, wrote one social worker in 1936, "is retreating step by step. Its liberalism, never very robust, threatens complete surrender to the reactionary demands of Hearst and his allies."[38]

WORK RELIEF

Those who charged that the FDR administration's liberalism was "never very robust" would no doubt have pointed to their capitulation on citizenship restrictions and preferences in work relief in the first New Deal. Though given equal access to *direct* relief by local, state, and federal authorities, European aliens often encountered barriers to public works jobs. But while federal work relief programs made distinctions based on citizenship, the American-born children of immigrants were still eligible. And federal authorities sometimes required higher direct relief payments to make up for any exclusion, suggesting that the restriction may have been more symbolic than real.[39]

Prohibitions against aliens on pre–New Deal local public work projects varied widely by region and were most severe in the West. At the end of 1932, eighteen states either barred aliens from *local* public works employment or gave preference to U.S. citizens. Full citizenship was necessary only in Arizona, California, Idaho, Illinois, Montana, Nevada, Oregon, Pennsylvania, and Washington. In Oregon this exclusion applied only to the Chinese and aliens who claimed exemption during World War I. In Wyoming only citizens and aliens with first papers were eligible. In Massachusetts, New Jersey, New York, and Wisconsin, state laws dictated that preference be given to U.S. citizens, but aliens were still permitted to work on these local projects.[40]

In addition to these local public works projects, the federal government also sponsored public works programs in the administration's first hundred days. The three principal work relief programs during the first New Deal were the Civilian Conservation Corps (CCC), the Public Works Administration (PWA), and the Civil Works Administration (CWA).

CCC

The Civilian Conservation Corps, signed into law in March 1933, put young men between the ages of eighteen and twenty-five to work in camps, primarily in rural areas. Much smaller than FERA, which served four million families and individuals at its height in 1934, the CCC employed only 505,000 young men. According to immigration advocates, Congress never entertained the idea that aliens would be included in this program: "From the first there was shown no disposition to include aliens among the beneficiaries of the plan; every draft . . . provided for the selection of workers from 'the unemployed citizens of the United States.'" The administration, usually a staunch defender of aliens' rights to assistance, did not protest this restriction. The exclusion of non-citizens disqualified approximately 3 percent of all young men between the ages of eighteen and twenty-five in 1933. And it disqualified roughly 5 percent of all aliens living in the United States. The American-born children of aliens, however, *were* eligible for the CCC, and as a result, aliens could benefit indirectly through the wages their children sent home. CCC workers were in fact *required* to send home more than 80 percent of their monthly wages.[41]

The CCC did not collect data on the second generation's use of its program, but 17 percent of qualified young men were the American-born children of two foreign-born parents and nearly a quarter of young men had at least one foreign-born parent. What is more, 18 percent of all alien-headed households had at least one household member who would have qualified for the program in 1933, compared to 20 percent of citizen-headed families. One study of young men from Cleveland who had participated in the CCC showed that nearly 60 percent of the family heads were foreign born, while they made up roughly 45 percent of family heads in Cleveland. Another study of 7,193 CCC enrollees at more than 240 camps scattered across the United States noted that 20 percent of the mothers and 21 percent of the fathers of the enrollees were foreign born. Many camp personnel took note of how heterogeneous the corps was. One officer who met new recruits as they disembarked from the train in Butte, Montana, remarked: "What a mob got off the train . . . they were large and small, Italians, Jews and every other nationality."[42] A CCC enrollee in Colorado colorfully portrayed the backgrounds of his fellow corps enrollees with a poem titled "Our League of Nations."

> We have Russians; We have Jews; We have good boys, bad are fews.
> We have Irish; We have Warps [*sic*]; You boys must use the barber shops.
> We have Frenchmen, we have Greeks; We have classes every weeks;
> We have Germans, we have Swedes. We have a mess hall where we feeds.[43]

The children of southern and eastern European immigrants in particular likely were well represented in the program if only because of the age structure of the population: 29 percent of families headed by southern and eastern Europeans had household members eligible for the program, compared to roughly 20 percent of native-white or black households, and just 15 percent of Mexican households. The first national director of the CCC in fact saw the assimilation of the second generation as a central aim of the program, describing the camps as "civic melting pots." The second director agreed, writing:

> They are from farms and cities, from Catholic, Protestant and Jewish homes, from English, German, Irish, Italian, Polish, Swedish, French and Indian ancestries. Some are illiterates, some college students. If they lived clannishly in their home communities, they have a new experience when they are all thrown together in the CCC. They must learn to live with other men of all faiths and backgrounds. They must learn to be tolerant of the opinions and respectful of the rights of others.

Writing to the president, one CCC veteran from Ohio evidently saw this objective fulfilled, observing that through their labor in the corps, "sec-

ond generation Poles, Slovaks, Italians, Hungarians, all are . . . finding a
new pride in saying, 'We are Americans!'"[44]

According to the historian Bryant Simon, "Six months in the wilder-
ness would, New Deal leaders . . . thought, strengthen teenaged city
boys, flush the tenements out of their systems, and transform them from
scrawny, unattractive revolutionaries and criminals into proud, dutiful
men." John Bartok, born in Cleveland of Bohemian parents, was just the
sort of young man New Dealers were targeting. His father had been working off and on for years, and rumor had it he was engaged in bootlegging.
Conditions at home were rough—his parents often fought—and he was
not doing well at school. He decided to enroll in the corps: "He stayed
14 months, doing various laboring jobs. He felt '100 per cent better in
camp' and gained 18 pounds in weight." Aside from the money he sent
home and his improved health, he also made "several lasting friendships.
'We were all like one happy family and they were a keen bunch,'" he recalled. When the International Institute in Gary, Indiana, got word of the
program, they went through their files to see how many of their clients
might qualify: "We got all those boys together and talked to them about
it. We went with them to make personal applications. Many of these boys
did not know that they were not citizens as they had lived in this country
so long. Many of them knew that they were aliens but had no money for
naturalization fees." For those who were eligible, though, the CCC was
"one of the most popular things that has ever struck Gary."[45]

Few blacks, however, benefited from the CCC, due largely to the discriminatory practices of southern administrative agencies. Though blacks
made up 10 percent of young men eligible for such assistance nationwide,
by the end of the first year of the program they represented only 5 percent
of CCC enrollees. While non-citizens could benefit indirectly through the
wages their American children sent home, this option was not available
for black families. What is more, while the corps acted self-consciously as
a civic melting pot for hyphenated Americans, federal policy *mandated*
that CCC camps segregate blacks from whites throughout the country.
The executive secretary of the Milwaukee Urban League protested this
policy, noting that "To my knowledge there are no units in Wisconsin
designated as Italian, Polish, German, or Jewish. Therefore we feel it well
within the fitness of things to raise the question as to why Negroes are
being set aside into so called Negro units." Few white communities, furthermore, were eager to accept all-black camps in their midst, fearing the
"anticipated . . . increases in drunkenness and other social vices" as well
as for "the safety of white women and children." Whites' aversion toward
blacks served to decrease the total number of black projects available and
therefore black slots in the program. And the federal policy of segregated
black and white camps helped further entrench a national segregationist
racial order.[46]

There are no data on the number of Mexican Americans who entered the CCC. Since most of those who entered the program were referred by a relief agency, relief officials' attitudes would have come into play, but some Mexican Americans did benefit from the program. Born in the United States, Frank Rodríguez was the son of a Mexican citizen. Though not old enough to qualify for the corps, Frank lied about his age and joined the CCC in Ely, Minnesota, at the age of fifteen. He sent home $25 each month to his parents, who worked in the beet fields surrounding St. Paul. Benito Montoya, a CCC worker in New Mexico, said that with the CCC money, "people started living again. . . . I had plenty to eat, I had clothes you know. I had brand new clothes when I went in the CCC camp." According to María Montoya, who studied the situation in New Mexico, the New Deal programs that targeted youth, including the CCC and the National Youth Administration, were important not only for the survival of their families but also in "exposing young *mexicanos* to the larger society."[47]

Though the CCC sometimes functioned as an assimilating force for *mexicanos* as well as second-generation European immigrants, Mexican Americans also faced discrimination in the corps. According to Montoya, "prejudice against Mexican Americans was not institutionalized" as it was for blacks. There was no federal policy of segregating Mexicans from whites. Nonetheless, "racist attitudes still permeated the ranks of the New Deal's administrators in New Mexico." Mexican Americans in Colorado and New Mexico often slept in segregated quarters. Suggestive of the conditions in one Colorado camp, an anonymous letter printed in the camp newsletter said, "we are all human, so let us act like humans. If you don't like the Mexican boys, leave them alone. Don't try to treat them like animals and make their camp life miserable." Still, when Anglo youth protested working with Mexicans in one New Mexico camp and asked for segregated work units, their requests were denied.[48]

PWA

The Public Works Administration, signed into law in June 1933, loaned money to state and local governments and private businesses to help finance the construction of public facilities and provide work for needy individuals. Of all the first New Deal programs, the PWA did the most to assist blacks. Run by Harold Ickes, who was, aside from Eleanor Roosevelt, "widely regarded as the best friend that blacks had in the new administration," the program was centrally controlled and therefore less susceptible to discrimination by local authorities. While all New Deal programs were supposed to be implemented without regard to race, only the PWA set quotas requiring that black workers be employed in proportion to their representation in the occupational census of 1930 for each city.[49]

The PWA did not specifically bar aliens from public works, but it established preferences for citizens and declarants—aliens who had taken out their first papers indicating their intention to naturalize. When the law was first passed by the House, it included a preference for U.S. citizens only. Immigrant advocates in the FLIS lobbied individual senators, however, to remove all distinctions based on citizenship: "The Senate, acting on a motion by Senator Costigan (D-CO), who characterized the arguments presented by the F.L.I.S. as 'convincing and indeed overwhelming', voted to eliminate this discrimination" against non-citizens. The House was eager to maintain some distinction, however, and so the House and Senate compromised by including declarants among those with preferences. In the end, preference was given first to "ex-service men with dependents," second to "citizens and declarants who are bona-fide residents of the locality or subdivision where the work is being done," and third to "citizens and declarants who are bona-fide residents of the State, provided, of course, they are qualified to perform the work." Under this system of preferences, aliens who had taken out their first papers and were county residents had preference over U.S. citizens who were only state residents. Aliens without first papers had "the same rights to such employment as citizens who are not residents of the state where the work is being done." While non-declarant aliens were not barred from these jobs, they (and transients with U.S. citizenship) were unlikely to receive them given that so many people were eager to fill the limited jobs.[50]

CWA

The largest federal work relief program during the first hundred days was the Civil Works Administration, described by Michael Katz as "the greatest public works experiment in American history." Though it was in operation for only a few months during the winter of 1934, it provided employment for over four million people at its peak. Because the CWA used PWA funds, Hopkins used the same eligibility preferences in the CWA as in the PWA. Federal officials did not have much control over the day-to-day administration of the CWA, and at a news conference, Hopkins acknowledged that he received thousands of letters each day with charges of graft and political corruption in the distribution of these jobs.[51]

While work relief programs such as the CWA gave preference to citizens and non-citizens with first papers, relief recipients who could not get work relief due to these preferences were granted higher FERA benefits to make up for being denied the opportunity to work. In some sense, then, giving preferences to citizens and declarants may have been somewhat of a symbolic measure, designed to appease vocal nativists. The Los

Angeles Superintendent of Charities, Rex Thompson, was indignant at this federal policy. In a letter to the local Mexican consulate, Thompson explained that the federal government had requested that counties "increase the amount of direct relief given to those cases for whom no Civil Works Projects are available, due to limited quotas, or who, because of nationality, cannot take part on Civil Works Projects."

> Therefore, we find a peculiar situation, and a most unsatisfactory one, where the Mexican alien's monthly budget has been increased 30% and yet we refuse to allow him to do any work in return for the same, even if he were willing to do so.

To "overcome these most unsatisfactory conditions," Thompson said, the Department of Charities had decided to provide a "small cash bonus to be delivered" to Mexicans when they reached their point of destination in Mexico "in order that we may encourage further repatriation."[52]

Prohibitions against discrimination on the grounds of race in work relief programs such as the CWA, as in direct relief, "varied greatly in their effectiveness," noted a Social Science Research Council report. "This was due in part to the more or less deliberate violation of national regulations by some local and state agencies." But it was also due "in part to the fact that Negroes, Mexicans and Indians, because of their geographic and occupational concentration and their relatively greater need, were affected more by the general limitation of work relief than was the white population." In addition, "Discrimination rarely took the form of open defiance of federal regulations. Because the determination of eligibility was so largely in the hands of local agencies . . . the introduction of local prejudices was inevitable." Local relief administrators, for example, applied non-race-based criteria "with especial vigor to Negroes and other minority groups in many communities in which prejudices were particularly strong."[53]

In many areas, officials would earmark a set number of work relief jobs for blacks or Mexicans, "either upon some arbitrary basis or according to their proportion in the local population." Little attention was paid to actual need. Work relief projects in the South and even sometimes the North were segregated. And many work relief projects were designed to benefit white rather than black neighborhoods: "In some communities in which there were large numbers of Negro and Mexican agricultural laborers, local opposition to the federally controlled, work relief wage policy resulted in a general reluctance to sponsor work relief employment." A peach grower in South Carolina, for example, said he had "300 Negro families living on his place, and he felt very resentful about their all 'going to work under CWA' because in the last two or three years he had spent between $35,000 and $40,000 to keep them fed. And now he felt they were deserting him." What's more, he complained that "Negro women wouldn't work in the fields as long as their husbands had CWA jobs." Similarly, a landlord in Mississippi complained that "this charity and CWA" had "made folks lazy and they won't work. There are a lot for [sic] women in town who sued [sic] to chop cotton every year. This year the charities is taking care of them. When we went in town and asked them to come out and chop they said they hands didn't fit a hoe." According to one report, county relief officials in Colorado did "'not believe in helping Mexicans at all.' . . . Once county people knew that a man put on a Civil Works job would have to be continuously employed, there seemed to be a widespread determination not to give any such jobs to Spanish-Americans." They assumed that if a Mexican earned fifty or sixty dollars a month in public work employment, "he would not work again until spring."[54]

Citizenship barriers were also sometimes erroneously applied to Mexican Americans. In 1933 Mexican Americans in Texas charged that they were being wrongfully denied government work relief on the grounds that they were not citizens, even though they were born in the United States. The federal government dismissed a county relief chairman in 1934 in Denver for "permitting" discrimination against "Spanish-Americans in the selection of men for CWA relief" because they were presumed to be aliens. Colorado relief officials denied the charges as "the veriest bunk," but, according to one report, "no one seems to doubt their truth. In fact, such discrimination would be praised rather than blamed. 'I should do the same,' one Denver business executive said, and his attitude was typical." Confirming that most Anglos did not perceive Mexican Americans to be Americans, a reporter noted that "Although it is generally felt that Spanish-Americans are Mexicans and therefore foreigners, probably not a quarter of all persons classed in the popular mind as 'Mexicans' are natives from the other side of the Rio Grande."[55]

CONCLUSION

In the final analysis, European non-citizens during the first New Deal had roughly equal access to direct relief but were sometimes excluded from work relief projects, like the CCC, or assigned a lower preference ranking than citizens in the PWA and CWA. When federal policy denied non-citizens work relief or placed them last (along with transients) in the preference queue, they were often given higher direct relief benefits to make up for such distinctions. Moreover their U.S.-born children could count on the CCC and any other program for which they were eligible. Since social workers in the Northeast and Midwest did not believe that foreign birth or lack of citizenship should bar needy individuals from relief, they did little to circumvent FERA's policy of non-discrimination. In fact, as the next chapter will show, local relief officials in the Northeast and Midwest sometimes found ways to work around federal mandates to exclude non-citizens that emerged in the second New Deal. Perhaps for these reasons, a FERA investigator in Homestead, Pennsylvania, just outside of Pittsburgh, "found only two pictures hanging in the home of one Croatian immigrant family on relief. The first rendered a vivid presentation of the Last Supper; the second was a newspaper portrait of the president."[56]

Citizenship requirements, where they existed, were often applied with special vigor to Mexicans and even misapplied to Mexican Americans, whom some Anglos simply presumed were foreign born. Though both blacks and Mexicans received greater access to relief than ever before, both groups confronted discrimination, especially in programs with the least federal oversight. Local administration severely undercut blacks' and Mexicans' access to direct relief and work relief in the South and Southwest. There, local relief officials' beliefs that blacks and Mexicans were not as worthy of assistance as native-born whites or European immigrants, combined with low political power and political pressure from planters and growers whose desire for cheap labor was nearly insatiable, helped seal their fate.

CHAPTER 9

The WPA and the (Short-Lived) Triumph of Nativism

IN 1936 CONGRESSMAN MARTIN DIES (D-TX) published an anti-alien screed in the *Washington Herald*. In it, he charged that a million and a half aliens were on relief, at a cost of half a billion dollars per year. "While European nations eject all jobless foreigners our Labor Department now coddles them," he charged. "These aliens write home joyfully declaring that they are better off here on relief than they ever were at home at hard work." But rather than express gratitude, Dies claimed, aliens complained and fomented dissent by demonstrating for more relief in cities across the country. "If we propose firm, fair dealing regarding aliens we are accused of intolerance and racial prejudice," he carped. "It is time for us to think as Americans, about Americans." Dies worried that "the average citizen" was "under the impression that the dangers of alien invasion" were long "past," and he made it his mission to bar non-citizens from relief and educate Americans about the ongoing menace.[1]

Dies need not have been so concerned. As the Depression raged on, with as many as fourteen million people out of work, anxious residents desperately searched for solutions to their misery. Spurred in part by the nativist rhetoric of individuals like Dies in the press and on the airwaves, many Americans came to blame *all* foreigners for their economic plight, especially those who "refused" to naturalize. Large-scale deportations and coerced repatriations would become early solutions, unevenly applied. But unlike Hoover, FDR's administration had no interest in mass deportation, and the number of removals plummeted soon after FDR entered office from nearly twenty thousand each year between 1931 and 1933 to less than half that number for the rest of the decade. But with no end to their economic woes in sight and nativism on the rise, congressmen—many of them from the South and Southwest—took matters into their own hands and slowly chipped away at aliens' access to one of the most esteemed relief programs: the Works Progress Administration (WPA).[2]

Welfare scholars have largely ignored how New Deal policies like the WPA affected non-citizens. Many have, in fact, unwittingly erased the issue from scholarly debate by interchangeably employing terms like "workers," "the needy," "Americans," or "citizens" when discussing the beneficiaries of New Deal programs. They can hardly be blamed—in his speeches, FDR did the same. Moreover, given that immigration had slowed to a trickle in the early 1920s and come to a virtual halt in 1929, it is reasonable to assume the country would have not been much concerned with non-citizens. Nevertheless, the treatment of aliens and even illegal immigrants was of considerable concern to New Deal officials, social workers, politicians, reporters, the general public, and especially non-citizens and their families. The issue became so contentious, in fact, that several national public opinion polls were fielded in the mid- to late 1930s about non-citizens' right to relief, and New Deal officials kept their own pulse on the issue, collecting hundreds of articles and editorials from newspapers around the country about "aliens and relief."[3]

Harry Hopkins and Frances Perkins generally protested these attacks on aliens and often tried to block restrictive legislation or soften its impact. They also tried to dampen the nativist flames by refusing to gather or publish statistics on aliens' use of relief. As a result, when the WPA was first authorized in 1935, there were no citizenship or legal status restrictions for access to the program. Just as with FERA, New Deal officials expressly forbade local WPA administrators from discriminating on the basis of race, color, religion, or non-citizenship. Because of these non-discrimination provisions (and their great need), blacks and Mexican Americans gained unprecedented access to WPA employment. Over time, however, Congress imposed successively harsher restrictions against aliens, barring the employment of illegal aliens on WPA projects in 1936 and imposing a full ban for legal non-citizens by 1939.

Whatever action federal officials took could be sustained or undermined at the local level. The local administration of relief had very different effects for blacks, Mexicans, and European immigrants. Relief officials in the South and Southwest defied federal orders and discriminated in the assignment of WPA jobs on the basis of race and color—a practice encouraged by growers in the South and Southwest and facilitated by each group's minimal political power and the power of rural interests in state legislatures. But local relief administrators in the North often made efforts to *keep* non-citizens on work relief, to certify other eligible household members instead, or to provide non-citizen-headed households with alternate forms of support when they were barred from the WPA. Relief officials engaged in no similar mitigating tactics for aliens in the Southwest. While these citizenship restrictions constituted the greatest challenge to aliens' access to the welfare state during this period, its impact was short-lived and its effects fell disproportionately on Mexican non-citizens.

ACCESS TO THE WPA: BLACKS AND MEXICAN AMERICANS

In 1935 the federal government attempted to get out of the business of providing relief for unemployable men and women who did not qualify for categorical assistance such as Aid to Dependent Children, Old Age Assistance, or Aid to the Blind. It abolished FERA and launched a massive work relief program called the Works Progress Administration (renamed the Work Projects Administration after 1939), with the aim of providing public works jobs for all employable adults. Relief for unemployables who did not qualify for categorical assistance would become, once again, a state and local responsibility. By 1936 the WPA was already employing three million people. The program "adhered to the concept of the family wage, enforced by the stricture that only one family member, usually expected to be a man, could receive WPA employment." Since the average WPA family had three or four household members, the total number of individuals reached by the WPA at any one time ran as high as eleven million.[4]

For black Americans, according to the historian Nancy Weiss, "the single most important event of the Second Hundred Days—indeed, perhaps of the whole New Deal—was the creation . . . of the Works Progress Administration." By 1939 nearly 390,000 black men and women were certified for continued WPA employment, representing 14 percent of all WPA workers, somewhat higher than their proportion (10 percent) in the general population. While they were certainly underrepresented relative to need, for blacks who held WPA jobs, and their dependents, the program provided a measure of protection against homelessness and severe malnutrition.[5]

Official data on Mexicans' use of the WPA are harder to come by. The Mexican embassy estimated that as many as 100,000 Mexicans benefited from WPA employment. One report described "Latin Americans" as perhaps "the most submerged and destitute group in the United States. Where these people are numerous, they are found on WPA and other forms of relief in higher proportion than other groups because of unemployment; lack of vocational training . . . [and] discriminatory job practices." By 1939, 3,600 Mexicans in Bexar County, Texas, worked in WPA jobs, representing 53 percent of the total caseload. More than 1,200 more were certified but awaiting assignment. Mexicans made up roughly 40 percent of the population in the county, and according to federal relief officials, without the public works employment and the surplus commodities program, "malnutrition and actual starvation would undoubtedly have taken a much heavier toll than they did in the Mexican community during the depression."[6]

Repeated federal mandates required that there be no discrimination in the allotment of WPA jobs, and Congress went so far as to declare that any "knowing" violation of mandates prohibiting discrimination on the basis of race would be considered "a felony punishable by fine of not more than $1,000 or imprisonment for not more than one year or both." Despite such orders and the "establishment of national, state and local advisory boards" to monitor such issues, the WPA was nonetheless "often plagued with discrimination." Federal relief administrators did not have a high degree of control over the implementation of the program nor the will to do what was necessary to enforce the mandate: "Left to their own devices, local relief administrators followed their own conservative instincts." As a result, there were sometimes different eligibility standards for blacks and whites. WPA projects were segregated, and blacks were not often assigned to employment in "executive and administrative capacities." As with direct relief, access to WPA work was better in the North: "In various southern communities, particularly in rural areas . . . Negro unemployed workers have had less chance of receiving work relief than white unemployed workers." Furthermore, WPA wages were set, more or less, to the prevailing wages in the community. As a result, they varied widely by region and skill level. Blacks tended to get lower wages on WPA work than whites because they lived in counties where the prevailing wages were lower and because they were less likely than whites to be rated as skilled laborers. Southerners also often opposed WPA work for black women, feeling they should be available for domestic work. One black man complained of discrimination in the administration of WPA jobs, reminding the state relief official that "the President promised all a fair deal." "He told me Dam the President and said he did not care any dam more for the President than he did for a dam nigger, and not as much. And said he was running the office down here and not the dam President or no one else."[7]

Some observers believed that the local racial context affected the degree of support for sponsoring work relief projects. "The racial composition in Williamson County," noted one Texas social worker, "seems undoubtedly to be an important factor in the often indifferent attitude and occasional opposition to sponsoring WPA projects." The fact that whites did not understand that blacks could "no longer get enough farm work to support themselves and their families . . . plus racial prejudice, keeps many people in Williamson County from actively supporting the Work Program." Similar concerns about large numbers of Mexicans also endangered the viability of certain work relief projects in San Antonio. Mexicans and non-citizens in Colorado were also threatened by native whites resentful that Mexicans were receiving assistance. A group calling themselves the Colorado State Vigilantes distributed leaflets near federal work relief sites warning "Mexicans and other aliens to leave the state."[8]

As they did with relief in the first New Deal, southern planters and western growers continued to try to get farm workers off the rolls when they needed laborers. In one county in Texas, WPA workers were dismissed if they "refused to accept farm jobs for mere subsistence—without wages." California State Chamber of Commerce officials called a meeting with state relief officials at the Biltmore Hotel in Los Angeles in 1936. Complaining of labor shortages, they secured a pledge from the state WPA director that "if and when the need arises . . . we will shut down WPA projects to furnish harvest workers." Thomas Mahony, who complained about grower pressures to remove migrant laborers from the FERA rolls, found similar problems with the WPA. He charged that "the WPA with its notorious 'hunger pressure' methods takes advantage of the destitution of our Catholic Spanish-speaking poor and forces them into the beet fields on the threat of starving their families. Their plight is worse than that of chattel slaves of the old plantation days. At least slaves were sure of food and shelter."[9]

Nativism on the Rise

An added problem for the Mexican community, as for all aliens living in the United States, involved citizenship requirements. When the WPA was first launched it made no distinctions between citizens and non-citizens. But as the Depression wore on, there were increasing calls to bar non-citizens from all forms of relief. A woman wrote a letter to Frances Perkins in 1933 expressing her concerns: "Here in Chicago, a fifth of those on the relief lists are aliens. . . . Can't some plan be devised whereby the foreign groups help their own needy?" The letter was signed on the back, "From a Chicago school teacher, unpaid for nearly a year." "We Americans worry along as best we can," she continued, "while many foreigners and those of foreign parentage are living on public help." A self-described "real white-man" complained that relief was extended to all racial groups but his. "From what we see around here not much of the money goes to those who actually are patriotic and Americans and real good-living people. Most of it is handed out to European Waps [sic]. Jews. and a certain class of Irish. Outside of these and the Niggers, a real White-man has very little chance for help." A California woman wrote to her senator asking "why Mr. Senator should Uncle Sam play God father to all the aliens & starve our own citizens. America should take care of our own." Making clear exactly what she meant by "our own," she added that she didn't understand why Mexican American families got the same amount of relief as white families. Ohio's senators in Washington were "deluged with 15,000 post cards" protesting "giving WPA jobs to foreigners while citizens are out of work." The postcards typically "showed a gentleman in Italian dress crying 'scramba' to another individual as he firmly booted him from the rear while the recipient protested he was 'born in this country.'"[10]

While immigration to the United States had been drastically curtailed by the 1921 and 1924 Immigration Acts and had virtually stopped in 1929 with the more stringent application of the public charge doctrine, the public at large was not at all convinced that the "immigration problem" had been solved. "The average American retains a mental vision of a vast stream of immigration pouring into the United States," wrote D. W. MacCormack, Commissioner of Immigration. "Consequently, the most exaggerated statements concerning numerical phases of the alien problem find ready credence." Estimates of the number of aliens in the United States ranged from 6 to 20 million, but the real number, according to MacCormack, was probably closer to 4.9 million. The number of illegal aliens subject to deportation was estimated in the press at somewhere between 3.5 and 10 million, but the true figure was probably closer to 100,000. In fact, since 1931, "more aliens have left the United States each year than have entered," and as a result, the alien population was decreasing. "I have hesitated long before undertaking to refute the allegations . . . and would not do so now did I not keenly feel that in times of stress such as the present no erroneous statements which might serve to feed the fires of prejudice, intolerance and antagonism . . . should be permitted to go unchallenged," he wrote. Speaking before the American Civil Liberties Union, another federal official noted that there were signs that the character of anti-alien sentiment had changed significantly since World War I. During and immediately after the war, nativism "was directed against particular national groups rather than against aliens as such and its appearance was more localized and sporadic, whereas current manifestations are more or less universal and are influentially directed. So the problem is greater now than it was then." Social workers, immigration advocates, and immigrants concurred with these assessments, noting that as the Depression wore on, anti-alien sentiment was increasing. The Russian newspaper *Rassviet* remarked in 1935 that "After several years of comparative quiet, a new campaign of agitation against foreigners is in progress . . . in newspapers, in various conventions, and in state legislative assemblies." The editorial also noted that special ire was directed at communist aliens on relief: "But, since many Americans, as a result of misinformation, regard every foreigner as a Bolshevik . . . they draw the conclusion that they must cease feeding all foreigners who have not taken out citizenship papers."[11]

Some newspapers and magazines fanned the flames of nativist sentiment, running pejorative stories about "alien reliefers." Many of the sen-
sational headlines associated aliens on relief with crime: "Alien Cheaters
on Relief Get Jail Sentences," "Alien Reliefer Gets Jail Term for Drunkenness," "Alien on Relief Tramples Flag; Police Save Him," and "Alien Defies Court after 6 Year Relief Fraud."[12]

Other news stories contrasted the "worthy veteran" with the "unworthy alien." Veterans felt they were not getting the support they deserved
for the sacrifices they had made for the nation. In 1932 a group of World
War I veterans—calling themselves the Bonus Expeditionary Force—
marched on Washington to demand that Hoover give them an early pay-
out on their "bonuses," which were not due until 1945. Rather than accede to their demands, Hoover sent the army to disperse the picketers.
Veterans continued to press for their bonuses when FDR entered office,
but it was not until 1936 that their demands were finally met. Angered
by the years of apparent disregard for their service and sacrifice, veterans'
organizations in cities big and small used the press effectively to highlight
their plight. There was perhaps no better juxtaposition than the "unworthy alien" receiving relief ahead of the "worthy veteran." In New York
the commander of an American Legion Post complained that aliens were
getting work relief jobs ahead of veterans. It released a report document-
ing the practice and declared that "Not only were aliens given preference
in the hiring of persons on relief projects but veterans were laid off and
aliens hired in their place." The chairman of the employment committee
of the Cook County Veteran's Relief Commission argued that "Millions
of veterans, fighters of American principles, have been walking the streets
for years; denied employment under the alphabetic agencies because they
did not apply for relief, while aliens, illegally in the United States, draw
government doles and send $300,000,000 annually to their homelands
for the support of their families and steamship fares to reunite them in
the United States." That many veterans of World War I were themselves
first- or second-generation immigrants was rarely mentioned. The *Los
Angeles Evening Herald and Express* ran an editorial in June 1936 titled
"Are Aliens Preferred?" "Is the Works Progress Administration discharg-
ing CITIZENS and WAR VETERANS, while retaining ALIENS on its
payroll," they asked. A cartoon accompanied the editorial, depicting a
WPA office with two doors. The first, marked "Aliens Preferred," was
wide open, with a stream of aliens walking through. The second, marked
"Citizens Only," bore a "closed" sign and was padlocked for good measure. Two men, one in an army uniform, sat despondently on the step, as
an alien in the line nearby held his hand up at them, as if signaling *they*
were not welcome.[13]

In 1936 the *Saturday Evening Post* carried an article by Raymond Carroll titled "Alien Workers in America," in which the indignant author listed the benefits under the second New Deal that aliens would be eligible to partake in: "Attorneys for the National Social Security Board say that aliens are eligible for the benefits of the new Social Security Act, including old age pensions (social security), unemployment compensation, and sick-benefit handouts." Aliens were also eligible for home loans through the Home Owner's Loan Corporation, federally financed housing projects, Agricultural Adjustment Act checks, and Federal Housing Administration help, as well as assistance through the Resettlement Administration. "The National Youth Administration's cash education aid to deserving students, and all the other implantations of New Deal paternalism have been placed at the disposal of aliens. . . . 'There shall be no unjust discrimination against our aliens' is the outcry of the foreign bloc in Congress, the Department of Labor, and the devotees of alienism in the New Deal," he complained.[14]

While a vocal minority—often members of patriotic societies or nativist organizations—was generally responsible for the most lurid statements, most American residents agreed that aliens should not receive relief. When Gallup asked a sample of American residents in 1939 whether relief should be given to needy "people" or "foreigners" "living in this country who are not citizens and have not applied for citizenship," 70 percent believed they should not receive relief. Men and women, young and old, were just as likely to believe relief should be reserved for U.S. citizens, and there were no significant regional differences in these attitudes.[15]

Social Workers Respond

The strength of anti-alien sentiment was so strong and so widespread that social workers in the Northeast and Midwest were forced to respond and articulate a clear rationale for including aliens in these benefit programs. They argued that if Americans expected—or demanded—that foreigners assimilate, they should not treat immigrants poorly: "Make the immigration restrictions as tight as the economic conditions demand it. But once an alien is admitted to the United States, treat him as a citizen of tomorrow, as a partner in the common American enterprise." Aliens, it was also argued, paid the same taxes as citizens; therefore, they should be entitled to the same benefits. One social worker decried that foreign-born workers who had "contributed so largely to the production of real wealth of the country and who suffered the most bitter exploitation" were now being made "the scapegoats" for the entire Depression. Social workers were also quick to point out that any discrimination against non-citizens often discriminated against their citizen children. To quantify the toll that anti-immigrant legislation would have on U.S. citizens if enacted, the National Council on Naturalization and Citizenship released a study in 1937 on adult aliens and their families in fifteen states. The report revealed that "three out of every four aliens studied had one or more American citizens (either spouse or child) in their immediate families."[16]

Advocates also argued that an alien's failure to naturalize did not necessarily signify any lack of allegiance to the United States. Rather, it might be due "to the bars which have been set up to prevent them from obtaining citizenship here," such as high naturalization fees or literacy requirements. Furthermore, some social workers objected to the time wasted in determining the citizenship of applicants, when need—and need alone— should be the paramount concern. Finally, they argued that providing relief to aliens was simply the decent thing to do: "When we admit an alien for permanent residence, we are accepting him, provisionally at least, as a member of our American society. . . . He and his children are part of our future as much as if they had settled in New England two or three hundred years ago. And that future will be a successful one for all of us, only as it is based on tolerance and equal opportunity."[17]

Social workers also took action to ensure that non-citizens would continue to have access to relief. When exaggerated claims were made about the number of aliens on relief, social workers made it their work to address these allegations in "speeches, in the press, [and] over the radio." "In Congress and in state legislatures," according to *Social Work Year Book*, social agencies "have opposed measures which threatened to discriminate against the foreign born and have worked for their equitable treatment, particularly in the matter of employment and relief."[18]

Hopkins and Perkins Resist Fanning Flames of Nativist Sentiment

While social workers in the Northeast and Midwest worked vigorously to defend non-citizens, FDR's administration was being accused by many of "alien coddling." Sympathy for aliens in the administration—especially in the Department of Labor—was said to be so strong that many charged that the administration was refusing to collect data on the number of aliens on relief. "No one knows, apparently, how many aliens are on relief," complained Representative Henry Stubbs (D-CA). "Administrator Hopkins has conducted almost every type of census under the sun, but he consistently has declined to cooperate with me in the matter of determining how many aliens are on relief." Finding little cooperation anywhere in the administration, Stubbs asked: "I am wondering if they realize that public opinion is being roused to the point where wholesale deportation of aliens is being suggested in some quarters." A former head of the National

Recovery Administration charged that FDR was unwilling to conduct a mandatory census of the unemployed because "any census would disclose hundreds of thousands of aliens—with their dependents perhaps millions—who are illegally in this country either on the relief rolls or holding jobs that could be taken by legal residents now on relief."[19]

In the absence of statistics, individuals made wild guesses, reprinted in newspapers all over the country. One *Saturday Evening Post* headline asked, "Are There a Million Aliens on Relief?" Other estimates put the number even higher. One news story charged that there were as many as five hundred thousand aliens on New York City's dole alone and that FERA was keeping such statistics secret. According to one newspaper, New York "relief officials expressed horror when asked if any effort had been made to tabulate the aliens on their lists" since relief was extended without "regard to citizenship or noncitizenship." "Meanwhile, exasperated taxpayers continue to dig into their pockets for contributions . . . to the 'emergency fund' with the discomfiting knowledge that nearly one-sixth of the persons they are being called upon to support are 'Russians, Germans, Turks, or Prussians'—aliens or persons who have only taken out their first citizenship papers." *New York Times* Washington bureau chief Arthur Krock also suggested that the administration was hiding important statistics from the public. The "President's aides," he claimed, were hesitant to conduct an unemployment census because they feared that "there are hundreds of thousands of aliens of illegal residential status on the rolls." Krock averred that the public would understand if, in the haste of providing emergency relief on such a large scale, some illegal aliens made their way onto the relief rolls. "But if a census should disclose what is feared by some in touch with the . . . relief activities in the United States, reason might fly out the window, and Mr. Hopkins and Secretary Perkins might find themselves the centers of a storm violent enough to sweep them both out of office."[20]

Understanding the power of data to frame the public debate, some organizations tried to persuade state and local governments to collect and release the numbers. The American Legion in New York pressured the city to disclose the number of aliens on relief. Interested in registering all aliens living in New York City and creating a list of those on relief, the New York City Board of Aldermen, largely controlled by the Tammany machine, and "anxious to embarrass" Mayor La Guardia, asked that the Emergency Relief Bureau (ERB) report the number of aliens on relief. The ERB replied that it "regretted that it was impossible to furnish the information sought within the time given" because it did not collect the information since citizenship was not a requirement for relief. The aldermen accused the ERB of foot-dragging, and one news editorial alleged that the ERB was run by foreigners who "cannot be expected to show zeal in compiling information about other aliens who may be receiving preferential treatment." This was likely a dig at the increasing number of Italians and Jews working in city government under La Guardia's reign. The ERB finally agreed to disclose the information but warned that any attempt to discriminate against aliens would put the city at risk of losing state relief funds, which expressly provided that there could be no discrimination based on citizenship.[21]

Administration critics were right about one thing: Hopkins did conduct "almost every type of census under the sun," and none of those studies asked recipients their citizenship status. At a news conference in 1936, a reporter asked Hopkins to respond to the *Saturday Evening Post*'s suggestion that one out of every seven people on relief was an alien. Hopkins disputed the figures: "I am sure that is incorrect. I do not know where anybody could ever find that out." No one could find that out because Hopkins refused to collect the data. When a reporter pressed, saying, "there is no question a large percentage [of those on relief] are aliens," Hopkins refused to concede the point. He suggested instead that aliens were probably underrepresented on the relief rolls because aliens were fearful of being deported if they went on the dole. "Certainly any figure of one to seven is ridiculous," he contended. When Hopkins was asked during Senate Committee hearings a few months later how many aliens were employed in WPA jobs, "he stated that, since prevailing law made no provision for discriminating against aliens, the WPA had no exact figures as to how many were employed." Hopkins did, however, estimate that in only "4 per cent of the total number of families on relief was the head of the family an alien who had not declared his intent to become a citizen. 'This is a smaller proportion than the proportion of aliens to the total population' he said." He then reminded the Senate that most of the alien-headed families had "American citizens who are dependent upon them." The administration never told the public why they were reluctant to collect or distribute these data, especially if they were so convinced that immigrants were underrepresented on the relief rolls. Staff members did express concern—behind the scenes—that the collection of such information might lead to the deportation of those on relief. And perhaps officials feared that cities in which aliens were overrepresented on relief would feel pressure to weed out their rolls. Whatever the motive, federal relief officials were reluctant to fan the nativist flames.[22]

Of course, not all local agencies were reluctant to disclose such data. Los Angeles relief officials were eager to release this information. Throughout the Depression, relief administrators conducted studies showing aliens' alleged overuse of relief. One study in 1934 counted 63,000 Mexicans on the relief rolls, only 23,000 of whom were American citizens. "The total cost incurred by the presence of these Mexican alien indigents," the superintendent of the local relief administration declared, "creates a financial burden the county can ill afford to carry at present." Every few months, it seemed, relief officials released data showing how aliens bulked on the rolls, and the subsequent headlines in the *Los Angeles Times* painted a clear picture: "Aliens Load Relief Roll," "Thomson Tells of Huge Cost of Relief for Aliens," "Aliens on County Dole Raise Grave Problem," and "Aliens Heavy Relief Burden" were but a few examples.[23]

The "alien relief burden" was hardly astronomical, however. Between July 1937 and December 1938 the California State Relief Administration (SRA) served approximately 13,100 aliens, or about 6 percent of its total caseload. Meanwhile, aliens made up roughly 6.5 percent of California's population in 1940. Many state relief officials, however, were frustrated that aliens (or non-whites) got any relief at all: "After years of daily contact with these people, we, as employees of the SRA, have made the following personal analysis of the clients." Relief recipients, they claimed, fell into "three nearly numerically equal groups." First, there were those who were "undoubtedly deserving," mostly comprising the "white American small family group formerly of adequate means." Next were the "doubtfully deserving," a group containing "many ignorant, semi-skilled or laborer families who have always lived more or less precariously and their resources are extremely difficult to check. Furthermore, they are usually of larger than average families and their present 'dole' constitutes to them a 'security wage' comparable with past earnings." Last was the "undoubtedly **not** deserving. . . . This group is composed of alien (or part alien) families (who constitute a very large percentage of the entire relief load), bums both masculine and feminine, habitual drunkards and dope users, and just plain 'chiselers'" (boldface in the original). According to the historian Richard Lester, the report angered the black community, who interpreted the reference to individuals with larger than average families to be a veiled reference to blacks. The author of the report was dismissed but later reinstated, causing blacks and Mexicans to "picket" his office, "urging that he be fired permanently."[24]

BARRING ILLEGAL ALIENS

Given the growing anti-immigrant sentiment, there were almost immediate efforts in Congress to bar non-citizens from the WPA, especially those who had "smuggled themselves in." When the WPA was first launched in 1935, applicants were not required to produce proof of citizenship to get a WPA job. In fact, illegal immigrants were neither expressly permitted nor prohibited from public works jobs. Hopkins testified at a congressional hearing that the WPA did not "knowingly have a person on the rolls who is here in violation of our laws." There was no policy to screen all WPA applicants to determine their legal status, but Hopkins indicated that his office was "constantly in touch with the Labor Department . . . and they are in touch with us about particular families that they think are here illegally, and which they are trying to find." Hopkins was a little fuzzy on the practices of individual agencies. From his "general knowledge" of things, he was fairly confident that WPA workers would report any applicant they suspected of being in the country in violation of the law to the Labor Department. But WPA workers did not make it a policy to check the citizenship or legal status of WPA applicants.[25]

When asked by a congressman whether there might be a way to improve the coordination between immigration authorities and the WPA, Hopkins was evasive. He likened hiring illegal immigrants to hiring individuals who had violated any law. If the WPA *knew*, for example, that a man had committed burglary, he thought it was the duty of the WPA to report him to the proper authorities. Similarly, if the WPA *knew* that an applicant was in the U.S. in violation of the law, they should report him to the INS. Hopkins was wary, however, of turning the WPA into a police or INS agency: "I agree fully that anybody who is here illegally and the fact is known. . . . [w]e should get him in the hands of the proper authorities and off the relief rolls." Hopkins insisted, however, that it was not the responsibility of the WPA to "run down and find out whether an alien had come in in violation of the quota laws. That is the responsibility of others." The fact that Hopkins did not want the WPA to turn into a police agency accounted for part of the administration's opposition to a congressional measure to bar illegal aliens from the WPA. He was also concerned about the administrative difficulties entailed in such a law. WPA officials were already overburdened, and having to check the citizenship and legal status of those applying for relief would take time away from the more important task of providing emergency work relief jobs to millions. It was "an enormous job," Hopkins testified, and it "is the job of another department."[26]

Despite administration objections, in May 1936 Representative Clifton Woodrum (D-VA) offered an amendment to restrict the employment of aliens who were known to be in the country illegally. In the course of the deliberations over this amendment, three congressmen rose to the defense of illegal immigrants. Representative Vito Marcantonio, a Republican from New York City who later switched to the American Labor Party, was one of the staunchest defenders of non-citizens in the House. He objected to the amendment because "it would leave all aliens on relief, subject to persecution by relief administrators." Likewise, Representative Gerald Boileau, a Progressive from Wisconsin who, like Marcantonio, was a member of the liberal bloc in Congress, argued that aliens who were in the country illegally and subject to deportation should be deported. But if they were not deported, then they should not be excluded from relief: "Are we going to deprive human beings who are here, whom we permit to stay here, and whom we do not force out of our country, of the only means they have of obtaining bread and meat? . . . Human beings who are in this country, either legally or illegally," Boileau continued, "should [have] an opportunity to eat. If we need to appropriate more money, let us do so, but we should not take such an un-Christian and un-American attitude as is expressed in this amendment."[27]

Representative Everett Dirksen, a moderate Republican from Illinois who supported the New Deal, joined the fray as well. While he was "entirely in sympathy with the idea of giving preference to American citizens," in practice, he agreed with Hopkins that there were a variety of complications to consider. If an illegal alien had a family "consisting of an American wife and American children, what are you going to do about him? If . . . you strike his name from the relief rolls, you have left a wife and her children, who are American citizens, high and dry and hungry." Dirksen was also concerned about the potential abuses that might result if relief administrators had too much power. "Do not forget that if you charge a relief supervisor with the responsibility of striking the names of aliens from the rolls, you also provide him with a weapon which in indiscriminate hands, could be an instrument of grave abuse."

> If the relief supervisor decided . . . he did not like the accent, the color of the hair, the slant of the nose, or the color of the skin of a relief applicant who was actually a citizen, he could cause so much trouble . . . by demanding undue proof of citizenship that the whole relief program purpose would be perverted or destroyed.[28]

Given the growing strength of anti-immigrant sentiment, however, few congressmen were willing to publicly defend illegal aliens. Indeed, the balance of opinion was toward denying illegal immigrants' access to the WPA. Representative Robert Bacon (R-NY) reminded his colleagues that illegal aliens were felons and as such should not benefit from relief: "We do not want to replace American citizens on the relief rolls [with] illegal aliens who have under our own laws committed a felony when they entered the United States. They are subject to deportation and should be deported." Similarly, Representative Jed Johnson (D-OK) averred that it was "somewhat surprising to hear a Member of this body actually defend an alien who is here illegally." He estimated that there were five million aliens in the country illegally, more than three hundred thousand of whom had "WPA jobs that belong to loyal American citizens. . . . These aliens ought to become American citizens or be deported." Both of these comments drew applause, and the amendment passed the House 136 to 19. However, the administration was able to qualify the ban in two significant ways. First, the language of the amendment was such that the WPA was prohibited from "knowingly" employing illegal aliens. Second, the WPA was "not absolutely forbidden to employ aliens even when they were known to be here illegally since the law specified that officials had only to make 'every reasonable effort consistent with prompt employment of the destitute unemployed' to see that such aliens were not given employment."[29]

Once the measure was passed, WPA officials were supposed to ascertain the place and date of the applicant's birth, naturalization, or declaration of intent to naturalize. Foreign-born individuals who were not naturalized or had not filed their first papers "were required to fill out a comprehensive questionnaire" prepared by the INS. "When information thus secured indicated irregular or illegal entry or when complaints or charges were brought against specific individuals WPA officials were responsible only for forwarding all available data for further checking by the proper authorities." According to one observer, "this provision was variously applied. In some localities there was little investigation of aliens, while in others extended inquiries were made into the circumstances of arrival in this country."[30]

As soon as the new law went into effect, Los Angeles officials began a "three-week campaign" to "slash from relief rolls all aliens who have entered the United States illegally." All WPA employees in the city were asked to fill out a questionnaire to determine their citizenship and legal status. Individuals who answered the questions falsely were subject to fines and imprisonment. Those who could not produce proof that they had entered the country legally would be thoroughly investigated by the INS. Similarly, in Arizona, the state WPA directed all employees to "cooperate with the immigration service in bringing about the elimination of Aliens illegally in this country." By August 1936, state officials estimated that 177 "aliens illegally in the United States" had been "removed from the WPA rolls." Many more refused to be investigated and were "placed in the inactive files."[31]

Press estimates of the number of illegal aliens on the WPA rolls nationwide varied from a low of 3,000 to a high of 1,000,000. Federal officials guessed there might be as many as 10,000. A year after this legislation passed, Hopkins reported that "out of about 2,000 separate charges that persons [employed in WPA] were in this country illegally, the Department of Labor had been able to establish this fact in only four cases."[32]

Upon hearing the news that the law banning illegal aliens from receiving WPA was to pass, one immigrant advocate suggested that "under the circumstances this was not very bad" since no action had been taken to ban legal aliens from the program, a minor miracle given all the anti-alien sentiment in the press and Congress. Efforts to bar legal immigrants had indeed started in 1936 when Representative Stubbs (D-CA) suggested that simply barring illegal aliens from WPA work did "not go far enough. It does not reach the bottom of this vital question." To his mind, it was a superfluous amendment since all illegal aliens should be deported. In California, Stubbs explained, the real problem was the *legal aliens*. Mexicans in particular, he argued, "come here in droves during the seasonal harvests, and after the work is done they simply go on relief." "I am reliably informed that in one part of my district 40 percent of those on relief are aliens. . . . they came here legally, but they have become a public burden." He asked his colleagues to remove all non-citizens from the WPA rolls in order "to protect the taxpayers and citizens of the United States from carrying the almost unbearable burden of relief—a burden heavily weighted with uninvited and unnecessary aliens."[33]

Various congressmen rose to the defense of the alien. Representative Marcantonio objected to Stubbs's proposal because "hundreds of thousands, or maybe a few thousand—I do not know how many aliens— would be deprived of the benefits of the bill. What would then happen? You cannot deport them. You have no right to. They are not cattle." Marcantonio also stressed the fact that alien heads of household often had American children: "Starve the alien father and you starve his American children." Discrimination against aliens, he continued, was against American ideals.

> I do not think that we are acting in the spirit of Americans. All of our ancestors were aliens. . . . Would you have wanted restrictions placed on your forefathers when they came to this country? My friends, these aliens are here legally. They are seeking to live peacefully, they are patriotic at heart, they love America, they want to build America. Give them a chance to live.

These arguments were successful, at least in 1936. The Stubbs amendment was defeated 93 to 45. The following year a similar amendment to deny all legal aliens' access to WPA jobs was also defeated but by a far slimmer margin: 116 to 112. A compromise amendment was then proposed, denying illegal aliens and legal aliens who had not taken out their first papers from the WPA and establishing preferences: first for veterans, second for American citizens, third for aliens who had taken out their first papers by the date the act became law, and fourth for aliens who had taken out their first papers after the act became law. Hopkins testified before the House against the proposal, and Hopkins and Perkins each wrote letters to Congress protesting the restrictions. Nevertheless, the amendment passed by a margin of 101 to 32.[34]

Since officials were projecting that 400,000 WPA jobs would be eliminated due to budgetary cuts, they estimated that all 120,000 aliens (including those with first papers and those without) would be dropped from the program. The FLIS, however, called on WPA officials to administer the law "as humanely as possible." They urged that WPA employees be given ample time to prove their legal status and that those awaiting receipt of their first papers not be stricken from the rolls. Ultimately, only 60 percent of the estimated 120,000 aliens were dropped. One observer noted that while a great many aliens were excluded by the ruling, "many of them continued to find WPA project employment, particularly in localities with large needy foreign populations."[35]

California

How local administrators chose to implement the ruling proved critical. California officials were eager to get to work. State WPA officials sent a telegram to Hopkins asking if they should await instructions or go ahead and interpret the act on their own. Los Angeles officials estimated that five thousand aliens—most of them Mexicans—would be dropped due to the tightened eligibility requirements. The county WPA administrator, Donald Connolly, an army engineer picked by federal officials to "ensure that the WPA had the image of being efficient and insulated from politics," gave aliens five days to take out their first papers before they would be dropped, and he assumed that those who did not file for first papers were illegal aliens, a dubious proposition given the tight cooperation between relief and immigration officials there. The dismissal of so many aliens brought the relief rolls "down far below the quota designated by Washington."[36]

People who got cut from the WPA could, in theory, receive state assistance through the State Relief Administration (SRA). Governor Frank Merriam, a right-wing Republican who was a staunch anti-communist and backed by the state's agricultural interests, "exercised political control over SRA." The SRA was not under civil service rules, and the governor appointed the State Relief Administrator and the Relief Commission. Merriam appointed Harold Pomeroy as head of the SRA. Under Pomeroy's watch, the SRA adopted lower relief budgets for Mexicans as well as a variety of other pro-grower policies. So close was Pomeroy to growers that after he resigned his post he became the executive secretary of the Associated Farmers of California.[37]

One month after the new citizenship ruling went into effect Pomeroy outlined two courses of action. Aliens removed from WPA projects would be given the choice of "getting their return passage home or going off the relief rolls. . . . If he agrees to leave the country, he will be given relief until arrangements are completed for his deportation. If he refuses to leave, the relief administration may decline to give him aid unless such action would work undue hardship." An opponent of the bill described the commission's action as "one of the most disgraceful in its history. . . . There is no other intent than this: aliens will be asked to please express a desire to leave or get the hell out and starve." He proposed an amendment to provide for relief to all eligible aliens removed from the WPA, but the amendment "died for want of a second." More than two hundred members of the Workers Alliance in Los Angeles marched on "dole headquarters" in protest of the policy.[38]

From the SRA's perspective, it already had 3,900 aliens on state rolls, and the dismissal of an additional 5,000 from WPA rolls would only add to their burden. As a result, the SRA asked that the federal government pay for the relief administered to aliens pending their removal, but it declined to do so. Determined to move ahead with their plans anyway, the SRA commissioned a study of alien cases in Los Angeles County. The study found that 28 percent of the caseload was comprised of aliens. Mexicans represented "23% of the total caseload and 80% of the alien caseload. Although we have generally conceded that the entire alien problem is limited to purely Mexicans, this survey has revealed that 44 other countries are contributing toward these problems." The survey also showed that over 70 percent of the aliens on relief had lived in the country more than seventeen years. Just over 40 percent indicated a desire to become American citizens, and 20 percent had already taken out their first papers. Only 9 percent indicated that they wanted to return to their country of birth. These facts—especially the "long period of time most . . . have been residents of the United States and the large number of American citizen members in the family cases"—complicated repatriation plans somewhat, but the relief administration maintained that it was "diligently pursuing every reasonable possibility for the repatriation of alien relief cases."[39]

Angered by the mounting costs of relief, the California state legislature and Governor Merriam sent another resolution to Congress in 1938 to expel undesirable aliens from the country. According to Merriam, "The problem of aliens in California has become a very serious one. It should be a matter of grave concern to every American citizen, particularly to every American wage earner in this state and to every taxpayer who is compelled to contribute to the mounting cost of supporting aliens on our relief rolls." He urged state residents to write their representatives in support of expulsion. Immigration officials in California got into the act as well and wrote to their supervisors in Washington, asking what might be done since "the relief charges for the maintenance of Mexicans" were "high." California's immigration officials were most concerned about devising a "plan that will make the Mexicans stick, once they cross the Border" and hoped it would be sponsored by the Mexican government. Though acknowledging that steps "toward the repatriation of Mexicans" would "be most heartily applauded on Capitol Hill," federal officials noted that the Mexican government was not in any position at the moment to fund or provide land for Mexican repatriates, and the condition of Mexican repatriates in Mexico was "a long way from being favorable." They nonetheless promised to communicate with the U.S. State Department to see what might be done. Ultimately, it appears that the SRA dropped its plans for any large-scale repatriation of Mexican families, though it did repatriate significant numbers of Filipino families. When Los Angeles County relief officials asked the SRA whether it would cooperate in repatriating Mexicans, the SRA told county officials that no one on its caseload wanted to be repatriated.[40]

Illinois

Illinois handled the congressional action to drop aliens without first papers from relief differently than California. The Illinois Emergency Relief Commission, the state agency charged with certifying WPA workers, had made plans to review its caseload in July 1937 to determine which employees were aliens, estimating that 5,200 might be dropped. Charles Miner, a social worker and the WPA administrator for Illinois, stressed, however, that they were not planning to "eliminate aliens in any wholesale or slashing fashion." And they promised to accept workers' statements about their birthplace. The IPL spent "hours and hours and hours since this legislation passed, advising with Directors and Supervisors of the Works Progress Administration" so as to minimize the harm to aliens. Local and regional WPA officials, according to the IPL, were "sympathetic toward the efforts and desires of the foreign born to achieve citizenship," and local supervisors "were anxious not to disrupt more than necessary, the degree of efficiency which they had been able to develop in personnel." One way in which they helped minimize harm was by getting assurances from WPA officials that a "declaration [of intent to naturalize] is a declaration no matter how long ago it was secured" even if it was no longer valid or the alien was unable to proceed with naturalization. More important, in August, a local WPA official informed the press that the review of the WPA rolls had been called off: "There will be no review made to find aliens except on the list of relief persons awaiting assignment to WPA. As to those now on WPA, we will take no action unless a signed complaint is sent to us challenging the right of a specific individual to hold his job." Local officials were taking advantage of the fact that the new law stipulated that the WPA "shall not *knowingly* permit the employment" of illegal aliens or those without first papers. The law did not require that any investigation be made, and Hopkins advised Illinois officials that they did not have to go through with the caseload review.[41]

While social workers in the city generally shared an ideological commitment to extending relief to individuals regardless of citizenship, WPA officials were all confirmed by the Senate, and "by usual courtesy procedures the appointees were typically favorable to at least one of the state's senators." As a result, many (though not all) big-city bosses had a considerable amount of power in controlling WPA administrators. FDR chose a longtime ally of Chicago's Mayor Edward Kelly to direct the Illinois program, effectively giving the Kelly-Nash machine control over nearly 68,000 WPA jobs in Cook County alone. Kelly denied that he used the WPA for political patronage and federal officials "insisted that the certification process" was "free from political influence." Despite the protestations, there is little doubt that the Kelly-Nash machine used WPA jobs to bolster its power: "WPA files abounded with letters attesting to the Kelly-Nash machine's willingness to threaten loss of employment for failure to support the organization candidate." The Women's Civic Council conducted a study of political coercion and found a "polling place where 'seventy per cent of the voters voted by assistance, and the men received from the Democratic precinct captain a blank filled out which constituted an 'OK' for the voters to go back upon their WPA jobs the day after election.'" Though the previous mayor had avoided meddling too much in the business of relief provision, public works jobs were another matter. Indeed, according to Steven Erie, "by 1936 two-thirds of the machine's lieutenants reported serving as employment and welfare brokers, up from one-third in 1928." What is more, by the Depression years, approximately 20 percent of precinct captains were foreign born and over two-thirds had at least one parent who was foreign born. According to Erie, Kelly "particularly targeted the city's Southern and Eastern Europeans for jobs and relief." Whether WPA administrators came to this commitment from a moral imperative or from electoral concerns, then, the effect was the same: The implementation of citizenship restrictions in Chicago was far less draconian than in Los Angeles.[42]

None of this is to say there were no calls in Illinois to deny aliens access to relief. In fact, a member of the American Legion, who was also on the Advisory Board of the Cook County Bureau of Public Welfare, introduced a recommendation in 1937 providing for the "speedy deportation of all aliens employed on public works or receiving direct or indirect

234 • Chapter 9

relief who have resided in the country for more than five years without applying for citizenship." The Bureau of Public Welfare, however, refused to heed the recommendation. According to the IPL, "There is no disposition on the part of the Cook County Bureau of Public Welfare itself, to proceed by the starvation method, of compelling citizenship among its clients. Like the League, it encourages citizenship, but appreciates the difficulties in the processes and the prohibitive costs of naturalization." That same year an alien registration bill was introduced in the Illinois General Assembly. Among the provisions, aliens who applied for or received relief would be guilty of a misdemeanor and subject to a fixed penalty of six months in the county jail, a $1,000 fine, or both. They would also be reported to the INS for possible deportation. The IPL lobbied members of the legislature from the Hull-House 17th Senatorial District, who "promised that it will be either kept sleeping or killed in committee." The measure did not pass.[43]

In 1935 a similar issue came up in the small community of Carlinville, a mining area about 250 miles southwest of Chicago, with the potential to affect aliens throughout the state. Local officials asked the state attorney general for an opinion as to whether "relief authorities have the right to furnish relief to people who are not citizens." While the state pauper law made no mention of citizenship—only residence—the state's attorney wondered how an alien could gain a residence in the state. He subsequently issued an opinion that the only aliens who should be granted relief were those who had not lived in the United States long enough to acquire citizenship or who had filed their first papers. Those who failed to become citizens when eligible should be reported to the INS for deportation. County relief administrators did not deny relief to aliens, however, nor did the Illinois Emergency Relief Commission. The opinion, unsupported by law, was subsequently nullified, and the IPL helped the Illinois Emergency Relief Commission craft a formal non-discrimination statement for aliens and relief, noting that under both state and federal law, discrimination on the basis of non-citizenship was prohibited.[44]

In its liberal treatment of aliens on WPA work relief, Illinois was probably somewhat of an exception. According to the American Committee for the Protection of Foreign Born, "wholesale dismissals of noncitizens" were "taking place all over the country." Indeed, in the summer of 1937 newspapers across the country from Spokane, Washington, to Belle Fourche, South Dakota, to Manchester, New Hampshire, and even Macon, Georgia, all reported on the aliens cut from WPA jobs in their communities. In Arizona local papers reported that more than one thousand aliens had been removed from the WPA rolls "and made available to cotton growers and other agricultural employers." WPA administrators in Milwaukee, Wisconsin, started their purge by combing through WPA and county relief records as well as "investigating anonymous letters accusing WPA workers of being aliens." They were amazed to find one thousand aliens on their WPA rolls when they had originally estimated that only two hundred were employed.[45]

New York

Because it was home to nearly a quarter of the total alien population in the country, New York suffered the heaviest layoffs. In June 1937 all "known" aliens who had failed to take out their first papers were given "pink slips" and dropped from the WPA rolls. Foreign-born WPA workers who thought they could prove their citizenship were given sixty days to do so—significantly longer than the five days non-citizens in Los Angeles received. Aliens with only first papers were fired. In just three months, over twenty thousand non-citizens had been laid off. New York City's WPA administrator admitted that he had "administrative discretion, aside from the law, to drop any persons he wished." Since budgetary cuts required the administrator to drop a large number of individuals from the WPA rolls regardless of citizenship status, he argued that "It is a question of whether we should lay off aliens or perfectly good citizens."[46]

Unlike in Illinois, where the WPA administrator was selected to curry favor with Mayor Kelly's patronage machine, Roosevelt ran the WPA through New York City's Fusion Reform mayor, Fiorello La Guardia, bypassing the Tammany machine completely. La Guardia was an Italian American who, as a representative in Congress, had fought hard against immigration restriction. He won his mayoral race with the strong support of the city's southern and eastern Europeans, who had long felt ignored by the Tammany machine. But to guard against charges of political favoritism, La Guardia selected Colonel Somervell, a non-partisan administrator with a background in the Army Corps of Engineers, to run the program. Somervell's reign over the WPA was regarded by many to have increased efficiency, discipline, and productivity, but, according to WPA workers, he (and other army officers in charge of WPA programs around the country) regarded and treated them "with insufferable contempt." Indeed, various groups and local politicians protested the alien relief cuts. The New York City Department of Public Welfare condemned the new policy, arguing that it defeated its own ends: "The isolation of hundreds or thousands of human beings from the economic structure of the country in which they live will hardly make for national unity and the effect on citizen children of aliens, born in this country, cannot be discarded." The American Committee for the Protection of Foreign Born and the City Projects Council, which along with the Workers Alliance had encouraged "most of the sit-down strikes and mass demonstrations in the past," got a court injunction to temporarily stop the alien purge, though ultimately to no avail. About a month after the cuts were made, however, there was a shortage of skilled workers for specific WPA projects. As a result, Somervell instructed the ERB that they should fill the slots with skilled aliens who had taken out their first papers.[47]

The Henry Street Settlement followed seventy-two aliens who had been stricken from New York's WPA rolls for a year after their dismissal. When they received their pink slips, these workers were described as "stunned, bewildered, disheartened, afraid." Having lived and toiled in the United States for so many years—twenty years, on average, for this group—these workers imagined they were just as much a part of the community as any other worker. Not a single WPA worker who had been dropped had ever experienced discrimination because of their citizenship status, and they believed that their non-citizenship was a mere "technicality associated with voting. They did not realize that they were 'aliens.'" If not through hard work and long residence, then surely the fact that nearly all of them had American children qualified them for support from the community. When Henry Street followed up a year later, they found that 83 percent had spent the year living entirely with home relief. Only three had been able to support themselves without any public assistance. Where they had once found shock and fear, settlement workers now found "frustration and hopelessness." Though city and state relief officials had always "taken the position that aid must be extended to all qualified persons, regardless of citizenship," many non-citizens still feared that they would soon be kicked off of home relief as well. They had heard rumors that "in California all aliens had been taken off relief and left in the streets to starve" and that those who were unable to find a job would be summarily deported. New York public relief administrators did not kick aliens off of home relief, however. In fact, dropping aliens from the WPA amounted, ultimately, to a reshuffling of relief recipients. Aliens dropped from the WPA were "expected to be absorbed on home relief" and "replaced in the WPA jobs by citizens now on home relief." Somervell in fact staggered the dismissals so as not to overwhelm the ERB. By 1940 aliens made up more than a quarter of the home relief rolls, costing the city almost $19 million per year.[48]

WPA administrators sometimes had, or felt they had, discretion in the way they would implement congressional mandates. Los Angeles officials reviewed their entire caseload and dropped all aliens who had failed to take out first papers immediately, even though this action brought them under quota. Cook County officials, meanwhile, decided to forgo reviewing the existing caseload and drop only those aliens for whom they had a "signed complaint . . . challenging the right of a specific individual to hold his job." New York's WPA administrator gave aliens much more time than did his counterpart in Los Angeles to prove their citizenship but ultimately made severe cuts in the caseload against the wishes of the city's local relief officials. But when there was a shortage of skilled workers, he rehired some of the aliens who had been dismissed. The fact that many WPA administrators had backgrounds in the Army Corps of Engineers may explain some of the generally tough treatment of aliens, even in cities where public and private relief officials objected to such treatment. There were big differences, too, in how local relief officials responded to aliens dropped from the WPA rolls. In California, elected officials and relief administrators contemplated mass expulsion. In New York, WPA administrators cooperated with local relief officials to stagger WPA dismissals so that aliens would have an easier time getting on home relief.[49]

THE POLITICS OF ALIEN EXCLUSION

In general it was congressmen from the South and the Southwest who were most in favor of denying non-citizens access to work relief, while those in the Northeast and Midwest—including Democrats, liberal Republicans, and progressive third-party candidates—were against such proposals. Robert Reynolds (D-NC), John Robsion (R-KY), Martin Dies (D-TX), Fritz Lanham (D-TX), and Henry Stubbs (D-CA) spoke frequently on the issue, and all opposed the extension of work relief to aliens. One congressman from Michigan speculated that "some gentlemen, especially from the South, who come from districts where they do not happen to have any aliens or people of foreign extraction, are not as well acquainted with the problem as some of us who come from the northern districts." Even though the South did not experience the rush of new immigrants, beginning in the 1890s a mix of nationalism, racism, anti-Catholicism, and anti-Semitism led southerners to become champions of immigration restriction during the first third of the twentieth century. Southerners also had little to gain and much to lose by including aliens in federal relief programs. Barring aliens from the WPA was consistent with their desire to "prevent excessive sums being spent in the rest of the country." In addition, because they did not have many aliens—or more to the point citizen family members of aliens—in their districts, voting for their exclusion was politically painless.[50]

The motives of southwestern congressmen were slightly more complicated. Restriction was also usually politically painless because Mexicans were not as likely as European immigrants to be politically incorporated. However, excluding aliens from WPA jobs would mean that they would generally become the responsibility of states and counties, increasing the tax burden on their constituents. To the extent that those localities could rid themselves of aliens altogether through deportation and repatriation programs or find other ways to exclude them from the relief rolls, the costs could be mitigated somewhat.

Northeastern and midwestern politicians often represented districts with large foreign-born populations. Marcantonio's constituency, for example, included many Italians, who "had a tendency to delay naturalization and were, therefore, in special need of protection." Indeed in cities such as New York, only one out of every five people had native-born white parents. Many families in these areas included U.S. citizens, non-citizens, and sometimes illegal immigrants. Excluding aliens from relief, therefore, would mean that American family members (current or potential voters) would bear the costs. Moreover, aliens in the Northeast and Midwest were almost always given general relief if dropped from the WPA. Contemporaries noted that states saddled with the responsibility of supporting aliens thrown off of relief were generally "the most vocal" in protesting "the barring of aliens from the WPA rolls." Finally, while aliens could not vote, they were counted for apportionment purposes. As a result, it was estimated that twenty-two members of Congress owed their positions to large numbers of aliens. These congressmen, one paper noted, "reside in large cities and constitute an active, strong block [sic] for or against any bill on immigration or naturalization." These regional divisions did not always break cleanly, of course, and in due time, as nativism increased, restriction came to rule the day. But on the whole the congressional drive to bar aliens from the WPA came from the South and Southwest.[51]

Barring Legal Immigrants

Because some states such as Illinois were circumventing the intent of Congress by refusing to investigate their relief rolls, Representative Lanham (D-TX) proposed an amendment in February 1938 to require that future applicants prove they had taken out their first papers or be denied WPA employment. Lanham complained that under the existing language of the law, the WPA could "employ many aliens without knowing that they are aliens and illegally within the borders of the United States." The law did not require an investigation, and as long as they did not know there were aliens "they are absolved." The new amendment, then, would put the burden of proof on the WPA applicant. The House approved the amendment 87 to 84. The House also passed an amendment barring *all* aliens from the WPA, but in conference the Senate "yielded to pressure from WPA officials" who opposed the amendment, and the House "finally receded on the question." The final bill included language that required that WPA applicants' declarations of intent to naturalize be valid in order for them to get employment. Furthermore, language was added specifying that aliens who had failed to declare their intent to naturalize before the enactment of the pending bill would not be eligible.[52]

In 1939 the House passed another "flat prohibition" against all aliens receiving WPA employment. There was little discussion this time. Representative Lyle Boren (D-OK) offered the amendment to reserve WPA jobs to U.S. citizens, "in the interest of the many thousands of deserving people who are denied portions of this fund who think enough of America to be citizens of the United States of America. [Applause.]" The only congressman to defend aliens this time was Representative Marcantonio, who equated the restrictions to "Nazi edicts against so-called non-Aryans" and declared: "It is not fair play to first make it almost impossible for the immigrant to become naturalized and then starve him because he is not naturalized. This is not patriotism, it is just plain rotten." The amendment still passed overwhelmingly, 144 to 41.[53]

The Senate, however, again rejected the ban on all aliens from the WPA. Citing the testimony of Colonel Harrington, the new WPA administrator, the Senate argued that the language of the House resolution would exclude aliens who had declared their allegiance to the United States by taking out their first papers. Furthermore, by removing the word "knowingly," the WPA would have to certify that every person under their employment was a U.S. citizen. That would mean that "each of the approximately 3,000,000 W.P.A. workers would be required to submit a birth certificate or naturalization papers . . . before payments could be effected." The whole process would take months, especially since "in many places no birth records or other evidence to establish citizenship are maintained." The House and Senate compromised, and Congress finally agreed that no person should be employed who had not made an "affidavit as to United States citizenship."[54]

The lack of discussion and overwhelming vote in favor of the amendment in the House reflected a number of factors. In 1938 Martin Dies's House Committee on Un-American Activities was investigating the possibility of Communist—which many equated with alien—infiltration of the WPA, the Federal Writers' Project, and the National Labor Relations Board. The committee hearings were front-page news in 1938 and 1939, and they helped "strengthen the opponents of the WPA." Economy-minded legislators in the House and Senate were also pushing through New Deal spending cuts, and many people were about to lose their jobs— the only question was who to cut. Another world war seemed imminent, and pogroms in Germany led to a small influx of Jewish refugees. Many Americans wrote letters to Washington, fearful that these refugees would take away "their" jobs and relief.[55]

Harrington sent a letter to all state WPA administrators describing the new law and indicated that all those who were "unable to comply with the requirements for making this citizenship affidavit shall be terminated on or before March 6, 1939." The law permitted up to a year's imprisonment and a fine of $1,000 for submitting false citizenship affidavits. But by August 1942, only twenty persons had been convicted: "Penalties inflicted were light . . . and in no case exceeded a short term in jail." Prior to the enactment of this new law, officials estimated that fewer than thirty thousand aliens remained on the relief rolls. In most states, officials argued, there were no aliens with first papers employed because the limited number of jobs went to those with higher preference ratings. In the final analysis, more than forty-five thousand were dismissed. Nearly 60 percent of the dismissals came from Ohio, Illinois, Michigan, California, and New York—states with the largest numbers of non-citizens.[56]

Effect of the Alien Ban

Citizenship exclusions were hard on many alien families. WPA workers had thirty days in which to prove their citizenship. In Alabama, Colorado, Atlantic City, and elsewhere, aliens disqualified from the ban found it hard to get any type of relief. Some communities only reluctantly abandoned direct relief to aliens as their local budgets bowed under the weight of the enormous need. Being cut off of WPA relief in Texas was an especially onerous fate. Since 1936, Texas state officials did not provide home relief to any of the able-bodied poor. Instead, counties were responsible for the care of their own indigent poor, whether or not they had the funds to do so. By the end of the decade, almost seventy thousand families in the state were surviving on surplus commodities alone. Where the average WPA family received $41.75 per month in wages, the total value of a month's worth of surplus commodities was only $3.88, amounting to "less than one cent per person per meal." One man lived off of potato peels for an entire week so that his family might eat the potatoes. Other families lived out of garbage cans. Texas social workers observed that some of their clients were literally starving to death, with starvation a factor in nearly 75 percent of the deaths in one county in one year. In El Paso "of the alien husbands interviewed" in May 1939, "none has found private employment other than a few odd jobs." Women typically "found work more readily than the men," often as domestics, "but their wages are so low that the family could not possibly live on their income, even if two members were thus employed."[57]

In response to the inability of their nationals to secure WPA employment or relief of any kind, the Mexican government made new plans to subsidize the repatriation of Mexicans. Between May and July 1939,

431 Mexican nationals and 698 Mexican Americans—mostly spouses, children, and other relatives—left Texas for Mexico. Official correspondence suggests that the movement was, under the circumstances, voluntary and that demand outstripped the ability of the Mexican government to accommodate the repatriates. The coercive nature of the repatriation program was clear elsewhere, however. In Kansas City, Mexican aliens who had been dropped from the WPA and were now receiving direct or categorical relief were told that they would no longer be eligible for relief. The county relief director reported that "we are instructing case workers to inform the Mexican families that they must return to their native country. Mexico has arranged to care for its citizens and there's no reason for them to continue to be an expense to Kansas City." The relief director acknowledged that "some appeared reluctant to accept the offer while others are glad of the chance. But we are going to make all return." Many of these families had lived in the United States for twenty years or more.[58]

In California yet another bill was proposed to deport aliens on relief in 1939. Under the terms of the bill, "the state relief administrator would be authorized to use funds for the deportation of indigent aliens to their native lands." It would also ban permanent relief to individuals "who are ineligible to become citizens or who declined to be citizens." The bill's author noted, bluntly, that deportable aliens "would be given the alternative of a 'free ride home or a voluntary, self-imposed starving death and a free burial in a pauper's grave, unless the relief administrator comes to their rescue and extends aid as an act of charity and mercy.'" The state legislature passed a slightly modified version of the measure. But after a high-profile meeting with Mexican government officials, Governor Culbert Olson (D), considerably more liberal than his predecessor, vetoed the measure with the support of some liberal organizations in the state.[59]

In Chicago the ban led to "a flood of questioners" to the IPL office who formed waiting lines that snaked down the street long before nine in the morning, asking for assistance in either proving their citizenship or to understand why they had not yet received their naturalization papers "when their applications were filed . . . sometimes as long as one or two years ago." According to the IPL, "it was a month of desperation for many . . . as they saw the means of livelihood for themselves and their families slip from under their feet." Social workers, if so inclined, could try to find ways to help those who lost WPA work get private employment. Relief officials also encouraged some of their clients to naturalize, wrote to federal officials on their behalf, and occasionally paid the naturalization fees of relief recipients so that they could qualify for the WPA. Governor Henry Horner (D-IL) created a committee that established citizenship and English-language classes with funds from the state and the Illinois Emergency Relief Commission. In Detroit the naturalization fee was included as a regular part of the relief budget. Explaining why they subsidized citizenship, one social worker said that "the foreign born workers have been largely responsible for the growth of our great automobile industries. Although many of them have not been able to become citizens, we do not believe it to the advantage of the community, to bar them from the benefits which they have earned by their life time of toil here in this country." While relief officials in California were contemplating mass expulsion, relief officials in Illinois and other parts of the North were trying to circumvent the impact of the citizenship restrictions.[60]

Despite all of the efforts of social workers in northern cities, the restrictions, they admitted, were "a hardship to many of our neighbors. In some instances it meant that school had to be given up and in others that the family had to try to get back on relief." Family members bickered and simmered, blaming each other for the loss of income. One New Yorker whose husband was cut from the WPA was frustrated that he was not being diligent about attending classes to improve his English so he could apply for his first papers: "He knows to speak [sic] and my girl could teach. But no, he goes to school two, three days, then stop. Says it is no good. Bah!" According to the settlement house worker recording this harangue, the woman then "turned away in a fit of disgust. 'I get so mad! But he go now,'" she said as "she waved a paring knife, with which she was peeling potatoes, high in the air. 'He go now. You see!'" Some individuals resorted to desperate measures. Harold Kimber, a forty-four-year-old husband and father of eight who was denied WPA work in Ohio because he was not a citizen, leaped from a nearby bridge to his death—the third suicide from the same spot that week. He had had no food for three consecutive days, he could not find a job, and his family was on the verge of eviction. While ineligible for WPA work, Kimber and his family were likely eligible for home relief. Prior to committing suicide, Kimber applied for home relief, but when caseworkers went to his home for their investigation, there was no one there, so they left a note on the door. "As far as we know," noted the caseworker, "the family never followed up the note and we are so swamped with cases we did not follow the case further."[61]

Non-citizens were eligible for home relief in Chicago, and by May 1939 there were 904 "WPA aliens" on city relief. But there were delays in getting aid, nearly 500 of those who applied for home relief did not qualify, and almost two months after they were cut from WPA, more than 60 percent had not yet applied for home relief. How those people survived is unclear. Even for the lucky who got on home relief, their futures were not certain. In July, the Chicago Relief Administration was forced, due to lack of funds, to cut *all* relief budgets to 65 percent of what it "formerly considered the minimum requirements for life." These cuts affected over one hundred thousand Chicago families, only a small portion of whom were non-citizens. "Alarmed by all too numerous reports that people are slowly starving and falling victim to diseases which assail their weakened bodies," the *Daily News* launched an investigation. "Mealtime interviews were the saddest," remarked one social worker. "The mothers sat by dumbly watching their ragged children fight over the last piece of day-old bread, gulping down their small plateful of black beans or sucking at the water the macaroni was boiled in to get some added nourishment." During the cold winter months, relief families sometimes didn't have enough bedding or coal to stay warm. Their clothes were in rags; children had no mittens.[62]

Non-citizens did not passively accept their treatment. Many protested the ban. Frustrated by their dismissal from the WPA, Mexicans in San Antonio apparently stoned their local WPA office. The First National Congress of Spanish-Speaking Peoples, which drew about a thousand delegates, met in Los Angeles in 1939 and issued a resolution calling for an end to discrimination in relief. Aliens, they said, were citizens of the United States "in every way except the possession of citizenship papers" and therefore deserved the same access to assistance. According to the group's Guatemalan-born leader, Luisa Moreno, "they have contributed their endurance, sacrifices, youth and labor to the Southwest. Indirectly, they have paid more taxes than all the stockholders of California's industrialized agriculture, the sugar beet companies and the large cotton interests that operate . . . with the labor of Mexican workers." Emma Tenayuca, a Mexican American woman, appointed to the National Executive Committee of the Workers Alliance for her organizing success in San Antonio, led mass demonstrations protesting citizenship and other eligibility standards that dropped Mexicans from the WPA rolls, arguing that their "historical rights in this territory" made their right to WPA employment "unchallengeable."[63] Progressive unions like the CIO and the Workers Alliance, who counted many non-citizens as members, strongly protested the dismissals. And hundreds of aliens wrote to Washington asking—sometimes begging—for assistance in proving their citizenship or for help in paying their naturalization fees so they could be reinstated.[64]

Non-citizens were not the only ones excluded from WPA work, of course. There were ten million unemployed in 1939, and the WPA only employed a quarter of these. As many as six to eight million, then, could not get a WPA job because they were unemployable or transients, funds for projects were lacking, or they were not quite destitute enough. Transients, in fact, often faced some of the worst conditions since settlement laws generally excluded them from home relief for one to three years, leaving few options for survival. The American Association of Social Workers reported widespread hunger and starvation among transient workers—many of them Dust Bowl migrants—in California's agricultural districts in 1938. One federal official reported that 90 percent or more of children in some districts suffered from significant malnutrition. In Tulare County, the children of migrant workers were "dying at a rate of one or two a day." Even in Colorado, private agencies would often provide assistance to aliens, but few would support transients. And of course, despite prohibitions against discrimination by race or color, blacks and Mexican Americans were often improperly denied WPA and other relief assistance.[65]

Getting around Restriction

Though the hardships among non-citizens, as others denied WPA employment, were real, WPA officials were quick to tell state relief officials that the regulations should not bar citizen members of families headed by aliens. Since usually only one person per family would be certified for work relief, certifying a secondary worker—a spouse or older child who had U.S. citizenship—was a simple solution to the problem of alien exclusion. A district WPA director in Ohio conceded that "members of families in which aliens are the family heads are given employment if they were born in this country and are employables." But this practice was not followed everywhere, and some alien-headed families had no citizen members living at home.[66]

The ban on aliens in the WPA also led communities in some states to develop local work relief projects "as a means of meeting the relief needs of large numbers of able-bodied aliens." In two upstate towns in New York, there were almost a hundred aliens who had been thrown off the WPA "now on the town's 'private' work projects, clearing off ice skating rinks, building cinder paths along the highways and doing multiple other odd jobs around the town." The men were said to be "more than willing to work," and their efforts helped cover the costs of their relief orders. Donald Howard, a charity official at the Russell Sage Foundation who published the first authoritative account of the WPA in 1943, explained, however, that "While it is agreed in most quarters that congressional discrimination against aliens constitutes less preferential treatment, it has sometimes been thought that it is the citizens rather than the aliens who [have] been discriminated against" by the citizenship ban. "Citizens given WPA jobs, it is argued, must 'work for what they get.' Aliens, on the other hand, are given relief without 'having to work for it.'—provided, of course, they are given relief." In New York this issue became heated. As the economy started to improve, white Americans were able to find work and the city relief rolls were increasingly composed of blacks and aliens. Consequently, support for relief started to wane. In 1939 Mayor

La Guardia "spearheaded a campaign" to make the "able-bodied people still on the dole," including aliens, work for relief. La Guardia was joined in his efforts by upstate Republican assemblymen. Three work relief bills passed the Republican-controlled state legislature in 1939, but all were vetoed by Governor Herbert Lehman (D), who worried about the cost of a work relief program and believed that relief recipients were on the dole "through no fault of their own." He was also following the advice of State Board of Social Welfare officials who feared the measure "would lead to the exploitation of welfare clients." Whether to give aliens more dignified forms of relief like WPA or whether simply to require aliens, like citizens, to work for their bread, the development of local work relief programs for aliens was another way to circumvent the effects of the federal ban.[67]

The WPA did not keep statistics on how many secondary workers were certified and there is not much systematic information on cities that developed local public works programs to help those disqualified by federal citizenship restrictions. But using the 1940 census, we can estimate the proportion of citizen- and alien-headed households with at least one member employed in a public works job. As it turns out, the differences between the two types of households were not large, given the ban. In 1940, 4.8 percent of alien-headed households had at least one member in a public works job compared to 6.8 percent of households headed by a citizen. The most common way to circumvent the citizenship requirement was through certifying secondary workers. Among citizen-headed households with public works jobs, it was the household head in 71 percent of the cases who held the job. But among alien-headed households, the household head held the job in only 21 percent of the cases. The difference between alien-headed and citizen-headed families was smallest in the Northeast and Midwest. There, citizen-headed households were 25 percent more likely than alien-headed households to have one member employed in a public works job; elsewhere, they were roughly twice as likely to have such jobs (see Table 9.1).[68]

These census data reveal that households headed by blacks (8.8 percent) and Mexicans (11 percent) were more likely than other groups to be employed in a public works job (see Table 9.2). For black households, the rates varied widely by region, however. A full 18 percent of black households were employed in public works jobs in the Northeast and Midwest compared to only 5 percent in the South, even though there were no substantial regional variations in public works employment rates.[69]

Even with the citizenship restrictions, southeastern European–headed households (6.5 percent) were just as likely as native-born white households (6.6 percent) to have a household member employed in public

TABLE 9.1
Percent of Households with at Least One Household Member Employed in a
Public Works Job, by Region and Citizenship Status of Household Head, 1940

	Alien-headed households	Citizen-headed households	% Difference
Northeast and Midwest	5.3	6.6	25
South	3.1	6.9	123
Southwest	2.9	5.7	97

Note: All household heads are 64 years or younger.
Source: Author's calculation, 1940 Census.

works. (Northwestern European immigrants had lower rates of participation, but they had slightly higher rates of employment in non-public
works jobs as well as higher incomes than other groups, including native-
born whites.) Significantly, the citizenship status of the head of household did not much affect the public works participation rate for southern
and eastern Europeans. Among that group, 6.1 percent of alien-headed
households had at least one family member employed in a public works
job compared to 6.7 percent for citizen-headed households. For Mexican
households, by contrast, the head's citizenship status made a large difference. Among this group, 4.8 percent of alien-headed households had at
least one household member employed in a public works job compared
to 15.7 percent of citizen-headed households. Part of the difference may
be due to the fact that Mexicans were younger than European immigrants as a group and therefore might not have had citizen children old
enough to be certified as secondary workers. But even if we control for
whether there were any adult citizens in the household who could potentially be certified as secondary workers, there is still evidence of a disparity. Among southern and eastern European households where at least one
household member was an adult citizen, slightly more alien-headed (8
percent) than citizen-headed (6.7 percent) households had public works
jobs. Among similar Mexican households, however, the reverse was true:
significantly more citizen-headed (17.2 percent) than alien-headed (8.3
percent) households had public works jobs (see Table 9.3).

A large part of this difference appears to be due to region-level bias.
When we assess all of these factors simultaneously—the household head's
race and citizenship, the presence of other adult citizens in the household
who could be certified instead, and region—non-citizen-headed households of all backgrounds were at a clear disadvantage in the Southwest
relative to their peers in the Northeast and Midwest. Exactly how Mexican households in particular fared in the Northeast and Midwest is hard

TABLE 9.2

Percent of Households with at Least One Household Member Employed in Public Works or Non-Public Works Job, by Race or Nativity of the Household Head, 1940

	Employed in public works job	Employed in non-public works job	No one employed
Native-born white	6.6	87.3	8.3
Foreign-born white	5.6	87.8	9.2
Northwestern European	4.2	88.4	9.2
Southeastern European	6.5	87.5	9.2
Black	8.8	85.3	9.3
Mexican[†]	11.0	75.8	16.0

Note: All household heads are 64 years or younger.
Source: Author's calculation, 1940 Census.
[†] Estimate of the Mexican-origin population constructed by IPUMS

TABLE 9.3

Percent of Households with at Least One Household Member Employed in Public Works Job, by Race or Nativity of the Household Head, 1940

	At least one adult citizen in household	
	Alien-headed households	Citizen-headed households
Southeastern European	8.0	6.7
Northwestern European	4.9	4.4
Mexican[†]	8.3	17.2

Note: All household heads are 64 years or younger.
Source: Author's calculations, 1940 Census.
[†] Estimate of the Mexican-origin population constructed by IPUMS

to tell. There were so few left after the repatriations of the 1930s that the sample sizes are simply too small to judge.[70]

In addition to variation in social worker benevolence, the political context likely played a significant role in the treatment of these alien-headed households across regions. To be sure, one could find elected officials in every region of the country who championed alien restriction. Nativism was strong everywhere and some politicians eagerly tried to capitalize on it. But the congressional drive to bar non-citizens, as we saw, was led by congressmen from the South and Southwest. And communities in the Northeast and Midwest often had at least some elected officials who defended non-citizens or their families. This was smart politics as well because southern and eastern Europeans were voting in record numbers by the early 1930s. Mexicans, on the other hand, had seen no similar electoral surge in this period, and there were far fewer elected officials who defended their interests or encouraged them to politically mobilize.[71]

The growing political power of the new immigrants in the big cities of the North meant that politicians had to increasingly include new immigrants in the city spoils system. Chicago's machine not only targeted southern and eastern Europeans for jobs, as we already saw, but various congressmen wrote to federal authorities to get assistance in proving the citizenship status of a constituent or somehow speed up the naturalization process, all with an eye to reinstate those dropped from the WPA. "Armed with federal relief," wrote Steven Erie, machines like those in Pittsburgh and Chicago or the Hague machine in New Jersey "brought the New Deal's newest ethnic recruits securely into the organization's fold." Over the life of the WPA, "up to one-quarter of all big-city registered voters were on the WPA payroll at one time or another." Perhaps that's why, when a naturalization examiner reportedly asked an alien, "Who elects the President?" he replied: "The WPA!" And with that answer, he became an American citizen. Because they were more likely to live in cities driven by machine politics, because they were far more politically incorporated, and because social workers were on their side, European immigrants were better able to circumvent citizenship restrictions.[72]

CONCLUSION

As the United States became embroiled in World War II, discrimination based on citizenship status became an even greater concern for the White House. The administration began to fear that aliens denied access to WPA jobs, relief, or defense work "might prove easy prey to subversive interests." Many of those denied assistance were not "enemy aliens" but rather nationals of allied governments. According Donald Howard, "To many observers, therefore, the nation's policy of refusing WPA employment to aliens was incompatible with its policy of all-out aid to opponents of aggression and with its policy of trying to be a good neighbor in the western world." Stressing the "hardship" that WPA policies exacted "upon a class of person whose private employment opportunities are becoming increasingly limited," in May 1941 the president urged Congress to end the restriction on employing aliens in the WPA. The House refused, voting down an amendment by Representative Lucien Maciora (D-CT) 71 to 15.[73]

Being cut from public works programs as a result of citizenship preferences or exclusions was a significant hardship for the aliens affected. But ultimately these restrictions did not last long. The full ban on aliens receiving WPA employment was not enacted until 1939, and the entire program was discontinued at the end of 1942. This triumph of nativistic forces, thus, was short-lived. It was also unevenly applied. Many European alien-headed families managed to get on work relief while the ban was in effect by having household members who were U.S. citizens certified as secondary workers, by enrolling their citizen children in the CCC, or because they lived in communities that chose to develop alternate local public works programs. And if they couldn't get work relief, they usually could get on direct relief. Citizenship barriers in WPA employment proved to be a far bigger problem for Mexicans than for European immigrants.

The regional segregation of each group combined with local control over the administration of work relief allowed for much of the different treatment of Mexicans, blacks, and European immigrants. Encouraged by agricultural interests alarmed that relatively generous federal relief was reducing their labor supply, southern and southwestern relief officials defied federal non-discrimination orders and often excluded blacks and Mexicans from direct relief and public works jobs. Though most American residents disapproved of extending relief to aliens, European immigrants were gaining greater political power, often living in cities where work relief jobs were distributed to them as political patronage. And they could also still count on the support of local and federal relief officials who remained adamantly opposed to citizenship restrictions. Despite persistent discrimination in access to direct relief and public works by local authorities especially in the South and Southwest, the advent of federally financed relief significantly increased African Americans' and Mexican Americans' access to means-tested assistance. As we will see in the next chapter, however, they would not be as lucky with social insurance.

CHAPTER 10

A New Deal for the Alien

WHEN FDR SIGNED THE SOCIAL SECURITY ACT ON AUGUST 14, 1935, he told the nation that "Today a hope of many years' standing is in large part fulfilled."

> This social security measure gives at least some protection to thirty millions of our *citizens*. . . . We can never insure one hundred percent of the population against one hundred percent of the hazards and vicissitudes of life, but we have tried to frame a law which will give some measure of protection to the *average citizen* and to his family against the loss of a job and against poverty-ridden old age. (italics added)

Though framed as legislation that would help the "average citizen," scholars have shown that the Social Security Act in fact excluded the vast majority of blacks from the most generous social insurance programs, relegating them to meager, decentralized, and demeaning means-tested programs. "From a Negro's point of view," noted an NAACP official, the Social Security legislation looked "like a sieve with the holes just big enough for the majority of Negroes to fall through." Scholars have identified two primary limitations of the Social Security legislation that put blacks at a disadvantage. Occupational exclusions—barring agricultural and domestic workers—disqualified large numbers of blacks from social insurance programs, including Social Security and Unemployment Insurance, forcing them to rely disproportionately on means-tested categorical assistance programs such as Aid to Dependent Children (ADC) and Old Age Assistance (OAA). What is more, the federal government failed to provide adequate safeguards to protect minorities in these programs, agreeing to accede to southern demands to jettison language mandating that benefit levels provide at minimum "a reasonable subsistence compatible with decency and health." Consequently, these means-tested programs were susceptible to the same forces that limited the access of blacks in other locally administered relief programs, including planter pressure, racism, and white domination of the political system.[1]

While many excellent studies have detailed the disparate effects of the Social Security Act on blacks and whites, little has been written about how it treated European immigrants or Mexicans. Occupational exclusions barred most Mexicans, like blacks, from the benefits of social insurance, forcing them to rely disproportionately on means-tested programs. Though southern and southwestern congressmen shared an interest in this sort of arrangement, it was southerners who were in a position to do something about it. Widespread black disenfranchisement and one-party rule in the South allowed southern whites to reelect racially conservative Democrats to Congress and thereby gain leadership positions in the congressional committees that oversaw the passage of the legislation. While many Mexicans were disenfranchised, too, there was more political competition in the Southwest. As a result, southwestern congressmen did not amass the same sort of political power at the national level. Federal officials deserve some of the blame for black and Mexican exclusion, too, however. Some expressed concern over the technical difficulties of including agricultural and domestic workers in social insurance programs, and certainly no one in the administration was willing to endanger the passage of the Social Security Act to solve "the race problem."

European immigrants, by contrast, benefited from many of the provisions of the Social Security Act, and in at least some respects, they benefited more than even native-born whites. European immigrants were more likely than native-born whites to work in manufacturing and other occupations covered by social insurance. They were also more likely to be nearing the age of sixty-five when Social Security was first established. Since the benefits formula was structured to grandfather in those at the cusp of retirement when the act passed, European immigrants ended up contributing little to the system but benefited almost as much as those who would contribute their whole working lives. For foreign-born whites, then, Social Security functioned more like a highly redistributive relief program but without the means test and without the stigma.

Ironically, while it excluded many American racial minorities from its most generous benefits, the Social Security Act extended social insurance benefits without regard to citizenship or even legal status. It could have turned out differently, however. Most competing proposals—including the famed Townsend Plan—barred aliens. And the same year that Congress barred non-citizens from the WPA, they tried—and failed—to bar them from Social Security. Though federal law did not prohibit aliens from receiving means-tested assistance, states were allowed to adopt citizenship requirements for these programs—a concession that federal officials made to stave off federal restriction. Few states chose to require citizenship for ADC but most required it for OAA. But citizenship requirements in OAA were generally short-lived, especially in the North. In the Southwest, however, states were far more reluctant to abandon such requirements.

Why didn't citizenship, like race, become a key boundary of social citizenship? There was far less organized support for alien exclusion. Nativism, though powerful, was not embedded in the political economy of the

North as racism was in the South and Southwest. In fact, there were many forces—immigrant advocates, social workers, politicians, and federal officials alike—working to ensure that non-citizens would benefit from the federal legislation. The net result of these policies was that blacks were disproportionately shunted into categorical assistance programs with low benefit levels, European immigrants were disproportionately covered under social insurance regardless of citizenship, and Mexicans were often shut out altogether.

The Social Security Act

In the first New Deal, FDR's administration was concerned with providing immediate relief for the jobless and those who were unemployable. For the second New Deal, they turned their sights on long-term economic security. The Social Security Act of 1935, which became the backbone of our modern welfare state, created two tiers of social assistance. Social insurance programs, including Social Security—often called Old Age Insurance—and Unemployment Insurance, were created to insure workers against the hazards of unemployment and old age. Means-tested public assistance programs, including Aid to the Blind, Aid to Dependent Children, and Old Age Assistance, were for those deemed unemployable.

Social insurance programs did not cover all workers, however. Occupational exclusions built into the act greatly limited the reach of these programs in the early years of their existence. The exclusion of workers from Old Age Insurance (OAI) took two primary forms. First, some workers were excluded because they worked in particular occupations or industries, like agriculture, domestic service, railroads, shipping, nonprofit organizations, and government. Second, workers who were self-employed were excluded regardless of occupation or industry. Similar exclusions applied to Unemployment Insurance. Overall, 56 percent of all workers in 1930 worked in what would soon become "covered employment." But rates of coverage varied significantly across groups. Blacks (38 percent) and Mexicans (39 percent) were least likely to work in covered employment while European immigrants (67 percent), especially southern and eastern Europeans (71 percent), were most likely to be covered. Native-born whites (57 percent) fell somewhere in between. While whites certainly benefited more than blacks as a result of these occupational exclusions, these data reveal that the real winners of this social insurance legislation were *foreign-born* whites, especially southern and eastern Europeans. Since Social Security was open from the start to non-citizens—including those who entered the country illegally—even recent immigrants who had failed to naturalize would have access to this more generous program. If the 1935 Social Security Act functioned like a sieve with the holes just big enough for the majority of blacks and Mexicans to fall through, it nonetheless managed to catch the vast majority of European immigrants.[2]

The Logic of Exclusion

Why did Congress create this sieve? Why were agricultural and domestic workers—and thus a large proportion of blacks and Mexicans—excluded from Social Security and Unemployment Insurance? And, then, why did Congress further imperil access by acceding to state demands for local control in the administration of means-tested benefits without federal standards?[3]

When the administration was devising its social insurance legislation, it looked to the practices of other countries for guidance. Most other countries against which the United States compared itself excluded agricultural and domestic workers when they first implemented their social insurance programs. The logic was that it was too administratively burdensome to collect contributions from persons who were "irregularly employed, from agricultural laborers, from those who are their own employers," and others. But there was division in the five-member Committee on Economic Security (CES)—formed to give the president and Congress recommendations for Social Security legislation—about whether to follow "precedent in excluding agricultural and domestic workers on administrative and actuarial grounds" or work toward the president's goal of getting "as close to universal coverage . . . as was legislatively possible." While Perkins and Hopkins were in favor of universal coverage, Treasury Secretary Henry Morgenthau became convinced that these technical difficulties were significant, and he urged the House Ways and Means Committee to exclude agricultural and domestic workers. Edwin Witte, the CES director, recalled that in agreeing with Morgenthau, however, the Ways and Means Committee—run by southerners—"was influenced far less by the difficulties of administration than by the fact that it was felt that the farmers would object to being taxed for old age insurance protection for their employees," since agricultural and domestic workers were "customarily excluded in this country from all types of laws regulating employment conditions." Had Morgenthau not suggested exclusion, it is quite likely that southerners would have insisted on it given their stand on related issues.[4]

Indeed, the decision to jettison language mandating that welfare benefit levels provide at minimum "a reasonable subsistence compatible with decency and health" was based largely on concerns of the southerners on these committees, who feared such protections might disturb the South's system of race and farm-labor relations. Paul Douglas, a University of Chicago economics professor who testified in Congress on social insurance legislation, argued that southern legislators pushed to drop the "decency and health" provision at least in part because they feared that it might be "used by authorities in Washington to compel Southern states to pay higher pensions to aged Negroes than the dominant white groups believed to be desirable." Virginia senator Harry Byrd led the effort to eliminate the health and decency provision from OAA. Byrd, "supported by nearly all of the southern members of both committees," complained that the bill vested too much power in the federal government to dictate state affairs. Director Witte agreed with Douglas, saying that "The southern members did not want to give authority to anyone in Washington to deny aid to any state because it discriminated against Negroes in the administration of old age assistance." Witte offered further that "it had never occurred" to the CES "that the Negro question would come up in this connection." But it soon became "apparent that the bill could not be passed as it stood and that it would be necessary to tone down all clauses relating to supervisory control by the federal government." Even after the Social Security Act had safely passed, federal officials continued to fear that southerners would "kill" the act because they believed blacks were benefiting too much from the legislation. Blacks, however, were not the only group targeted for exclusion. "In fairness to the south," noted Douglas, "it should be added that there were Congressmen from [other] sections of the country where there were unpopular racial or cultural minorities who wanted to have their states left more or less free to treat them as they wished." Unfortunately, Douglas did not elaborate on exactly which sections of the country he was referring to. The Senate Finance Committee and the House Ways and Means Committee were the two bodies that most directly influenced the structure of the Social Security legislation, and both were chaired by southern Democrats. Both committees also included Texans (Rep. Morgan Sanders [D-TX] and Sen. Tom Connally [D-TX]), and the House Committee included Frank Buck, a "Bourbon" Democrat from Vacaville, California. Buck was a lawyer but also a large fruit grower who had had run-ins with his Mexican and Filipino workers over wages and who, by all accounts, did what he could to represent the interests of California farmers in Washington. And certainly by 1935, growers in California no longer wanted migrant laborers to have access to any form of relief. Buck's influence over the shape of the Social Security Act, beyond giving the act its name, is not entirely clear. Nevertheless, because of their control of key congressional committees—the legacy of the one-party system in the South—it was Southern legislators who were in the best position to help shape legislation that would be in line with their interests.[5]

While powerful interests were working behind the scene to exclude blacks and other minorities from federal protection, there were only a few individuals or groups who were working actively for their inclusion or protection. While the bill was still in committee, black leaders in the NAACP and the Urban League lobbied the administration hard to include agricultural and domestic workers. One editorial in the NAACP's journal *The Crisis*, bluntly titled "Social Security—for White Folk," expressed the frustration of many blacks.

> Just as Mr. Roosevelt threw the Negro textile workers to the wolves . . . so he and his advisers are preparing to dump overboard the majority of Negro workers in this [Social] security legislation program by exempting from pensions and job insurance all farmers, domestics and casual labor. . . . It may be a bitter pill for trusting Negroes to swallow . . . but they ought to realize by now that the powers-that-be in the Roosevelt administration have nothing for them.[6]

Mexican American leaders did not testify before Congress on the exclusion of agricultural or domestic workers, but Senator Dennis Chávez (D-NM), who was a member of the League of United Latin American Citizens and the only Spanish-speaking senator, lobbied for their inclusion. But neither blacks nor Mexicans had enough political power to have their interests or needs met.[7]

Interestingly, public opinion data from the period actually show wide support, even in the South and Southwest, for the inclusion of agricultural and domestic workers in social insurance legislation. Nearly three-quarters of American residents in 1937 and 1939 agreed that Social Security should cover household help, farmhands, and sailors. What is more, some non-elite southern whites believed that any proposals that made blacks exceptionally vulnerable also undermined their own economic interests. The Old Age Pension Society in Biloxi wrote to the Ways and Means Committee, urging them not to give the states too much power in the administration of OAA, fearful that certain southern employers would "make a howling farce of security legislation, and by doing that could keep a plenty of cheap labor on hand, and in hand. . . . No white man will be paid a decent wage while there is cheap colored labor," they explained. Instead, the society advocated the passage of a competing measure because "it gives control and administration to Federal Departments."[8]

It did not help matters, however, that "the most active private advocate of social insurance," Abraham Epstein, who was the executive secretary of the American Association for Social Security, had essentially told federal officials "that the inclusion of [agricultural and domestic workers] might endanger the long-term prospects of the entire social security program." Indeed, one NAACP leader recounted that Epstein "said frankly that he was interested, first, in social insurance and that he did not see how we can solve the Negro problem through social insurance; in other words, there are realities existing with respect to Negroes and whites in this country which no program of social insurance can undertake to correct."[9]

Ultimately, the efforts of black leaders came to naught. FDR's administration was racially conservative and "acutely sensitive to the political context of the times." It was never the administration's intent to use federal welfare programs to fundamentally alter race relations. Neither blacks nor Mexicans had much political power, nor did they have many advocates working on their behalf who did. According to Weiss, federal officials were simply not interested in expending much political capital to solve the "race problem."

> What they *were* interested in was "securing old age legislation and . . . antagonizing as few persons in the process as possible." Social security itself was sufficiently controversial; its proponents had no interest in further complicating the delicate effort to win support for the program by adding provisions certain to raise southern hackles. . . . No wonder, then, that proponents of the legislation shied away from explicit protections for blacks that seemed certain to sabotage the entire program.

The failure of the Social Security legislation to fully incorporate blacks and Mexicans and protect them from discrimination in the implementation of the program can be attributed perhaps as much to the lack of will among federal officials as to the direct influence of southern and southwestern legislators.[10]

Aliens and Social Insurance

While the Social Security Act excluded agricultural and domestic laborers from social insurance programs, it did not exclude aliens. Social Security and Unemployment Insurance were open from the start to non-citizens. No Gallup polls during this period asked American residents whether aliens should receive Social Security or Unemployment Insurance, but given the widespread nativism, it seems safe to assume that many would have been opposed to it. After all, the vast majority of American residents did not support the extension of relief to non-citizens, most believed that all aliens on relief should be deported, and many were opposed to having alien coworkers. Letters poured into Washington, complaining not only of aliens on relief but worse, aliens who were employed when so many citizens went without.[11]

To be sure, a few people wrote to federal officials in support of aliens' access to Social Security legislation. An Italian American whose father was not a citizen because he did not speak English wrote to his congressional representative, asking if a foreigner like his father, who "bred three natural born citizens" and who toiled in this country for forty-seven years, would be provided for in his old age under the terms of the legislation then under debate. But if we can infer from the evidence still in the archives, these sorts of letters were few and far between. More common were letters that called on federal officials to bar aliens from the benefits of the Social Security Act. A woman from White Plains, New York, worried that aliens would start flooding the country in order to benefit from the new legislation. She asked that a clause be added to the old age pension bill "that would provide a definite length of time, such as forty years, for an applicant to have been a naturalized citizen of the United State [*sic*], before they could be eligible to obtain said pension." One union member argued that only native-born or naturalized citizens should be eligible for pensions, and foreigners who immigrated "to the United States after the Federal Old Age Pension is enacted into law," and who were over thirty-five at the time of arrival, should be permanently barred from the pension. Congressman William Brunner (D-NY) forwarded a letter from one of his constituents, which was "similar to hundreds of letters I have been receiving in connection with the Social Security and Old Age ension Bill." His constituent demanded that no pensions be extended to individuals who had not seen fit to have become naturalized "prior to 1930." When Frances Perkins spoke to a slightly hostile audience of women at an Episcopal church in New York City in the spring of 1935, one woman demanded to know whether "the social security program would benefit aliens who lingered here 'when they ought to be deported.'" She would certainly have been unsatisfied with Perkins's response.[12]

Indeed, despite such nativism, Perkins and Hopkins had been working tirelessly to ensure that aliens would be included in social welfare programs. And they were "the two most active members" on the five-member executive committee. Though no record of the CES's discussion on this matter appears to have survived, we do know the issue of non-citizens was on their minds. To come up with recommendations, Witte had his staff investigate the practices of other nations. They found that most countries provided social insurance benefits to citizens and aliens alike. Equal treatment of foreign nationals in contributory social insurance programs had become an international norm in recent years. In addition, virtually all of the competing proposals to the Social Security Act, including the principal alternative old age insurance bill—the Townsend Plan—specifically excluded aliens. The CES estimated that half a million elderly non-citizens would not receive a pension should the Townsend Plan pass instead. Such a prospect even stirred a rush on the naturalization office, as non-citizens lined up for their first papers to ensure they would not be left out. Ultimately neither the bill that the administration sent to Congress nor the text of the 1935 Social Security Act specifically included or excluded aliens from the benefits of Social Security and Unemployment Insurance. But the Ways and Means report on the legislation clarified that this silence meant that "Services performed by aliens, whether resident or nonresident, within the United States are included; but services performed outside the United States, whether by a citizen or an alien, are not included." Despite the clarification, many people remained confused about whether aliens were eligible for social insurance. As a result, the Social Security Board (SSB) had to repeatedly assure noncitizens that they would be eligible for social insurance on the same basis as citizens.[13]

To further clarify that these benefits would be made available to noncitizens (and specifically alien seamen employed on an American vessel), the SSB proposed an amendment to the Social Security Act in 1939, specifying that neither the employee nor the employer need have U.S. citizenship for a worker to be covered under the act. The amendment would specifically define employment to mean "any service, of whatever nature, performed . . . by an employee for the person employing him, irrespective of the citizenship or residence of either, (A) within the United States, or (B) on or in connection with an American vessel." Opposition to this amendment came from many of the same legislators who opposed extending work relief to aliens. Frank Carlson (R-KS) offered an amendment in the House to strike the words "irrespective of citizenship" from the bill: "As long as we have millions of American citizens who are not under the old-age insurance provision and receiving the protection of this Government, I for one will absolutely not stand on this floor and permit this bill to go through without my vote being cast against it." His colleagues pointed out, however, that non-citizens were already covered under social insurance legislation and that the new language would only add alien seamen. Carlson's amendment was therefore rejected. The following month, however, Robert Reynolds (D-NC) offered an amendment in the Senate to exclude aliens from all of the Social Security Act's provisions. "I think the time has arrived when we should pay more attention to our own people and quit worrying about the citizens of other countries of the world," argued Reynolds. "I do not see why American taxpayers should support citizens of other countries." Offering that he would be happy to "help people in Europe and every other continent" after he had provided for the millions of jobless Americans, Reynolds added, "I am for the American citizens first, and then for the 'furriner' second."[14]

The details of the Reynolds amendment were somewhat complicated. He suggested that the government would continue to collect wage contributions of alien workers toward Social Security and Unemployment Insurance and then return to aliens their contributions without giving them any additional federal or state benefits from the programs. The employer's contribution toward alien workers would not be returned to employers, however, but kept as a "special privilege tax." The tax would ensure that the cost of hiring aliens and citizens remained equivalent so as not to give employers incentives to hire aliens over citizens. Senator David Walsh (D-MA) was "sympathetic" toward Reynolds's idea, noting that his first "impulse is to be for it." "But it is far reaching and important," he added, and he suggested they adjourn and consider it again in the morning. "I personally do not feel like going on record without an opportunity to study it . . . I do not know how many people it would affect; I do not know what distress it might cause; I do not know how far reaching it would be." The chairman of the Finance Committee, Senator Byron "Pat" Harrison (D-MS), had been informed by the SSB that excluding aliens would create administrative difficulties, but he suggested the whole thing go to conference committee where they could better sort out the details. Much of the short discussion revolved around the administrative burdens and the possible international implications, since the finance committee was unsure whether the United States was a party to any international treaties on the matter. There was no passionate defense of the alien in Congress as there had been in years past. A slightly modified version of the Reynolds amendment passed by a voice vote, and the Social Security bill, as amended, passed the Senate 57 to 8 with thirty-one members abstaining.[15]

Shortly after Reynolds offered his amendment, the *New York Times* ran an editorial against the proposal, describing it as "bigoted" and "malicious." The National Emergency Conference, an organization concerned about the rash of anti-alien legislation proposed since the outbreak of war in Europe, opined that the Reynolds amendment amounted to a tax on the employment of aliens and called it "fascist in conception and content." A member of the Roland German-American Democratic Society wrote a letter to the editor arguing that to "persecute" aliens as the Reynolds amendment would do "would mean to make them the non-Aryans of the United States," suggesting that to discriminate against aliens was tantamount to racializing them. Similarly, writing on behalf of the American Association for Social Security, Abraham Epstein, himself a naturalized Russian immigrant, denounced that portion of the bill. "We are bitterly opposed to this amendment because it is contrary to all established social policy, is inhuman and vicious as well as most uneconomical," wrote Epstein. "The amendment goes counter to our historically established national policy and seeks to inaugurate a new cleavage in our midst which will only bring about new hates. It seeks to discriminate against beings at a time of their greatest need, not because of any crime they committed, but because they have been unable, for one reason or another, to comply with certain required forms." Since communities, according to Epstein, would not allow any person—whether alien or citizen—to starve, denying non-citizens the benefits of Social Security and Unemployment Insurance would simply shift the burden to the taxpayers. Epstein reminded readers that states could choose whether to bar aliens from categorical assistance programs and he implored: "Why not let the States continue to determine what is wise for them? In the name of justice and elementary decency the Reynolds amendment should be eliminated."[16]

Contrasting Epstein's views on the exclusion of blacks with his views on the inclusion of aliens in social insurance is instructive. He was opposed to including agricultural and domestic workers in social insurance because he thought the administrative difficulties of inclusion were too large. But he and other old age security advocates were also not interested in solving "the race problem" through social insurance. Gareth Davies and Martha Derthick argue that Epstein was "scarcely an exemplar of southern racism." And indeed Epstein did lament the fact that blacks would not only fail to benefit from social insurance legislation because of the occupation exclusions but would be forced to pay for it, since employers would simply pass their portion of the tax onto their consumers through higher prices. But solving the race problem was not high on his agenda either. And it may very well have been an impossible fight given the power of southern Democrats in Congress. Discrimination against aliens, however, was another matter as Epstein saw no benefit to inaugurating *new* cleavages, nor did he see any administrative need for their exclusion. Nativism was strong indeed, but the issue was also more tractable because it was not deeply embedded in the political economy of the North. Industrial employers were not lobbying for alien exclusion. And northern politicians were not leading the charge for citizenship restrictions either.[17]

Ultimately the Reynolds amendment was eliminated in conference committee. There is no surviving record of the committee's deliberations on this point. In its newsletter, the American Association for Social Security counted the "bigoted" amendment's defeat as "one of the most encouraging achievements of the Association. . . . This amendment would have evoked great bitterness in the country and would have raised impossible administrative problems as well as endless international complications."[18]

Why did the Reynolds amendment fail in the same year that the ban on aliens in the WPA succeeded? Federal officials argued in both cases that aliens should be included and that the administrative burdens of excluding aliens were too onerous. Congressmen wanting to exclude non-citizens were, in both cases, at least initially unimpressed by the purported administrative difficulties involved in exclusion. It is possible that the administrative burdens *were* more difficult to overcome with social insurance. By allowing aliens to sign an affidavit swearing that they were American citizens, the complications involved in checking the immigration status of every WPA employee were removed. Furthermore, most countries included non-citizens in their social insurance legislation but there was far less consistency in how non-nationals were treated in means-tested programs. Finally, there may have been less public opposition to including aliens on social insurance than in WPA employment. Since the benefits of social insurance did not come from general tax revenues, social insurance may not have been perceived in stark zero-sum terms. With finite resources, a WPA job for an alien meant one less job for an American citizen. But including aliens in social insurance would not deny American citizens an opportunity for benefits.

Illegal Aliens and Social Insurance

As originally passed, the Social Security Act not only made no mention of the citizenship status of potential social insurance beneficiaries, it was also silent on their *legal status*. And for decades, Social Security officials interpreted this silence to mean that illegal immigrants were eligible for these programs. Had the SSB reported illegal immigrants who applied for Social Security numbers or who tried to collect benefits to the INS, the Social Security Act's silence on this subject would be unremarkable. But the SSB did not report such information. In fact, it took steps to ensure that immigration inspectors would not have access to information about Social Security applicants.[19]

Concerned that legal and illegal aliens were hesitant to apply for Social Security numbers, the FLIS put out a press release in 1937 to clarify the rules under which the SSB was operating. Acknowledging that aliens might see Social Security numbers as a way to register them or that the information supplied to the SSB might be used by other branches of government to "check up on the applicants," the FLIS assured its readers that this was not the case. The SSB did not collect information that could be used to track down aliens: "The application forms . . . ask only a few simple questions: name, address, date, and place of birth, color, sex, employer's name and address, and father's and mother's names. They do not ask whether the applicant is a citizen or an alien, or, if an alien, when or in what manner he or she entered the United States." More important, however, the SSB promised that whatever information they did collect would not be disclosed to anyone. "As a matter of fact," wrote the FLIS, "the Social Security Board has given assurance that the information submitted by an applicant for a Social Security account will be regarded as confidential. 'Only government employees having official responsibility in connection with the Social Security files will have access to this information.'" Even if the SSB were to allow the INS access to its records, the FLIS did not believe that the government would engage in any wholesale purging of the Social Security rolls: "To suppose that the government will investigate every applicant, or even every worker who says he was born abroad, is fantastic." The FLIS suggested, in fact, that it would appear more suspicious if illegal aliens refrained from applying for a Social Security number: "his failure to make application is more likely than not to call attention to himself and to raise questions as to why he seeks to evade the law providing for his own social security." Perhaps to ensure that aliens would feel more comfortable filing for Social Security numbers, the FLIS encouraged aliens to file under the name "by which the applicant is known on the payroll of his employer. For record identification purposes, it does not matter whether this is the alien's true name, or a name assumed since arrival in America." Being able to file under their "American" name was critical because it decreased the likelihood the INS would use the information in the Social Security files if it were ever granted such permission.[20]

There were instances in which the INS did request such permission. In 1937 a post office in Minneapolis, working on behalf of an immigration inspector, requested "certain information from the files furnished the Social Security Board." Because the SSB regarded the information they collected on their applicants as confidential, they had previously rejected requests for such information. Perkins, who as secretary of labor oversaw the INS, did not protest the decision, noting that "it is not the intention of the Department of Labor to make any applications for information which are contrary to this well established [confidentiality] policy." She then instructed immigration field officers to "refrain from requesting information from the Social Security Board for immigration, naturalization or other purposes." The federal government was sending a clear message that illegal aliens need not worry about applying for social insurance benefits.[21]

The net effect of the social insurance legislation was that most European immigrants—even those not authorized to live and work in the United States—were extended the security and benefits of social insurance, while most blacks and Mexicans were denied these benefits. It is not clear whether anyone made this explicit connection at the time the legislation passed. CES members certainly understood how occupational exclusions would have affected blacks, Mexicans, and European immigrants. But the Social Security Act was hastily conceived and it is at least possible that CES members did not have time to think through all of its implications. If they knew when they crafted the legislation, they certainly did not say so. Given the tenor of the times, the fact that many immigrants—some of whom had yet to become citizens—would benefit disproportionately from some of the most generous provisions of the Social Security Act would not have been something federal officials wanted to advertise.[22]

Aliens and Categorical Assistance

Unlike Social Security, categorical assistance programs like Aid to Dependent Children and Old Age Assistance were funded by a mixture of state and federal funds. Partly because of this joint funding, the authors of the Social Security Act gave states leeway in designing their public assistance plans. Before the Social Security Act was passed, states with old age pension programs in place not only limited their benefits to U.S. citizens, they also required recipients to have been U.S. citizens for at least fifteen years. The Social Security Act, however, stipulated that means-tested programs could not be denied to any otherwise eligible individual who was a U.S. citizen. In order to receive federal matching funds, most states had to amend their laws to take out provisions disqualifying recently naturalized citizens. The Social Security Act thus represented a liberalization of existing state laws. But the law did not go so far as to mandate that states cover non-citizens.[23]

Allowing states to exclude aliens from means-tested assistance did not reflect federal officials' belief that aliens *should* be excluded. Instead, CES members were simply realistic about the strength of anti-immigrant sentiment. Witte feared that "there is some possibility" that the Senate would amend the Social Security bill to preclude states from covering aliens in OAA: "The federal bill is being attacked because under its provisions aliens may be granted pensions by the states, and I anticipate that at least an attempt will be made to limit the federal aid to cases where pensions are granted to citizens. If an amendment to this effect is offered, I expect it will be adopted." Instead of forcing states to cover non-citizens, federal officials tried to convince states to pass more lenient provisions. When writing up model state legislation or reviewing state plans, federal officials reminded states that they did not have to bar aliens from means-tested programs, at times suggesting alternative residency provisions instead. And federal officials repeatedly called on states to extend means-tested benefits to non-citizens.[24]

Given that nativism was so strong, the FLIS was not sanguine that states would include aliens in their welfare programs. However, most states refrained from adopting citizenship restrictions on all of their categorical assistance programs and quickly dropped whatever citizenship requirements they had adopted. Few states, for example, ever adopted citizenship requirements for ADC, which was the successor to the Mothers' Pension programs. It provided funds to states on a matching basis (66 percent state, 33 percent federal, increased to 50/50 in 1939) for needy and dependent children. By 1940 only Connecticut, the District of Columbia, Illinois, Mississippi, and Texas had some sort of citizenship requirement for such children. Illinois had not yet passed ADC, so its citizenship requirement was part of its old Mothers' Pension plan. Noting the hardships involved in such discrimination, social workers there were "urging the passage of a new aid-to-dependent-children law in which the elimination of the citizenship requirement will be one of the benefits." In the meantime, the IPL called on social workers to help non-citizens naturalize. When the ADC program became effective in Illinois in 1941, the citizenship requirement was lifted.[25]

Though humanitarian concerns were often weighed in these decisions, cost considerations also played a role. Allowing aliens into ADC programs was probably not very costly for most states. By the time the Social Security Act was implemented, very few children in the United States were foreign born, and even fewer were aliens. While 5 percent of female-headed households in 1940 were headed by a non-citizen, only 4 percent of these households had children who were aliens. But even if there had been more non-citizens eligible for ADC, providing it was financially advantageous in most states since these children would generally be covered by General Assistance (GA) if they were not qualified for ADC, and GA was entirely funded by state and local funds. Children on ADC often received less assistance than the average individual on GA. And in all but one state (Missouri) the state contribution for ADC payments, even at the 66 percent rate, would be less than what it would probably have provided under GA. Once the federal government agreed to pay up to half of ADC payments in 1939, the financial incentives to cover aliens increased. Confirming that financial considerations were important, Abraham Epstein noted in 1939 that practically all states had removed citizenship requirements from their Mothers' Pension or ADC laws "because it was found more economical as well as more just to provide for these needy children under the dependent children's allowances." By 1947 Texas was the only state that still required citizenship for ADC. The SSB urged Texas to drop the requirement, but Texas was unique in that its eligibility criteria for public assistance were written into the state constitution. The only way to alter eligibility criteria was therefore to amend the constitution, which required a public vote. In 1951 Texans were asked to vote on an amendment that would have dropped citizenship requirements for their means-tested programs but the amendment failed. In fact, Texas only dropped its citizenship requirement in 1971 when the Supreme Court found such state restrictions to be unconstitutional.[26]

While states were generally quick to provide ADC benefits to alien children or their alien parents, they were initially more hesitant to extend OAA to aged aliens. The stakes with OAA were higher because the program was bigger. In 1947 over two million needy elderly individuals received OAA compared to just over one million children on ADC. OAA also had a larger potential pool of alien recipients than ADC. The curtailment of immigration in the 1920s left a rapidly aging alien population with few sources of replenishment. By 1940 nearly 13 percent of aliens were sixty-five years and older, compared to only 7 percent of all U.S. citizens. The financial incentives to cover aged aliens on OAA instead of General Assistance, however, were even greater than in the case of ADC. While the federal government only covered a third of ADC payments before 1939, it covered half of OAA benefits from the start. Most states covered indigent elderly aliens on GA, so it would have been fiscally prudent to move them to OAA. Indeed, because of the federal matching, in fifteen out of the nineteen states reporting data in 1940 it would have been cheaper to carry an aged alien on OAA than on GA.[27]

A number of factors appear to have caused states to adopt citizenship requirements for OAA despite the potential savings. OAA benefits were quite generous, and even though the benefits were means tested, many chose to think of the program early on as a pension—or something earned—and not as welfare. While children could less easily be blamed for their parents' failure to naturalize, many people wondered why immigrants failed to declare allegiance to the country that had been their home for so many years. In addition, aliens had generally been excluded from the state-run Old Age Pension programs prior to the second New Deal. Therefore, when states were required to amend their OAA plans to comply with the Social Security Act they would have had to drop a citizenship requirement that was already in place. (Since relatively few states had had citizenship requirements for Mothers' Pensions, they would have had to add such a provision.) With anti-alien sentiment so high in the late 1930s, it was politically difficult to drop a citizenship requirement, even if it would save taxpayer money.[28]

By 1939, then, twenty-five states plus the District of Columbia had citizenship requirements for OAA. In addition, six states had alternate requirements, usually a durational residence requirement (ten to twenty-five years) for aliens only (see Figure 10.1). All told nearly 77 percent of elderly aliens lived in a state with a strict citizenship requirement for OAA in 1939, and only 20 percent lived in a state with no requirement whatsoever. Fairly quickly, however, many states dropped these citizenship requirements. Within ten years, only fifteen states still had flat restrictions. In six additional states, long-term residency could be substituted for the citizenship requirement (see Figure 10.2). Consequently, only 40 percent of elderly aliens were still affected by strict restrictions by 1948.[29]

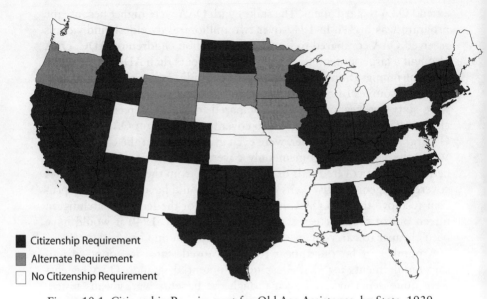

Figure 10.1: Citizenship Requirement for Old Age Assistance, by State, 1939

Source: Hugh Carter and Bernice Doster, "The Foreign-Born Population and Old-Age Assistance," INS Monthly Review 7, no. 6 (1949): 75.

Why did states drop their citizenship requirements? For one, social workers, relief officials, immigrant advocacy organizations, and immigrant groups lobbied their state legislators to eliminate the exclusion. Abraham Epstein worked for ten years with a variety of organizations serving the foreign born and eventually with the State Aid Charities Organization to eliminate citizenship requirements for New York's OAA program. Immigrant advocates in New York estimated that approximately ten thousand elderly aliens were being denied pensions for which they might otherwise be eligible. As early as 1941, a bill eliminating the citizenship requirement made it through the Republican-controlled legislature by "overwhelming majorities" only to be vetoed by Governor Lehman (D), who maintained that the legislature had not voted additional appropriations to cover the costs of implementing the law. While Lehman acknowledged that many of the aliens that would be covered under OAA would come from the GA rolls, he was not convinced that federal contributions would completely cover the additional costs. But two years later, Governor Thomas Dewey, a liberal Republican, signed a bill allowing aliens access to OAA, acknowledging that the legislation would lighten the tax burden on New Yorkers. Describing it as a "most worthwhile extension," he said "this change in the law will . . . cost the

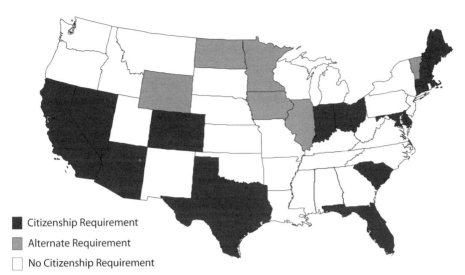

Figure 10.2: Citizenship Requirement for Old Age Assistance, by State, 1948

Source: Hugh Carter and Bernice Doster, "The Foreign-Born Population and Old-Age Assistance," *INS Monthly Review* 7, no. 6 (1949): 75.

State less than if the change were not made." "Public charges or persons in dire need," he explained, "are entitled to the care of the community, whether they be citizens or aliens." Similarly, when Chicago's welfare commissioner urged, in 1945, that the state OAA law be amended to include aliens, he explained that the "Removal of the citizenship requirement would admit 1,500 Chicagoans to old age pensions who must now be cared for through general relief," a move that would result in $360,000 a year in local and state savings. While there was little mention that dropping citizenship restrictions on elderly aliens might please their citizen children, the political power of second-generation whites no doubt played an important role.[30]

Not all states dropped their citizenship restrictions for OAA, however. Southwestern states proved especially stubborn in this regard. Only New Mexico had no citizenship requirement in 1948. As a result, 91 percent of elderly Mexican aliens lived in states with strict citizenship restrictions in 1948 compared to just 36 percent of white aliens. Why were southwestern states more reluctant to abandon citizenship restrictions? Reformer Joanna Colcord suggested that OAA programs were "powerfully wrought upon by the pioneer philosophy of the West. . . . To have survived to the age of sixty-five in these far west communities means that the applicant presumably has participated in the upbuilding of the

268 • Chapter 10

region from its early days. Far from regretting the necessity of accepting public assistance, the applicant and his friends, if he is denied this accolade of pioneership, demand belligerently to know what's wrong with his record." This philosophy may help explain why OAA benefit levels were especially high in the West. While the national average benefit level for OAA in 1947 was $37, the average benefit level was $48 in Arizona, $57 in California, and $85 in Colorado—the highest, by far, of any state in the nation. However, western residents rarely acknowledged that Mexicans had "participated in the upbuilding of the region." "It must be said," Colcord added, "that the term 'pioneers' is reserved for the dominant race. There was a great to-do in the Arizona papers when the first OAA grant was made to a Mexican." In fact, in contrast to the South, which typically had uniformly low benefit levels, whether for OAA or GA, many southwestern states had a stratified benefits system, with high benefits for OAA, from which most Mexicans were excluded, and low benefits for GA, upon which they were forced to rely. And because OAA benefits were so high and GA benefits so low in these states, the fiscal incentives to drop the citizenship requirements were smaller.[31]

Without much political power, Mexicans faced an uphill battle in trying to get state laws in the Southwest amended. It was not until 1961, in fact, that California finally dropped its citizenship requirement for OAA, after more than eight years of organizing and lobbying by a Mexican American group called the Community Service Organization (CSO). According to the historian Mark Brilliant, recognizing that "the Mexican-American population of California" was "the largest, least civically active, least organized minority in the region," the CSO undertook a massive voter registration and mobilization campaign, which registered 92,000 voters of Mexican descent between 1949 and 1954 alone. By 1960 the organization claimed to have assisted 40,000 Mexican nationals to naturalize. The CSO launched a letter-writing campaign and in 1961 "dispatched Dolores Huerta to Sacramento . . . 'the first time in the history of California the Spanish-speaking community had one of their own as a full-time legislative advocate at the State Capitol working towards the solution of their problems.'" Ending the bar on aliens in OAA was her main objective in 1961.[32]

By 1961 California social workers, as a group, were also no longer the champions of Mexican exclusion that they once had been. In fact, by the late 1930s, California relief providers had already begun to split on the issue of relief to aliens. In 1937 the Los Angeles County Chapter of the American Association of Social Workers formally protested the restrictions on aliens in the WPA. And in 1939 the California Conference of Social Work passed a resolution against proposed legislation to bar aliens from state relief and lobbied the governor to veto the measure.

Certainly not all social workers in the state believed aliens deserved relief. In 1940 the Legislative Committee of the State Relief Administration put out the report describing relief recipients as falling into three categories: undoubtedly deserving, doubtfully deserving, and undoubtedly not deserving groups. Aliens, they said, fell into the last category. But the split in attitudes was a noteworthy change and was likely caused by a shift in the composition of California social workers over the course of the Depression. Carey McWilliams explained that in the 1930s there was an "influx of young, idealistic, college-trained social workers" in California, "unable to find work elsewhere, whose liberal ideals clashed with those of the more traditional department old-timers and with the then-widely-held conservative notions about welfare." A rift developed between the older social workers and the younger ones. The younger social workers, "who were drawn into social work as an emergency, many of them with no thought of making a career of it at all," were more radical and believed that relief should "have standards" and be "fairly administered." In some cases, they made converts of "the more conventionally trained older social worker types" but "in some cases they aroused nothing but opposition," creating tension. When Governor Edmund "Pat" Brown (D) signed the law eliminating citizenship restrictions from OAA, the head of the California Department of Social Welfare "described the bill as 'simple justice' to the non-citizen 'long-term residents of this state who have contributed greatly to the progress and development of California during their working lives.'" A noteworthy change indeed.[33]

CONSEQUENCES OF THE SOCIAL SECURITY ACT

Benefits for the Elderly

While non-citizens were formally incorporated into social insurance programs, to what extent did they actually use them? The SSB did not collect any data on this issue, but the census did. By 1940, 36 percent of aliens had received a Social Security number compared to 39 percent of citizens, a relatively small disparity. In fact, among those in the labor force, aliens were slightly more likely than citizens (66 percent versus 62 percent, respectively) and much more likely than black Americans (41 percent) to have received a number. All in all, non-citizens appear to have been on track to take advantage of the Social Security program.[34]

Due to the ravages of the Depression, between 1930 and 1940 all racial and nativity groups experienced some decline in the fraction of members working in covered occupations, but the decline was slightly more pronounced among European immigrants, especially southern and eastern Europeans (see Table 10.1). Nonetheless, southern and eastern European

Table 10.1

Percent of Individuals in the Labor Force Covered by Social Security, by Race and Nativity

	Works in covered occupation (1930)	Works in covered occupation (1940)	Has Social Security number (1940)	Federal Old Age Insurance or Railroad Retirement funds deducted from pay (1940)*
Native-born white	57	56	64	63
Foreign-born white	67	62	67	67
SE European	71	64	69	71
NW European	62	60	63	63
Black	38	35	41	38
Mexican	39	N/A	N/A	N/A
Mexican†	40	40	58	49
2nd generation SE European	79	68	74	73
2nd generation NW European	60	56	63	64

Source: Author's calculation, 1930 and 1940 Censuses.

* 14 years of age and older with an income > $0

† Estimate of the Mexican-origin population constructed by IPUMS

workers were still more likely to work in a covered occupation in 1940 (64 percent) than native-born whites (56 percent), Mexicans (40 percent), or blacks (35 percent). They were also, therefore, more likely than others to be enrolled in the Social Security program and to have had OAI (or Railroad Retirement funds) deducted from their pay. Furthermore, second-generation southern and eastern Europeans were slightly more likely than their parents to work in these covered occupations (68 percent versus 64 percent) and to benefit from the social insurance program.[35]

The age structure of the European immigrant population was also such that most white immigrants in the labor force were in their later working years. Nearly half (48 percent) of all foreign-born whites were between the ages of forty-five and sixty-four in 1940 compared to only 17 percent of native-born whites. This is significant because those who designed the Social Security program wanted to be sure that workers who had already been in the labor force and were nearing retirement would still be able to enjoy the benefits of the Social Security program. Therefore they structured the benefit payments such that even those who had contributed to the Social Security program for only a few years would still receive the benefits at the end. Frances Perkins recalled that one of the reasons that

OAI was "an extremely complicated provision to write" was because "the necessity for providing benefits of a reasonable amount for people who were already close to the old age and retirement period was most difficult." "But," she added, "the Government of the United States is not an insurance company. And so it could be done."[36]

The way the benefit payments were structured, the rate of annuities was highest at the lowest levels of total income, and the system favored those with smaller lifetime earnings. According to Paul Douglas, this would benefit "those who are now relatively old and have only a few years remaining in which to receive wages and salaries." For workers in their later years, then, Social Security was not just an insurance program but also functioned as an assistance program akin to OAA, except without the means test. That is, all covered workers would receive the benefits regardless of need.[37]

Furthermore, when the Social Security Act was amended in 1939, the payouts, which had been set to begin in 1942, were moved up to 1940. And the formula was revised to ensure even bigger payments for workers who retired relatively soon after the act was passed. As originally designed, a covered worker with an average monthly wage of $50 and who had made contributions for five years would receive a pension of $15 per month. With the 1939 amendments, he would receive $21. If that same worker contributed for thirty years instead of five, he would receive only $5 extra per month. Clearly, then, those with only a few years left to work before retirement would gain the most. Furthermore, the 1939 amendments added "supplementary benefits to the aged wives of retired workers" and dependent children, ensuring that the dependents of covered workers would be covered by the program too.[38]

Though coverage was not extended to agricultural and domestic workers in 1939, it was extended to individuals who had reached the age of sixty-five by 1936 who were also excluded under the terms of the 1935 act. According to the director of the SSB, "This means that 750,000 people who are for the first time given protection will be the claimants, not in the distant future, but primarily in the first years of this program, during 1940 and 1941." Given the age structure of the population, this change would benefit proportionately more European immigrants than blacks, native-born whites, or Mexicans, as 18 percent of foreign-born whites were sixty-five and over in 1940 compared to just 6 percent of native-born whites, 5 percent of blacks, and 3 percent of Mexicans. Immigrant advocacy organizations were in fact counseling aged immigrants that if they were "strong enough to work six quarters (one year and a half) in some industrial job, earning as little [as] 50 dollars every three months," then they could qualify for OAI and receive benefits for the rest of their lives.[39]

The director of the SSB acknowledged that as designed, the social insurance legislation would pay relatively generous benefits to older workers who had contributed very little to the program. But he believed this was necessary because if they did not receive adequate benefits, they would have to be supported through emergency relief. For some workers at or near the age of retirement during the Depression, the social insurance program served as a redistributive program, except under the guise of a federal right. The CES, its staff, and even FDR saw it that way, understanding that by supporting newly retired workers who had yet to contribute much to OAI, the program would reduce the costs of OAA. But Witte worried at the end of 1939 that the fact that the Social Security system provided "large unearned benefits to a part of the population only" not only violated "the sense of fairness but will prove a source of great dissatisfaction with the existing law."[40]

Not all European aliens qualified for OAI, however. Those who did not work in covered occupations or were too old and feeble to work when the Social Security Act passed were left out. These folks had to seek means-tested assistance instead. The citizenship restrictions for OAA therefore would have had a tremendous impact on these people. Data on the citizenship status of OAA recipients confirm that few aliens were able to make use of the program. More than half a million recipients were added to the OAA rolls during 1937–38. Of these, only 3 percent were aliens even though aliens represented 5 percent of the total elderly population. The vast majority of aliens on OAA in fact came from just three states: Michigan, Pennsylvania, and Washington. Michigan never had a citizenship requirement for OAA, and Pennsylvania and Washington each removed their citizenship requirements in 1937.[41]

In most states, elderly aliens who were excluded from OAA and did not qualify for OAI were eligible for GA. But the difference between OAA benefits and GA varied widely across communities. In New York, home to 26 percent of all elderly aliens, GA payments were only 3 percent lower than OAA benefits in 1940. But the disparity was much larger in most other states. In Illinois and New Jersey, GA benefits were roughly 25 percent lower than OAA benefits. But in some states, especially out West, including Arizona, California, and Washington, GA benefits were less than half the value of OAA benefits.[42]

How did Social Security benefits compare to OAI? When the programs first started, the average OAI grant was higher than the average OAA grant by about 10 percent. Relatively quickly, however, OAA payments outpaced OAI benefits, at least outside the South. But this happened at exactly the same time that citizenship requirements for OAA were being dropped. By 1948 when the vast majority of European non-citizens lived in states that had abandoned strict citizenship requirements (but 91 percent of Mexican aliens did not), benefit payments were 34 percent higher for OAA than what they might receive through OAI. For those who could not survive on the old age annuities alone, states could supplement the insurance benefits with means-tested assistance.[43]

Agricultural workers excluded from OAI generally made far too little to support themselves in old age and relied heavily on means-tested assistance as a result. Because most blacks were ineligible for OAI, they were overrepresented in OAA relative to their numbers in the general population. Roughly 14 percent of those accepted for OAA in 1937–38 were black, while blacks made up roughly 7 percent of aged individuals. But OAA benefit levels varied widely by state, from a high of $85 in Colorado to a low of $16 in Mississippi. Edwin Amenta and Jane Poulsen have shown that OAA benefit levels were highly correlated with political and institutional context. States with stronger restrictions on the franchise had lower benefit levels. But states with strong patronage party organizations also had lower benefits, as machines were suspicious of entitlement programs over which they had no control. Nevertheless, this sort of variation still advantaged native and foreign-born whites more than blacks, as benefit levels in southern states were almost half the benefit levels of northeastern and midwestern states ($21 versus $39 per month, respectively, in 1947). Indeed another factor that kept southern OAA benefits so low was planter pressure. In the South, therefore, OAA grants were lower in cotton than non-cotton counties. One southerner explained opposition to state funding of OAA (which she calls a pension) in a letter to the president:

> The *main* reason that the Old Age Pension fund will *never* be paid from the *state* funds is that they claim it will effect [*sic*] the labor situation. I have heard some say that they . . . strongly opposed the Old Age Pension because if they paid them, why the negroes getting them, the entire family would live off the money, and they could not get them to work for us on our farms. . . . They would be too independent if they should get a Federal old age pension.

In the South, blacks also typically received lower benefits than whites. This was the result, according to one observer, of the fact that blacks were more likely to live on farms, and farm families typically received lower benefit levels than non-farm families. But in addition to this, he added that another factor was "The general belief in the South . . . that Negroes can get along on less than whites." Because discrimination on the basis of race was prohibited, southerners found ingenious ways to give whites higher benefits. They used different criteria for determining need for blacks or stipulated that the few remaining Confederate veterans (who were almost all white) should receive the highest benefits. But in order to be sure that OAA did not disrupt their labor system, they kept OAA benefits low for all.[44]

Elderly Mexicans were often shut out altogether. Many were ineligible for OAI because of occupational exclusions, but they were also ineligible for OAA because of citizenship restrictions. By the time the Social Security Act passed, roughly half of Mexican-origin individuals over the age of sixty-five were foreign born, representing 0.3 percent of all elderly individuals in the United States. Federal data indicate that only 0.05 percent of those accepted into OAA in 1936–37 were Mexican immigrants. There are no federal data on the use of OAA among Mexicans born in the United States because federal officials no longer distinguished Mexican Americans from whites. But states sometimes continued to collect the data nonetheless. In California 2.5 percent of the elderly were of Mexican origin, but Mexicans represented only 0.5 percent of new OAA cases accepted in the first year of the program. Federal officials in San Antonio found that out of the more than four thousand persons receiving OAA in 1938, roughly 20 percent had Spanish surnames, most of whom relief officials assumed were "of Mexican extraction." Since Mexicans represented just under 40 percent of the population in the county, they concluded that "the citizenship requirement excluded many of the Mexicans, the most needy group in the city, from the rolls." Furthermore, very few Mexicans in the city benefited from OAI, and when they did their annuities were low, "usually . . . only about $10 or $12," because their work in agriculture was not covered and their "wages in covered industries" were so "very low."[45]

Benefit levels for OAA in the Southwest averaged $43, well above the $21 average for the South and even slightly higher than the average for the Northeast and Midwest ($39). But these high benefits did little for Mexicans since citizenship was a prerequisite for OAA in every southwestern state except New Mexico. Moreover, Mexicans were especially unlikely to naturalize. As a result, in California of the more than 4,700 naturalized immigrants who were accepted for OAA in the first few years of the program, more than 3,800 were European; only 19 were Mexican.[46]

In Texas—home to significant numbers of blacks and Mexicans—OAA benefit levels were fairly low ($30), but additional steps were taken to ensure that blacks and Mexicans would receive even less. Elected officials in the state feared that should either receive OAA payments that were too high, they might choose not to work. "An acrid subject of debate" in the Texas legislature was whether "$30 a month would be likely to raise the standard of living" of the state's estimated one hundred thousand elderly blacks and Mexicans "above their accustomed status. Accordingly, the Legislature provided for payments either above or below the [state] limit of $15 in order that sums could be disbursed to allow for 'customary standards of living.'" As a result, Mexican Americans in Texas got lower OAA benefits than whites, while Mexican aliens were shut out altogether by the citizenship requirements. Whites in Texas showed little concern for the plight of those left out of the safety net. It was not uncommon for white residents there to say, "Oh, well—all they need are a few tortillas and frijoles and they're satisfied." A public official in San Antonio evinced that if Mexicans "earned more than $1 a day, they'd just spend their money on tequila and on worthless trinkets in the dime stores."[47]

Benefits for Braceros

In 1942 FDR negotiated a bilateral treaty with Mexico for the temporary importation of contract laborers, and soon there were hundreds of thousands of contract workers laboring in twenty-six states, mostly as agricultural workers. These braceros were guaranteed transportation, housing, food, and repatriation. Their wages were set at the prevailing domestic rate, but not less than $0.30 per hour, and they were guaranteed work for 75 percent of the contract period. Though only temporary residents, in theory they had greater protection than the permanent agricultural labor force already in the United States. In practice, however, the work was hard, the conditions were poor, and many braceros complained of substandard housing, mistreatment, threats, and especially underpayment or illegal deductions. The "prevailing wage" that braceros were promised was often in practice whatever the growers decided to pay.[48]

Mexican braceros, however, had no formal access to American social welfare programs. One of the primary benefits of the bracero program to American communities was that it provided cheap labor to employers without the social costs that Mexican laborers were alleged to cause. Because braceros were supposed to return to Mexico after the growing season, they would not be dependent on public assistance between harvests. For growers who felt stung by the labor militancy of Mexicans during the Depression—made possible at times by the availability of relatively generous federal relief—the bracero program was a good remedy. As President Truman's Commission on Migratory Labor explained: "[Growers] want a labor supply which, on one hand, is ready and willing to meet the short-term work requirements and which, on the other hand, will not impose social and economic problems on them or on their community when the work is finished. . . . The demand for migratory workers is thus essentially twofold: To be ready to go to work when needed; to be gone when not needed."[49]

When the Mexican government negotiated the bracero contract, it insisted that Mexicans have access to a form of unemployment insurance. The contract required that braceros unemployed for more than 25 percent of the contract period—usually the length of a growing season—would be paid a subsistence wage of $3 per day. For workers who were unemployed for less than 25 percent of the contract period, "Mexican officials insisted on the payment of whatever unemployment benefits U.S. farm workers received," not realizing, apparently, that farm workers were not covered by Unemployment Insurance.[50]

As farm workers, braceros did not accumulate wage credits in the OAI system, but they were nonetheless required to participate in a forced savings plan. The U.S. government deducted 10 percent of each bracero's paycheck. The wages would be paid after braceros returned to Mexico, functioning as a mechanism to ensure braceros returned to Mexico after the termination of their contract. However, few braceros who returned ever received their money, and sixty years later some brought suit against the Mexican government and the banks involved in hopes of collecting their back wages. In 2008 a California judge held that former braceros had been cheated and were entitled to compensation amounting to $3,500 per worker.[51]

Migrant laborers who were not braceros often could not count on any assistance at all. One study of more than 300 Mexican migratory workers in Crystal City, Texas, published in 1941, showed that the median yearly cash earnings of these families, whose average family size was 6.6 members, was $350, considerably lower than the $480 the Texas Social Welfare Association had deemed necessary to sustain a family with 4.2 members "in health and decency." "Despite their very low incomes," the report said, "the people received little aid from public relief or work programs because of the limited extent to which provisions had been made in Texas . . . for assistance to needy families." Ineligible for Social Security and Unemployment Insurance because of their agricultural labor status, many were also ineligible for OAA and WPA work because of citizenship requirements. Because Texas had not yet funded any ADC or Aid to the Blind program and had no GA program, Mexicans in this south Texas community were forced to subsist on surplus commodities and whatever casual employment they could find.[52]

Benefits for Dependent Children

Mexican children had trouble accessing ADC, too. Almost 2 percent of households headed by a single mother in 1940 were Mexican, almost half of whom were non-citizens. National data on the participation of Mexican American children are lacking as the SSB classified them as white. We do know that when the program first started, only 0.07 percent of ADC children were foreign-born Mexicans. Texas was reluctant to fund ADC in large part because state legislators there feared that the "provisions regarding dependent children are entirely too broad and 'might easily be applicable to all children.'" Many believed that "a large Mexican or negro family might easily receive from $100 to $150 and $175 per month," which might discourage them from working in the fields. Once Texas appropriated funds in 1941, they excluded children who were not citizens. Average benefit levels were also quite low: $38 in 1947 compared to the nationwide average of $63. Elsewhere, residency restrictions limited access for migratory workers even in generous states like California, where average ADC benefits were higher than any other state in the nation. Meanwhile, two-tiered benefit levels continued to persist in some states. Federal officials who visited Arizona noted that "budgetary standards used for determining need and the amount of [ADC] grants for Mexicans [were] distinctly lower than those employed for other nationalities." They recommended that "a firm stand be taken by the Board to discourage deliberate discrimination against applicants who are Mexicans and to encourage the granting of assistance on the basis of need irrespective of nationality."[53]

Black children represented fewer than 11 percent of ADC beneficiaries by 1939. But blacks were likely underrepresented relative to need as 21 percent of households headed by a single mother in 1940 were black. As with OAA, local administration of ADC made room for discrimination in the implementation of the program. Many states had "suitable home" provisions, which were often used to exclude blacks. Black women were also more likely to be found employable and therefore ineligible for welfare. Access to ADC was particularly difficult in the South. In Georgia in 1940, roughly 14 percent of white families eligible for ADC received it compared to only 1.5 percent of black families. Benefit levels were also considerably lower in the South ($39) than in the Northeast and Midwest ($74). As with OAA, scholars have shown that benefit levels were low because of planter pressure and because restrictions on the franchise prevented blacks from making their voices heard. Furthermore, in the South, average benefit levels were typically lower for black families than for white families. Scholars at Howard University's School of Social Work observed in 1950 that:

> If it is the prevailing attitude that Negro families either need less to get along on, or deserve less, this attitude may be reflected in the items allowed in the family budget—no sheets allowed in the household budgets of Negro families, as was found in one county for instance—or a lower ceiling on budgets, based, supposedly, upon need, or the habitual granting of lesser amounts to families with similar requirements.

State plans in the South were never openly discriminatory since this was against federal law. Nevertheless, "experience has shown . . . that community attitudes and traditions which favor differential treatment are strong enough to hold their own where rules and regulations are not sufficiently explicit or leave too much to the initiative of individuals, and this unfortunately is widely evident in the case of needy children."[54]

ADC benefits in the North were generous relative to other sections of the country, but we do not know the extent to which European immigrants used this program. When the ADC program started, 99.6 percent of covered children were native born; only 0.13 percent were born in Europe. This is not surprising given that immigration from Europe had been sharply curtailed in the early 1920s. The SSB did not collect nativity data from parents who claimed ADC for their children, however. According to the census, 14 percent of female-headed households with children were headed by a white foreign-born immigrant. There is reason to believe, however, that relatively few of these parents had children on the ADC rolls after the 1939 amendments to the Social Security Act made widows and dependents of covered workers eligible for survivors' benefits from social insurance. Not only were European immigrants more likely to work in covered occupations, white foreign-born female heads were more likely than others to be widows (75 percent and 61 percent, respectively), making them eligible for Old Age and Survivors Insurance after 1939. Consequently, European immigrant women were more likely to benefit from the more generous survivors' benefits.[55]

CONCLUSION

Anton Kmet, a native of Slovenia, moved to America in 1890. Though he never became a U.S. citizen, he worked for twenty-five years at the American Steel and Wire Company in Cleveland, and for twenty-five years since his retirement, he had received a pension from the company, which in 1940 amounted to $21 per month. When the American social critic Louis Adamic paid a visit to Mr. Kmet, he mentioned to the old man that "there were people in the United States, including members of Congress . . . who were disturbed about the aliens and non-citizens, and that some wanted to deport all the foreign-born who did not have their naturalization papers."

> *Taku?*—so? . . . Well, maybe I was wrong in not taking out the citizenship paper. Mind you, I don't say I was. But I tell you what you do: You bring those people here on the first of the month . . . and *I'll show them my American paper*, which says that I worked all right and did what was expected of me. I didn't ask for this paper [the pension check]. . . . I worked until I did enough for one man's lifetime, and America has been giving me this paper once a month now for twenty-five years. (italics added)[56]

Could a pension, whether from the American Steel and Wire Company or the American government, make an alien an American, if not in fact then in substance? Conversely, could the denial of a pension—a social right to assistance—undermine any substantive claims of citizenship? In his testimony at the Senate hearings on the proposed Social Security Act, the NAACP's Charles Houston insisted that the bill be amended to ensure that the vast majority of black Americans would be covered under social insurance and shielded from discrimination. "We Negroes are United States citizens," he said, "who have never failed to shoulder our full share of the national burden." He demanded the opportunity to work and benefit from social legislation "the same as any other citizen regardless of color or creed." Formal citizenship was not sufficient, however, nor was it even necessary for social citizenship.[57]

State and local control in the administration of means-tested programs allowed for continued discrimination against blacks and Mexicans. Though there was little discrimination in the federally controlled OAI program, most blacks and Mexicans were excluded from this insurance because they were disproportionately represented in non-covered occupations, especially agriculture and domestic service. That these occupations were not initially covered under the Social Security Act was the result in part of the legacy and continued significance of racial divisions in America—a racial caste system in the South and many parts of the Southwest, widespread disenfranchisement of blacks and many Mexican Americans, few affirmative efforts to politically incorporate Mexican immigrants, and the influence of planters and growers who wanted a cheap and willing labor force. These combined forces ultimately left these groups with too little political power to have their interests, concerns, or basic needs met.

Though Mexicans and blacks did not benefit much from the Social Security Act, the mechanisms of exclusion were not always the same. While both groups experienced discrimination by local welfare providers, many blacks also lived in communities with extremely low benefit levels for categorical assistance. Benefit levels were not uniformly low in the Southwest as they were in the South, but Mexican aliens were blocked by citizenship restrictions and Mexican migrants by stiff residency provisions. What is more, the U.S. government imported millions of Mexican braceros with no recognized claim to social assistance. These differences had important consequences for the structure of the social welfare system that was established in each region. In the South there was less overall redistribution. In the Southwest there was welfare chauvinism.

In contrast to both blacks and Mexicans, southern and eastern European immigrants were more likely than even native-born whites to work in covered occupations. These immigrants had greater access to industrial

jobs covered under social insurance both because they were more likely
to live in industrialized areas and because they faced less employment-
related discrimination than blacks or Mexicans. They were also more
likely to be nearing the age of retirement, ensuring they would put little into the Social Security program but reap most of its early rewards.
Whatever the motivations behind the decisions to exclude agricultural
and domestic workers and yet include aliens under social insurance, the
consequences were important both in their practical repercussions and in
their symbolic statements about the contours of social citizenship in the
United States.

CHAPTER 11

The Boundaries of Social Citizenship

A POPULAR "NATIONAL RECOVERY PEP SONG" during the Depression titled "Marching Along Together" tried to galvanize the nation to face the crisis with unity, optimism, and confidence that better times were ahead. Its collective, hopeful theme was reflected in much of the New Deal's iconography. A Social Security Board poster showed a stream of smiling, well-dressed adults, working-class types and professionals—old and new immigrant stock alike—all marching together out of a teeming industrial city. The poster urged the public to "Join the March to Old Age Security," which they could do by filing their application for a Social Security number (see Figure 11.1). Highlighting blacks' exclusion from this sea of faces and from many New Deal programs, the renowned black artist Romare Bearden depicted a similar stream of workers "marching along together" toward "recovery" while "Negro Americans" stood on a hill watching the group march away without them (see Figure 11.2). Bearden's political cartoon, which appeared in a 1935 issue of *The Crisis*, illustrates one of the most rigid and enduring boundaries of social citizenship during the first half of the twentieth century: the limited inclusion—and sometimes near wholesale exclusion—of blacks in the relief programs of both the Progressive Era and the New Deal. Mexicans were on the march, too, during this period of course but not toward Social Security. They were on a march south—by train, by car, or by foot—across the border and out of the country in a movement that was sparked by the actions of local relief officials who no longer wanted to support these "unwelcome visitors" (see Figure 11.3).[1]

Taken together, the treatment of blacks, Mexicans, and European immigrants provides a nuanced picture of how race, citizenship, and nativity served as dividing lines between those who were judged worthy of assistance and those who were not. Despite persistent and widespread nativism, European immigrants were included within the boundaries of social citizenship while Mexicans were left on the periphery, granted limited inclusion at times, completely excluded at other times, and in some instances expelled from the nation entirely.

The different treatment of blacks, European immigrants and Mexicans reflected the worlds each group inhabited—worlds bound by both regional political economies and each group's social position. Blacks, Eu-

Figure 11.1: Join the March to Old Age Security

Source: "Join the March to Old Age Security," United States Social Security Board, 1936.

Figure 11.2: Marching Along Together

Source: Romare Bearden, "Marching Along Together," *The Crisis* (March 1935): 84. Art © Romare Bearden Foundation/Licensed by VAGA, New York, NY.

ropean immigrants, and Mexicans were concentrated in separate regions of the country, and within each region there developed starkly different political systems and race and labor market relations. The vast majority of blacks lived in the South, typically in rural areas, where they worked disproportionately in agriculture and domestic service under a labor system governed by debt peonage and an ethos of paternalism. They were deemed racially inferior and inassimilable, and were subject to exclusion and segregation. They had virtually no political power, the result of widespread disenfranchisement and white Democratic rule.

By contrast, the majority of European immigrants lived in the Northeast and Midwest, where they settled in cities and into industrial occupations. The cities in which they lived were often rife with machine politics. While southern and eastern European immigrants were deemed

Figure 11.3: Mexican Migrants on the Road with Tire Trouble, California, February 1936

Source: Farm Security Administration Project. Photograph by Dorothea Lange; Library of Congress, Prints & Photographs Division, FSA/OWI Collection, LC-USF347-002464.

racially inferior to northern and western Europeans, they were nonetheless treated as white by most American institutions. And indeed a variety of forces in those cities encouraged their assimilation and naturalization and helped incorporate them into the polity as well as the welfare state.

Mexicans lived overwhelmingly in the Southwest, where, like blacks, they tended to live in rural areas and work disproportionately in agriculture. Unlike blacks, they labored under a system of migratory wage labor—not debt peonage and paternalism. Mexicans occupied a more liminal position in the American racial and color hierarchy, too. Guaranteed many of the privileges of whiteness by law, they nonetheless suffered from many of the liabilities of non-whiteness in practice. But the color line they faced in the Southwest was not as insidious as the one blacks faced in the South. And unlike blacks, Mexicans were seen as foreign and "alien" even when they were U.S. citizens. Unlike European immigrants,

Mexican immigrants were dissuaded from naturalizing and incorporating politically because southwestern cities were often governed by Anglo municipal reformers who preferred business efficiency and government by the city's leading experts over party politicians who courted working-class and immigrant voters.

Because each group lived in largely different worlds, local control over relief administration had profoundly different consequences for each group, affecting the size, form, and function of the welfare state that developed in each region, as well as the treatment each group would receive. In every way a product of these distinct worlds, but by no means confined to them, social workers in the first third of the twentieth century developed very different ideas about each group's propensity to become dependent on relief and right to legitimately claim assistance from the public purse.

Formal citizenship on its own was not a significant obstacle to access most social welfare programs during this period. Formal citizenship and even legal status were relatively unimportant for access to Progressive Era relief programs. Most people in need of assistance received help from public and private indoor and outdoor relief agencies where the primary criteria for assistance were need and county residence, not citizenship. Relief providers did, however, sometimes use citizenship, legal status, or simply the perception that one was alien to justify expelling those who requested relief. During the first third of the twentieth century, relief officials cooperated with immigration authorities to expel dependent individuals from the nation. In the most extreme cases, the local welfare office quite literally turned into an immigration bureau or became an extralegal arm of the Immigration Service, expelling those whom even immigration laws could not touch. While there was widespread public support for such efforts, the tactics were unevenly applied: Mexicans and Mexican Americans were targeted for expulsion while European immigrants were usually spared.

Mexicans were not subject to expulsion because they presented a greater relief burden than did European immigrants. If anything, European immigrants made greater use of relief than did Mexicans prior to the New Deal. Yet despite the fact that Mexicans' use of assistance was not especially high, relief providers increasingly saw them as a dependent population incapable of racial assimilation. Social workers viewed Mexicans as culturally or even biologically indolent, thriftless, and diseased and therefore incapable of rising out of poverty or becoming true Americans. Rather than seeing the extension of relief to this group as the natural humanitarian response to people in need, social workers portrayed it as an illegitimate burden and an economic subsidy to the agricultural industry. Though race scientists and much of the general public believed that southern and eastern Europeans were racially inferior and chronic paupers, too, social workers firmly rejected both assertions. They publicly refuted claims that southern and eastern Europeans were biologically inferior and believed they possessed the cultural traits—thrift, ambition, and a strong work ethic—necessary to move out of any present dependent condition.

Social workers were important because they functioned as gatekeepers to relief and as intermediaries with the Immigration Service. Each decision to include, exclude, or expel was colored by social workers' perceptions about their clients. While their attitudes were products of the labor, racial, and political environment in which they lived, relief officials were not passively responding to local public opinion or simply taking orders from politicians. Rather, they actively constructed populations as deserving and undeserving, wielded data to support their beliefs, and made sustained efforts to convince legislators and the broader public of their "expert" opinions. Social workers had considerable agency and discretion, of which they took full advantage. And they consistently worked to alter such constraints to better suit their objectives.

As the Depression took hold, nativism increased and a desperate public looked for easy solutions to the unfolding national calamity. This nativism was not targeted narrowly on Mexicans, even though the expulsions generally were. Since it had reemerged during World War I, the content of nativism in the United States had been shifting from a kind of racial nationalism, which conditioned inclusion primarily on racial fitness, to a conservative civic nationalism, which mandated loyalty, patriotism, and naturalization to warrant the fruits of American citizenship.[2] Where nativism once targeted southern and eastern Europeans, Asians, and Mexicans as putatively inferior racial groups, it was now *also* broadly directed against all non-citizens. Though federal relief officials like Frances Perkins and Harry Hopkins and elected officials from the North were generally keen to include aliens in their recovery program, they found their efforts occasionally thwarted by southern and southwestern members of Congress. The result was citizenship preferences or restrictions in work relief and state discretion in citizenship restrictions on categorical assistance.

Citizenship restrictions—when and where enacted—could be devastating for those who could not get around them, but there were many ways to do so, especially for European immigrants who were perceived by relief officials to be worthy of assistance and whose position in the labor market and growing political power put them in a particularly advantageous position relative to Mexicans. Alien-headed families could have family members certified as secondary workers in work relief programs. They could also send their American sons to the Civilian Conservation Corps or take advantage of local work relief projects their communities developed that did not have such restrictions. If older aliens did not qualify for Old Age Assistance because their state had adopted a citizenship restriction, they might qualify for Old Age Insurance. In fact, European immigrants were more likely than native-born whites to work in occupations covered by social insurance. What is more, most states with large numbers of white immigrants would cover aged aliens on General Assistance and quickly dropped their citizenship requirements for OAA. Households headed by a woman who was white and a non-citizen could generally count on ADC or, better yet, survivor's benefits for the widows of workers in covered employment.

European aliens, moreover, could always naturalize. Indeed, one of the biggest effects of citizenship restrictions on the WPA and OAA was a rush on the naturalization office. Starting in 1935, cities across the country reported impressive increases in the number of people declaring their intent to initiate or finalize naturalization. An assistant secretary of labor described the naturalization offices in 1939 as "literally swamped."[3] Recognizing that citizenship might become increasingly important for access to government benefits, the federal government took pains to ease the process. Congress cut naturalization fees in half in 1934. The INS promised a "New Deal for the Alien," easing some of the "cruel and unnecessary hardships involved in the administration" of deportation and naturalization laws. And WPA adult educators were put to work in many cities to help thousands of aliens complete their first or second papers.[4]

In some areas, these efforts produced truly remarkable results that virtually nullified the effects of any citizenship restrictions. State legislators in Pennsylvania passed a law in June 1939 barring non-citizens who had failed to take out their first papers from General Assistance. Aliens in the state were still eligible for ADC and OAA, but the new law could have hurt more than forty thousand aliens already on General Assistance statewide. Social workers disapproved of the new policy, but to their delight, the attorney general advised the State Department of Assistance that the provisions of the new bill would not be retroactive, so aliens already on relief would not be affected. Aliens not already on the rolls had to apply for their first papers by the end of the year in order to be eligible for assistance. Social agencies, therefore, had six months in which to help needy aliens start the naturalization process. In the interim, the State Department of Assistance gave alien applicants without first papers referrals to the American Citizenship League, which could assist them with the process of securing the necessary documents. Private nationality organizations raised funds to help immigrants pay the costs of their first papers. In addition, social welfare agencies joined forces to create a coordinating committee on aliens. Using a census of aliens constructed by the Pittsburgh Board of Education, they fanned out into immigrant communities to help non-citizens take out their first papers in the comfort of their own homes, thereby "saving carfare and avoiding congestion and a long waiting period." By December 31—the last day before the new law was set to take effect—a local paper declared that the state relief rolls would remain largely unchanged due to the "biggest mass naturalization drive" in the state's history. "The amended relief law will have virtually no immediate effect here," the paper confirmed, "because there's scarcely anyone left eligible to be affected."[5]

All told, more than 1.7 million immigrants were issued certificates of naturalization during the Depression decade. Not everyone could take advantage of these sorts of naturalization projects, however. Chinese and Japanese immigrants, among others, were racially ineligible for citizenship. While technically "nationals" of the United States, Filipinos were not considered citizens and were barred from WPA employment once citizenship restrictions went into effect. Not every community was as enthusiastic about starting a massive naturalization project either. While Mexicans were racially eligible for citizenship, the Southwest remained, for the most part, ambivalent toward naturalization and political incorporation projects, a product of local racism and the municipal reform movement's hostility to immigrants. What is more, despite the reduced naturalization fees, some non-citizens could not afford the costs. This was especially true in areas with lower benefit levels or where applicants did not receive assistance with their naturalization fees. And yet, the fraction of the adult Mexican-origin population in the United States who were non-citizens declined precipitously over the Depression decade from roughly 60 percent in 1930 to less than 40 percent by 1940. This was not so much because of any special effort to incorporate those who were here—fewer than nine thousand Mexican nationals were issued certificates of naturalization during the Depression decade. Rather, it was because the repatriation and deportation campaigns were so effective.[6]

Once they had naturalized, European immigrants faced few barriers in accessing the welfare state. Discrimination based on race or color—rather than citizenship—was harder to circumvent, and citizenship restrictions were harder for Mexicans to overcome. If blacks or Mexicans were denied work relief during the Depression because of racial discrimination, certifying secondary workers in their household was not an option. Nor were communities in which there were large numbers of blacks or Mexicans likely to look for alternate ways to help them get by. One reason racial discrimination was more intractable was that it often occurred at the local level and at the level of implementation. Communities with large numbers of blacks and Mexicans often defied federal non-discrimination orders or failed to live up to their intent. Blacks were concentrated in areas where benefits were low, and relief providers sometimes denied blacks and Mexicans any assistance at all. The denial of assistance or reduction of relief budgets was due to relief providers' beliefs about who was deserving and who was not—attitudes that were buttressed by community norms in the South and Southwest. But it was also the result of requests from planters and eventually growers who feared a labor shortage and wanted to maintain a steady supply of willing, even desperate workers. The large-scale disenfranchisement of blacks and many Mexican Americans and their overall lack of political power meant that their exclusion and poor treatment had few electoral costs. Federal authorities often ignored these local practices, and in some cases federal policies themselves were responsible for exclusion. Indeed it was because of occupational exclusions from Old Age and Unemployment Insurance that so many blacks and Mexicans were forced to rely on the whims of local officials administering ADC, OAA, and GA.

As bleak and desperate as the situation often was for blacks and Mexicans in the 1930s and 1940s, it represented a significant improvement, in some ways, over the situation before 1933. Prior to the New Deal, blacks were concentrated in regions with almost no public relief and were generally relegated to segregated underfunded charities or excluded altogether. That was why, despite the Roosevelt administration's refusal to advance civil rights initiatives, blacks turned away from the party of Lincoln and voted in large numbers for the Democrat from Hyde Park. The New Deal brought some improvement in the circumstances of Mexicans as well. There was a temporary respite in the massive repatriations and deportations of the Hoover years. Repatriations continued under FDR but not on the same scale. Mexicans would soon again become the targets of deportation drives—such as "Operation Wetback" in the 1950s—but the degree of cooperation between the INS and welfare offices substantially decreased. This was due in large part to the federal privacy and confidentiality provisions of the Social Security Act, which prohibited agencies receiving such funds from divulging the names of beneficiaries to other government agencies. While cooperation with the INS decreased, citizenship requirements for OAA—and even ADC in Texas—endured in the Southwest. And unlike European immigrants, few Mexicans could turn to Old Age or Unemployment Insurance if they were excluded from state-administered means-tested assistance.[7]

What do Mexicans' experiences with the welfare state tell us about their place in the nation's racial and color hierarchy? Was their experience more similar to that of blacks or southern and eastern European immigrants? Clearly the experience of Mexicans was unlike that of southern and eastern Europeans. They lived in largely different worlds, social workers generally perceived them differently, and their access to benefits was unequal. European immigrants lived in areas with more relief spending, more public investment, and more liberal access to social welfare programs, only marginally and briefly affected by their citizenship or legal status. Mexicans, in contrast, lived in cities with lower relief spending and lower public investment prior to the New Deal, and they were offered limited access to relief, strongly mediated by their citizenship and legal status (or perceived citizenship and legal status).

Neither did the Mexican experience parallel the black experience. Attitudes about the two groups' welfare dependence often differed. Prior to the Depression, social workers and relief providers were far more concerned about dependence among Mexicans than among blacks. Part of the reason was Mexicans' racially liminal status. Even during a period in which Mexicans were increasingly racialized as non-white, they did not fit neatly into a black-white or white–non-white racial binary. Social workers and relief providers never assumed that blacks were capable of assimilation and therefore excluded them from much early social welfare provision. However, social workers in California were at least initially optimistic that they could Americanize Mexicans, and as a result, Mexicans became (not entirely willing) objects of social worker Americanization efforts there when they first started immigrating in large numbers. Soon, however, these social workers concluded that Mexicans could not assimilate, and their use of relief, previously encouraged, was used as proof that they were an economic and social burden. It was at least in part because of Mexicans' racially in-between status, therefore, that social workers constructed them as a "dependency problem."

Mexicans were also more likely to be migrant laborers and therefore outside the system of debt peonage and paternalism that governed much of the Old South. Unlike southern planters, western growers were seldom threatened by their laborers' use of social assistance, at least until federal intervention pushed relief benefits above wage levels. Consequently, southwestern growers had fewer reasons to oppose the growth of a public or private relief system during the first third of the twentieth century, and Mexicans had slightly greater access to relief than did blacks.

Finally, the large-scale expulsion of black Americans during this period was never a real option. Whatever social workers or relief officials thought of blacks' use of relief, they could choose to give them access on equal terms, give them less, or give them none at all. For Mexicans, however, there was always the threat of harassment from immigration officials at the relief office or pressure by caseworkers to just "go home," even if their home, from birth, was the United States. Furthermore, their very access to the nation was sometimes conditioned on whether or not they could (or would be allowed to) become dependent on relief. To speak of a single "minority" experience during these years is inappropriate, as is any attempt to make Mexicans fit the southeastern European trajectory.

IMPLICATIONS

What are the implications of this history for our thinking about contemporary social policies? How should we think, for example, about recent efforts to impose citizenship restrictions on access to social services? It is clear, for one, that such efforts are not unprecedented. Although the federal government never imposed a citizenship requirement on ADC (or its successor, AFDC) until 1996, when it became Temporary Assistance to Needy Families,[8] the federal government had previously imposed citizenship requirements on work relief programs and it had permitted states to impose citizenship requirements on ADC, OAA, and Aid to the Blind. While citizenship restrictions in the welfare state are not unprecedented, neither were they ubiquitous. In fact, but for a brief period, most non-citizens had access to welfare state services.

Local welfare officials have, however, had a history of singling out Mexicans for different treatment. We need to think about both our welfare and immigration policies in light of this historical pattern. Ever since the late 1920s, public officials have been trying to reconcile their desire for a large labor force to meet the demands of employers with their desire to minimize any perceived social and economic costs. This is the logic behind the bracero program and other contract worker proposals, and it is the logic behind permitting an undocumented population, perhaps ten to twelve million strong as of this writing, to live in the United States without any recognized right to non-emergency means-tested assistance or social insurance programs.

This book also highlights the fact that decentralized policymaking can have substantially different consequences for disparate groups of claimants. Blacks and Mexicans were generally disadvantaged when programs were administered at the local level. For European immigrants—even non-citizens—local control generally did not present the same barriers and was sometimes an advantage. Even when the federal or state government passed a law that disadvantaged non-citizens, local administration and control often led to greater overall welfare spending, protection from discriminatory legislation, and access to quite generous relief assistance. European immigrants fared well under local control at least in part because social workers believed that citizenship should not determine access to welfare services and that these immigrants were capable of racial assimilation and therefore rightful claimants on the public purse. In addition, the political context in which European immigrants lived encouraged naturalization and political incorporation, giving them greater power to ensure that their needs were considered. To be sure, even in the North there were elected officials who tried to capitalize on the rising nativist sentiment. But some of their colleagues, more dependent on the votes of new immigrants, or perhaps new immigrants themselves, invariably came to the aliens' defense.

This history suggests that we should be wary about romanticized notions of the bootstrapping "white ethnic" who got ahead without government help. During the first forty years of the last century, many people believed that European immigrants were a social and economic liability, draining hospital funds and swamping relief rolls. How soon we forget! We forget at least in part because social workers did such a good job of constructing European immigrants as thrifty, hardworking and self-sufficient—a direct response to popular claims to the contrary. European immigrants were also understandably quick to seize on assertions that their group was not as undesirable as others claimed. When historians rely on evidence from social workers or immigrants themselves to argue that "ethnic populations shied away from outside help" and that they exhibited "a deep distrust of public assistance," they ignore the context in which such claims were made. Prior to the Depression, most people in the United States thought it was shameful to ask for assistance, and European immigrants were probably no different in that respect than any other group.[9] Of course many European immigrants worked hard and did what they could to get ahead. But they also got a lot of help. They were more likely than other groups to use assistance, and certainly more likely than blacks or Mexicans during the Progressive Era. Furthermore, where blacks and Mexicans were disproportionately shunted into demeaning means-tested programs during the Depression and largely excluded from the more generous social insurance programs, European immigrants had the opposite experience. They received almost unfettered access to Social Security, even though many made few contributions to the system. For them, Social Security functioned more like a giant welfare program—except without the means test and without the stigma. Furthermore, whenever they were stymied by citizenship restrictions, they were given alternative forms of support or received assistance in naturalizing. Exactly what long-term consequences this may have had for the groups in question is not yet entirely clear. But in an era when welfare is so thoroughly connected in the white mind with blacks and increasingly (again) Mexicans, allusions to European immigrants in the first half of the twentieth century as bootstrapping and self-sufficient immediately call to mind the present-day and highly misleading comparison.

What are the implications for our theories about the role of race in the American welfare state? Previous attempts to explain racial disparities in social welfare provision have at times been framed in stark either/or terms. One debate, for example, pits racial divisions against states' rights considerations or southern labor market concerns to explain the differential treatment of African Americans in the New Deal.[10] While such debates have been indisputably valuable in advancing our understanding of the determinants of social welfare provision, they have also at times masked the ways in which race, labor, and politics were so thoroughly entangled in this period. The focus here on worlds was an explicit attempt to think about racial, political, and labor market contexts as whole systems rather than separate, mutually exclusive variables. Indeed, by looking at the intersection of race, labor, and politics, we can better see exactly how high the deck was stacked against blacks and Mexicans and how much it favored European immigrants.

Despite increased attention to immigrants and welfare, most scholars continue to portray the origins of the American welfare state in black and white. Such a portrait vastly oversimplifies the role of racial divisions in the politics of redistribution. This book shows how important it is to look beyond black-white relations to understand how diversity influenced the development, scope, and function of the American welfare system. And yet this study also casts doubt on recent suggestions that all diversity—whether racial, ethnic, linguistic, or religious—may discourage redistribution. Many of these "diversity tradeoff" studies proceed on the assumption that all diversity has the same effect on redistribution for the same reasons and through the same means.[11] The racial and ethnic patterning of relief provision in 1929, however, belies that assumption. On the eve of the Depression, cities with more European immigrants spent considerably *more* on relief than did cities with more native-born whites. Cities with more blacks or Mexicans spent considerably *less* but for different reasons. These spending differences were not the result of differences across cities in levels of urbanization, industrialization, need, or a city's ability to fund relief programs. Rather, they were a product of the political economies of the different regions and the growing resentment against Mexicans' perceived greater use of relief. There is no universal tradeoff between diversity and redistribution. The relationship between diversity and social welfare spending is context dependent and mediated by a host of different social and political institutions.

Looking beyond the outcomes welfare scholars have typically studied can also provide a fuller picture of the relationship between race, diversity, and redistribution. The share of public or private funding in a city's relief system is but one example. Cities with more Mexicans were more likely to fund their relief system privately, even after controlling for a host of other factors. While relief officials and the general public resented the use of tax dollars to support Mexican migratory labor, employers of such labor nonetheless subsidized private charities to keep a large labor pool nearby between harvests. Non-citizens' access to welfare is another example. In *Spheres of Justice*, Michael Walzer wrote that political philosophers who study distributive justice presuppose "a bounded world within

294 • Chapter 11

which distributions [take] place. . . . We assume an established group and a fixed population, and so we miss the first and most important distributive question: How is that group constituted?"[12] Similarly, welfare state scholars have thought too little about the intersection of immigration and welfare policies. We need to pay closer attention to citizenship and legal status exclusions, the degree of coordination between relief officials and immigration authorities, and policies that condition formal citizenship on showing that one will not become a public charge. None of this is to say that immigrant-native relations may not affect welfare spending or other standard outcomes—they clearly did. But we should be mindful of how the very possibility of expulsion could moderate the effects of diversity on these more standard measures. Indeed, if we focus simply on benefit levels, we might erroneously come away with the impression that Mexicans in the Southwest, where Old Age Assistance benefits were highest, fared far better than blacks in the South, where benefits were lowest. Indeed, we would miss that citizenship restrictions barred many Mexicans from any benefits at all.

And yet, despite rampant nativism, citizenship and legal status restrictions, on their own, were not significant boundaries of social citizenship during this era, nor for much of the twentieth century. Indeed, for nearly four decades after the passage of the Social Security Act, there continued to be no federal citizenship or legal status restrictions for access to virtually any of our welfare state programs. As new programs such as Food Stamps and Medicaid were passed, they followed earlier precedent and had no citizenship restrictions. All of that began to change only in the 1970s. Between 1972 and 1976, the federal government for the first time barred undocumented immigrants from nearly every major welfare and social insurance program. And since then these policies have been growing increasingly restrictive. The 1996 welfare reforms, which barred recent legal immigrants from many social welfare programs, was in many ways the culmination of this restrictive turn in federal policy. Legal status and formal citizenship are relatively new boundaries of social citizenship. To make sense of these new boundaries, we must first make sense of the old.[13]

Abbreviations in the Notes

1930 Census	Steven Ruggles, J. Trent Alexander, Katie Genadek, Ronald Goeken, Matthew B. Schroeder, and Matthew Sobek. *Integrated Public Use Microdata Series: Version 5.0* [Machine-readable database]. Minneapolis: University of Minnesota, 2010. 1% Sample, 1930 Census.
1940 Census	Ruggles et al. *Integrated Public Use Microdata Series*. 1% Sample, 1940 Census.
1950 Census	Ruggles et al. *Integrated Public Use Microdata Series*. 1% Sample, 1950 Census.
Abbott Papers	Edith and Grace Abbott Papers, University of Chicago, Hyde Park, IL.
ACLU Papers	American Civil Liberties Union Archives, 1917–50: The Roger Baldwin Years, Microfilm. Wilmington, DE: Scholarly Resources.
ACNS Records	Records of the American Council for Nationalities Service, 1921–71, Microfilm. Bethesda, MD: University Publications of America.
AFII Papers	American Federation of International Institutes, Immigration and Refugee Services of America Records, 1918–85, Microfilm. Woodbridge, CT: Primary Source Microfilm.
AFL Minutes	Minutes of the Executive Council of the American Federation of Labor, 1893–1955, Microfilm. Bethesda, MD: University Publications of America.
Burgess Papers	Ernest Burgess Collection, University of Chicago, Hyde Park, IL.
CD	*Chicago Defender*
CDT	*Chicago Daily Tribune*
CR	*Congressional Record*
Clements Papers	George P. Clements Papers, University of California, Los Angeles.
Dean Papers	Jessie E. Dean Papers, Social Welfare Archives, University of Southern California, Los Angeles.
DIR Papers	California Department of Industrial Relations Papers, Bancroft Library, University of California, Berkeley.
Dimock Papers	Marshal Dimock Papers, FDR Library, Hyde Park, NY.

FDR Papers   Franklin Delano Roosevelt Papers, Franklin Delano Roosevelt Library, Hyde Park, NY.

FLIS Papers   Foreign Language Information Service Papers, Immigration and Refugee Services of America Records, 1918–85, Microfilm. Woodbridge, CT: Primary Source Microfilm.

Ford Papers   John Anson Ford Papers, Huntington Library, San Marino, CA.

Foreign Press Survey   Chicago Foreign Language Press Survey, University of Chicago, Hyde Park, IL.

Gallup Poll   Adam Berinsky and Eric Schickler. National Science Foundation, Political Science Program Grant SES-0550431, "Collaborative Research: The American Mass Public in the 1930s and 1940s." 2006–8. American Institute of Public Opinion Polls, #1936-0062, #1938-0141, #1939-0144.

Hall Papers   Helen Hall Papers, Social Welfare History Archives, University of Minnesota, Minneapolis.

Hilliard Papers   Raymond M. Hilliard Papers, Chicago Historical Society.

Hopkins Papers   Harry Hopkins Papers, Franklin Delano Roosevelt Library, Hyde Park, NY.

IPL Papers   Immigrants' Protective League Papers, University of Illinois, Chicago.

INS Records   Records of the Immigration and Naturalization Service, Series A: Subject Correspondence Files, Part 2: Mexican Immigration, 1906–30, Microfilm. Bethesda, MD: University Publications of America.

Interpreter Release   FLIS, Interpreter Releases and Clip Sheets, Records of the American Council for Nationalities Service, 1921–71, Microfilm. Bethesda, MD: University Publications of America.

Kohn Papers   Esther Loeb Kohn Papers, University of Illinois, Chicago.

LACBS Decimal Files   Los Angeles County Board of Supervisors, Los Angeles.

LAT   *Los Angeles Times*

McDowell Papers   Mary McDowell Papers, Chicago Historical Society.

McWilliams Papers   Carey McWilliams Papers, University of California, Los Angeles.

McWilliams Oral History	Carey McWilliams Oral History, California State Archives, Sacramento.
NCCC Proceedings	National Conference of Charities and Correction Proceedings, 1874–1984, University of Michigan Library Repository (http://porter.umdl.umich.edu/n/ncosw/).
NCSW Proceedings	National Conference of Social Welfare Proceedings, 1874–1984, University of Michigan Library Repository (http://porter.umdl.umich.edu/n/ncosw/).
NYT	*New York Times*
Race Relations Records	Register of the Survey of Race Relations Records, 1924–27, Hoover Institution Archives, Stanford University, Palo Alto, CA.
RG 46	Records of the United States Senate, National Archives, Washington, DC.
RG 47	Records of the Social Security Administration, National Archives, College Park, MD.
RG 59	Records of the Department of State, National Archives, College Park, MD.
RG 69	Records of the Federal Emergency Relief Administration and Work Projects Administration, National Archives, College Park, MD.
RG 73	Records of the President's Organization on Unemployment Relief, National Archives, College Park, MD.
RG 85	Records of the Immigration and Naturalization Service, National Archives, Washington, DC.
RG 174	Records of the Department of Labor, National Archives, College Park, MD.
RG 233	Records of the House Committee on Ways and Means, National Archives, Washington, DC.
Ross Papers	Fred Ross Papers, Special Collections, Stanford University, Palo Alto, CA.
SRA Papers	State Relief Administration Archives, California State Archives, Sacramento.
SSH online	Social Security History, online collection of materials on the history of the Social Security Administration (http://www.ssa.gov/history/history.html).

Taylor Papers   Paul S. Taylor Papers, Bancroft Library, University of California, Berkeley.

TSLAC Papers   Texas State Library and Archives Commission, Austin.

United Charities Papers   United Charities Papers, Chicago Historical Society.

WP   *Washington Post*

Notes

CHAPTER 1

1. Kitty Calavita, "The New Politics of Immigration: 'Budget-Balanced Conservatism' and the Symbolism of Proposition 187," *Social Problems* 43, no. 3 (1996): 284–305; Tanya Broder, "State and Local Policies on Immigrant Access to Services: Promoting Integration or Isolation?" *National Immigration Law Center* (Los Angeles, 2009); National Immigration Law Center, *State Measures Requiring Applicants for Public Benefits Verify Status (2004-09), Part I: Language Provisions*, November 2009, Los Angeles. http://www.nilc.org/dc_conf/flashdrive09/Access-to-Public-Benefits/pb9_comparison-chart-formal-bill-language-2009-11-121.pdf.

2. Lena Sun, "GOP Proposals Could Sever Noncitizens' Benefit Lifeline," *WP*, May 30, 1995, p. A01; Abby Goodnough, "Massachusetts Takes a Step Back from Health Care for All," *NYT*, July 15, 2009, p. A10.

3. Lynn Fujiwara, *Mothers without Citizenship: Asian Immigrant Families and the Consequences of Welfare Reform* (Minneapolis: University of Minnesota Press, 2008); Calavita, "The New Politics of Immigration"; Susan Okie, "Immigrants and Health Care—At the Intersection of Two Broken Systems," *New England Journal of Medicine* 357, no. 6 (2007): 525–29; Michael Fix and Ron Haskins, "Welfare Benefits for Non-Citizens," *Brookings Institution*, Brief No. 15 (Washington, DC, 2002).

4. Michael Alvarez and Tara Butterfield, "The Resurgence of Nativism in California? The Case of Proposition 187 and Illegal Immigration," *Social Science Quarterly* 81, no. 1 (2000): 167–79; James Edwards Jr., "Public Charge Doctrine: A Fundamental Principle of American Immigration Policy" (Washington, DC: Center for Immigration Studies, 2001); House Committee on Ways and Means, Subcommittee on Human Resources, *President's Fiscal Year 1998 Budget: Hearings*, 105th Cong., 1st sess., 1997, pp. 49–55.

5. Desmond King, *Making Americans: Immigration, Race, and the Origins of the Diverse Democracy* (Cambridge, MA: Harvard University Press, 2000), A1; Census Bureau, *Fifteenth Census of the United States, 1930, Population* (Washington, DC: GPO, 1933), vol. 2, p. 25.

6. Unless otherwise specified, I follow common usage of the period and use the term "Mexican" to refer to both Mexican immigrants and Mexican Americans.

7. Gøsta Esping-Andersen, *The Three Worlds of Welfare Capitalism* (Princeton: Princeton University Press, 1990), 55; Ira Katznelson, *When Affirmative Action Was White: An Untold History of Racial Inequality in Twentieth-Century America* (New York: W. W. Norton, 2005); Melvin Oliver and Thomas Shapiro, *Black Wealth/White Wealth: A New Perspective on Racial Inequality* (New York: Routledge, 1995).

8. Richard Alba and Victor Nee, *Remaking the American Mainstream: Assimilation and Contemporary Immigration* (Cambridge, MA: Harvard University

Press, 2003); Joel Perlmann, *Italians Then, Mexicans Now* (New York: Russell Sage Foundation, 2005); Ian Haney-López, "Race and Erasure: The Salience of Race to Latinos/as," in *The Latino/a Condition: A Critical Reader*, ed. R. Delgado and J. Stefanic (New York: New York University Press, 1998), 180–95; Marcelo Suárez-Orozco and Mariela Páez, *Latinos: Remaking America* (Berkeley: University of California Press, 2002); Edward Telles and Vilma Ortiz, *Generations of Exclusion: Mexican Americans, Assimilation, and Race* (New York: Russell Sage Foundation, 2008).

9. Alberto Alesina, Reza Baqir, and William Easterly, "Public Goods and Ethnic Divisions," *Quarterly Journal of Economics* 114, no. 4 (1999): 1243–84; Linda Gordon, *Pitied But Not Entitled: Single Mothers and the History of Welfare* (Cambridge, MA: Harvard University Press, 1994); Gwendolyn Mink, *The Wages of Motherhood: Inequality in the Welfare State, 1917–1942* (Ithaca: Cornell University Press, 1995); Alberto Alesina, Edward Glaeser, and Bruce Sacerdote, "Why Doesn't the United States Have a European-Style Welfare State?" Brookings Papers on Economic Activity (Washington, DC, 2001); Martin Gilens, *Why Americans Hate Welfare* (Chicago: University of Chicago Press, 1999), 70; Robert Lieberman, *Shifting the Color Line: Race and the American Welfare State* (Cambridge, MA: Harvard University Press, 1998); Jill Quadagno, *The Color of Welfare: How Racism Undermined the War on Poverty* (New York: Oxford University Press, 1994); Katznelson, *When Affirmative Action Was White*.

10. James Davis and Tom Smith, *General Social Surveys, 1972–2008* (Chicago: National Opinion Research Center; Storrs, CT: Roper Center for Public Opinion Research, University of Connecticut, 2009); Michael Beyer, "Immigration Plan Is Noble, But Who's Going to Pay for It?" *Buffalo News*, May 23, 2006, p. A9; William Woo, "Opinion Roundup: Immigration and Welfare," *Atlanta Journal Constitution*, May 11, 1995, p. 11a; Lina Newton, *Illegal, Alien or Immigrant: The Politics of Immigration Reform* (New York: New York University Press, 2008); Lizabeth Cohen, *Making a New Deal: Industrial Workers in Chicago, 1919–1930* (Cambridge: Cambridge University Press, 1990), 56–64; Jonathan Rieder, *Canarsie: The Jews and Italians of Brooklyn against Liberalism* (Cambridge, MA: Harvard University Press, 1985), 27–28, 35.

11. T. H. Marshall, "Citizenship and Social Class," in *Class, Citizenship and Social Development: Essays by T. H. Marshall* (Garden City, NY: Doubleday, 1964), 65–122.

12. Robert McElvaine, ed., *Down and Out in the Great Depression: Letters from the "Forgotten Man"* (Chapel Hill: University of North Carolina Press, 1983), 153.

13. David Roediger, *Working toward Whiteness: How America's Immigrants Became White* (New York: Basic Books, 2005). See also Karen Brodkin, *How Jews Became White Folks: And What That Says about Race in America* (New Brunswick: Rutgers University Press, 2000).

14. Lieberman, *Shifting the Color Line*, 308; Katznelson, *When Affirmative Action Was White*; Jill Quadagno, "From Old-Age Assistance to Supplemental Security Income: The Political Economy of Relief in the South, 1935–1972," in *The Politics of Social Policy in the United States*, ed. Margaret Weir, Ann Shola Orloff, and Theda Skocpol (Princeton: Princeton University Press, 1988), 235–64.

15. At least one scholar has argued that southern and eastern European immigrants' access to federal housing policy had a lasting effect. Roediger, *Working toward Whiteness*, 224–34.

16. For the view that the significance of race in welfare state development has been overemphasized, see Michael Brown, *Race, Money and the American Welfare State* (Ithaca: Cornell University Press, 1999); Gareth Davies and Martha Derthick,"Race and Social Welfare Policy: The Social Security Act of 1935,"*Political Science Quarterly* 112, no. 2 (1997): 217–35.

17. Lee Alston and Joseph Ferrie, *Southern Paternalism and the American Welfare State: Economics, Politics, and Institutions in the South, 1865–1965* (Cambridge: Cambridge University Press, 1999). See also Quadagno, "From Old-Age Assistance to Supplemental Security Income"; Ellen Reese, *Backlash against Welfare Mothers: Past and Present* (Berkeley: University of California Press, 2005).

18. Mink, *The Wages of Motherhood*, 8, 51; Gordon, *Pitied But Not Entitled*.

19. For differing perspectives on the agency of social workers, see Michael Lipsky, *Street-Level Bureaucracy: Dilemmas of the Individual in Public Services* (New York: Russell Sage Foundation, 1980); Helen Marrow, "Immigrant Bureaucratic Incorporation: The Dual Roles of Professional Missions and Government Policies," *American Sociological Review* 74, no. 5 (2009): 756–76; Frances Fox Piven and Richard Cloward, *Regulating the Poor: The Functions of Public Welfare* (New York: Vintage Books, 1971).

20. Joseph Carens,"Immigration and the Welfare State,"in *Democracy and the Welfare State*, ed. Amy Gutmann (Princeton: Princeton University Press, 1988), 209; Martin Johnson, "Racial Context, Public Attitudes, and Welfare Effort in the American States," in *Race and the Politics of Welfare Reform*, ed. Sanford Schram, Joe Soss, and Richard Fording (Ann Arbor: University of Michigan Press, 2003), 151–67; Alesina, Glaeser, and Sacerdote,"Why Doesn't the United States Have a European-Style Welfare State?"; Robert Brown,"Party Cleavages and Welfare Effort in the American States,"*American Political Science Review* 89, no. 1 (1995): 23–33; Joe Soss, Sanford Schram, Thomas Vartanian, and Erin O'Brien,"Setting the Terms of Relief: Explaining State Policy Choices in the Devolution Revolution,"*American Journal of Political Science* 45, no. 2 (2001): 378–95; Alesina, Baqir, and Easterly,"Public Goods and Ethnic Divisions"; Robert Putnam, "E Pluribus Unum: Diversity and Community in the Twenty-First Century," *Scandinavian Political Studies* 30, no. 2 (2007): 137–174; Gary Freeman,"Migration and the Political Economy of the Welfare State,"*Annals of the American Academy of Political and Social Science* 485 (1986): 51–63; David Goodhart,"Too Diverse?"*Prospect Magazine*, February 2004; David Goodhart,"Diversity Divide,"*Prospect Magazine*, April 2004.

21. Gilens, *Why Americans Hate Welfare*; Yueh-Ting Lee, Victor Ottati, and Imtiaz Hussain,"Attitudes toward 'Illegal' Immigration into the United States: California Proposition 187,"*Hispanic Journal of Behavioral Sciences* 23, no. 4 (2001): 430–43; Jack Citrin, Donald Green, Christopher Muste, and Cara Wong,"Public Opinion toward Immigration Reform: The Role of Economic Motivations," *Journal of Politics* 59, no. 3 (1997): 858–81.

22. Esping-Andersen, *The Three Worlds of Welfare Capitalism*, 2; Mink, *The Wages of Motherhood*; Piven and Cloward, *Regulating the Poor*; Loïc Wacquant,

Punishing the Poor: The Neoliberal Government of Social Insecurity (Durham: Duke University Press, 2009).

23. Thomas A. Guglielmo, *White on Arrival: Italians, Race, Color, and Power in Chicago, 1890–1945* (New York: Oxford University Press, 2004).

24. On local control, see Lieberman, *Shifting the Color Line*; Robert Lieberman and John Lapinski,"American Federalism, Race and the Administration of Welfare,"*British Journal of Political Science* 31, no. 2 (2001): 303–29.

25. Walter Trattner, *From Poor Law to Welfare State: A History of Social Welfare in America* (1974; New York: The Free Press, 1999), 233–72.

26. Lipsky, *Street-Level Bureaucracy*; Anne Schneider and Helen Ingram, "The Social Construction of Target Populations: Implications for Politics and Policy," *American Political Science Review* 87, no. 2 (1993): 334–47.

27. Esping-Andersen, *The Three Worlds of Welfare Capitalism*.

CHAPTER 2

1. Cohen, *Making a New Deal*; Neil Foley, *The White Scourge: Mexicans, Blacks, and Poor Whites in Texas Cotton Culture* (Berkeley: University of California Press, 1997); Evelyn Nakano Glenn, *Unequal Freedom: How Race and Gender Shaped American Citizenship and Labor* (Cambridge, MA: Harvard University Press, 2002).

2. Census Bureau, *Fifteenth Census of the United States, 1930, Population*, vol. 2, p. 32, and vol. 5, pp. 74–76; Census Bureau, *Fifteenth Census of the United States: 1930, Agriculture*, vol. 2, part 1 (Washington, DC: GPO, 1932), 35; Author's calculation, 1930 Census; Leon F. Litwack, *Trouble in Mind: Black Southerners in the Age of Jim Crow* (New York: Vintage Books, 1998), 125–29, 164; Neil McMillen, *Dark Journey: Black Mississippians in the Age of Jim Crow* (Urbana: University of Illinois Press, 1990), 128–30; Jacqueline Jones, *Labor of Love, Labor of Sorrow: Black Women, Work, and the Family from Slavery to the Present* (New York: Basic Books, 1985), 93–95; Glenn, *Unequal Freedom*, 101. All calculations of the "South" include the following states: Alabama, Arkansas, Florida, Georgia, Kentucky, Louisiana, Maryland, Mississippi, North Carolina, South Carolina, Tennessee, Virginia, and West Virginia.

3. Author's calculation, 1930 Census; Jones, *Labor of Love, Labor of Sorrow*, 82–83, 90, 127–37; Litwack, *Trouble in Mind*, 124–25, 169; Glenn, *Unequal Freedom*, 106; McMillen, *Dark Journey*, 160–63.

4. McMillen, *Dark Journey*, 130–33, 143–44; Lee Alston and T. Hatton, "The Earnings Gap between Agricultural and Manufacturing Laborers, 1925–1941," *Journal of Economic History* 51, no. 1 (1991): 83–99; Dan Green and Edwin Driver, eds., *W.E.B. Du Bois on Sociology and the Black Community* (Chicago: University of Chicago Press, 1980), 163; Litwack, *Trouble in Mind*, 131–40; W.E.B. Du Bois, *The Souls of Black Folk* (1903; New York: Vintage Books, 1990), 111; Glenn, *Unequal Freedom*, 102; William Cohen, "Negro Involuntary Servitude in the South, 1865–1940: A Preliminary Analysis," *Journal of Southern History* 42, no. 1 (1976): 31–60.

5. Litwack, *Trouble in Mind*, 139–41, 270–75; McMillen, *Dark Journey*, 141–50; Glenn, *Unequal Freedom*, 101–5; Cohen, "Negro Involuntary Servitude in

the South"; Du Bois, *The Souls of Black Folk*, 111–12; James Cobb, *The Most Southern Place on Earth: The Mississippi Delta and the Roots of Regional Identity* (New York: Oxford University Press, 1992), 104, 121; Jones, *Labor of Love, Labor of Sorrow*, 83–84.

6. Alston and Ferrie, *Southern Paternalism and the American Welfare State*, 15, passim; Lee Alston and Joseph Ferrie, "Labor Costs, Paternalism, and Loyalty in Southern Agriculture: A Constraint on the Growth of the Welfare State," *Journal of Economic History* 45, no. 1 (1985): 95–117; McMillen, *Dark Journey*, 162–63; Du Bois, *The Souls of Black Folk*, 112.

7. Cobb, *The Most Southern Place on Earth*, 103, 112; Lee Alston and Joseph Ferrie, "Paternalism in Agricultural Labor Contracts in the U.S. South: Implications for the Growth of the Welfare State," *American Economic Review* 83, no. 4 (1993): 856.

8. Harold Hoffsommer, *Landlord-Tenant Relations and Relief in Alabama* (Washington, DC: Federal Emergency Relief Administration, 1935); Cobb, *The Most Southern Place on Earth*, 122; McMillen, *Dark Journey*, 131.

9. Author's calculation, 1930 Census; Green and Driver, *W.E.B. Du Bois on Sociology and the Black Community*, 162; Du Bois, *The Souls of Black Folk*, 102–3; Cobb, *The Most Southern Place on Earth*, 119–20; Jones, *Labor of Love, Labor of Sorrow*, 86; T. J. Woofter, *Landlord and Tenant on the Cotton Plantation* (Washington, DC: Works Progress Administration, 1936), 91–106; Henry J. Kaiser Family Foundation, "Key Facts: Race, Ethnicity, and Medical Care" (Menlo Park, CA, 1999); Stanley Lieberson, *A Piece of the Pie: Black and White Immigrants since 1880* (Berkeley: University of California Press, 1980), 46.

10. Census Bureau, *Fifteenth Census of the United States: 1930, Agriculture*, vol. 2, part 1, 35; Litwack, *Trouble in Mind*, 118–19.

11. Litwack, *Trouble in Mind*, 230–36, 328; C. Vann Woodward, *The Strange Career of Jim Crow* (1955; New York: Oxford University Press, 2002), 33, 100–102, 116–18; McMillen, *Dark Journey*, 8–18; John Dittmer, *Black Georgia in the Progressive Era, 1900–1920* (Urbana: University of Illinois Press, 1977), 16–22; J. Douglas Smith, *Managing White Supremacy: Race, Politics, and Citizenship in Jim Crow Virginia* (Chapel Hill: University of North Carolina Press, 2002), 100–102; Jones, *Labor of Love, Labor of Sorrow*, 149–50; David Hollinger, "Amalgamation and Hypodescent: The Question of Ethnoracial Mixture in the History of the United States," *American Historical Review* 108, no. 5 (2003): 1363–90; Peggy Pascoe, "Miscegenation Law, Court Cases, and Ideologies of 'Race' in Twentieth-Century America," *Journal of American History* 83, no. 1 (1996): 44–69.

12. Litwack, *Trouble in Mind*, 238, 249, 254, 283–312; McMillen, *Dark Journey*, 28–32, 205, 221–22; Steward Tolnay, E. M. Beck, and James Massey, "Black Lynchings: The Power Threat Hypothesis Revisited," *Social Forces* 67, no. 3 (1988): 605–23; Gunnar Myrdal, *An American Dilemma: The Negro Problem and Modern Democracy* (1944; New York: Harper and Row, 1962), 535, 549–53, 560–62; Steven Hahn, *A Nation under Our Feet: Black Political Struggles in the Rural South from Slavery to the Great Migration* (Cambridge, MA: Harvard University Press, 2003), 426.

13. Woodward, *The Strange Career of Jim Crow*, 107; Litwack, *Trouble in Mind*, 230, 238–39; Myrdal, *An American Dilemma*, 580; Glenn, *Unequal Free-*

304 • Notes to Chapter 2

304 • Notes to Chapter 2

dom, 142; Smith, *Managing White Supremacy*, 84; Paul Finkleman, "The Color of Law," *Northwestern University Law Review* 87 (1993): 955n96; Melissa Nobles, *Shades of Citizenship: Race and the Census in Modern Politics* (Stanford: Stanford University Press, 2000), 61–72; Hollinger, "Amalgamation and Hypodescent"; Teresa Zackondik, "Fixing the Color Line: The Mulatto, Southern Courts, and Racial Identity," *American Quarterly* 53, no. 3 (2001): 420–51, 442–43.

14. Thomas Sugrue, *Sweet Land of Liberty: The Forgotten Struggle for Civil Rights in the North* (New York: Random House, 2008); Woodward, *The Strange Career of Jim Crow*, 98, 115; McMillen, *Dark Journey*, 155–66; Litwack, *Trouble in Mind*, 133, 142–43.

15. Douglas Massey and Nancy Denton, *American Apartheid: Segregation and the Making of the Underclass* (Cambridge, MA: Harvard University Press, 1993), 36, 41–42; Woodward, *The Strange Career of Jim Crow*, 100–101; McMillen, *Dark Journey*, 13; Thomas Philpott, *The Slum and the Ghetto: Immigrants, Blacks, and Reformers in Chicago, 1880–1930* (1978; Belmont, CA: Wadsworth Publishing Company, 1991), xv, 169.

16. Du Bois, *The Souls of Black Folk*; Hahn, *A Nation under Our Feet*, 431–46; Woodward, *The Strange Career of Jim Crow*, 60–64, 78–84; Myrdal, *An American Dilemma*, 452, 479–86; Alexander Keyssar, *The Right to Vote: The Contested History of Democracy in the United States* (New York: Basic Books, 2000), 111–13; V. O. Key, *Southern Politics in State and Nation* (1949; Knoxville: University of Tennessee Press, 1984), 537–40; McMillen, *Dark Journey*, 43.

17. Keyssar, *The Right to Vote*, 111–13; Key, *Southern Politics in State and Nation*, 504–8, 537–38, 542–50; Glenn, *Unequal Freedom*, 111–13; Woodward, *The Strange Career of Jim Crow*, 84; Litwack, *Trouble in Mind*, 226; McMillen, *Dark Journey*, 45; Smith, *Managing White Supremacy*, 25–26, 59; Paul Kleppner, *Who Voted? The Dynamics of Electoral Turnout, 1870–1920* (New York: Praeger, 1982), 66.

18. Key, *Southern Politics in State and Nation*, 620–21.

19. Hahn, *A Nation under Our Feet*, 445, 450; Woodward, *The Strange Career of Jim Crow*, 85; Dittmer, *Black Georgia in the Progressive Era*, 103; Keyssar, *The Right to Vote*, 115; *Historical Statistics of the United States, Colonial Times to 1970* (Washington, DC: GPO, 1975); Myrdal, *An American Dilemma*, 474–75, 478–79; Glenda Gilmore, *Gender and Jim Crow: Women and the Politics of White Supremacy in North Carolina, 1896–1920* (Chapel Hill: University of North Carolina Press, 1996), 119–20, 129–30; Smith, *Managing White Supremacy*, 60–67; Key, *Southern Politics in State and Nation*, 504–8; Lieberman, *Shifting the Color Line*; Katznelson, *When Affirmative Action Was White*.

20. Glenn, *Unequal Freedom*, 113; McMillen, *Dark Journey*, 60; Smith, *Managing White Supremacy*, 60–61; Lieberson, *A Piece of the Pie*, 63.

21. Census Bureau, "Region of Birth of the Foreign-Born Population: 1850 to 1930 and 1960 to 1990," table 2, http://www.census.gov/population/www/documentation/twps0029/tab02.html; author's calculation, 1930 Census; Harold Gosnell, "Non-Naturalization: A Study in Political Assimilation," *American Journal of Sociology* 33, no. 6 (1928): 930–39; Lieberson, *A Piece of the Pie*,

22–24; Helen Marrow, "Race and the New Southern Migration, 1986–present," in *Beyond the Border: The History of Mexico-US Migration*, ed. M. Overmyer-Velázquez (New York: Oxford University Press, 2011). I follow the Dillingham Commission's definition for the distinction between southern and eastern versus northern and western European. U.S. Immigration Commission, *Reports of the Immigration Commission: Abstracts* (Washington, DC: GPO, 1911), vol. 1, p. 61. All calculations for the Northeast and Midwest include: Connecticut, Delaware, D.C., Illinois, Indiana, Iowa, Maine, Massachusetts, Michigan, Minnesota, Missouri, New Hampshire, New Jersey, New York, Ohio, Pennsylvania, Rhode Island, Vermont, and Wisconsin. All calculations for the North include the former states plus Colorado, Idaho, Kansas, Montana, Nebraska, Nevada, North Dakota, Oklahoma, Oregon, South Dakota, Utah, Washington, and Wyoming.

22. Census Bureau, *Fifteenth Census of the United States, Population*, vol. 5, p. 74; Julie Greene, *Pure and Simple Politics: The American Federation of Labor and Political Activism, 1881–1917* (Cambridge: Cambridge University Press, 1998), 22–23; Cohen, *Making a New Deal*, 13, 187; Dominica Pacyga, *Polish Immigrants and Industrial Chicago: Workers on the South Side, 1880–1922* (Columbus: Ohio State University Press, 1991), 59–62, 88–96, 106.

23. Pacyga, *Polish Immigrants and Industrial Chicago*, 95; Thomas Göbel, "Becoming American: Ethnic Workers and the Rise of the CIO," *Labor History* 29, no. 2 (1988): 173–98; Francis Ianni, "Residential and Occupational Mobility as Indices of the Acculturation of an Ethnic Group," *Social Forces* 36, no. 1 (1957): 65–72; Lieberson, *A Piece of the Pie*, chapter 11, especially 329, 334–39; John Hinshaw, *Steel and Steelworkers: Race and Class Struggle in Twentieth-Century Pittsburgh* (Albany: State University of New York Press, 2002), 73–74; Roediger, *Working toward Whiteness*, 220; Mark Reisler, *By the Sweat of Their Brow: Mexican Immigrant Labor in the United States, 1900–1940* (Westport, CT: Greenwood Press, 1976), 105; Cohen, *Making a New Deal*, 186–87; Sumner Slichter, "The Current Labor Policies of American Industries," *Quarterly Journal of Economics* 43, no. 3 (1929): 393–435.

24. Michael B. Katz, *In the Shadow of the Poorhouse: A Social History of Welfare in America* (New York: Basic Books, 1986), 192–97; Irving Bernstein, *The Lean Years: A History of the American Worker, 1920–1933* (New York: Da Capo Press, 1960), 170–89; Cohen, *Making a New Deal*, 159–211; David Montgomery, *The Fall of the House of Labor: The Workplace, the State, and American Labor Activism, 1865–1925* (Cambridge: Cambridge University Press, 1987); Slichter, "The Current Labor Policies of American Industries."

25. Author's calculation, 1930 Census; Humbert Nelli, *Italians in Chicago, 1880–1930: A Study in Ethnic Mobility* (New York: Oxford University Press, 1970), 77.

26. Cohen, *Making a New Deal*, 17; Lieberson, *A Piece of the Pie*, chapter 9, p. 278; William Yancey, Eugene Ericksen, and Richard Juliani, "Emergent Ethnicity: A Review and Reformulation," *American Sociological Review* 41, no. 3 (1976): 391–403; Philpott, *The Slum and the Ghetto*, 23, 141; Howard Chudacoff, "A New Look at Ethnic Neighborhoods: Residential Dispersion and the Concept of Visibility in a Medium-Sized City," *Journal of American History* 60, no. 1 (1973): 76–93; Massey and Denton, *American Apartheid*, 32.

27. Jacob Riis, *How the Other Half Lives: Studies among the Tenements of New York* (1901; New York: Penguin Books, 1997), 6, 19; Katz, *In the Shadow of the Poorhouse*, 177–184; Philpott, *The Slum and the Ghetto*, 23–33; Pacyga, *Polish Immigrants and Industrial Chicago*, 43–110; Lieberson, *A Piece of the Pie*, 46.

28. Author's calculation, 1930 Census; Lieberson, *A Piece of the Pie*, 46; Philpott, *The Slum and the Ghetto*.

29. Nobles, *Shades of Citizenship*, 72; Guglielmo, *White on Arrival*, 30; Ariela Gross, *What Blood Won't Tell: A History of Race on Trial in America* (Cambridge, MA: Harvard University Press, 2008), 7, 230–36.

30. Guglielmo, *White on Arrival*, 6, 27–29; Roediger, *Working toward Whiteness*, 180.

31. Guglielmo, *White on Arrival*, 8–9, 30; Matthew Jacobson, *Whiteness of a Different Color: European Immigrants and the Alchemy of Race* (Cambridge, MA: Harvard University Press, 1998), 6.

32. King, *Making Americans*; Jennifer Hochschild and Brenna Powell, "Racial Reorganization and the United States Census, 1850–1930: Mulattoes, Half Breeds, Mixed Parentage, Hindoos and the Mexican Race," *Studies in American Political Development* 22, no. 1 (2008): 75, 76–77; Joel Perlmann, "Race or People": Federal Race Classification for Europeans in America, 1898–1913 (Jerome Levy Economics Institute Working Paper No. 320, 2001).

33. David Roediger and James Barrett, "Making New Immigrants 'Inbetween': Irish Hosts and White Panethnicity, 1890 to 1930," in *Not Just Black and White: Historical and Contemporary Perspectives on Immigration, Race, and Ethnicity in the United States*, ed. N. Foner and G. Fredrickson (New York: Russell Sage Foundation, 2004), 167–96; Guglielmo, *White on Arrival*, 27; Roediger, *Working toward Whiteness*, 171–73, 198.

34. Paul McGouldrick and Michael Tannen, "Did American Manufacturers Discriminate against Immigrants before 1914?" *Journal of Economic History* 37, no. 3 (1977): 723–46; Roediger, *Working toward Whiteness*, 75–78, 106; John Higham, *Strangers in the Land: Patterns of American Nativism, 1860–1925* (1955; New Brunswick: Rutgers University Press, 1994), 278, 286; King, *Making Americans*.

35. *Historical Statistics of the United States, Colonial Times to 1970*; Keyssar, *The Right to Vote*.

36. Keyssar, *The Right to Vote*, 129–58, 168–69, 355–79; Steven Erie, *Rainbow's End: Irish-Americans and the Dilemmas of Urban Machine Politics, 1840–1985* (Berkeley: University of California Press, 1988), 92; author's calculation, 1930 Census; Arthur Bromage, "Literacy and the Electorate," *American Political Science Review* 24, no. 4 (1930): 946–62; Michael McGerr, *The Decline of Popular Politics: The North, 1865–1930* (New York: Oxford University Press, 1986), 46–52; Evelyn Savidge Sterne, "Bringing Religion into Working-Class History: Parish, Public, and Politics in Providence, 1890–1930," *Social Science History* 24, no. 1 (2000): 171–73.

37. McGerr, *The Decline of Popular Politics*, 47–51, 207–9, 285n72; Amy Bridges and Richard Kronick, "Writing the Rules to Win the Game: The Middle-Class Regimes of Municipal Reformers," *Urban Affairs Quarterly* 34, no. 5

(1999): 698; Bromage, "Literacy and the Electorate," 955, 959–61; Kleppner, *Who Voted?* 60–61, 68, 80; Keyssar, *The Right to Vote*, 170.

38. Paul Kleppner, *Continuity and Change in Electoral Politics, 1893–1928* (New York: Greenwood Press, 1987), 165; Leon Aylsworth, "The Passing of Alien Suffrage," *American Political Science Review* 25, no. 1 (1931): 114–16; Keyssar, *The Right to Vote*, 136, 371–72; Virginia Harper-Ho, "Noncitizen Voting Rights: The History, the Law and Current Prospects for Change," *Law and Inequality* 18 (2000): 282; Higham, *Strangers in the Land*, 214; Erie, *Rainbow's End*, 92; author's calculation, 1930 Census; Irene Bloemraad, "Citizenship Lessons from the Past: The Contours of Immigrant Naturalization in the Early Twentieth Century," *Social Science Quarterly* 87, no. 5 (2006): 936; William Bernard, "Cultural Determinants of Naturalization," *American Sociological Review* 1, no. 6 (1936): 943–53; John Gavit, *Americans by Choice* (New York: Harper and Brothers, 1922), 241, 245.

39. McGerr, *The Decline of Popular Politics*; Robert Dahl, *Who Governs? Democracy and Power in an American City* (1961; New Haven: Yale University Press, 2005), 32–36; M. Brown Craig and Charles Halaby, "Machine Politics in America, 1870–1945," *Journal of Interdisciplinary History* 17, no. 3 (1987): 587–612; Jessica Trounstine, *Political Monopolies in American Cities: The Rise and Fall of Bosses and Reformers* (Chicago: University of Chicago Press, 2008), 241–43; Amy Bridges, *Morning Glories: Municipal Reform in the Southwest* (Princeton: Princeton University Press, 1997); Bridges and Kronick, "Writing the Rules to Win the Game"; Thomas Dye and Susan Macmanus, "Predicting City Government Structure," *American Journal of Political Science* 20, no. 2 (1976): 257–71; Daniel Gordon, "Immigrants and Urban Governmental Form in American Cities, 1933–1960," *American Journal of Sociology* 74, no. 2 (1968): 158–71.

40. Sonya Forthal, "The Precinct Worker," *Annals of the American Academy of Political and Social Science* 259 (1948): 30–45; Evelyn Savidge Sterne, "Beyond the Boss: Immigration and American Political Culture from 1880 to 1940," in *E Pluribus Unum? Contemporary and Historical Perspectives on Immigrant Political Incorporation*, ed. G. Gerstle and J. Mollenkopf (New York: Russell Sage Foundation, 2001), 39–41; Bruce Stave, *The New Deal and the Last Hurrah: Pittsburgh Machine Politics* (Pittsburgh: University of Pittsburgh Press, 1970), 11, 16; Nelli, *Italians in Chicago*, 95, 114; Dorothee Schneider, "Naturalization and United States Citizenship in Two Periods of Mass Migration: 1894–1930, 1965–2000," *Journal of American Ethnic History* 21, no. 1 (2001): 54; Erie, *Rainbow's End*, 94–95; Harold Gosnell, *Machine Politics, Chicago Model* (Chicago: University of Chicago Press, 1937), 71.

41. Harold Gosnell, *Getting Out the Vote: An Experiment in the Stimulation of Voting* (Chicago: University of Chicago Press, 1927), 46–80; Nelli, *Italians in Chicago*, 89, 95, 103; Keyssar, *The Right to Vote*, 129, 157; Erie, *Rainbow's End*, 95; Kenneth Finegold, *Experts and Politicians: Reform Challenges to Machine Politics in New York, Cleveland, and Chicago* (Princeton: Princeton University Press, 1995); Pacyga, *Polish Immigrants and Industrial Chicago*, 197–98, 204.

42. McGerr, *The Decline of Popular Politics*, 52–68; Kleppner, *Who Voted?* 68–80, 88–89; Kleppner, *Continuity and Change in Electoral Politics*, 191–93;

Charles Merriam and Harold Gosnell, *Non-Voting: Causes and Methods of Control* (Chicago: University of Chicago Press, 1924), 6, 28, 40.

43. Erie, *Rainbow's End*, 101; Dahl, *Who Governs?* 43; Stefano Luconi, "Machine Politics and the Consolidation of the Roosevelt Majority: The Case of Italian Americans in Pittsburgh and Philadelphia," *Journal of American Ethnic History* 15, no. 2 (1996): 32–59; Giovanni E. Sciavo, *The Italians of Chicago: A Study in Americanization* (Chicago: Italian American Publishing, 1928), 103–6; Pacyga, *Polish Immigrants and Industrial Chicago*, 200–201; Nelli, *Italians in Chicago*, 113–16; Alex Gottfried, *Boss Cermak of Chicago: A Study of Political Leadership* (Seattle: University of Washington Press, 1962); Marian Schibsby, "New York's Foreign Language Newspapers and the Mayoralty Campaign," *Interpreter Release Clip Sheet* 10, no. 19 (1933): 81–85; Lieberson, *A Piece of the Pie*, 78–88.

44. Higham, *Strangers in the Land*, 235–42; Philpott, *The Slum and the Ghetto*, 108; Frank Thompson, *Schooling of the Immigrant* (New York: Harper and Brothers, 1920), 57; "Confidential List of International Institutes," National Department of Immigration and Foreign Communities, National Board, YWCA, January 1, 1925, folder 7, box 288, reel 195, AFII Papers; International Institute of St. Louis, "The International Institutes: A National Movement of Resettlement and Inclusion," http://www.iistl.org/history.html.

45. Higham, *Strangers in the Land*, 241–45; James Barrett, "Americanization from the Bottom Up: Immigration and the Remaking of the Working Class in the United States, 1880–1930," *Journal of American History* 79, no. 3 (1992): 996–1020; William Leiserson, *Adjusting Immigrant and Industry* (New York: Harper and Brothers, 1924), 80–81, 120–25; Thompson, *Schooling of the Immigrant*, 56–57, 99–106; King, *Making Americans*, 98–100; Olivier Zunz, *The Changing Face of Inequality: Urbanization, Industrial Development, and Immigrants in Detroit, 1880–1920* (Chicago: University of Chicago Press, 1982), 311–17; Gosnell, "Non-Naturalization," 932–33; Cohen, *Making a New Deal*, 165.

46. Nancy Cott, "Marriage and Women's Citizenship in the United States, 1830–1934," *American Historical Review* 103, no. 5 (1998): 1456, 1462–63, 1465; Gavit, *Americans by Choice*, 297; Thompson, *Schooling of the Immigrant*, 54, 109; Zunz, *The Changing Face of Inequality*, 317; King, *Making Americans*, 107–9; Higham, *Strangers in the Land*, 238, 245, 251; Sterne, "Bringing Religion into Working-Class History"; Sterne, "Beyond the Boss," 55.

47. David Tuack, "Schools for Citizens: The Politics of Civic Education from 1790 to 1990," in *E Pluribus Unum? Contemporary and Historical Perspectives on Immigrant Political Incorporation*, ed. G. Gerstle and J. Mollenkopf (New York: Russell Sage Foundation, 2001), 347–50; Thompson, *Schooling of the Immigrant*, 282–326; King, *Making Americans*, 88–90, 105, 108, 113–15; Frank Ross, *School Attendance in 1920*, Census Monographs, vol. 5 (Washington, DC: GPO, 1924), 39, 76–77; Lieberson, *A Piece of the Pie*, 135–37; Gosnell, "Non-Naturalization," 935; Higham, *Strangers in the Land*, 248.

48. Higham, *Strangers in the Land*, 242–49, 255; King, *Making Americans*, 87–120; Leiserson, *Adjusting Immigrant and Industry*, 249–53; Roediger, *Working toward Whiteness*, 208–9; Lieberson, *A Piece of the Pie*, 339–41; Hinshaw, *Steel and Steelworkers*, 20–22; Schneider, "Naturalization and United States

Citizenship in Two Periods of Mass Migration"; Keyssar, *The Right to Vote*, 139; Erie, *Rainbow's End*, 92; Gavit, *Americans by Choice*, 77–142, 177–80, 232–33; Bloemraad, "Citizenship Lessons from the Past," 941; Gosnell, "Non-Naturalization," 935–36; Thompson, *Schooling of the Immigrant*, 46–48.

49. Higham, *Strangers in the Land*, 253–54; Schneider, "Naturalization and United States Citizenship in Two Periods of Mass Migration," 61.

50. *Historical Statistics of the United States, Millennial Edition*, Naturalization, Series Ad1030-1071, Washington, DC, http://hsus.cambridge.org/HSUS-Web/toc/showTable.do?id=Ad1030-1071.

51. Census Bureau, *Fifteenth Census of the United States, Population*, vol. 2, p. 25; author's calculation, 1930 Census. These numbers underestimate the number of Mexican-origin individuals since the census included in their designation of Mexican only first- and second-generation Mexicans who were "not definitely white, Negro, Indian, Chinese, or Japanese." Third-plus generation individuals of Mexican origin were not supposed to be included, although in practice many census enumerators did include these individuals as Mexican. All calculations of the "Southwest" include Arizona, California, New Mexico, and Texas.

52. Author's calculation, 1930 Census; Foley, *The White Scourge*; David Montejano, *Anglos and Mexicans in the Making of Texas, 1836–1986* (Austin: University of Texas Press, 1987); Census Bureau, *Fifteenth Census of the United States, Population*, vol. 5, pp. 76, 86; Cybelle Fox, "Three Worlds of Relief: Race, Immigration and Public and Private Social Welfare Spending, 1929," *American Journal of Sociology* 116, no. 2 (2010): 464.

53. Reisler, *By the Sweat of Their Brow*, 5, 78, 129, 131; Glenn, *Unequal Freedom*, 151; Zaragosa Vargas, *Labor Rights Are Civil Rights: Mexican American Workers in Twentieth-Century America* (Princeton: Princeton University Press, 2005), 27–34; Carey McWilliams, *Ill Fares the Land: Migrants and Migratory Labor in the United States* (Boston: Little, Brown and Company, 1942), 39, 224; House Committee on Immigration and Naturalization, *Immigration from Countries of the Western Hemisphere*, 70th Cong., 1st Sess., 1928, p. 318; David Gutiérrez, *Walls and Mirrors: Mexican Americans, Mexican Immigrants, and the Politics of Ethnicity* (Berkeley: University of California Press, 1995), 49.

54. Vargas, *Labor Rights Are Civil Rights*, 30, passim; Reisler, *By the Sweat of Their Brow*, 89, 138; McWilliams, *Ill Fares the Land*, 76, 247; Glenn, *Unequal Freedom*, 153; Mario Barrera, *Race and Class in the Southwest: A Theory of Racial Inequality* (Notre Dame: University of Notre Dame Press, 1979), 78–79; Carey McWilliams, *Factories in the Field: The Story of Migratory Farm Labor in California* (1935; Berkeley: University of California Press, 1999), 130; Montejano, *Anglos and Mexicans in the Making of Texas*, 9; House Committee, *Immigration from Countries of the Western Hemisphere*, 325.

55. House Committee, *Immigration from Countries of the Western Hemisphere*, 305; Paul Taylor, "Mexican Labor in the United States Valley of the South Platte Colorado," in *Mexican Labor in the United States*, vol. 1 (Berkeley: University of California Press, 1928–34), 95–235; Paul Taylor, "Mexican Labor in the United States: Dimmit County, Winter Garden District, South Texas," in *Mexican Labor in the United States*, vol. 1, pp. 293–464; Montejano, *Anglos and Mexicans in the Making of Texas*, 206–7; CCIH, *Annual Report of the Commission*

of Immigration and Housing of California (Sacramento, CA, 1927), 17; McWilliams, *Factories in the Field*, 126, 232–33.

56. Alston and Ferrie, *Southern Paternalism and the American Welfare State*, 28–30; Josiah Folsom, *Perquisites and Wages of Hired Farm Laborers* (Washington, DC, 1931); Taylor, "Mexican Labor in the United States Valley of the South Platte Colorado," 182.

57. Laura Parker, "Migratory Children," in *NCSW Proceedings*, 1927, pp. 302–9; Vargas, *Labor Rights Are Civil Rights*, 35; Reisler, *By the Sweat of Their Brow*, 57, 80; Census Bureau, *Fifteenth Census of the United States, Population*, vol. 5, p. 76.

58. Author's calculation, 1930 Census; Glenn, *Unequal Freedom*, 156; Sarah Deutsch, *No Separate Refuge: Culture, Class, and Gender on an Anglo-Hispanic Frontier in the American Southwest, 1880–1940* (Oxford: Oxford University Press, 1987), 146–47.

59. McWilliams, *Ill Fares the Land*, 77, 231–35, 251–54, 264–71; Montejano, *Anglos and Mexicans in the Making of Texas*, 171, 200, 205, 219; CCIH, *Annual Report of the Commission of Immigration and Housing of California*; Paul Taylor, "Mexican Labor in the United States Imperial Valley," in *Mexican Labor in the United States*, vol. 1, pp. 55–58; Vargas, *Labor Rights Are Civil Rights*, 22, 36; Lawrence Waters, "Transient Mexican Agricultural Labor," *Southwestern Social Science Quarterly* 22 (1941): 52.

60. Albert Camarillo, *Chicanos in a Changing Society: From Mexican Pueblos to American Barrios in Santa Barbara and Southern California, 1848–1930* (1979; Dallas: Southern Methodist University Press, 1996), 202–3; Jet Winters, *A Report on the Health and Nutrition of Mexicans Living in Texas* (Austin: University of Texas Bulletin, 1931); Vargas, *Labor Rights Are Civil Rights*, 23; California, Mexican-Fact Finding Committee, *Mexicans in California: Report of Governor C. C. Young's Mexican Fact-Finding Committee* (Sacramento, CA, 1930), 206, passim; Natalia Molina, *Fit to Be Citizens? Public Health and Race in Los Angeles, 1879–1939* (Berkeley: University of California Press, 2006); Census Bureau, *Birth, Stillbirth, and Infant Mortality Statistics for the Birth Registration Area of the United States, 1931* (Washington, DC: GPO, 1934), 4, 36.

61. Tomás Almaguer, *Racial Fault Lines: The Historical Origins of White Supremacy in California* (Berkeley: University of California Press, 1994), chapter 2; Linda Gordon, *The Great Arizona Orphan Abduction* (Cambridge, MA: Harvard University Press, 1999), 99–100; Camarillo, *Chicanos in a Changing Society*, chapter 3; O. Douglas Weeks, "The Texas-Mexican and the Politics of South Texas," *American Political Science Review* 24, no. 3 (1930): 606–27; Robert Foerster, "The Racial Problems Involved in Immigration from Latin America and the West Indies to the United States" (Washington, DC: GPO, 1925), 11.

62. Hochschild and Powell, "Racial Reorganization and the United States Census, 1850–1930"; Census Bureau, *Fifteenth Census of the United States, Population*, vol. 2, p. 27; Mario Garcia, "Mexican Americans and the Politics of Citizenship: The Case of El Paso, 1936," *New Mexico Historical Review* 59, no. 2 (1984): 187–204; Thomas Guglielmo, "Fighting for Caucasian Rights: Mexicans, Mexican Americans, and the Transnational Struggle for Civil Rights in World War II Texas," *Journal of American History* 92, no. 4 (2006): 1212–37; Patrick

Espinosa, "Mexico, Mexican Americans and the FDR Administration's Racial Classification Policy: Public Policy in Place of Diplomacy" (Ph.D. diss., Arizona State University, 1999); Natalia Molina, "'In a Race All Their Own': The Quest to Make Mexicans Ineligible for U.S. Citizenship," *Pacific Historical Review* 79, no. 2 (2010): 167–201.

63. Espinosa, "Mexico, Mexican Americans and the FDR Administration's Racial Classification Policy"; "Indian Blood Bars Mexicans as Citizens," *NYT*, December 12, 1935, p. 4; Secretary to Acting Commissioner of Immigration and Naturalization, May 5, 1937, Immigration, box 71, RG 174; Davis to Johnson, February 14, 1929, carton 10:1, Taylor Papers; Molina, "In a Race All Their Own."

64. Gary Greenfield and Don Kates Jr., "Mexican Americans, Racial Discrimination, and the Civil Rights Act of 1866," *California Law Review* 63, no. 3 (1975): 662–731; Reisler, *By the Sweat of Their Brow*, 140–41; Taylor, "Mexican Labor in the United States: Dimmit County," 416–21; Jorge Rangel and Carlos Acala, "Project Report: De Jure Segregation of Chicanos in Texas Schools," *Harvard Civil Rights—Civil Liberties Law Review* 7, no. 2 (1972): 307–91; Paul Taylor, *An American-Mexican Frontier: Nueces County, Texas* (New York: Russell and Russell, 1934), 250–55, 250n1, 264n13, 265; Taylor, "Mexican Labor in the United States: Imperial Valley," 83–94; Dionicio Valdés, *Barrios Norteños: St. Paul and Midwestern Mexican Communities in the Twentieth Century* (Austin: University of Texas Press, 2000), 62–63; Rubén Donato, "Theory, Research, Policy, and Practice: Sugar Beets, Segregation, and Schools: Mexican Americans in a Northern Colorado Community, 1920–1960," *Journal of Latinos and Education* 2, no. 2 (2003): 69–88; Foley, *The White Scourge*; Pauline Kibbe, *Latin Americans in Texas* (New York: Arno Press, 1974), 208–12; Guglielmo, "Fighting for Caucasian Rights"; Taylor, "Mexican Labor in the United States of the South Platte Valley," 222; Selden Menefee and Orin Cassmore, *The Pecan Shellers of San Antonio* (Washington, DC: GPO, 1940), 51; Juan García, *Mexicans in the Midwest, 1900–1932* (Tucson: University of Arizona Press, 1996).

65. Vicki Ruiz, "South by Southwest: Mexican Americans and Segregated Schooling, 1900–1950," *OAH Magazine of History* 15, no. 2 (2001): 23–27; Gilbert Gonzalez, "Segregation of Mexican Children in a Southern California City: The Legacy of Expansionism and the American Southwest," *Western Historical Quarterly* 16, no. 1 (1985): 55–76; Valdés, *Barrios Norteños*, 63; Taylor, "Mexican Labor in the United States: Imperial Valley," 83–86; Reisler, *By the Sweat of Their Brow*, 141; E. B. Fincher, *Spanish-Americans as a Political Factor in New Mexico, 1912–1950* (New York: Arno Press, 1974), 76–79; Taylor, "Mexican Labor in the United States: Dimmit County," 388; Taylor, *An American-Mexican Frontier*, 216–25; Neil Foley, "Straddling the Color Line: The Legal Construction of Hispanic Identity in Texas," in *Not Just Black and White: Historical and Contemporary Perspectives on Immigration, Race, and Ethnicity in the United States*, ed. N. Foner and G. Fredrickson (New York: Russell Sage Foundation, 2004), 350; Foley, *The White Scourge*, 41; Rangel and Acala, "Project Report," 314–15.

66. Taylor, "Mexican Labor in the United States of the South Platte Valley," 209, 216–17; Taylor, "Mexican Labor in the United States: Dimmit County," 396–98; Taylor, "Mexican Labor in the United States, Imperial Valley," 79–83;

California, *Mexicans in California*, 176–77; Michael Jones-Correa, "The Origins and Diffusion of Racial Restrictive Covenants," *Political Science Quarterly* 115, no. 4 (2000–2001): 541–68; Camarillo, *Chicanos in a Changing Society*, 205, 209; Kibbe, *Latin Americans in Texas*, 229; Taylor, *An American-Mexican Frontier*, 226–29; Norman Williams Jr., "Discrimination and Segregation in Minority Housing," *American Journal of Economics and Sociology* 9, no. 1 (1949): 85–102; William Ming Jr., "Racial Restrictions and the Fourteenth Amendment: The Restrictive Covenant Cases," *University of Chicago Law Review* 16, no. 2 (1949): 203–38.

67. Pascoe, "Miscegenation Law, Court Cases, and Ideologies of 'Race' in Twentieth-Century America"; Hollinger, "Amalgamation and Hypodescent"; Glenn, *Unequal Freedom*, 165–69; Taylor, "Mexican Labor in the United States: Dimmit County," 388–92, 424, 428; Taylor, *An American-Mexican Frontier*, 257–60, 266–69, 296–97; Deutsch, *No Separate Refuge*, 175; Taylor, "Mexican Labor in the United States of the South Platte Valley," 228–32; Taylor, "Mexican Labor in the United States: Imperial Valley," 92; Foley, *The White Scourge*, 208–10.

68. Bridges, *Morning Glories*, 7–8, passim; author's calculation. The index tallies the number of government reforms a city adopted by 1929 and runs from 0 to 3. Reforms include at large instead of ward-based elections, nonpartisan elections, and commission or council-manager as opposed to mayoral-council style government. The idea for the index came from Terry Clark, "The Irish Ethic and the Spirit of Patronage," *Ethnicity* 2 (1975): 319. Data on the index come from: Bureau of Governmental Research, *The Form of Government in 288 American Cities: A Summary of a Questionnaire Sent Cities over 30,000 Population, August, 1929* (Detroit, 1931); "The Municipal Year Book, 1934," International City Managers' Association, Chicago (1934). See also Fox, "Three Worlds of Relief," 470–74.

69. Bridges, *Morning Glories*, 8, 18–19, 55; Martin Shefter, "Regional Receptivity to Reform: The Legacy of the Progressive Era," *Political Science Quarterly* 98, no. 3 (1983): 459–83; Bridges and Kronick, "Writing the Rules to Win the Game," 693; Keyssar, *The Right to Vote*, 146–56, 368–79, 380–89; Dudley McGoveney, *The American Suffrage Medley* (Chicago: University of Chicago Press, 1949), 59–60, 92, 142; John Burma, *Spanish-Speaking Groups in the United States* (1954; Detroit: Blaine Ethridge Books, 1974), 104–5.

70. Montejano, *Anglos and Mexicans in the Making of Texas*, 144–47; Key, *Southern Politics in State and Nation*, 273; Taylor, "Mexican Labor in the United States: Dimmit County"; "Bars Voting by Mexicans," *NYT*, July 27, 1934, p. 6; Kibbe, *Latin Americans in Texas*, 227; Allred to Blalock, July 25, 1934, Opinions No. 65, p. 548, Archives and Information Services Division, TSLAC Papers; State Department Memorandum, September 12, 1941, p. 30, 811.4016, 1940–44, RG 59.

71. Taylor, "Mexican Labor in the United States: Imperial Valley," 91; author's calculation, 1930 Census; Bridges, *Morning Glories*, 19; Bridges and Kronick, "Writing the Rules to Win the Game"; *Historical Statistics of the United States, Colonial Times to 1970*; Fox, "Three Worlds of Relief."

72. Fincher, *Spanish-Americans as a Political Factor in New Mexico*, 116–29, 243–60; Joan Jensen, "'Disfranchisement Is a Disgrace': Women and Politics in

New Mexico," *New Mexican Historical Review* 56, no. 5 (1981): 5–35; Mc-Goveney, *The American Suffrage Medley*, 59; Keyssar, *The Right to Vote*, 372; Taylor, "Mexican Labor in the United States: Dimmit County," 398; Audrey Granneberg, "Maury Maverick's San Antonio," *Survey Graphic* 1, no. 28 (1939): 423–30; Richard Garcia, *Rise of the Mexican American Middle Class, San Antonio, 1929–1941* (College Station: Texas A&M University Press, 1991), 211–14; Richard Henderson, *Maury Maverick: A Political Biography* (Austin: University of Texas Press, 1970), 199; Vargas, *Labor Rights Are Civil Rights*, 129.

73. Author's calculation, 1930 Census; Cybelle Fox and Irene Bloemraad, "White by Law, Not in Practice: Explaining the Gulf in Citizenship Acquisition between Mexican and European Immigrants, 1930" (Paper presented at the Law and Society Association Conference, San Francisco, June 4, 2011).

74. Fox and Bloemraad, "White by Law, Not in Practice"; Manuel Gamio, *Mexican Immigration to the United States: A Study of Human Migration and Adjustment* (1930; New York: Dover Publications, 1971), 128; Emory Bogardus, "The Mexican Immigrant and Segregation," *American Journal of Sociology* 36, no. 1 (1930): 78; Mae Ngai, *Impossible Subjects: Illegal Aliens and the Making of Modern America* (Princeton: Princeton University Press, 2004), 8.

75. Raphael Sonenshein, *Los Angeles: Structure of a City Government* (Los Angeles: League of Women Voters of Los Angeles, 2006), 27; Thomas Sitton, "Urban Politics and Reform in New Deal Los Angeles: The Recall of Mayor Frank L. Shaw" (Ph.D. thesis, University of California, Riverside, 1983), 78; Ross, *School Attendance in 1920*, 68, 201; Frances Cahn and Valeska Bary, *Welfare Activities of Federal, State, and Local Governments in California, 1850–1934* (Berkeley: University of California Press, 1936), 346; Leiserson, *Adjusting Immigrant and Industry*, 257–58; Thompson, *Schooling of the Immigrant*, 50–51; Higham, *Strangers in the Land*, 241; Jess Walsh, "Laboring at the Margins: Welfare and the Regulation of Mexican Workers in Southern California," *Antipode* 31, no. 4 (1999): 398–420, 403–4; George J. Sánchez, *Becoming Mexican American: Ethnicity, Culture and Identity in Chicano Los Angeles, 1900–1945* (New York: Oxford University Press, 1995), 95, chapter 4; Gayle Gullett, "Women Progressives and the Politics of Americanization in California," *Pacific Historical Review* 64, no. 1 (1995): 71–94; Edythe Tate Thompson, "Cost of Importing Mexican Labor," *Sacramento Region News*, January 21, 1928, 4–5, carton 2:12, DIR Papers; California, *Mexicans in California*; Robin Scott, "The Mexican-American in the Los Angeles Area, 1920–1950: From Acquiescence to Activity" (Ph.D. thesis, University of Southern California, Los Angeles, 1971); Don Mitchell, *The Lie of the Land: Migrant Workers and the California Landscape* (Minneapolis: University of Minnesota Press, 1996), 121–23; Christina Ziegler-McPherson, "Americanization: The California Plan: The Commission of Immigration and Housing of California and Public Policy, 1913–1923" (Ph.D. thesis, University of California, Santa Barbara, 2000); Hanna to Shortridge, February 24, 1926, folder 36, box 4, DIR Papers.

76. Reisler, *By the Sweat of Their Brow*, 178–79; Sánchez, *Becoming Mexican American*; Bridges, *Morning Glories*; Valdés, *Barrios Norteños*, 74.

77. Agnes Hanna, "Social Services on the Mexican Border," *NCSW Proceedings*, 1935, pp. 692–702; Gamio, *Mexican Immigration to the United States*,

118–19; Reisler, *By the Sweat of Their Brow*, 82, 108, 114, 141, 158; Leo Grebler, Joan W. Moore, and Ralph Guzman, *The Mexican American People: The Nation's Second Largest Minority* (New York: The Free Press, 1970), 449–53; Gilberto Hinojosa, "Mexican-American Faith Communities in Texas and the Southwest," in *Mexican Americans and the Catholic Church, 1900–1965*, ed. J. Dolan and G. Hinosa (Notre Dame: University of Notre Dame Press, 1994), 38–45; Valdés, *Barrios Norteños*, 72–74, 115–16; author's calculation, 1930 Census; Donato, "Theory, Research, Policy, and Practice"; Bureau of Labor Statistics, "Survey of Child Labor in Agriculture in California, 1924," *Monthly Labor Review* 21 (1925): 88–89; Ross, *School Attendance in 1920*, 67, 78, 84–85, 89; Gonzalez, "Segregation of Mexican Children in a Southern California City," 57, 63; Taylor, "Mexican Labor in the United States Valley of the South Platte Colorado," 195; Mario Garcia, "Americanization and the Mexican Immigrant, 1880–1930," *Journal of Ethnic Studies* 6, no. 2 (1978): 28–30.

78. Vargas, *Labor Rights Are Civil Rights*, 236; Robin Scott, "Wartime Labor Problems and Mexican-Americans in the War," in *The Mexican Americans: An Awakening Minority*, ed. M. Servin (Beverly Hills, CA: Glencoe Press, 1970), 136–37; Sonenshein, *Los Angeles*, 27–28; Kibbe, *Latin Americans in Texas*, 227–28; Burma, *Spanish-Speaking Groups in the United States*, 105; Taylor, *An American-Mexican Frontier*, 235, 237; Fincher, *Spanish-Americans as a Political Factor in New Mexico*, 243–60, 267–70; Jensen, "Disfranchisement Is a Disgrace," 23–24; Montejano, *Anglos and Mexicans in the Making of Texas*, 248.

CHAPTER 3

1. For a more technical version of this chapter, see Fox, "Three Worlds of Relief." Sydnor Walker, "Privately Supported Social Work," in *Recent Social Trends in the United States: Report of the President's Research Committee on Social Trends II* (New York: McGraw-Hill, 1933), 1192–96.

2. Thomas Krainz, "Culture and Poverty: Progressive Era Relief in the Rural West," *Pacific Historical Review* 74, no. 1 (2005): 87–120.

3. Katz, *In the Shadow of the Poorhouse*, 15; Elna Green, *This Business of Relief: Confronting Poverty in a Southern City, 1740–1940* (Athens: University of Georgia Press, 2003); Elizabeth Wisner, *Social Welfare in the South: From Colonial Times to World War I* (Baton Rouge: Louisiana State University Press, 1970). See also Fred Hall, ed., *Social Work Year Book, 1935* (New York: Russell Sage Foundation, 1935), 661–67; Russell Kurtz, ed., *Social Work Year Book, 1937* (New York: Russell Sage Foundation, 1937), 673–79; Jessica H. Barr, "Directory of Members of the American Association of Social Workers" (New York: American Association of Social Workers, 1936).

4. Homer Borst, "Rural Family Welfare Service in the Gulf Division," *NCSW Proceedings*, 1920, p. 285; Gilens, *Why Americans Hate Welfare*; Ange-Marie Hancock, *The Politics of Disgust: The Public Identity of the Welfare Queen* (New York: New York University Press, 2004); Katznelson, *When Affirmative Action Was White*; Lieberman, *Shifting the Color Line*; Mink, *The Wages of Motherhood*; Quadagno, *The Color of Welfare*.

5. Theda Skocpol, *Protecting Soldiers and Mothers: The Political Origins of Social Policy in the United States* (Cambridge, MA: Harvard University Press, 1992).

6. Katz, *In the Shadow of the Poorhouse*; Census Bureau, *Paupers in Almshouses: 1923* (Washington, DC: GPO, 1925).

7. Katz, *In the Shadow of the Poorhouse*; Census Bureau, *Relief Expenditures by Governmental and Private Organizations, 1929 and 1931* (Washington, DC: GPO, 1932); Mink, *The Wages of Motherhood*, 49–52; Children's Bureau, *Mother's Aid, 1931*, No. 220 (Washington, DC: GPO, 1933), 7–11; Paul Douglas, *Social Security in the United States: An Analysis and Appraisal of the Federal Social Security Act* (New York: Whittlesey House, McGraw-Hill, 1936).

8. Edwin Amenta, *Bold Relief: Institutional Politics and the Origins of Modern American Social Policy* (Princeton: Princeton University Press, 1998), 64; Kenneth Kusmer, *Down and Out and on the Road: The Homeless in American History* (Oxford: Oxford University Press, 2002).

9. Charles Persons, "Calculation of Relief Expenditures," *Journal of the American Statistical Association* 28, no. 181 (1933): 68; Department of Commerce, *Financial Statistics of Cities Having a Population of over 30,000* (Washington, DC: GPO, 1932); "Method of Collecting Financial Statistics of Cities and States," *Journal of the American Statistical Association* 18, no. 140 (1922): 517–19; Census Bureau, *Relief Expenditures by Governmental and Private Organizations, 1929 and 1931*.

10. Census Bureau, *Relief Expenditures by Governmental and Private Organizations, 1929 and 1931*.

11. Ibid. Cost of living adjustments come from: Jeffrey Williamson and Peter Lindert, *American Inequality: A Macroeconomic History* (New York: Academic Press, 1980).

12. Katz, *In the Shadow of the Poorhouse*, 68–83; Kenneth Kusmer, "The Functions of Organized Charity in the Progressive Era: Chicago as a Case Study," *Journal of American History* 60, no. 3 (1973): 657–78.

13. Katz, *In the Shadow of the Poorhouse*, 68–83; Frank Watson, *The Charity Organization Movement in the United States: A Study in American Philanthropy* (Philadelphia: University of Pennsylvania, 1922).

14. Katz, *In the Shadow of the Poorhouse*, 83–87; Gertrude Vaile, "Public Administration of Charity in Denver," *NCSW Proceedings*, 1916, p. 417; Green, *This Business of Relief*, 143–44.

15. Author's calculation, 1930 Census; Woofter, *Landlord and Tenant on the Cotton Plantation*, 151; Wiley Sanders, "Training for Rural Leadership: II. The North Carolina Plan," *Journal of Social Forces* 2, no. 1 (1923): 42–45; Aubrey Williams, "Social Work in the Southwest," *Social Service Review* 7, no. 3 (1933): 375–82.

16. Joseph Mayer, "Municipal Public Welfare Administration in a City of 200,000 to 750,000 Population," *Journal of Social Forces* 2, no. 2 (1924): 213–20; Chicago Council of Social Agencies, *Social Service Directory, Chicago, 1926* (Chicago, 1926); T. J. Woofter, "Organization of Rural Negroes for Public Health," *NCSW Proceedings*, 1923, pp. 72–75; Benson Landis, "Rural Social

Work," in *Social Work Year Book, 1929*, ed. F. Hall and M. Ellis (New York: Russell Sage Foundation, 1929), 393; Walker, "Privately Supported Social Work," 1190, 1193.

17. John Tombs, "The New Health Law and the Department of Health of New Mexico," *NCSW Proceedings*, 1920, pp. 188–91; Deutsch, *No Separate Refuge*; Sandra Schackel, *Social Housekeepers: Women Shaping Public Policy in New Mexico, 1920–1940* (Albuquerque: University of New Mexico Press, 1992).

18. Green, *This Business of Relief*, 202; "Help for Rural Children Will Be Society's Program," *Atlanta Constitution*, December 4, 1927, p. C10; Howard Jensen, "The County as an Administrative Unit in Social Work," *Journal of Social Forces* 2, no. 4 (1924): 552–59; Dwight Sanderson, "Community Organization for Rural Social Work," *Journal of Social Forces* 1 (1923): 156–61; George Warfield, "The County as a Unit in Charity Administration: Outdoor Relief," *NCSW Proceedings*, 1918, pp. 250–51; Georgia State Department of Public Welfare, "Georgia's Progress in Social Welfare" (Atlanta, GA, 1927), 12, 58–66.

19. Cahn and Bary, *Welfare Activities of Federal, State, and Local Governments in California*; California State Board of Charities and Corrections, "County Outdoor Relief in California" (Sacramento, CA, 1918); Robert Rapp, "Some Aspects of the Rural Relief Problem in California as Revealed in Ten Selected Counties" (Ph.D. thesis, Stanford University, 1937); California Department of Social Welfare, *Second Biennial Report of the Department of Social Welfare of the State of California* (Sacramento, CA, 1928–30), 10; CCIH, *Annual Report of the Commission of Immigration and Housing of California*, 17–20; Children's Bureau, *The Welfare of Children in Cotton-Growing Areas of Texas* (Washington, DC, 1924), 71.

20. Elizabeth Dinwiddie, "Illustrations from the Annals of the Gulf Division—American Red Cross," *NCSW Proceedings*, 1920, p. 294; Schackel, *Social Housekeepers*, 33; Wilma Van Dusseldorp, "The Uses of Committees and Volunteers in Rural Social Work," *NCSW Proceedings*, 1927, pp. 272–76; Jesse Steiner, "The Basis of Procedure in Rural Social Work," *Social Forces* 4, no. 3 (1926): 508; Jesse Steiner, "Education for Social Work," *American Journal of Sociology* 26, no. 6 (1921): 744–66; Jesse Steiner, "Modification of Home Service Standards to Meet Conditions in Small Cities and Towns and Rural Communities," *Journal of Social Forces* 2, no. 1 (1923): 69–73; Jesse Steiner, "Interrelation between City and Rural Life," *Social Forces* 6, no. 2 (1927): 242–47.

21. J. Byron Deacon, "The Future of Red Cross Home Service," *NCSW Proceedings*, 1919, pp. 365–71; J. B. Gwin, "Present Status of the American Red Cross," *Journal of Social Forces* 2, no. 4 (1924): 533–36; Robert Bondy, "American National Red Cross," in *Social Work Year Book, 1935*, ed. F. Hall (New York: Russell Sage Foundation, 1935), 41; Anna King, "The Present Opportunity of the City Home Service Section," *NCSW Proceedings*, 1919, p. 379; G. Wyckoff, "Louisiana Notes," *Journal of Social Forces* 1 (1923): 411.

22. Senate Committee on Immigration, *Restriction of Western Hemisphere Immigration*, 70th Cong., 1st Sess., 1928, p. 61; Taylor, "Mexican Labor in the United States: Imperial Valley," 62; Reynolds McKay, "Texas Mexican Repatriation during the Great Depression" (Ph.D. thesis, University of Oklahoma, Nor-

man, 1982); Irvin Taubkin, "Texas Relief Work Not Well Managed," *NYT*, December 25, 1932, p. E5; Taylor, "Mexican Labor in the United States: Dimmit County," 359–60.

23. Schackel, *Social Housekeepers*, 29–36; Skocpol, *Protecting Soldiers and Mothers*, 480–524; "Department of Public Welfare, Biennial Report for the Years 1927 and 1928" (Atlanta, GA, 1929), 35; Georgia State Department of Public Welfare, "Georgia's Progress in Social Welfare," 14.

24. Hoffsommer, *Landlord-Tenant Relations and Relief in Alabama*; Green, *This Business of Relief*, 132–33.

25. Cahn and Bary, *Welfare Activities of Federal, State, and Local Governments in California*; Martha Chickering, "The Part Social Workers Have Taken in Promoting Social Legislation in California," *NCSW Proceedings*, 1935, pp. 505–11; Census Bureau, *Paupers in Almshouses: 1923*, 6–7, author's calculation. The correlation coefficient between percent Mexican and real per capita relief spending across large cities (30,000 residents or more) in California in 1929 was -0.41 and -0.38 for cities in the Southwest as a whole.

26. Putnam, "E Pluribus Unum"; Goodhart, "Diversity Divide"; Goodhart, "Too Diverse?"

27. Harold Wilensky and Charles Lebeaux, *Industrial Society and Social Welfare: The Impact of Industrialization on the Supply and Organization of Social Welfare Services in the United States* (New York: Russell Sage Foundation, 1958); Cook County Board of Commissioners, *Charity Service Reports, Cook County, IL, Fiscal Year 1927* (Chicago) 277; "Municipal Charities in the United States: An Account of the Charitable Activities of the 73 Cities in the United States Having a Population of More than 40,000 in 1890," *NCCC Proceedings*, 1898, pp. 106–81; Wisner, *Social Welfare in the South*, 122–23.

28. To control for urbanization, I include a measure of city size. To control for need, I include the state infant mortality rate, the estimated state per capita income, and the average low temperature in February. To control for fiscal capacity, I include real per capita city revenues, real per capita state revenues, real per capita state debt, and real per capita state wealth. For more detail on the data, models, and results, see Fox, "Three Worlds of Relief."

29. Edwin Amenta and Jane Poulsen, "Social Politics in Context: The Institutional Politics Theory and Social Spending at the End of the New Deal," *Social Forces* 75, no. 1 (1996): 36; Mink, *The Wages of Motherhood*, 36–41.

30. Michael Heymann, "Conditions and Needs of the South," *NCCC Proceedings*, 1903, pp. 370–72; Key, *Southern Politics in State and Nation*; Theda Skocpol, Marjorie Abend-Wein, Christopher Howard, and Susan Lehmann, "Women's Associations and the Enactment of Mothers' Pensions in the United States," *American Political Science Review* 87, no. 3 (1993): 686–701.

31. Sonya Forthal, *Cogwheels of Democracy: A Study of the Precinct Captain* (New York: William-Frederick Press, 1946), 55–66; Gosnell, *Machine Politics, Chicago Model*, 71; Cohen, *Making a New Deal*, 63–64; Erie, *Rainbow's End*, 103–4.

32. Forthal, *Cogwheels of Democracy*; Erie, *Rainbow's End*; Terrence McDonald, "The Problem of the Political in Recent American Urban History:

Liberal Pluralism and the Rise of Functionalism," *Social History* 10, no. 3 (1985): 343–44; Jon Teaford, "Finis for Tweed and Steffens: Rewriting the History of Urban Rule," *Reviews in American History* 10, no. 4 (1982): 133–49; Trounstine, *Political Monopolies in American Cities*, 141, 139–71.

33. Trounstine, *Political Monopolies in American Cities*, 153–54; Finegold, *Experts and Politicians*, 20; Clark, "The Irish Ethic and the Spirit of Patronage," 339; Harriet Vittum, "Politics from the Social Point of View," *NCSW Proceedings*, 1924, pp. 423–24; Boyle interview by Heitmann, March 27, 1934, folder 19, box 3, McDowell Papers; Bridges, *Morning Glories*, 8; Bonnie Schwartz, *The Civil Works Administration, 1933–1934: The Business of Emergency Employment in the New Deal* (Princeton: Princeton University Press, 1984), 86; Oscar Handlin, *The Uprooted* (Boston: Little, Brown and Company, 1951), 188–90.

34. Daniel Elazar, *American Federalism: A View from the States* (New York: Harper and Row, 1972); Ira Sharkansky, "The Utility of Elazar's Political Culture: A Research Note," *Polity* 2, no. 1 (1969): 69.

35. Alston and Ferrie, *Southern Paternalism and the American Welfare State*; Hoffsommer, *Landlord-Tenant Relations and Relief in Alabama*. See also Woofter, *Landlord and Tenant on the Cotton Plantation*.

36. Walsh, "Laboring at the Margins"; Donald Zelman, "Mexican Migrants and Relief in Depression California: Grower Reaction to Public Relief Policies as They Affected Mexican Migration," *Journal of Mexican American History* 5 (1975): 1–23; CCIH, *Annual Report of the Commission of Immigration and Housing of California*, 17; Senate Committee, *Restriction of Western Hemisphere Immigration*, 28–29.

37. Reisler, *By the Sweat of Their Brow*, 85; Cobb, *The Most Southern Place on Earth*, 120; Litwack, *Trouble in Mind*, 482–92; Key, *Southern Politics in State and Nation*; Dwight Billings, "Class Origins of the 'New South': Planter Persistence and Industry in North Carolina," *American Journal of Sociology* 88 (1982): S52–S85; Wisner, *Social Welfare in the South*, 116; Ada Baker, *A Preliminary Report of the Social Security Survey* (Atlanta, GA, 1936), 15; Elna Green, "National Trends, Regional Differences, Local Circumstances: Social Welfare in New Orleans, 1870s–1920s," in *Before the New Deal: Social Welfare in the South, 1830–1930*, ed. E. Green (Athens: University of Georgia Press, 1999), 83.

38. Gilens, *Why Americans Hate Welfare*.

39. James Hoffman Batten, "New Features of Mexican Immigration: The Case against Further Restrictive Legislation," *Pacific Affairs* 3, no. 10 (1930): 956–66; Theodore Rice, "Some Contributing Factors in Determining the Social Adjustment of the Spanish-Speaking People in Denver and Vicinity" (Master's thesis, University of Denver, 1932), 79; Sister Marineil Mahony, S.L., "Some Approaches to the Problems of the Mexican Migratory Beet Laborer in Colorado (1923–1933) by the Knights of Columbus Colorado Mexican Welfare Committee Under the Chairmanship of Thomas F. Mahony, Longmont, Colorado" (Master's thesis, University of Notre Dame, 1961), 41; Robert McLean, *That Mexican! As He Really Is, North and South of the Rio Grande* (New York: Fleming H. Revell Company, 1929), 161.

40. McWilliams, *Ill Fares the Land*, 122; Senate Committee, *Restriction of Western Hemisphere Immigration*, 61; Taylor, "Mexican Labor in the United States: Imperial Valley," 62; Mansfield to Commissioner-General, February 5, 1921, INS Records.

CHAPTER 4

1. R. R. Miller, "The Mexican Dependency Problem," *Municipal League Bulletin of Los Angeles* 6, no. 7 (Los Angeles, 1929).

2. Camarillo, *Chicanos in a Changing Society*, 66; Immigration Commission, *Reports of the Immigration Commission*, vol. 1, p. 691; Charles Blanpied, "Report of Special Immigration Survey of the Pacific Coast," *NCCC Proceedings*, 1913, p. 48. For a challenge, see Victor Clark, *Mexican Labor in the United States* (Washington, DC: Bureau of Labor, 1908). A keyword search of the *Los Angeles Times* for 1890–1920 turned up only a few articles associating Mexicans with relief or charity. See, for example, "Santa Barbara County: Able Bodied Indigents," *LAT*, February 2, 1895, p. 3; "Refugee Horde Called Danger," *LAT*, April 4, 1916, p. II2; "Brake Is Applied to This Charity," *LAT*, June 14, 1916, p. I10; "The Mexican 'Invaders' of El Paso," *The Survey* 36 (1916): 380–82. For more on the Dillingham Commission's attitude toward Mexicans, see Katherine Benton-Cohen, "Other Immigrants: Mexicans and the Dillingham Commission of 1907–1911," *Journal of American Ethnic History* 30, no. 2 (2011): 33–57.

3. Louis Bloch, "Facts about Mexican Immigration before and since the Quota Restriction Laws," *Journal of the American Statistical Association* 24, no. 165 (1929): 50–60; California, *Mexicans in California*, 31; Sánchez, *Becoming Mexican American*, 97; LACBS, *Annual Report of the Board of Supervisors of the County of Los Angeles for the Fiscal Year Ending June 30, 1925*, 57. On Bogardus, see also Gilbert González, *Culture of Empire: American Writers, Mexico, & Mexican Immigrants, 1880–1930* (Austin: University of Texas Press, 2004), 130–31.

4. Emory Bogardus, "The Mexican Immigrant," *Journal of Applied Sociology* 11, no. 5 (1927): 482; Charles Thomson, "Restriction of Mexican Immigration," *Journal of Applied Sociology* 11, no. 6 (1927): 576; Wilson Wallis, "The Mexican Immigrant of California," *Pacific Review* 2, no. 3 (1921): 449.

5. Author's calculation, 1930 Census; Hanna to Shortridge, February 24, 1926, folder 36, box 4, DIR Papers; Douglas Monroy, "Like Swallows at the Old Mission: Mexicans and the Racial Politics of Growth in Los Angeles in the Interwar Period," *Western Historical Quarterly* 14, no. 4 (1983): 450; C. Goethe, "Other Aspects of the Problem," *Current History* 28 (1928): 768.

6. Burch to Doak, April 11, 1931, 167/255B, RG 174; Barry Mehler, "A History of the American Eugenics Society, 1921–1940" (Ph.D. diss., University of Illinois, Urbana, 1988), 315–16; Alexandra Stern, *Eugenic Nation: Faults and Frontiers of Better Breeding in Modern America* (Berkeley: University of California Press, 2005); Alexandra Stern, "Sterilized in the Name of Public Health: Race, Immigration, and Reproductive Control in Modern California," *American Journal of Public Health* 95 (2005): 1128–38; Emily Abel, "From Exclusion

to Expulsion: Mexicans and Tuberculosis Control in Los Angeles, 1914–1940," *Bulletin of Historical Medicine* 77 (2003): 834; Bogardus, "The Mexican Immigrant," 482.

7. Bogardus, "The Mexican Immigrant," 488; Elizabeth Fuller, "The Mexican Housing Problem in Los Angeles," *Studies in Sociology Monograph* 17, no. 5(1920): 4; Alfred White, *The Apperceptive Mass of Foreigners as Applied to Americanization: The Mexican Group* (San Francisco: R and E Research Associates, 1923), 13, 56.

8. White, *The Apperceptive Mass of Foreigners as Applied to Americanization*, 55; McLean, *That Mexican!* 142.

9. Linna Bresette, *Mexicans in the United States: A Report of a Brief Survey* (Washington, DC: National Catholic Welfare Conference, 1929), 18; Charles Thomson, "Mexicans—An Interpretation," *NCSW Proceedings*, 1928, p. 501; Robert McLean, "Mexican Workers in the United States," *NCSW Proceedings*, 1929, p. 537; McLean, *That Mexican!*; Wallis, "The Mexican Immigrant of California," 451. See also Batten, "New Features of Mexican Immigration."

10. Christine Lofstedt, "The Mexican Population of Pasadena California," *Journal of Applied Sociology* 7 (1923): 267; Paul Taylor, "Industrial Relations and Labor Conditions: Mexican Labor in the Imperial Valley, Calif.," *Monthly Labor Review* 28, no. 3 (1929): 59–65, p. 63; Paul Taylor, "Mexican Labor in the United States, Chicago and the Calumet Region," in *Mexican Labor in the United States*, vol. 2 (Berkeley: University of California Press, 1932), 129.

11. Carey McWilliams, "Getting Rid of the Mexican," *American Mercury* 28, no. 3 (1933): 322–24; Los Angeles Social Service Commission, "Second Annual Report of the Municipal Charities Commission" (Los Angeles, CA, 1915), 55; Vernon McCombs, "Rescuing Mexican Children in the Southwest," *Missionary Review of the World* 46 (July 1923): 529–32; Gullett, "Women Progressives and the Politics of Americanization in California," 83; Sánchez, *Becoming Mexican American*, 99, 103.

12. CCIH, *An Experiment Made in Los Angeles in the Summer of 1917 for the Americanization of Foreign-Born Women* (Sacramento, CA, 1917); Ricardo Romo, *East Los Angeles: History of a Barrio* (Austin: University of Texas Press, 1983); Anne Woo-Sam, "Domesticating the Immigrant: California's Commission of Immigration and Housing and the Domestic Immigration Policy Movement, 1910–1945" (Ph.D. thesis, University of California, Berkeley, 1999); Martinez interview, September 5, 1928, carton 10:9, Taylor Papers; "Draft Article," p. 29, California, Orange County, 1930, carton 10:36, Taylor Papers; Fuller, "The Mexican Housing Problem in Los Angeles," 4.

13. Bogardus, "The Mexican Immigrant," 480; Thompson, "Cost of Importing Mexican Labor," 4; Sánchez, *Becoming Mexican American*, 106; Miller, "The Mexican Dependency Problem;" Charles Thomson, "What of the Bracero?" *The Survey*, June 1, 1925, 292; McLean, *That Mexican!* 138.

14. Miller, "The Mexican Dependency Problem"; Bogardus, "The Mexican Immigrant," 480.

15. McLean, *That Mexican!* 141–42; Wallis, "The Mexican Immigrant of California"; Batten, "New Features of Mexican Immigration"; Thompson, "Cost

of Importing Mexican Labor," 4–5; Waters, "Transient Mexican Agricultural Labor," 60–61.

16. McLean, *That Mexican!*; Thomson, "Restriction of Mexican Immigration"; Myra Nye, "Of Interest to Women," *LAT*, October 8, 1925, p. A7; "Admitting Mexicans Discussed," *LAT*, February 14, 1928, p. A22; "Mexican Immigration," *LAT*, February 7, 1928, p. A14.

17. Sánchez, *Becoming Mexican American*; "Mexicans in Los Angeles," *The Survey* 44 (1920): 715–16; Bromley Oxnam, *The Mexican in Los Angeles: Los Angeles City Survey* (San Francisco: R and E Research Associates, 1920); Bromley Oxnam, "The Mexican in Los Angeles from the Standpoint of the Religious Forces of the City," *Annals of the American Academy of Political and Social Science* 93 (1921): 130–33.

18. Sánchez, *Becoming Mexican American*, 156–57; Scott, "The Mexican-American in the Los Angeles Area, 1920–1950"; Bresette, *Mexicans in the United States*, 18; Donald Gavin, *The National Conference of Catholic Charities, 1910–1960* (Milwaukee: Catholic Life Publications, 1962), 143.

19. California, *Mexicans in California*; Los Angeles Social Service Commission, "Second Annual Report of the Municipal Charities Commission"; LACBS, *Annual Report of the Board of Supervisors of the County of Los Angeles* (Los Angeles, 1927), 77; Abel, "From Exclusion to Expulsion," 829; "Cities Menace of Mexican Problem," *Star News*, February 10, 1928; House Committee, *Immigration from Countries of the Western Hemisphere*, 775.

20. Carey McWilliams, *North from Mexico: The Spanish-Speaking People of the United States* (New York: Monthly Review Press, 1948), 206–7.

21. California, *Mexicans in California*.

22. Ibid., 192; California Department of Social Welfare, *First Biennial Report of the Department of Social Welfare of the State of California* (Sacramento, CA, 1927–28), 55.

23. California, *Mexicans in California*, 177–78; Cybelle Fox, "The Boundaries of Social Citizenship: Race, Immigration and the American Welfare State, 1900–1950" (Ph.D. diss., Harvard University, 2007), 145; "The Future of Mexican Immigration," folder 5, box 20, Race Relations Records; Bogardus, "The Mexican Immigrant."

24. Hanna to Shortridge, February 24, 1926, Davis to Hanna, March 8, 1926, both in folder 36, box 4, DIR Papers; CCIH, *Annual Report of the Commission of Immigration and Housing of California*; "Check Urged on Mexican Influx," *LAT*, January 10, 1926, p. 10.

25. Edwin Bamford, "The Mexican Casual Problem in the Southwest," *Journal of Applied Sociology* 86 (1924): 371; Miller, "The Mexican Dependency Problem"; Abel, "From Exclusion to Expulsion"; Emily Abel, "'Only the Best Class of Immigration': Public Health Policy toward Mexicans and Filipinos in Los Angeles, 1910–1940," *American Journal of Public Health* 94, no. 6 (2004): 932–39; Bogardus, *The Mexican in the United States*; Thomson, "Mexicans—An Interpretation"; Cahn and Bary, *Welfare Activities of Federal, State, and Local Governments in California*, 345; Walsh, "Laboring at the Margins," 406.

26. McLean, *That Mexican!* 157–58; James Batten, "Southwest and Center: The Mexican Conference at Pomona," *The Survey* 61 (1929): 475; Emory Bogar-

dus, "The Mexican Immigrant and the Quota," *Sociology and Social Research* 12 (1928): 373; Molina, *Fit to Be Citizens?* 116–17.

27. Thomson, "Restriction of Mexican Immigration," 577.

28. Miller, "The Mexican Dependency Problem." See also LACBS, *Annual Report of the Board of Supervisors of the County of Los Angeles* (Los Angeles, CA, 1928).

29. LACBS, *Annual Report of the Board of Supervisors of the County of Los Angeles* (Los Angeles, CA, 1927), 65; House Committee, *Immigration from Countries of the Western Hemisphere*, 89–90.

30. Jeremy Attack and Peter Passell, *A New Economic View of American History from Colonial Times to 1940* (New York: W. W. Norton, 1994), 564–66; García, *Mexicans in the Midwest*, 41–48; Zaragosa Vargas, *Proletarians of the North: A History of Mexican Industrial Workers in Detroit and the Midwest, 1917–1933* (Berkeley: University of California Press, 1993), 78–84.

31. "Denver Is Crowded with Mexicans Who Are Near Starving," *Denver Post*, January 26, 1921; "Denver's Safety Menaced by 3,500 Starving Mexicans," *Denver Post*, January 19, 1922; McWilliams, *Ill Fares the Land*, 118.

32. Bloch, "Facts about Mexican Immigration"; Jay Stowell, "The Danger of Unrestricted Mexican Immigration," *Current History* 28 (1928): 763–64; García, *Mexicans in the Midwest*, 42, 46; Vargas, *Proletarians of the North*, 79, 82–83; Inspector in Charge to Commissioner of Immigration, February 22, 1921, INS Records; Deutsch, *No Separate Refuge*, 124–25.

33. McWilliams, *North from Mexico*, 206.

34. LeeRoy Bowman, "Social Workers Broaden Their Conception of Community," *Social Forces* 4, no. 1 (1925): 103–4; J. Gwin, "Social Problems of Our Mexican Population," *NCSW Proceedings*, 1926, p. 332; Don Lescohier, "The Vital Problem in Mexican Immigration," *NCSW Proceedings*, 1927, p. 551; McLean, "Mexican Workers in the United States"; Thomson, "Mexicans—An Interpretation."

35. Taylor, *An American-Mexican Frontier*, 163–64; Newlin interview, August 14, 1928, carton 11:33, Taylor Papers; Taylor, "Mexican Labor in the United States, Chicago and the Calumet Region," 129–30.

36. Robert Jones, "The Religious Life of the Mexican in Chicago," 1929, p. 5, carton 11:51, Taylor Papers; Cook County Board of Commissioners, *Charity Service Reports, Cook County, IL, 1917–27*; Anita Jones, *Conditions Surrounding Mexicans in Chicago* (Chicago: University of Chicago, 1928), 99–100; Taylor, "Mexican Labor in the United States, Chicago and the Calumet Region," 124–25.

37. David Weber, "Anglo Views of Mexican Immigrants: Popular Perceptions and Neighborhood Realities in Chicago, 1900–1940" (Ph.D. thesis, Ohio State University, 1982), 242, 248; Sarles and Kembell interviews, June 11, 1928, both in carton 11:32, Taylor Papers; Gabriela Arredondo, *Mexican Chicago: Race, Identity, and Nation, 1916–1939* (Urbana: University of Illinois Press, 2008), 102.

38. McLean, *That Mexican!* 143; Robert McLean, *The Northern Mexican* (New York: Home Missions Council, 1930).

39. Taylor, "Mexican Labor in the United States: Dimmit County," 358; McKay, "Texas Mexican Repatriation during the Great Depression"; House Commit-

tee, *Immigration from Countries of the Western Hemisphere*, 376, 725–26; Census Bureau, *Paupers in Almshouses*; Taylor, *An American-Mexican Frontier*, 163; "The Future of Mexican Immigration," folder 5, box 20, Race Relations Records.

40. House Committee on Immigration and Naturalization, *Seasonal Agricultural Laborers from Mexico*, 69th Cong., 1st Sess., 1926; House Committee, *Immigration from Countries of the Western Hemisphere*; Senate Committee, *Restriction of Western Hemisphere Immigration*; Charles Teague, "A Statement on Mexican Immigration," *Saturday Evening Post* 200 (1928): 169–70.

41. Gutiérrez, *Walls and Mirrors*, 51–68, 85–86; Bogardus, "The Mexican Immigrant and the Quota"; Ernest Galarza, "Life in the United States for Mexican People," *NCSW Proceedings*, 1929, pp. 400, 404; letter to Edward Hanna, unsigned, translated, Los Angeles, March 1926, folder 36, box 4, DIR Papers; Martinez interview, September 5, 1928, carton 10:9, Taylor Papers.

42. To my knowledge, there are no data on the number of Mexican social workers in 1930, but I created upper and lower bound estimates using 1930 census data. In 1930 there were 97 social workers classified as "other race." Mexicans represented 70 percent of those classified as "other race," suggesting 68 social workers might have been Mexican. But social workers were also lumped under the larger category of "other professional pursuits." We know there were 186 Mexicans classified as engaged in "other professional pursuits." Since social workers represent 17 percent of this other category, this yields an estimate of only 32 Mexican social workers. Census Bureau, *Fifteenth Census of the United States, Population*, vol. 5, pp. 84, 90. Other sources confirm that there were few Mexican social workers in California or elsewhere. See María Aranda, "The Development of the Latino Social Work Profession in Los Angeles," *Research on Social Work Practice* 11, no. 2 (2001): 254–65; Fox, "The Boundaries of Social Citizenship," 152n308, 155n313. Vargas, *Labor Rights Are Civil Rights*, 236; Sonenshein, *Los Angeles*; Francisco Balderrama, *In Defense of La Raza: The Los Angeles Mexican Consulate and the Mexican Community, 1929 to 1936* (Tucson: University of Arizona Press, 1982); García, *Mexicans in the Midwest*; José Hernández, *Mutual Aid for Survival: The Case of the Mexican American* (Malabar, FL: Robert Krieger Publishing Company, 1983); Romo, *East Los Angeles*, 145–52; Schackel, *Social Housekeepers*, 94–96; Zaldivares interview, June 9, 1928, carton 11:33, Taylor Papers; Francisco Balderrama and Raymond Rodriguez, *Decade of Betrayal: Mexican Repatriation in the 1930s* (Albuquerque: University of New Mexico Press, 1995); Douglas Monroy, *Rebirth: Mexican Los Angeles from the Great Migration to the Great Depression* (Berkeley: University of California Press, 1999), 129.

43. Richard Childe, "Our Open Back Doors," *American Legion Monthly* 5 (October 1928): 18–19; S. Holmes, "Perils of the Mexican Invasion," *North American Review* 227, no. 5 (1929): 615–23; Robert McLean, "A Dyke against Mexicans," *New Republic* 59 (1929): 334–37; "To Put Mexico on a Quota Basis," *Literary Digest*, April 7, 1928, p. 14; Stuart Ward, "Gain from Peon Influx Weighed against Losses," *Christian Science Monitor*, March 24, 1928; "Secret Treaty Said to Cause Issues in East," *Christian Science Monitor*, August 14, 1928; House Committee, *Immigration from Countries of the Western Hemisphere*, 194; Raymond Mohl, "The *Saturday Evening Post* and the 'Mexican Invasion,'"

Journal of Mexican American History 3 (1973): 131–38; Alan Nourie and Barbara Nourie, *American Mass-Market Magazines* (New York: Greenwood Press, 1990); Kenneth Roberts, "Wet and Other Mexicans," *Saturday Evening Post* 200 (1928): 10; Kenneth Roberts, "Mexicans or Ruin," *Saturday Evening Post* 200 (1928): 14–; Kenneth Roberts, "The Docile Mexican," *Saturday Evening Post* 200 (1928): 39–.

44. "St. Paul Studies Its Mexicans," *Quarterly Bulletin for the International Institutes I(9)*, May 1937, folder 6, box 288, reel 195, AFII Papers.

CHAPTER 5

1. Grace Abbott, *The Immigrant and the Community* (New York: Century, 1917), 188, 191–92.

2. King, *Making Americans*; Mink, *The Wages of Motherhood*; Gordon, *Pitied But Not Entitled*; Katrina Irving, *Immigrant Mothers: Narratives of Race and Maternity, 1890–1925* (Urbana: University of Illinois Press, 2000).

3. Gilens, *Why Americans Hate Welfare.*

4. Kenneth Roberts, "Ports of Embarkation," *Saturday Evening Post* 193 (1921): 72; see also Kenneth Roberts, "Lest We Forget," *Saturday Evening Post* 195, no. 44 (1925): 3–. Prescott Hall, *Immigration and Its Effects upon the United States* (New York: H. Holt, 1908); Edward Ross, *The Old World in the New: The Significance of Past and Present Immigration to the American People* (New York: Century, 1914); Harry Laughlin, "Analysis of America's Melting Pot," Hearings Before the House Committee on Immigration and Naturalization, 67th Cong., 3rd Sess., November 21, 1922.

5. Daniel Kelves, *In the Name of Eugenics: Genetics and the Uses of Human Heredity* (New York: Alfred A. Knopf, 1985); King, *Making Americans*; Stern, *Eugenic Nation*; Nicole Rafter, *White Trash: The Eugenic Family Studies, 1877–1919* (Boston: Northeastern University Press, 1988), 5–6, passim.

6. Harry Laughlin, "Biological Aspects of Immigration," Hearings Before the Committee on Immigration and Naturalization, 66th Cong., 2nd Sess., April 16, 1920, pp. 4–5.

7. Hall, *Immigration and Its Effects upon the United States.* Though Laughlin thought they were racially inferior, like most race scientists, he categorized southeastern European immigrants as "white." Laughlin, "Analysis of America's Melting Pot," 731, 753; King, *Making Americans*, 181.

8. Laughlin, "Analysis of America's Melting Pot," 748.

9. King, *Making Americans*, 174–75; Laughlin, "Analysis of America's Melting Pot," 731, 747–48. See also Ross, *The Old World in the New*, 244.

10. Roberts, "Lest We Forget," 160–61.

11. National Industrial Conference Board, *Social Adequacy of Foreign Nationals in the United States: A Critical Review of "Analysis of America's Modern Melting Pot"* (New York, 1924), 24.

12. William Schieffelin, "Immigration: Report of Committee," *NCCC Proceedings*, 1912, pp. 234–37; Graham Taylor, "Distribution and Assimilation of Immigrants," *NCCC Proceedings*, 1913, pp. 27–28, 30. See also Isaac Hourwich,

Immigration and Labor: The Economic Aspects of European Immigration to the United States (New York: G. P. Putnam's Sons, 1912).

13. Pearl's was one of the only studies to refute the contention that Mexicans were dependent, and his data were never cited in the discussions of the Mexican "dependency problem." Raymond Pearl, "The Racial Origin of Almshouse Paupers in the United States," *Science* 60, no. 1557 (1924): 395, 397.

14. Marian Schibsby, "Is There an Undue Proportion of Aliens on Relief?" *Interpreter Releases* 13, no. 48 (1936): 289–94.

15. Higham, *Strangers in the Land*, 130; Immigration Commission, *Reports of the Immigration Commission*, vol. 1, pp. 35–36, vol. 34–35.

16. Immigration Commission, *Reports of the Immigration Commission*, vol. 2, pp. 87–158; Census Bureau, *Thirteenth Census of the United States Taken in the Year 1910* (Washington, DC: GPO, 1912); Fox, "The Boundaries of Social Citizenship," 191–93.

17. *Annual Report of the Family Society of Philadelphia* (Philadelphia, 1927, 1930); Weber, "Anglo Views of Mexican Immigrants," 268; Cook County Board of Commissioners, *Charity Service Reports, Fiscal Years 1908–1928.*

18. Florence Nesbitt, *Standards of Public Aid to Children in Their Own Homes* (Washington, DC, 1923), 84–85. See also Gordon, *Pitied But Not Entitled*, 47–48.

19. Kate Claghorn, "Immigration and Its Relation to Pauperism," *Annals of the American Academy of Political and Social Science* 24 (1904): 192, 204.

20. Ibid., 190, 194, 200; Amos Warner, *American Charities* (New York: Thomas Crowell Company, 1894). See also Hall, *Immigration and Its Effects upon the United States*, 164–65.

21. Lee Frankel, "Jewish Charities," *Annals of the American Academy of Political and Social Science* 21 (1903): 47–64.

22. Robert Hunter, *Poverty* (New York: Macmillan, 1904), 281–83.

23. Ibid., 281–83; Claghorn, "Immigration and Its Relation to Pauperism," 187. See also Maurice Davie, *World Immigration, With Special Reference to the United States* (New York: MacMillan, 1936), 281–82; Cyrus Sulzberger, "Immigration," *NCCC Proceedings*, 1912, pp. 239–49.

24. Joseph Stella, "The Immigrant Madonna," *The Survey*, December 1, 1922, cover; E. Benedict, "A Bohemian Immigrant Mother," *The Survey*, October 11, 1913, p. 56; Helen Dwight, "The Immigrant Madonna, a Poem," *The Survey*, December 11, 1915, p. 281; Irving, *Immigrant Mothers*; *Thirty-Third Annual Report of the Philadelphia Society for Organization Charity*, (Philadelphia, 1911).

25. Blanpied, "Report of Special Immigration Survey of the Pacific Coast," 42–72; Irving, *Immigrant Mothers*; Joseph Remenyi, "Unemployment and the Immigrant," *NCSW Proceedings*, 1921, pp. 308–12; Jerome Davis, *The Russians and Ruthenians in America: Bolsheviks or Brothers?* (New York: G. H. Doran, 1922); Paul Fox, *The Poles in America* (New York: G. H. Doran, 1922); Kenneth Miller, *The Czecho-Slovaks in America* (New York: G. H. Doran, 1922); Philip Rose, *The Italians in America* (New York: G. H. Doran, 1922); Frank Beck, "The Italian in Chicago," *Bulletin of the Department of Public Welfare, City of Chicago* 2, no. 3 (1919): 3–32; Robert Kelso, "The Problem of Rural and Village

Areas in Massachusetts," *NCSW Proceedings*, 1928, pp. 538–41; Grace Abbott, "A Study of the Greeks in Chicago," *American Journal of Sociology* 15, no. 3 (1909): 379–93; Frederic Almy, "The Huddled Poles of Buffalo," *The Survey*, February 4, 1911, pp. 25–. The frugal stereotype was not always flattering. Irving, *Immigrant Mothers*, 57–59; Sophonisba Breckinridge, *New Homes for Old* (New York: Harper and Brothers, 1921), 85–87.

26. Clark, *Mexican Labor in the United States*; Taylor, "Mexican Labor in the United States Valley of the South Platte Colorado," 171; Rice, "Some Contributing Factors," v–vi; Fred Janette, untitled article, *Detroit News*, February 17, 1921, carton 11:69, Taylor Papers; Bogardus, *The Mexican in the United States*; Gamio, *Mexican Immigration to the United States*; Abraham Hoffman, "The Repatriation of Mexican Nationals from the United States during the Great Depression" (Ph.D. thesis, University of California, Los Angeles, 1970).

27. Lilian Brandt, "The Causes of Poverty," *Political Science Quarterly* 23, no. 4 (1908): 637–51; Higham, *Strangers in the Land*; James Patterson, *America's Struggle against Poverty in the Twentieth Century* (Cambridge, MA: Harvard University Press, 1981); Edith Abbott, *Historical Aspects of the Immigration Problem* (New York: Arno Press, 1926), 539; Abbott, *The Immigrant and the Community*; Cahn and Bary, *Welfare Activities of Federal, State, and Local Governments in California*, 145; Hunter, *Poverty*, 283; Claghorn, "Immigration and Its Relation to Pauperism," 202; Jacob Hollander, *The Abolition of Poverty* (Boston: Houghton Mifflin, 1914), 5.

28. Eva White, "The Immigrant Family," *Annals of the American Academy of Political and Social Science* 77 (1918): 167.

29. Edith Abbott, "Immigration Legislation and the Problems of Assimilation," *NCSW Proceedings*, 1924, pp. 82–91; Frankel, "Jewish Charities," 53; Ruth Crocker, *Social Work and Social Order: The Settlement Movement in Two Industrial Cities, 1889–1930* (Urbana: University of Illinois Press, 1992); Gordon, *Pitied But Not Entitled*; Mink, *The Wages of Motherhood*; Irving, *Immigrant Mothers*.

30. Irving, *Immigrant Mothers*, 78; Gordon, *Pitied But Not Entitled*, 30; Breckinridge, *New Homes for Old*; Mink, *The Wages of Motherhood*; Nesbitt, *Standards of Public Aid to Children in Their Own Homes*, 78; Suzanne Wasserman, "'Our Alien Neighbors': Coping with the Depression on the Lower East Side," *American Jewish History* 88 (2000): 229; Crocker, *Social Work and Social Order*, 158.

31. Mark Reisler, "Always the Laborer, Never the Citizen: Anglo Perceptions of the Mexican Immigrant during the 1920s," in *Between Two Worlds: Mexican Immigrants in the United States*, ed. David G. Gutiérrez (Wilmington, DE: Scholarly Resources, 1996); Katherine Benton, "What about Women in the White Man's Camp? Gender, Nation, and the Redefinition of Race in Cochise County, Arizona, 1853–1941" (Ph.D. thesis, University of Wisconsin, Madison, 2002), 581–82; Thompson, "Cost of Importing Mexican Labor," 4–5; CCIH, *Annual Report of the Commission of Immigration and Housing of California* (Sacramento, CA, 1916), 239; Gibbs interview, 1927, carton 11:25, Taylor Papers; Newlin interview, August 14, 1928, carton 11:33, Taylor Papers; Valdés, *Barrios Norteños*, 72.

32. Edith Bremer, "Immigrants and Foreign Communities," *Social Work Year Book* (New York: Russell Sage Foundation, 1929), 214–21; Edith Bremer, "The Foreign Language Worker in the Fusion Process," *NCSW Proceedings*, 1919, pp. 740–47; Virginia Murray, "The Training and Use of Nationality Workers," *NCSW Proceedings*, 1922, pp. 484–87; Breckinridge, *New Homes for Old*; Census Bureau, *Fifteenth Census of the United States, Population*, vol. 5, p. 84; author's calculation, 1930 Census.

33. William Bremer, *Depression Winters: New York Social Workers and the New Deal* (Philadelphia: Temple University Press, 1984), 4.

34. Abbott, "Immigration Legislation and the Problems of Assimilation"; Graham Taylor, "The Social Settlements' Influence Upon Public Policies," *NCSW Proceedings*, 1923, pp. 526–29; Bremer, "Immigrants and Foreign Communities," 217; Edith Bremer, "Immigrants and Foreign Communities," in *Social Work Year Book, 1933*, ed. F. Hall (New York: Russell Sage Foundation, 1933), 238–46; FLIS, *The Work of the Foreign Language Information Service: A Summary and Survey* (New York, 1921).

35. Bremer, "Immigrants and Foreign Communities" (1929); Joanne L. Goodwin, *Gender and the Politics of Welfare Reform: Mothers' Pensions in Chicago, 1911–1929* (Chicago: University of Chicago Press, 1997), 132, 138; see also Cecilia Razovsky, "Humanitarian Effects of the Immigration Law," *NCSW Proceedings*, 1927, pp. 518–30; Gudrun Rom, "Family Problems Resulting from the Present Deportation System," *NCSW Proceedings*, 1927, pp. 568–72.

36. Bremer, "Immigrants and Foreign Communities" (1929); Schieffelin, "Immigration: Report of Committee"; Correspondence between the AFII and Congress, folders 9, 14, box 287, reel 194, AFII Papers; Clarke Chambers, *Seedtime of Reform: American Social Service and Social Action, 1918–1933* (Westwood, CT: Greenwood Press, 1963); Jane Addams, "Social Consequences of the Immigration Law," *NCSW Proceedings*, 1927, pp. 102–6; Frank Bruno, *Trends in Social Work, 1874–1956* (New York: Columbia University Press, 1957); Jane Clark, "American Deportation Procedure: An International Social Problem," *NCSW Proceedings*, 1927, pp. 559–72; Razovsky, "Humanitarian Effects of the Immigration Law."

37. Abbott, "Immigration Legislation and the Problems of Assimilation"; Allen Davis, *Spearheads for Reform: The Social Settlements and the Progressive Movement, 1890–1914* (New York: Oxford University Press, 1967); Schieffelin, "Immigration: Report of Committee"; Martin Anderson, "Legislation to Prevent the United States from Being Made a Receptacle for Foreign Paupers" in *Proceedings of the First Annual Conference of Charities* (New York, 1874), 170–85; New York State Board of Charities, "Thirteenth Annual Report of the State Board of Charities of the State of New York," in *Historical Aspects of the Immigration Problem*, ed. E. Abbott (New York: Arno Press, 1880), 685–87; Charles Hoyt, "Report on Immigration," *NCCC Proceedings*, 1881, pp. 217–27; Abbott, *The Immigrant and the Community*; Clark, "American Deportation Procedure"; Rom, "Family Problems Resulting from the Present Deportation System"; Higham, *Strangers in the Land*, 120.

38. Roberts, "The Docile Mexican," 41.

39. Alvin Kogut, "The Negro and the Charity Organization Society in the Progressive Era," *Social Service Review* 44, no. 1 (1970): 11–21; Green, *This*

Business of Relief, 112, 160; Watson, *The Charity Organization Movement in the United States*, 357n4; Hoffsommer, *Landlord-Tenant Relations and Relief in Alabama*; Pearl, "The Racial Origin of Almshouse Paupers in the United States," 395; Eugene Jones, "Social Work among Negroes," *Annals of the American Academy of Political and Social Science* 140 (1928): 292; *White House Conference on Child Health and Protection: Preliminary Committee Reports* (New York: Century, 1930), 512.

40. Laughlin, "Analysis of America's Melting Pot," 748.

41. L. Hammond, "The White Man's Debt to the Negro," *Annals of the American Academy of Political and Social Science* 49 (1913): 68.

42. Cook County Board of Commissioners, *Charity Service Reports, Fiscal Year of 1917*, 74; Cook County Board of Commissioners, *Charity Service Reports, Fiscal Year of 1918*, 253; Steven Diner, "Chicago Social Workers and Blacks in the Progressive Era," *Social Service Review* 44, no. 4 (1970): 393–410; LACBS, *Annual Report of the Board of Supervisors of the County of Los Angeles* (Los Angeles, 1927).

43. Pearl, "The Racial Origin of Almshouse Paupers in the United States"; Census Bureau, *Paupers in Almshouses*; Nesbitt, *Standards of Public Aid to Children in Their Own Homes*; Children's Bureau, *Mother's Aid, 1931*, 26.

44. Immigration Commission, *Reports of the Immigration Commission*, vol. 2; Fox, "The Boundaries of Social Citizenship," 192, 233–36; Watson, *The Charity Organization Movement in the United States*, 358; Gordon, *Pitied But Not Entitled*, 85.

45. Gordon, *Pitied But Not Entitled*, 87; Jones, "Social Work among Negroes"; James Hubert, "Urbanization and the Negro," *NCSW Proceedings*, 1933, pp. 418–25; Katz, *In the Shadow of the Poorhouse*, 183; discussion following R. R. Wright, "What Does the Negro Want in Our Democracy," *NCSW Proceedings*, 1919, pp. 539–45; Diner, "Chicago Social Workers and Blacks in the Progressive Era"; Mink, *The Wages of Motherhood*; Sandra Stehno, "Public Responsibility for Dependent Black Children: The Advocacy of Edith Abbott and Sophonisba Breckinridge," *Social Service Review* 62, no. 3 (1988): 485; Philip Jackson, "Black Charity in Progressive Era Chicago," *Social Service Review* 52, no. 3 (1978): 400–417.

46. W.E.B. Du Bois, *Efforts for Social Betterment among Negro Americans* (Atlanta: Atlanta University Press, 1909); Karen Ferguson, *Black Politics in New Deal Atlanta* (Chapel Hill: University of North Carolina Press, 2002); Goodwin, *Gender and the Politics of Welfare Reform*; Gordon, *Pitied But Not Entitled*; Jackson, "Black Charity in Progressive Era Chicago"; Jones, "Social Work among Negroes"; Dorothy Salem, *To Better Our World: Black Women in Organized Reform, 1890–1920* (Brooklyn, NY: Carlson Publishing, 1990); Census Bureau, *Fifteenth Census of the United States, Population*, vol. 5, p. 84; "The Southern Negro and Social Work," *The Survey*, September 7, 1918, p. 643; George Haynes, "Migration of Negroes into Northern Cities," *NCSW Proceedings*, 1917, pp. 494–97; George Haynes, "Negro Labor and the New Order," *NCSW Proceedings*, 1919 , pp. 531–38.

47. Jackson, "Black Charity in Progressive Era Chicago"; "A Conference of Negro Women," *The Survey*, August 3, 1918, pp. 513–14; Forrester B. Washing-

ton, "A Program of Work for the Assimilation of Negro Immigrants in Northern Cities," *NCSW Proceedings*, 1917, pp. 497–500; James Robinson, "The Cincinnati Negro Survey and Program," *NCSW Proceedings*, 1919, pp. 524–31; Diner, "Chicago Social Workers and Blacks in the Progressive Era"; Ferguson, *Black Politics in New Deal Atlanta*; E. K. Jones, "The Negro in Industry," *NCSW Proceedings*, June 1917, pp. 494–503; Gordon, *Pitied But Not Entitled*.

48. Robinson, "The Cincinnati Negro Survey and Program"; W.E.B. Du Bois, *The Philadelphia Negro: A Social Study* (Philadelphia: University of Philadelphia, 1899).

49. Kogut, "The Negro and the Charity Organization Society in the Progressive Era"; Helen Pendleton, "Negro Dependence in Baltimore," *Charities and the Commons* 15, no. 1 (1905): 50–58.

50. Marvin Karlins, Thomas Coffman, and Gary Walters, "On the Fading of Social Stereotypes: Studies in Three Generations of College Students," *Journal of Personality and Social Psychology* 13 (1969): 1–16; Litwack, *Trouble in Mind*, 172; Laughlin, "Analysis of America's Melting Pot," 748.

51. Amos Warner, "The Causes of Poverty Further Considered," *Publications of the American Statistical Association* 4, no. 27 (1894): 66.

52. Pearl, "The Racial Origin of Almshouse Paupers in the United States," 395; Percy Clark, "Almshouse Paupers in the United States," *Science* 61, no. 1576 (1925): 284–85.

53. Niles Carpenter, "Feebleminded and Pauper Negroes in Public Institutions," *Annals of the American Academy of Political and Social Science* 140 (1928): 75; Du Bois, *Efforts for Social Betterment among Negro Americans*, 46–47.

CHAPTER 6

1. "Family of Ten Sent Back to Mexico," *LAT*, October 23, 1935, p. A2.

2. Confidential Statement by the Board of Trustees of the United Charities, March 21, 1930, folder 1930–1931, box 8, United Charities Papers.

3. Isaac Marcosson, "The Alien and Unemployment," *Saturday Evening Post* 202 (June 14, 1930): 6–7; Annual Report of the Director, February 27, 1936, p. 2, folder 66, box 5, Supplement II, IPL Papers; Ngai, *Impossible Subjects*, 54–55.

4. Watkins to White, February 8, 1931, 55739, pp. 674/674A, RG 85; "Law Body Hits Methods Used in Alien Cases," *WP*, August 8, 1931, p. 1; Fitzpatrick, Statement on Deportation and Registration of Aliens, September 12, 1931, folder 128, box 11, series I, IPL Papers.

5. Wilson of Morristown to Doak, December 17, 1930, Deportations, 167/255C, RG 174; Englert to Doak, Deportations, 167/255B, RG 174; Kesney to Doak, November 1, 1931, Deportations, 167/255C, RG 174; Jones to Doak, December 18, 1930; Alber to Doak, July 24, 1931; Chenoweth to Hoover, December 16, 1930; Kuester to Doak, April 12, 1931, all in Deportations, 167/255B, RG 174; Reese to Doak, May 23, 1931, 20/46, Employment of Aliens, RG 174; McElvaine, *Down and Out in the Great Depression*, 149–50.

6. "Defeat the Attacks on Chicago Workers," District Committee Communist Party USA, Unemployed Relief, 1927–July 1932, box 114; "Defeat the Dies-Fish

Anti-Labor Bill!" Unemployed Relief, August–November 1932, box 114, both in Hilliard Papers; "Resolution on the Persecution of Foreign Born Workers," 167/255, Deportation Sundry, 1920–1930, RG 174; Federation of the Slovenian National Benefit Society, "Resolution of Protest against the Increased Terror . . . ," January 25, 1932; Schmidt to Doak, March 21, 1932; Halanen to Doak, June 6, 1931; Taylor to Doak, January 25, 1932, all in Deportations, 167/255C, RG 174; *Annual Reports of the Commissioner General of Immigration to the Secretary of Labor for the Fiscal Year Ended June 30* (Washington, DC: GPO, 1906–32); *Statistical Abstract of the United States, 1940* (Washington, DC: GPO, 1941), 100.

7. Abraham Hoffman, *Unwanted Mexican Americans in the Great Depression: Repatriation Pressures, 1929–1939* (Tucson: University of Arizona Press, 1979), 42.

8. Visel to Woods, January 6, 1931, box 62, #118, Clements Papers; Watkins to White, February 8, 1931, 55739 674/674A, RG 85; Visel to the Crime and Unemployment Committee of the Chamber of Commerce, January 7, 1931, box 62, #118, Clements Papers.

9. Woods to Visel, January 8, 1931, box 62, #118, Clements Papers; Visel to Doak, January 12, 1931, 040, "Labor," RG 73; Visel to Doak, March 19, 1931, 55739 674/674A, RG 85. The details of the plan were discussed between Visel, the chief of police, the sheriff, and the local immigration bureau. Watkins to White, February 8, 1931, 55739 674/674A, RG 85; Hotchkiss to Woods, January 9, 1931, 040, "Labor," RG 73; Visel to Doak, January 11, 1931, box 62, #118, Clements Papers; Hoffman, *Unwanted Mexican Americans in the Great Depression*, 84.

10. Visel to Woods, and press release, January 19, 1931, 040, "Labor," RG 73; Hoffman, *Unwanted Mexican Americans in the Great Depression*, pp. 48, 170–71; Carr to Commissioner General, re: "Deportation—Mexican Newspaper Articles," June 17, 1931; "11 Mexican Prisoners Taken at a Sudden Raid at the Plaza," *La Opinión* (translation), February 27, 1931, both in 55739, 674/674A, RG 85.

11. Clements to Arnoll, January 31, 1931, box 80, #188, Clements Papers; Harris to District Director, June 9, 1931; "Deportations Continue" *Excelsior* (translation), May 11, 1931; "The Abuses Continue in California," *El Universal* (translation), February 24, 1931, all in 55739 674/674A, RG 85; Hoffman, *Unwanted Mexican Americans in the Great Depression*, 48–66.

12. Hoffman, *Unwanted Mexican Americans in the Great Depression*, 64–65; Watkins to White, February 21, 1931; Carr to Commissioner General, June 17, 1931, both in 55739 674/674A, RG 85; "Exodus of 75,000 Mexicans Alarms Western Growers," *WP*, June 21, 1931, p. M13.

13. Balderrama, *In Defense of La Raza*, 62–64; Hoffman, *Unwanted Mexican Americans in the Great Depression*, 73–76; Caroline Walker, "Jane Addams Decries Mex. Deportations," *Los Angeles Herald*, March 25, 1931, box 80, #188, Clements Papers; California Conference of Social Work, "Proceedings of the Twenty-Third Annual Meeting, Berkeley, May 17 to 21, 1931," *Conference Bulletin* 14, no. 4 (1931): 55–56. But see "Mexican Labor Scare Rapped," *LAT,* June 8, 1931, p. A2.

14. Editorial, "Deportation," *The Nation* 132, no. 3433 (1931): 437; Gardner Jackson, "Doak the Deportation Chief," *The Nation* 132, no. 3428 (1931):

295–96; Report of the Director, July–November 1931, pp. 12–14, folder 65, box 5; Rich, "Memorandum on the United States Deportation Drive," December 12, 1931, folder 54a, box 4; Report of the Director, April–June 1931, p. 14, folder 65, box 5, all in Supplement II, IPL Papers.

15. In Chicago, the raids were blamed on federal immigration officials. Report of the Director, July–November 1931, p. 13, folder 65, box 5, Supplement II, IPL Papers.

16. Brown to the Commissioner, August 16, 1934, 55598/568A, RG 85; Kevin Johnson, *The "Huddled Masses" Myth: Immigration and Civil Rights* (Philadelphia: Temple University Press, 2004); Ruben Klainer, "Deportation of Aliens," *Boston University Law Review* 15 (1935): 663–722; Benjamin Klebaner, *Public Poor Relief in America, 1790–1860* (New York: Arno Press, 1976); Gerald Neuman, "The Lost Century of American Immigration Law (1776–1875)," *Columbia Law Review* 93 (1993): 1833–1901; Gerald Neuman, *Strangers to the Constitution: Immigrants, Borders and Fundamental Law* (Princeton: Princeton University Press, 1996); Ngai, *Impossible Subjects*; Kunal Parker, "State, Citizenship and Territory: The Legal Construction of Immigrants in Antebellum Massachusetts," *Law and History Review* 19 (2001): 583–643; David Schneider, *The History of Public Welfare in New York State, 1609–1866* (Chicago: University of Chicago Press, 1938); David Schneider and Albert Deutsch, *The History of Public Welfare in New York State, 1867–1940* (Chicago: University of Chicago Press, 1941).

17. *Henderson et al. v. Mayor of the City of New York et al.*; *Commissioners of Immigration v. North German Lloyd*, 92 U.S. 259 (1876); Richard Boswell, "Restrictions on Non-Citizens' Access to Public Benefits: Flawed Premise, Unnecessary Response," *UCLA Law Review* 42 (1995): 1475; Edwards, "Public Charge Doctrine"; Klainer, "Deportation of Aliens"; Klebaner, *Public Poor Relief in America*; *Annual Report of the Commissioner General of Immigration to the Secretary of Labor for the Fiscal Year Ended June 30* (Washington, DC: GPO, 1906–32). The data on public charge exclusions are calculated for 1906 to 1923 only. After 1923, immigrants were pre-screened at embassies overseas. Those determined to be liable to become a public charge were not granted visas. No statistics were kept on the number of individuals excluded by this method.

18. Jane Clark, *Deportation of Aliens from the United States to Europe* (New York: Columbia University Press, 1931), 121–22; Wickersham Commission, *Report on the Enforcement of the Deportation Laws of the United States* (Washington, DC: GPO, 1931); William Van Vleck, *The Administrative Control of Aliens: A Study in Administrative Law and Procedure* (New York: The Commonwealth Fund, 1932).

19. Commissioner General to all Commissioners of Immigration, September 27, 1923, 54951, box 4038, RG 85; Shaughnessy to all District Directors, August 7, 1934, INS, 55598/568A, box 412, RG 85. The responses to the Bureau of Immigration inquiries can be found in 54951, box 4038 and 55598/568A, box 412, both in RG 85. See also Report of the Director, April–November 1932, pp. 30–31, folder 65, box 5, Supplement II, IPL Papers; Edith Terry Bremer, "The Jobless 'Alien'—A Challenge to Social Workers," *The Survey* 65 (December 15, 1930): 316–17.

20. Commissioner General to all Commissioners and Inspectors, June 30, 1920, 54951, RG 85; Commissioner Hull to all Commissioners and District Directors, February 5, 1926, 55598/568A, RG 85; Report of the Director, April–November 1932, pp. 30–31, folder 65, box 5, Supplement II, IPL Papers; Clark, *Deportation of Aliens from the United States to Europe*, 109–14.

21. Burnett to Commissioner General, October 24, 1923, 54951, RG 85.

22. Cahn and Bary, *Welfare Activities of Federal, State, and Local Governments in California*, 342; Waymire to Husband, October 23, 1923, May 15, 1924, and January 3, 1925; Commissioner General to Waymire, October 9, 1923, November 2, 1923, and January 10, 1925; Commissioner General to Inspector in Charge, Los Angeles, California, October 9, 1923; Riley to Waymire, August 23, 1923, all in 54915, RG 85.

23. Annual Reports of the Department of Charities, Fiscal Year Ending June 30, 1925, 1926, 1929, 1931, Dean Papers; "Bureau of Indigent Relief," September 1937, folder bb aaa 5, box 64, Ford Papers. See also Molina, *Fit to Be Citizens?* 141.

24. Annual Report of the Department of Charities, Fiscal Year Ending June 30, 1931, Dean Papers.

25. Shaw to District Director, INS, August 15, 1934, 55598/568A, RG 85.

26. Annual Reports of the Department of Charities, Fiscal Year Ending June 30, 1925, 1926, 1929, 1931, 1933, 1935, Dean Papers; Hanna, "Social Services on the Mexican Border."

27. Rom, "Family Problems Resulting from the Present Deportation System," 569–72. Rom was right that social welfare agencies had many opportunities to mitigate the effects of the pubic charge deportations but wrong when she said that reporting was mandatory in theory. See Bremer, "The Jobless 'Alien.'" On cooperation between relief offices and immigration authorities, see also Report of the Director, April–November 1932, pp. 30–31, folder 65, box 5, Supplement II, IPL Papers.

28. Inspector in Charge, Chicago, to Commissioner General, October 1, 1923, 54951, RG 85; Annual Report of the Director, October 25, 1933, folder 65, box 5, Supplement II, IPL Papers.

29. Inspector in Charge, Chicago, to Commissioner General, October 1, 1923; Ebey to Husband, March 6, 1923; Commissioner General to Ebey, March 3, 1923 and March 13, 1923, all in 54951/13, RG 85. Report of the Director, January–May 1929, folder 67, box 5; Report of the Director, October 1929–January 1930, folder 65, box 5, both in Supplement II, IPL Papers.

30. Inspector in Charge, Chicago, to Commissioner General, October 1, 1923; Ebey to Husband, March 6, 1923; Commissioner General to Ebey, March 3, 1923 and March 13, 1923, all in 54951/13, RG 85; "Hope to Deport 20,000 This Year," attached to Alber to Doak, July 24, 1931, 167/255B, RG 174; Davis to Doak, November 2, 1931, box 4, folder 54a, Supplement II, IPL Papers; "Shakeup of High Immigration Officers Begins," *CDT*, January 22, 1932, p. 22.

31. "Find Thousands of Aliens Fed by Relief Fund," *CDT*, October 15, 1932, p. 6; Report of the Director, April–November 1932, folder 65, box 5, Supplement II, IPL Papers; "Memorandum of Meeting of Committee Representing the Advisory Board of the Immigration Service," September 26, 1932, Joseph Moss,

folder 49, box 3, Kohn Papers; Minutes of the Meeting of the Advisory Board of Cook County Bureau of Public Welfare, September 29, 1932, folder 10, box 6, Burgess Papers.

32. "Find Thousands of Aliens Fed by Relief Fund."

33. "County Official Defends Relief for the Aliens," *CDT*, October 16, 1932, p. 14; Report of the Director, April–November 1932, folder 65, box 5, Supplement II, IPL Papers; Minutes of the Meeting of Advisory Board of the Cook County Bureau of Public Welfare, September 29, 1932.

34. "Discuss Pleas to Cut Pay of Relief Workers," *CDT*, October 21, 1932, p. 19; "U.S. May Deport Aliens on Poor Relief Rolls," *CDT*, October 19, 1932, p. 11. On the careers of Sears and Kelly, see "Amelia Sears Dies," *CDT*, March 28, 1946, p. 30; "Peter M. Kelly Is Dead," *CDT*, March 1, 1936, p. 25.

35. "Sees $450,000 Relief Saving in Deportation," *CDT*, October 30, 1932, p. 6.

36. "Jobless Parade in Loop," *CDT*, November 1, 1932, p. 11; "Mayor Replies to Demands of Jobless Group," *CDT*, November 2, 1932, p. 22; "10,000 Chicagoans Join 'Hunger March,'" *NYT*, November 1, 1932, p. 3; "'Reds' Storm City in Food Plea," *CD*, November 5, 1932, p. 1; "Unemployed Chicagoans Protest Relief Cut," *Ada Evening News*, November 3, 1932, p. 1; "Chicago's Hunger March," *Syracuse Herald*, November 3, 1932, p. 32; "More Relief to Unemployed in Chicago Area," *Burlington Daily Times News*, November 2, 1932, p. 6; "Chicago Idle Stage Gigantic Parade," *Galveston Daily News*, November 1, 1932, p. 1; "Thousands of Jobless Go on March in Chicago," *LAT*, November 1, 1932, p. 1; "10,000 of Chicago's Idle Cry for Bread," *WP*, November 1, 1932, p. 7.

37. "For the Clubs of Unemployed Men . . . ," November 1, 1932, Mexican Work, box 21, McDowell Papers; "Jobless Parade in Loop," *CDT*, November 1, 1932, p. 11; "Mayor Replies to Demands of Jobless Group," *CDT*, November 2, 1932, p. 22; Digest of Meeting of the Illinois Emergency Relief Commission, November 4, 1932, Unemployed Relief, box 114, Hilliard Papers.

38. "Mayor Replies to Demands of Jobless Group."

39. Digest of Meeting of the Illinois Emergency Relief Commission, November 4, 1932.

40. "May Alter Law to Bare Names of Needy Aliens," *CDT*, October 20, 1932, p. 3; Editorial, "Thousands of Aliens," *The Nation*, 135, no. 3518 (1932): 544; "Offers Bill in House to Create Illinois Housing Commission," *CDT*, November 16, 1932, p. 8; Report of the Director, April–November 1932, folder 65, box 5, Supplement II, IPL Papers.

41. "Family of Ten Sent Back to Mexico," *LAT*, October 23, 1935, p. A2.

42. "Raps New Deal for Failure to Deport Aliens," *CDT*, October 11, 1936, p. NW2; Melvin Fagen, "The Families of Aliens" (New York: National Council on Naturalization and Citizenship, 1937), 4n2.

43. "Prepare to End Relief Board's Activities May 1," *CDT*, February 8, 1936, p. 3; Sophonisba Breckinridge, "Voice of the People: County Relief," *CDT*, April 3, 1931; Philip Kinsley, "County Welfare Work Built Up under Cermak," *CDT*, March 15, 1931, p. 3; Philip Kinsley, "Cermak Handles 'Poorhouse' on Business Basis," *CDT*, March 17, 1931, p. 6; Katherine Kelley, "Charity Chiefs Tell

Why They Back Cermak," *CDT*, March 28, 1931, p. 4; Gosnell, *Machine Politics, Chicago Model*, 78; Goodwin, *Gender and the Politics of Welfare Reform*, 152; Gene Jones, "The Chicago Catholic Charities, the Great Depression, and Public Monies," *Illinois Historical Journal* 83, no. 1 (1990): 17; Forthal, *Cogwheels of Democracy*, 55–66.

44. "Grand Jury Report Accusing County Charity Head Comes Up before Supervisors Today," *LAT*, October 24, 1927, p. A1; "Board Delays Charities Move," *LAT*, October 25, 1927, p. A1; "Bureau Scores Charities Head," *LAT*, January 5, 1928, p. A1; "Hearing on Charities Postponed," *LAT*, June 18, 1929, p. A11; "Charity Head's Ousting Asked," *LAT*, October 22, 1927, p. A1; Alma Whitaker, "Relief Ouster Protested," *LAT*, June 14, 1929, p. A1. See also Richard Lester, "Building the New Deal State on the Local Level: Unemployment Relief in Los Angeles County during the 1930s" (Ph.D. thesis, University of California, Los Angeles, 2001), 53–57, 68–72, 133; Eva Hance, "Report of Los Angeles County, California," July 30, 1934, box 26, 401.3–420, CA State Series, FERA, RG 69.

45. "Bureau Scores Charities Head," *LAT*, January 5, 1928, p. A1; Lester, "Building the New Deal State on the Local Level," 72.

46. Miller, "The Mexican Dependency Problem"; "Outdoor Relief Hearing Heated," *LAT*, June 25, 1929, p. A1; "Supervisors Will Reopen Ouster Row," *LAT*, June 19, 1929, p. A3; Whitaker, "Relief Ouster Protested"; Alma Whitaker, "The Outdoor Relief Problem," *LAT*, June 15, 1929, p. A4; "Shall We 'Give 'Em What They Want'?" *Bulletin of Municipal League of Los Angeles* 6, no. 10 (July 1, 1929): 1–2; "Board Delays Charities Move," *LAT*, October 25, 1927, p. A1; "Holland Hands in Resignation," *LAT*, August 25, 1931, p. A1. For more on the interference of the Department of Charities by the Board of Supervisors, see "Price Will Fight Ouster," *LAT*, August 28, 1931, p. A1; "County Charity Cut Short," *LAT*, June 5, 1931, p. A1; "Welfare Staff Feels Ax," *LAT*, August 12, 1933, p. A1;"Charity Quiz Demanded," *LAT*, June 11, 1931, p. A1; Lester, "Building the New Deal State on the Local Level," 53–57, 68–72, 133, 157, 160–72; Hance, "Report of Los Angeles County, California."

47. Rich, "The Present Field of the IPL," February 1933, folder 159, box 13, Kohn Papers; Report of the Director, April–November 1932, folder 66, box 5, Supplement II, IPL Papers.

48. Rom, "Family Problems Resulting from the Present Deportation System," 571–72; Mary-Claire Johnson, "Special Methods of Treatment in Family Case Work with Non-Citizens," *Illinois Conference on Social Welfare*, East St. Louis, October 28–31, 1935, pp. 154–59. Report of the Director, June–September 1929, October 1929–January 1930, April–June 1931, folder 65, box 5; Report of the Director, November 1940–February 1941, March–April 1941, 3–4, folder 69, box 6; Report of the Director, November 20, 1934, April–November 1932, folder 66, box 5, all in Supplement II, IPL Papers.

49. Sophonisba Breckinridge, "The Family in the Community, But Not Yet of the Community," *NCCC Proceedings*, 1914, p. 73.

50. Rom, "Family Problems Resulting from the Present Deportation System," 570–72; Harriette Ryan, "The Community's Interest in Fair Play to the Foreign-Born," *Illinois Conference on Social Welfare* (East St. Louis, 1935), 149–53.

51. Average calculated for years 1907–13. Cook County Board of Commissioners, *Charity Service Reports, Fiscal Years, 1908–1913*; "Fourth Annual Re-

port of the Immigrants' Protective League, for Year Ending Jan. 1, 1913," folder 59A, box 4, Supplement II, IPL Papers.

52. In 1915 fifteen people were deported, but the numbers trailed off after that. In 1920 there were eight deportations, and there were only three in each year from 1921 to 1923. In 1926 Cook County referred 111 tuberculosis cases to the Immigration Service for possible deportation, but the Immigration Service deported only five in that year and only one the year after. Cook County Board of Commissioners, *Charity Service Reports, Fiscal Years 1916–23, 1926–27*; Jones, *Conditions Surrounding Mexicans in Chicago*, 101; Weber, "Anglo Views of Mexican Immigrants," 264–65.

53. Marian Schibsby, "Immigrants and Their Children," in *Social Work Year Book, 1937*, ed. R. H. Kurtz (New York: Russell Sage Foundation, 1937), 215; Kate Claghorn, "The Work of the Voluntary Immigrant Protective Agencies," *Proceedings*, 1919, pp. 747–52; George Warren, "Some International Aspects of Immigration: The Widening Horizon of Our Service to Foreign Born Families," *NCSW Proceedings*, 1931, pp. 459–60.

54. Clark, *Deportation of Aliens from the United States to Europe*; Clark, "American Deportation Procedure," 567–68.

55. Shaw to District Director, INS, August 15, 1934; Kuykendall to District Director, Los Angeles, August 15, 1934, both in 55598/568A, RG 85; Clark, "American Deportation Procedure," 562; *Proceedings of the Tenth New York State Conference of Charities and Correction, Albany, New York, November 16–18, 1909* (Albany: J. B. Lyon Company, 1910), 126; Wickersham Commission, *Report on the Enforcement of the Deportation Laws of the United States*, 53.

56. Thomson to Board of Supervisors, June 15, 1939, 40.36/10, LACBS Decimal Files; Marian Schibsby, "The Medical-Social Worker and the United States Deportation Law," *Interpreter Release* 10, no. 29 (1933): 169–73.

57. *Fifty-Eighth Annual Report of the State Board of Charities for the Year 1924* (Albany: J. B. Lyon Company, 1925).

58. Hanna, "Social Services on the Mexican Border." For the work of the National Catholic Welfare Conference at one border crossing, see Marjorie Sánchez-Walker, "Migration Quicksand: Immigration Law and Immigration Advocated at the El Paso–Ciudad Juárez Border Crossing, 1933–1941" (Ph.D. thesis, Washington State University, 1999).

59. Ziegler-McPherson, "Americanization"; Walsh, "Laboring at the Margins," 404; Hanna to Shortridge, February 24, 1926, folder 36, box 4, DIR Papers; Willa Baum, Amelia Fry, and Hannah Josephson, "Oral History of Carey McWilliams," *California's Olson-Warren Era: Migrants and Social Welfare*, California State Archives Research Room.

60. Balderrama, *In Defense of La Raza*, 7, 18. On the ambivalence of some Mexican Americans toward Mexican immigrants, see Gutiérrez, *Walls and Mirrors*. There is little evidence that the lack of support from labor made the difference here. Even in Chicago, demands to stop deportations and prevent cooperation between welfare and immigration officials came *after* welfare officials promised not to cooperate.

61. Rom, "Family Problems Resulting from the Present Deportation System," 569. Mansfield to Commissioner General, December 6, 1921, and January 20, 1922; "Denver's Safety Is Menaced by 3,500 Starving Mexicans," *Denver*

Post, January 19, 1922; Chief of Police to Quijano, no date, all in INS Records; Deutsch, *No Separate Refuge*, 138.

62. Mansfield to Commissioner General, December 6, 1921 and January 20, 1922, both in INS Records; Mansfield to Commissioner General, August 8, 1924, box 4339, 55091/6, RG 85.

63. D. Dinwoodie, "Deportation: The Immigration Service and the Chicano Labor Movement in the 1930s," *New Mexico Historical Review* 52, no. 3 (1977): 200; Robb to Adar, April 6, 1921; Hart to Husband, April 13, 1921; Bondy to Husband, April 15, 1921, and May 16, 1921; Husband to Bondy, May 23 and 28, 1921; Persons to Husband, May 9, 1921; Husband to Immigration Service, El Paso, May 2, 1921; Fieser to Persons, April 12, 1921, all in INS Records; House Committee, *Immigration from Countries of the Western Hemisphere*, 376; Whalen to Commissioner of Immigration, August 30, 1933, 55739, 674/674A, RG 85; "U.S. to Probe Aliens Upon Relief Rolls," *Greeley Daily Tribune*, July 11, 1935, p. 2.

64. Kuykendall to District Director, August 15, 1934, 55598/568A, RG 85. For cooperation in Imperial Valley, see Spurlock to District Director, August 15, 1934, 55598/568A, RG 85.

65. Spurgeon to District Director, May 12, 1934, 311.1215/57, RG 59. There was a report claiming little cooperation between immigration and welfare agencies in Phoenix. Collaer to District Director, El Paso, May 8, 1934, 311.1215/57, RG 59.

66. Klainer, "Deportation of Aliens"; Ngai, *Impossible Subjects*; Van Vleck, *The Administrative Control of Aliens*.

67. For Figure 6.1, I excluded 1906–7 and 1931–32 because these years had exceptionally low numbers of documented Mexican admissions. As a result, Mexican public charge deportations as a percent of document admissions appear abnormally high: 4.3 percent for 1906–7 and 13.5 percent for 1931–32. By truncating the time series, not only am I able to present a more conservative estimate, but I am also better able to show the trends for the years between these outliers. United States Bureau of Immigration, *Annual Reports of the Commissioner General of Immigration to the Secretary of Labor for the Fiscal Year Ended June 30* (Washington, DC: GPO, 1906–32).

68. Bremer, "The Jobless 'Alien.'"

69. Ibid.

Chapter 7

1. McWilliams, "Getting Rid of the Mexican."

2. Hoffman, *Unwanted Mexican Americans in the Great Depression*; Balderrama and Rodriguez, *Decade of Betrayal*; Balderrama, *In Defense of La Raza*; Norman Humphrey, "Mexican Repatriation from Michigan: Public Assistance in Historical Perspective," *Social Service Review* 15 (1941): 497–513; García, *Mexicans in the Midwest*; Camille Guerin-Gonzales, *Mexican Workers and American Dreams: Immigration, Repatriation and California Farm Labor, 1900–1939*

(New Brunswick: Rutgers University Press, 1994); McKay, "Texas Mexican Repatriation during the Great Depression." Unlike these works, I focus solely on repatriation sponsored by relief agencies.

3. Hull to Brodie, March 28, 1933, 55739/674, RG 85; Klainer, "Deportation of Aliens"; Annual Report of the Department of Charities, Fiscal Year Ending June 30, 1933, Dean Papers; McWilliams, "Getting Rid of the Mexican."

4. Watkins to White, February 8, 1931, 55739 674/674A, RG 85.

5. John Littell, interview with Rex Thompson, May 11, 1934, 311.1215/55, RG 59.

6. Annual Report of the Department of Charities, Fiscal Year Ending June 30, 1931, Dean Papers; McWilliams, "Getting Rid of the Mexican."

7. Annual Report of the Department of Charities, Fiscal Year Ending June 30, 1931; Annual Report of the Department of Charities, Fiscal Year Ending June 30, 1933; Hoffman, *Unwanted Mexican Americans in the Great Depression*, 83–115.

8. Carr to Commissioner General, June 17, 1931; Watkins to White, February 21, 1931, both in 55739 674/674A, RG 85; Balderrama, *In Defense of La Raza*, 23; Matson to Arnoll, June 4, 1931, box 62, #118, Clements Papers; House Committee, *Immigration from Countries of the Western Hemisphere*, 325; "State against Mexican Bars," *LAT*, February 24, 1932, p. 5.

9. Hoffman, *Unwanted Mexican Americans in the Great Depression*, 76–77; "Can Find No Record of Shaw's Citizenship," *LAT*, May 23, 1933, p. A1; Lester, "Building the New Deal State on the Local Level," 83.

10. Carr to Commissioner General, June 17, 1931; Harris to District Director, Los Angeles, June 9, 1931; translated article, *Excelsior*, May 11, 1931, all in 55739 674/674A, RG 85. Clements to Arnoll, January 21, 1931; Clements to Woods, February 2, 1931, both in box 62, #118, Clements Papers. Balderrama, *In Defense of La Raza*.

11. Balderrama, *In Defense of La Raza*, 21; Sánchez, *Becoming Mexican American*, 215–21; García, *Mexicans in the Midwest*, 106.

12. Balderrama and Rodriguez, *Decade of Betrayal*, 105; Guerin-Gonzales, *Mexican Workers and American Dreams*, 145; Clements to Arnoll, August 17, 1931, box 62, #118, Clements Papers; Hoffman, "The Repatriation of Mexican Nationals from the United States during the Great Depression," appendix C; Schreiber to Board of Supervisors, January 21, 1941, 40.36/24.3, LACBS Decimal File; Molina, *Fit to Be Citizens?*

13. Translation of Thompson to Secretary of Agriculture and Public Works in Mexico, May 4, 1934, 311.1215/65, RG 59; Annual Report of the Department of Charities, Fiscal Year Ending June 30, 1931; Fox, "The Boundaries of Social Citizenship," 303.

14. Annual Report of the Department of Charities, Fiscal Year Ending June 30, 1933; Berkshire to INS Commissioner, June 23, 1934, 311.1215/65, RG 59; Besig to "Dear Friend," June 8, 1931, box 62, #118, Clements Papers; translation of Thompson to Secretary of Agriculture and Public Works in Mexico, May 4, 1934, 311.1215/65, RG 59; Littell interview with Thompson.

15. Gamio, *Mexican Immigration to the United States*; Sánchez, *Becoming Mexican American*, 209–26; Grebler, Moore, and Guzman, *The Mexican American People*, 523–26; Gutiérrez, *Walls and Mirrors*, 72–74; Hoffman, "The Repatriation of Mexican Nationals from the United States"; Abraham Hoffman, "Stimulus to Repatriation: The 1931 Federal Deportation Drive and the Los Angeles Mexican Community," *Pacific Historical Review* 42 (1973): 205–19; Hoffman, *Unwanted Mexican Americans in the Great Depression*, 83–115; Humphrey, "Mexican Repatriation from Michigan"; Carr to Commissioner General, June 17, 1931, 55739 674/674A, RG 85; Balderrama, *In Defense of La Raza*, 2, 22.

16. Emory Bogardus, "Repatriation and Readjustment," in *The Mexican-Americans: An Awakening Minority*, ed. M. Servin (Beverly Hills, CA: Glencoe Press, 1970), 93; Clements to Arnoll, August 13, 1931, box 62, #118, Clements Papers; "Aliens Depart as Relief Cut Off," *Herald and Express*, October 11, 1937, p. 11A, box 195, Division of Information, RG 69; Ford quoted in Sánchez, *Becoming Mexican American*, 223; Littell interview with Thompson; "Repatriation Drive Begun," *LAT*, March 31, 1934, p. A12; "Thomson Tells of Huge Cost of Relief for Aliens," *LAT*, June 6, 1937, p. 2.

17. Clements to Arnoll, August 17, 1931, box 62, #118, Clements Papers; Littell interview with Thompson; "Mexican Labor Scare Rapped"; Balderrama, *In Defense of La Raza*, 21.

18. Yost to Secretary of State, November 12, 1931, 311.1215/28, RG 59; Hanna, "Social Services on the Mexican Border"; Sánchez-Walker, "Migration Quicksand"; Warner to Hopkins, September 18, 1933, and October 2, 1933; Lewis to Hopkins, October 10, 1933, all in AZ 1933, box 9, FERA Central Files, State Series, RG 69. On conditions of repatriates in Mexico, see Balderrama and Rodriguez, *Decade of Betrayal*.

19. Hanna, "Social Services on the Mexican Border"; Sánchez-Walker, "Migration Quicksand."

20. Russel to FDR, April 3, 1933, 55739 674/674A, RG 85; Department of Labor, *Twenty-Fourth Annual Report of the Secretary of Labor for the Fiscal Year Ended June 30, 1936* (Washington, DC: GPO, 1936), 97. See also, Molina, *Fit to Be Citizens?* 131.

21. Carrie MacCarthy, "A Survey of the Mexican Hardship Cases Active in the Los Angeles County Department of Charities, Los Angeles, California" (Master's thesis, University of Southern California, School of Social Work, 1939), 49–52.

22. Besig to "Dear Friend," June 8, 1931; Hoffman, *Unwanted Mexican Americans in the Great Depression*, 89, 97–98.

23. Sánchez, *Becoming Mexican American*, 209–26.

24. Hoffman, *Unwanted Mexican Americans in the Great Depression*, 97–98; "New Aid Urged for Mexicans," *LAT*, December 4, 1932, p. C9.

25. Grebler, Moore, and Guzman, *The Mexican American People*, 458, 481n40; *Second Biennial Report of the Department of Industrial Relations of the State of California, 1930–1932* (Sacramento, CA, 1932), 135–48; California Conference of Social Work, "Proceedings of the Twenty-Third Annual Meeting, Berkeley, May 17 to 21, 1931," *Conference Bulletin* 14, no. 4 (1931): 55–56; "Mexican Labor Scare Rapped"; California Conference of Social Work, "Pro-

ceedings of the Twenty-Fourth Annual Meeting, Riverside, May 1 to 5, 1932," *Conference Bulletin* 15, no. 4 (1932): 30–32; California Conference of Social Work, "Proceedings of the Twenty-Fifth Annual Meeting, Sacramento, May 14 to 18, 1933," *Conference Bulletin* 16, no. 4 (1933): 22–23; Sánchez, *Becoming Mexican American*, 222–23. A resolution for the repatriation of Filipinos was put before the social workers in 1933 but they refused to vote on it. Abel, " 'Only the Best Class of Immigration,'" 937.

26. Hopkins and Perkins to FDR, "Aliens and Relief," January 15, 1935, Official File 444, FDR Papers; Hoffman, *Unwanted Mexican Americans in the Great Depression*, 106–7, 115, 172–73; Marian Schibsby, "Deportation in 1933," *Interpreter Release* 11, no. 6 (1934): 46–52; Berkshire to INS Commissioner, June 23, 1934, 311.1215/65, RG 59.

27. Carr to Immigration Bureau, May 13, 1931, 55739 674/674A, RG 85; Sánchez, *Becoming Mexican American*, 210, 314n3; Guerin-Gonzales, *Mexican Workers and American Dreams*, 143.

28. Leonardo Macias Jr., "Mexican Immigration and Repatriation during the Great Depression" (Master's thesis, Arizona State University, 1992); McKay, "Texas Mexican Repatriation during the Great Depression," 220–56; Sánchez-Walker, "Migration Quicksand"; "WPA Aliens Are Flayed," *San Antonio Sunday Light*, October 11, 1936, p. 1; "May Remove Aliens from Relief Payrolls," *El Paso Herald-Post*, September 13, 1933, p. 7; Reynolds McKay, "The Impact of the Great Depression on Immigrant Mexican Labor: Repatriation of the Bridgeport, Texas, Coalminers," *Social Science Quarterly* 65, no. 2 (1984): 358, 361.

29. Donald Young, "Research Memorandum on Minority Peoples in the Depression" (New York: Social Science Research Council, 1937), 43–44.

30. Superior Democrat Committee to President et al., March 10, 1933, 55739 674/674A, RG 85; Abraham Hoffman, "The Federal Bureaucracy Meets a Superior Spokesman for Alien Deportation," *Journal of the West* 11, no. 4 (1975): 91–106; Clark to FDR, January 17, 1934, 311.1215/48, RG 59. "Why Every Native-Born American Should Be a Member of the Junior Order United American Mechanics"; Petition, citizens of Jamestown to Copeland, March 24, 1936; "Help Save America for Americans," all in SEN 74A-J12, RG 46. Maynard to Department of Labor, November 30, 1931, 55739 674/674A, Patton to FDR, February 8, 1935, 55875/462C, 85-58A734; Quaill to FDR, January 12, 1939, 55789/979, all in RG 85. McElvaine, *Down and Out in the Great Depression*, 149–54.

31. "Round 'Em Up," *CDT*, June 22, 1935, p. 1; Junior Order United American Mechanics pamphlet, 74A-J12, RG 46.

32. Hadley Cantril, *Public Opinion: 1935–1946* (Princeton: Princeton University Press, 1951), 894; author's calculation, Gallup Polls #1936-0062, #1938-0141. Data presented with phone weights. Adam Berinsky, "Public Opinion in the 1930s and 1940s: The Analysis of Quota Controlled Sample Survey Data," *Public Opinion Quarterly* 70, no. 4 (2006): 530–64.

33. Adena Rich, "Outline for Cooperation with Social Agencies in Repatriation Cases," December 30, 1937, folder 67, box 5, Supplement II, IPL Papers.

34. Hopkins and Perkins to FDR, "Aliens and Relief," January 15, 1935; Marian Schibsby, "The Repatriation of Destitute Aliens," *Interpreter Release* 12, no.

24 (1935): 201–14; Fred Hall, ed., "International Social Case Work," in *Social Work Year Book, 1935*, 215–16; Hoffman, *Unwanted Mexican Americans in the Great Depression*, 101.

35. Schibsby, "The Repatriation of Destitute Aliens." But see Dwight Morgan, "Foreign-Born on Relief," *Social Work Today* 4 (1936): 11–13.

36. Rich, "Outline for Cooperation with Social Agencies in Repatriation Cases," December 30, 1937; Schibsby, "The Repatriation of Destitute Aliens"; Ambelang to MacCormack, August 9, 1933, Aliens, Repatriation of, Old General Subject Series, RG 69. Davis to Hopkins, August 27, 1935; Hallberg to FDR, July 26, 1935; Barber, Ohio to ?, July 8, 1935; Vincent Garibaldi to ?, August 20, 1935; Benson to FERA, October 3, 1935, all in 003 Aliens, box 7, FERA, New General Subject Series, RG 69.

37. Adena Rich, "Case Work in the Repatriation of Immigrants," *Social Service Review* 10, no. 4 (1936): 569, 574, 604. See also Rich, "Outline for Cooperation with Social Agencies in Repatriation Cases," December 30, 1937; Johnson, "Special Methods of Treatment in Family Case Work with Non-Citizens," 154–59.

38. Rich, "Case Work in the Repatriation of Immigrants," 580, 588–89. See also Marian Schibsby, "Repatriation by the United States Government of Aliens Who Are in Need of Public Aid," *Interpreter Release* 8, no. 8 (1931): 62–64.

39. Report of the Director, April–June 1931, p. 10; Report of the Director, April–November 1932, both in folder 65, box 5; Report of the Director, May 16, 1935, November 20, 1934, and December 17, 1935, all in folder 66, box 5, Supplement II, IPL Papers.

40. Report of the Director, July–November 1931; Report of the Director, April–November 1932, both in folder 65, box 5, Supplement II, IPL Papers; Marian Schibsby, "Repatriation to Home Lands," *Interpreter Release Clip Sheet* 10, no. 16 (1933): 64–66; Louise Kerr, "The Chicano Experience in Chicago: 1920–1970" (Ph.D. thesis, University of Illinois, Chicago, 1976); Rich, "Case Work in the Repatriation of Immigrants," 596; Annual Report of the Director, February 27, 1936, folder 66, box 5, Supplement II, IPL Papers.

41. Annual Report of the Director, October 25, 1933, folder 65, box 5, Supplement II, IPL Papers; Arletta Weimer, "Dreams of Happiness in America Shattered by Depression," *Akron Saturday Evening*, July 29, 1933; Ambelang to MacCormack, August 9, 1933, Aliens, Repatriation of, Old General Subject Series, RG 69; Marian Schibsby, "Concerning the Repatriation of Indigent Aliens," *Interpreter Release* 10, no. 6 (1933): 26–35; Morgan, "Foreign-Born on Relief"; Rich, "Case Work in the Repatriation of Immigrants," 605. For more letters from repatriates, see Annual Report of the Director, February 27, 1936, folder 66, box 5, Supplement II, IPL Papers.

42. Schibsby, "Repatriation to Home Lands"; Morgan, "Foreign-Born on Relief"; David Maynard, "Indigent Americans in Europe," 003-Aliens, New General Subject Series, RG 69; Warren to Lee, February 20, 1931, Labor Department Folder, 040, RG 73; Committee of Experts on Assistance to Indigent Foreigners, January 8, 1934, "Report to the Council on the Work of the Session Held from December 4–9, 1933," Official No.: C.10.M.8., 1934, IV, League of Nations: Geneva, 555.M1/63, RG 59; Committee of Experts on Assistance to Indigent Foreigners, December 20, 1935, "Suggestions for Drawing up a Conven-

tion on Assistance to Indigent Foreigners," A.E./22, League of Nations: Geneva, 555.M1, RG 59.

43. Katherine Lawless, "Brief Digest of New Arrival Report, 1926–1930," June 1933, *Proceedings of the National Conference of International Institutes, Detroit, MI, June 10–12, 1933*, folder 16, box 270, reel 175, AFII Papers.

44. Census Bureau, *Fifteenth Census of the United States*, vol. 2, p. 414; Marian Schibsby, "Certain State Legislation Affecting Aliens," *Interpreter Release* 10, no. 20 (1933): 120–25; Karnuth to Commissioner General, May 12, 1933; Shaughnessy to Commissioner General, May 29, 1933, both in 05/33, 55816/810, 85-58A334, RG 85; New York State, *General Laws of the State of New York* (St. Paul, MN: West Publishing, 1940), 600–601; Schneider and Deutsch, *The History of Public Welfare in New York State*, 372–73.

45. New York State, *General Laws of the State of New York* (St. Paul, MN: West Publishing, 1933), 270; New York State, *General Laws of the State of New York* (1940), 600–601; Harry Hirsch and Robert Axel, "The Drifting Poor Return Home," *Social Welfare Bulletin* 6, no. 8–9 (1935): 6–8; New York Department of Social Welfare, State of New York, *Sixty-Second Annual Report of the State Board of Charities for the Year Ending June 30, 1928* (Albany: J. B. Lyon Company, 1929); *Sixty-Ninth Annual Report of the State Board of Social Welfare for the Year Ended June 30, 1935* (Albany: J. B. Lyon Company, 1936), 178; *Seventieth Annual Report of the State Board of Social Welfare for the Year Ended June 30, 1936* (Albany: J. B. Lyon Company, 1937), 19; Department of Public Welfare, City of New York, *Annual Report for the Year 1934* (New York, 1935), 62.

46. Department of Public Welfare, City of New York, *Annual Report for the Year 1934* (New York, 1935), 62–65; Department of Public Welfare, City of New York, *Annual Report*, 1930 (New York, 1931); Department of Public Welfare, City of New York, *Annual Report*, 1931 (New York, 1932); Willard Edwards, "N.Y. Supporting Army of Aliens on Relief Rolls," March 13, 1935, p. 5; Willard Edwards, "200,000 Aliens on N.Y. Relief; 10 PCT. Are Reds," *CDT*, March 17, 1935, p. 5; McElvaine, *Down and Out in the Great Depression*, 151.

47. New York, State Board of Charities, *Annual Reports of the State Board of Charities* (Albany: J. B. Lyon Company, 1880–1929); New York Department of Social Welfare, State of New York, *Annual Reports of the State Board of Social Welfare for the Year Ended June 30* (Albany: J. B. Lyon Company, 1930–41); Fox, "The Boundaries of Social Citizenship," 329–33. This figure does not include the insane poor repatriated by the Deportation Bureau of the State Hospital Board.

48. New York State, *Fifty-Eighth Annual Report of the State Board of Charities for the Year 1924* (Albany: J. B. Lyon Company, 1925), 51; State of New York, *Annual Report of the State Board of Charities for the Year 1914*, vol. 1 (Albany: J. B. Lyon Company, 1915), 154–67.

49. "1,500,000 Aliens on U.S. Doles," *CDT*, April 25, 1935, p. 15; MacCormack to Williams, November 30, 1934, 003 Aliens, FERA Central Files, New General Subject Files, RG 69; "Concerning Aliens and Relief," *Syracuse Herald*, December 1, 1934, p. 8. The IPL estimated the cost to be $75. IPL, Report of the Director, December 17, 1935, folder 66, box 5, Supplement II, IPL Papers.

50. Census Bureau, *Fifteenth Census of the United States: 1930, Unemployment*, vol. 2 (Washington, DC: GPO, 1932); Census Bureau, "Table 19: Nativity of the Population for the 50 Largest Urban Places: 1870–1990," http://www.census.gov/population/www/documentation/twps0029/tab19.html; Census Bureau, *Fifteenth Census of the United States*, vol. 2, p. 463; Emma A. Winslow, *Trends in Different Types of Public and Private Relief in Urban Areas, 1929–1935* (Washington, DC: GPO, 1937); Department of Commerce, *Financial Statistics of Cities Having a Population of over 30,000* (Washington, DC: GPO, 1929–34); Fox, "The Boundaries of Social Citizenship," 334–37.

51. California Assembly Joint Resolution Nos. 31 and 32, 1935, 74th Cong., SEN 74A-J12, RG 46; Marian Schibsby, "Legislative Bulletin No. 1," *Interpreter Release* 7, no. 2 (1935): 47; Marian Schibsby, "Legislative Bulletin No. VI," *Interpreter Release* 12, no. 16 (1935): 140–43; "Age-Aid Vote Postponed," *LAT*, March 19, 1935, p. 1; Marian Schibsby, "Legislative Bulletin No. III," *Interpreter Release* 12, no. 8 (1935): 47–48; Fagen, "The Families of Aliens," 4n2.

52. Hopkins to MacCormack, July 14, 1933; Branion to Hopkins, September 19, 1933; Bookman to Branion, October 9, 1933, all in Aliens, Repatriation of, Old General Subject Series, RG 69. Memo from MacCormack, November 30, 1934; Williams to Haber, July 12 and 21, 1934, all in box 7, 003 Aliens, FERA Central Files, New General Subject Series, RG 69.

53. Memo from MacCormack, November 30, 1934, 003 Aliens, FERA Central Files, New General Subject Files, RG 69; Hopkins and Perkins to FDR, "Aliens and Relief," January 15, 1935; Mary Anne Thatcher, *Immigrants and the 1930s: Ethnicity and Alienage in Depression and On-Coming War* (New York: Garland, 1990), 135; Clements to Williams, May 1, 1935; "Deportation of Aliens on Relief," *Denver Post*, April 30, 1935, both in 406 CO Field Reports, box 39, FERA Central Files, State Series, RG 69; Wilmoth to Warner, November 12, 1934; Warner to Hopkins, November 15, 1934; Hopkins to Warner, November 21, 1934; Hopkins to Perkins, November 21, 1934, all in AZ Official FERA, box 9, FERA Central Files, State Series, RG 69.

54. Schibsby, "Concerning the Repatriation of Indigent Aliens"; Schibsby, "Repatriation by the United States Government of Aliens Who Are in Need of Public Aid"; Klainer, "Deportation of Aliens"; Comptroller General to the Secretary of Labor, February 12, 1931, Deportations, 167/255B, RG 174; Rich, "Case Work in the Repatriation of Immigrants"; *Statistical Abstract of the United States* (1940), 100; *Annual Report of the Commissioner General of Immigration to the Secretary of Labor, Fiscal Year Ended June 30, 1931* (Washington, DC: GPO, 1931); *Annual Report of the Commissioner General of Immigration to the Secretary of Labor, Fiscal Year Ended June 30, 1932* (Washington, DC: GPO, 1932), 6–7; Thatcher, *Immigrants and the 1930s*; Report of the Director, November 20, 1934, folder 66, box 5, Supplement II, IPL Papers; Rich, "Outline for Cooperation with Social Agencies in Repatriation Cases," December 30, 1937; Report of the Director, April–October 1937, folder 67, box 5, Supplement II, IPL Papers.

55. Hopkins and Perkins to FDR, "Aliens and Relief," January 15, 1935; Schibsby, "Concerning the Repatriation of Indigent Aliens"; Schibsby, "Legislative Bulletin No. III"; Chester Sipkin, "Removal of Distressed Aliens from the United States," *INS Monthly Review* 8 (1950): 12–13; Thatcher, *Immigrants*

and the 1930s, 125–39; Mrs. Kenneth Rich, "Why There Is 'Standing Room Only' at the Immigrants' Protective League," December 2, 1937, folder 67, box 5, Supplement II, IPL Papers; Aristide Zolberg, *A Nation by Design: Immigration Policy in the Fashioning of America* (Cambridge, MA: Harvard University Press, 2006), 269.

56. J. Colcord and R. Kurtz, eds., "Back to the Homeland," *The Survey* 69 (January 1933): 39; Norman Goldner, "The Mexican in the Northern Urban Area: A Comparison of Two Generations" (Master's thesis, University of Minnesota, 1959); Lorraine Pierce, "Mexican Americans on St. Paul's Lower West Side," *Journal of Mexican American History* 4 (1974): 1–18; "To Transfer Mexicans Now on Relief Back Home," *Brainerd (MN) Daily Dispatch*, June 15, 1937, p. 1; García, *Mexicans in the Midwest*, 223–44; Humphrey, "Mexican Repatriation from Michigan"; Valdés, *Barrios Norteños*, 87–100, 125–26; Vargas, *Proletarians of the North*, 176–90; "Aliens Will Be Returned Home," *Chronicle Telegram*, April 3, 1934, p. 5; Waters, "Transient Mexican Agricultural Labor," 61.

57. "The Present Situation in Foreign Communities," *Proceedings of the National Conference of International Institutes, Detroit, MI, June 10–12, 1933*, folder 16, box 270, reel 175, AFII Papers; Raymond Mohl and Neil Betten, "Discrimination and Repatriation: Mexican Life in Gary," in *Forging a Community: The Latino Experience in Northwest Indiana, 1919–1975*, ed. J. Lane and E. Escobar (Chicago: Cattails Press, 1987), 161–86; Francisco Rosales and Daniel Simon, "Mexican Immigrant Experience in the Urban Midwest: East Chicago, Indiana, 1919–1945," in *Forging a Community*, 137–60; Valdés, *Barrios Norteños*, 93–94.

58. Mohl and Betten, "Discrimination and Repatriation," 177–78; Balderrama, *In Defense of La Raza*, 24; Valdés, *Barrios Norteños*, 93–94.

59. García, *Mexicans in the Midwest*, 234–35; Kerr, "The Chicano Experience in Chicago"; Weber, "Anglo Views of Mexican Immigrants," 249–69; Report of the Director, April–June 1931, folder 65, box 5, Supplement II, IPL Papers; Arredondo, *Mexican Chicago*, 96, 105; Sánchez-Walker, "Migration Quicksand"; Valdés, *Barrios Norteños*, 96.

60. Zubrick to Commissioner General, October 20 and December 5, 1932, both in 55784/585, RG 85; Humphrey, "Mexican Repatriation from Michigan"; Louis Murillo, "The Detroit Mexican Colonia from 1920 to 1932: Implications for Social and Educational Policy" (Ph.D. thesis, Michigan State University, 1981); Weber, "Anglo Views of Mexican Immigrants."

61. Humphrey, "Mexican Repatriation from Michigan"; Murillo, "The Detroit Mexican Colonia from 1920 to 1932."

62. "Repatriation," State Welfare Department, Lansing, MI (n.d.), Harvard Library, Cambridge, MA; Humphrey, "Mexican Repatriation from Michigan"; Fox, "The Boundaries of Social Citizenship," 344–47.

63. Hopkins and Perkins to FDR, "Aliens and Relief," January 15, 1935; Gutiérrez, *Walls and Mirrors*, 72; Hoffman, *Unwanted Mexican Americans in the Great Depression*, ix, 2; Ngai, *Impossible Subjects*, 72, 75; Voluntary Report, John Littell, "Foreign Immigration into and Emigration from Mexico, 1930–1933," April 4, 1934, Subject Correspondence, 55609/551A, box 439, RG 85.

CHAPTER 8

1. "Senator Seeks Deporting of Race Citizens," *CD*, June 4, 1938, p. 7; "'God Created Only Whites,' Bilbo Raves," *CD*, June 11, 1938, p. 6; Edward Sholson, "What the People Say," *CD*, August 27, 1932, p. 14; "Church Opposes Deporting Relief Clients South," *CD*, June 24, 1939, p. 2; Mohl and Betten, "Discrimination and Repatriation," 173.

2. Amenta, *Bold Relief*, 85, 157–59; John David, "A Black Inventory of the New Deal," *The Crisis* 42 (May 1935): 141–, reprinted in H. Zinn, ed., *New Deal Thought* (Indianapolis: Bobbs-Merrill, 1966); Forrester Washington, "The Negro and Relief," *NCSW Proceedings*, 1934, pp. 178–94.

3. On blacks and the New Deal, see especially Ferguson, *Black Politics in New Deal Atlanta*; Katznelson, *When Affirmative Action Was White*; Lieberman, *Shifting the Color Line*; Nancy Weiss, *Farewell to the Party of Lincoln: Black Politics in the Age of FDR* (Princeton: Princeton University Press, 1983). The only works that cover immigrants are Donald Howard, *The WPA and Federal Relief Policy* (New York: Russell Sage Foundation, 1943) and Thatcher, *Immigrants and the 1930s*.

4. *Historical Statistics of the United States, Colonial Times to 1970*, 126; Trattner, *From Poor Law to Welfare State*, 273, 276; Winslow, *Trends in Different Types of Public and Private Relief in Urban Areas, 1929–1935*, 10; Amenta, *Bold Relief*, 71.

5. Katz, *In the Shadow of the Poorhouse*, 224–29; R. Clyde White and Mary White, "Research Memorandum on Social Aspects of Relief Policies in the Depression" (New York: Social Science Research Council, 1937), 73; Weiss, *Farewell to the Party of Lincoln*, 50.

6. Federal Emergency Relief Administration, "Unemployment Relief Census, October 1933" (Washington, DC: GPO, 1934), 34; Fox, "The Boundaries of Social Citizenship," 356–57.

7. Washington, "The Negro and Relief," 178. See also Hoffsommer, *Landlord-Tenant Relations and Relief in Alabama*; Woofter, *Landlord and Tenant on the Cotton Plantation*, xxx, 145–53, 156; Brown, *Race, Money and the American Welfare State*, 76–81.

8. Washington, "The Negro and Relief," 184–85.

9. Edward Lewis, "The Negro on Relief," *Journal of Negro Education* 5 (1936): 73.

10. "Alleges FERA Has Failed to Deport Aliens," *Greeley Daily Tribune*, April 30, 1935, p. 10; Letter to the Editor, by an American Citizen, "About Americans in Mexico," *San Antonio Light*, May 19, 1933, p. 16B; "Immigration Hearings End Tomorrow," *Hammond Times*, March 12, 1934, p. 2; Selden Meneffee, "The Free State of Bexar: A Profile of San Antonio," box 110, WPA, RG 69; Deutsch, *No Separate Refuge*, 175–77; Rice, "Some Contributing Factors," 74; Ric ard Lowitt and Maurine Beasley, eds., *One Third of a Nation: Lorena Hickok Reports on the Great Depression* (Urbana: University of Illinois Press, 1981), 230; Federal Emergency Relief Administration, "Unemployment Relief Census, October 1933"; translation from "Universal Grafico," Novem-

ber 9, 1933, p. 18, box 62, #118, Clements Papers; Balderrama and Rodriguez, *Decade of Betrayal*, 81.

11. Senate Committee on Education and Labor, *Violations of Free Speech and Rights of Labor: Hearings on S. Res. 266*, 76th Cong., 3rd Sess., 1940, 19673-5; Walsh, "Laboring at the Margins"; Zelman, "Mexican Migrants and Relief in Depression California."

12. Cobb, *The Most Southern Place on Earth*, 186, 193–94; Woofter, *Landlord and Tenant on the Cotton Plantation*, xxx, 148–51; Jill Quadagno, *The Transformation of Old Age Security: Class and Politics in the American Welfare State* (Chicago: University of Chicago Press, 1988), 131–37.

13. Lowitt and Beasley, *One Third of a Nation*, ix–x, xxiii, 225–28.

14. Hoffsommer, *Landlord-Tenant Relations and Relief in Alabama*, 5; Deutsch, *No Separate Refuge*, 177.

15. Balderrama and Rodriguez, *Decade of Betrayal*, 82–83; John Charnow, "Work Relief Experience in the United States" (Washington, DC: Committee on Social Security, Social Science Research Council, 1943), 40–41; Deutsch, *No Separate Refuge*, 176–78; Lester, "Building the New Deal State on the Local Level"; Quadagno, *The Transformation of Old Age Security*, 131–34; Valdés, *Barrios Norteños*, 106; Walsh, "Laboring at the Margins"; Woofter, *Landlord and Tenant on the Cotton Plantation*, 150–52; Zelman, "Mexican Migrants and Relief in Depression California"; Goyette to Warner, October 2, 1934, AZ Official CWA, Work Division, 1934–1935, box 9; Glassberg to Hopkins, February 3, 1934, and Beet Worker Application for Federal Relief, Weld County, 406 CO Field Reports, box 39; Hopkins to Pierce, July 19, 1933, CO Official FERA, box 37, all in FERA Central Files, State Series, RG 69. Mahony to Taylor, July 14, 1934, carton 10:3, Taylor Papers.

16. "Some Attitudes toward Relief in Rural Areas," January 1935, folder 7, box 132, Burgess Papers; Cobb, *The Most Southern Place on Earth*, 188, 193; Hoffsommer, *Landlord-Tenant Relations and Relief in Alabama*; Woofter, *Landlord and Tenant on the Cotton Plantation*, 148–51.

17. "Some Attitudes toward Relief in Rural Areas," January 1935; Malcolm Brown and Orin Cassmore, *Migratory Cotton Pickers in Arizona* (Washington, DC: GPO, 1939), 61; Cobb, *The Most Southern Place on Earth*, 194; Goyette to Warner, October 2, 1934, AZ Official CWA, Work Division, 1934–1935, box 9, FERA Central Files, State Series, RG 69.

18. Deutsch, *No Separate Refuge*, 177–78. See also McWilliams, *Ill Fares the Land*, 120.

19. Haigh, Elliott, and Fauver to Commissioner of Immigration, October 23, 1933; Borstadt to Inspector in Charge, INS, Fresno, January 4, 1934, both in 55853/737, RG 85.

20. Frances Cahn and Malcolm Davisson, "The Administrative and Financial Aspects of Certain Types of Outdoor Relief in California," *Social Service Review* 9, no. 3 (1935): 498–510; Walsh, "Laboring at the Margins," 414; Lester, "Building the New Deal State on the Local Level," 375–85; California State Unemployment Commission, *Report and Recommendations of the California State Unemployment Commission* (Sacramento, CA, 1933); Quadagno, "From Old-Age

Assistance to Supplemental Security Income," 241, 244; Key, *Southern Politics in State and Nation*.

21. Charnow, "Work Relief Experience in the United States," 40–41; Quadagno, *The Transformation of Old Age Security*, 131–37; "Some Attitudes toward Relief in Rural Areas," January 1935.

22. Warner to Goldschmidt, September 19, 1934, AZ Official FERA, box 9, FERA Central Files, State Series, RG 69.

23. "Green Wants Board to Oust Service Head," *El Paso Herald-Post*, April 3, 1935; "Some Attitudes toward Relief in Rural Areas," January 1935. See also Green, *This Business of Relief*, 198–201.

24. Souers to Warner, August 11, 1933; Childers to Hopkins, September 16, 1935, both in AZ Complaints, 460, box 13, FERA Central Files, State Series, RG 69; California, *Report and Recommendations of the California State Unemployment Commission*; Deutsch, *No Separate Refuge*, 181; Lester, "Building the New Deal State on the Local Level"; Lewis, "The Negro on Relief"; Valdés, *Barrios Norteños*, 106–7; Pomeroy to State Relief Commission, May 18, 1938, Meeting Files, January–May 1938, F2519, Controller, SRA Papers.

25. Lowitt and Beasley, *One Third of a Nation*, 240; Arthur to Persons, November 6, 1933, Employment Service, box 58, RG 174; Patricia Sullivan, *Days of Hope: Race and Democracy in the New Deal* (Chapel Hill: University of North Carolina Press, 1996), 54.

26. White and White, "Research Memorandum on Social Aspects of Relief Policies in the Depression," 72, 74.

27. Moss to Matthews, January 28, 1935; Courtney to Sears, February 5, 1934; Illinois House Bill 583; "Two Decades of Service, 1916–1936," Chicago Urban League, 1936, all in General Admin., 1934–1937, box 36, Hilliard Papers; Cohen, *Making a New Deal*, 260.

28. "Bosses Advocate Sterilization for Working Women," *Chicago Hunger Fighter*, July 4, 1932, Unemployed Relief 1927–July 1932, box 114, Hilliard Papers; Entry 2-16-36, "Sunday Afternoon Mexican Discussion Group, February to August, 1936," Mexican Work, box 25, University of Chicago Settlement, McDowell Papers; Foster to Moss, November 16, 1934; Paige to Moss, October 24, 1932; Director to Commissioner Busse, October 29, 1932; Brooke to Moss, October 22, 1932, all in General Admin., box 36, Hilliard Papers; leaflet, "Demonstrate: Friday July 29th, 10am, Charity Station," Unemployment Relief, 1927–July 1932; leaflet, "Demand, Xmas Relief, Demonstrate!"; Unemployed and Part Time Workers of Roseland and Vicinity to Cermak, Horner, and Moss, January 27, 1933, Unemployment Relief, August–November 1932, all in box 114, Hilliard Papers.

29. Moss to Foster, December 17, 1932; Foster to Moss, December 16, 1932, both in Unemployed Relief, December 1932–January 1933, box 114; Meaney to Sears, December 30, 1926, United Charities, 1926–1952, box 139; Moss to Matthews, January 28, 1935, General Administration 1934–1937, box 36; Ortleb to Moss, October 11, 1932; Davis to Moss, September 27, 1932, Unemployment Relief, August–November 1932, box 114; Moss to Davis, October 12, 1932; "Two Decades of Service, 1916–1936," Chicago Urban League, 1936, General

Administration, 1934–1937, box 36, all in Hilliard Papers; Chicago Commission on Race Relations, *The Negro in Chicago: A Study of Race Relations and a Race Riot* (Chicago: University of Chicago Press, 1922), 644.

30. Charles Henderson, "Poor Laws of the United States," *NCCC Proceedings*, 1897, pp. 256–71; Robert Hebberd, "Uniform Settlement Laws," *NCSW Proceedings*, 1914, p. 420. For a brief period in the nineteenth century Massachusetts had a citizenship requirement in its settlement law. Parker, "State, Citizenship and Territory"; George Warren, "Draft Proposal for the Reply of the United States Government to the Report of the Committee of Experts on Assistance to Indigent Foreigners," 1934, 555.M 1/77, RG 59.

31. Six states barred aliens from Mothers' Pensions. An additional six required either U.S. citizenship or evidence of intent to naturalize. Children's Bureau, Chart No. 3, "A Tabular Summary of State Laws Relating to Public Aid to Children in Their Own Homes in Effect January 1, 1929 and the Test of the Laws of Certain States" (Washington, DC: GPO, 1929); Marian Schibsby, "The Alien and Old Age Pension Laws," *Interpreter Release* 10, no. 19 (1933): 111–119b. The U.S. Children's Bureau estimated that in 1926 fewer than two out of five children in need received it. Mink, *The Wages of Motherhood*, 49. Similarly, Old Age Pensions served only 3 percent of individuals over sixty-five by 1934. Historical Background and Development of Social Security, Pre-Social Security Period, SSH online. White and White, "Research Memorandum on Social Aspects of Relief Policies in the Depression," 74; Schibsby, "Is There an Undue Proportion of Aliens on Relief?" 292.

32. Bremer, "Immigrants and Foreign Communities" (1933); Read Lewis, "Immigrants and Their Children," in *Social Work Year Book, 1935*, ed. F. Hall (New York: Russell Sage Foundation, 1935), 197–206; Schibsby, "Immigrants and Their Children"; Thatcher, *Immigrants and the 1930s*; Howard, *The WPA and Federal Relief Policy*, 313–14; YWCA, "Public Affairs: Program for the Biennium, 1938–1939," 811.144 YMCA/5, RG 59.

33. Hopkins and Perkins to FDR, "Aliens on Relief," January 21, 1935, Official File 444, FDR Papers; Clements to Braught, April 1, 1935, and excerpt from Mrs. Clements's Report on Activities, March 25, 1935, CO Official FERA, box 37; Clements to Williams, May 1, 1935, 406 CO Field Reports, box 39, both in FERA Central Files, State Series, RG 69. On the federal government protesting discrimination against aliens, see Warner to Williams, July 24, 1935; Brown to Warner, August 2, 1935; and Gill to Hayden, January 20, 1935, all in AZ Official FERA, box 9, FERA Central Files, State Series, RG 69.

34. Wilson to Secretary of State and attachment, July 10, 1931, JA 555, M 1/7, RG 59; George Warren, "Assistance to Aliens—in America," *Interpreter Release Clip Sheet* 10, no. 12 (1933): 39–46; Department of State to Amlegation, August 8, 1931, JA 555, M 1/9, RG 59; Department of State, Division of Western European Affairs, September 13, 1933, JA 555, M 1/17, RG 59; Perkins to Secretary of State, September 5, 1933, JA 555, M 1/16, RG 59; MacCormack to Secretary of State, September 28, 1933, 555, M 1/21, RG 59; Chamberlain and Warren to Secretary of State, September 15, 1933, JA 555, M 1/54, RG 59; Perkins to the Secretary of State and attachment, August 16, 1935, 555, M 1/83, RG 59; Warren

to Morin and attachment, December 10, 1934, 555, M 1/77, RG 59; Edith Abbott, "Is There a Legal Right to Relief?" *Social Service Review* 12, no. 2 (1938): 260–75.

35. Hopkins and Perkins to FDR, "Aliens on Relief," January 21, 1935.

36. John Allswang, *A House for All Peoples: Ethnic Politics in Chicago, 1890–1936* (Lexington: University Press of Kentucky, 1971); David Burner, *The Politics of Provincialism: The Democratic Party in Transition, 1918–1932* (Westport, CT: Greenwood, 1967); Richard Jensen, "The Cities Reelect Roosevelt: Ethnicity, Religion, and Class in 1940," *Ethnicity* 8, no. 2 (1981): 189–95; Marian Schibsby, "Immigration Questions and the Presidential Election," *Interpreter Release* 9, no. 33 (1932): 260–62; Marian Schibsby, "Certain Issues of Special Interest to the Foreign-Born Voter in the Presidential Campaign Just Ended," *Interpreter Release* 9, no. 36 (1932): 273–78; Marian Schibsby, "Legislative Bulletin No. VIII," *Interpreter Release* 9, no. 16 (1932): 146–47; Gary Gerstle, *American Crucible: Race and Nation in the Twentieth Century* (Princeton: Princeton University Press, 2001) , 129, 138–40, 154; Franklin Roosevelt, *The Public Papers and Addresses of Franklin D. Roosevelt* (New York: Random House, 1938), vol. 1, pp. 842–55, vol. 5, pp. 544–46.

37. Gerstle, *American Crucible*, 138, 185; Harold Ickes, *The Secret Diary of Harold L. Ickes*, vol. 2 (New York: Simon and Schuster, 1953–54), 591; George Martin, *Madam Secretary, Frances Perkins* (Boston: Houghton Mifflin, 1976), 294. See also Richard Steele, "'No Racials': Discrimination against Ethnics in American Defense Industry, 1940–42," *Labor History* 32, no. 1 (1991): 66–90.

38. Vocaire to Roosevelt, January 24, 1938, and Ise to President, August 11, 1937, both in 23/30675, RG 85; Sconyamillo to FDR, February 10, 1935, 55875/462C, 85-58A743, RG 85; author's calculation, 1930 Census, 1940 Census. Even among those who voted for FDR in 1936, 68 percent believed aliens on relief should be returned to their own countries compared to 76 percent who did not vote for him. Author's calculation, Gallup Poll #1936-0062. Data presented with phone weights. Baldwin Memo, October 26, 1934, re: Perkins, reel 106: 690, ACLU Papers; Dinwoodie, "Deportation"; Steele, " 'No Racials'"; FLIS Press Release, "Important Changes in Deportation Laws Proposed," Index No. 4031, May 31, 1935, reel 17, ACNS Records; Morgan, "Foreign-Born on Relief." See also Colonel D. MacCormack, "The New Deal for the Alien," *NCSW Proceedings*, 1934, pp. 465–72; Salvatore LaGumina, "The New Deal, the Immigrants and Congressman Vito Marcantonio," *International Migration Review* 4, no. 2 (1970): 57–75; Thatcher, *Immigrants and the 1930s*.

39. White and White, "Research Memorandum on Social Aspects of Relief Policies in the Depression," 74–76. See also Thatcher, *Immigrants and the 1930s*, 164–65.

40. Read Lewis, "Have We Still an Immigration Problem," *Interpreter Release* 10, no. 25 (1933): 150–57; Harold Fields, "Where Shall the Alien Work?" *Social Forces* 12, no. 2 (1933): 217.

41. Katz, *In the Shadow of the Poorhouse*, 232; Marian Schibsby, "Legislative Bulletin No. I: 73rd Congress," *Interpreter Release* 10, no. 16 (1933): 86–89; CR, 73rd Cong., 1st Sess., March 28, 1933, pp. 914–15; author's calculation, 1930 Census.

42. Author's calculation, 1930 Census; Helen Walker, *The CCC through the Eyes of 272 Boys: A Summary of a Group Study of the Reactions of 272 Cleveland Boys to Their Experience in the Civilian Conservation Corps* (Cleveland: Western Reserve University Press, 1938); Kenneth Holland, "Youth in American Work Camps" (Washington, DC: American Council on Education, 1941), 106; N. Maher, "A New Deal Body Politic: Landscape, Labor, and the Civilian Conservation Corps," *Environmental History* 7, no. 3 (2002): 446.

43. "Our League of Nations," *Bay State Sentinel*, March 21, 1940; Julia Brock, "Creating Consumers: The Civilian Conservation Corps in Rocky Mountain National Park" (Master's thesis, Florida State University, 2005), 62.

44. Author's calculation, 1930 Census; Robert Fechner, *Annual Report of the Director of the Civilian Conservation Corps, Fiscal Year Ended June 30, 1939* (Washington, DC: GPO), 8; James McEntee, *Now They Are Men* (Washington, DC, 1940), 28; Maher, "A New Deal Body Politic," 448–49.

45. Bryant Simon, "'New Men in Body and Soul': The Civilian Conservation Corps and the Transformation of Male Bodies and the Body Politic," in *Seeing Nature through Gender*, ed. V. Lawrence (Lawrence: University Press of Kansas, 2003), 80–102; "The Present Situation in Foreign Communities"; Walker, *The CCC through the Eyes of 272 Boys*.

46. Author's calculation, 1930 Census; Weiss, *Farewell to the Party of Lincoln*, 54; John Salmond, "The Civilian Conservation Corps and the Negro," *Journal of American History* 52, no. 1 (1965): 80, 86.

47. Valdés, *Barrios Norteños*, 102; María Montoya, "The Roots of Economic and Ethnic Divisions in Northern New Mexico: The Case of the Civilian Conservation Corps," *Western Historical Quarterly* 26, no. 1 (1995): 21; Francisco Rosales and Daniel Simon, "Mexican Immigrant Experience in the Urban Midwest: East Chicago, Indiana, 1919–1945," in *Forging a Community: The Latino Experience in Northwest Indiana, 1919–1975*, ed. J. Lane and E. Escobar (Chicago: Cattails Press, 1987), 149.

48. Montoya, "The Roots of Economic and Ethnic Divisions in Northern New Mexico," 28; Brock, "Creating Consumers," 61; "Equality," *The Four and One Times*, August 4, 1934, p. 2. See also Julie Pycior, *LBJ & Mexican Americans: The Paradox of Power* (Austin: University of Texas Press, 1997), 28–29.

49. Marc Kruman, "Quotas for Blacks: The Public Works Administration and the Black Construction Worker," *Labor History* 16, no. 1 (1975): 37–51; Katz, *In the Shadow of the Poorhouse*, 232–33; Weiss, *Farewell to the Party of Lincoln*, 51–52; Sullivan, *Days of Hope*, 55.

50. FLIS, "Aliens Eligible for the 3,000,000 Public Works Jobs," Index 3504, July 8, 1933, reel 16, ACNS Records; Marian Schibsby, "Legislative Bulletin No. III: 73rd Congress," *Interpreter Release* 10, no. 24 (1933): 143–48. See also Lewis, "Have We Still an Immigration Problem."

51. Katz, *In the Shadow of the Poorhouse*, 233; "New Arrest Here Spurs Inquiry of CWA Graft," *WP*, January 25, 1934, p. 1; Michael Lewis, "No Relief from Politics: Machine Bosses and Civil Works," *Urban Affairs Quarterly* 30, no. 2 (1994): 210–26; Schwartz, *The Civil Works Administration*, 44.

52. Thompson to Martinez, January 29, 1934, 311.1215/65, RG 59; "Aliens Load Relief Roll," *LAT,* March 4, 1934; Balderrama and Rodriguez, *Decade of Betrayal*, 75.

53. Charnow, "Work Relief Experience in the United States," 40.

54. Ibid.; Guy Johnson, "Does the South Owe the Negro a New Deal," in *New Deal Thought*, ed. H. Zinn (Indianapolis: Bobbs-Merrill, 1966), 100–103; Lester, "Building the New Deal State on the Local Level"; Lowitt and Beasley, *One Third of a Nation*, 181–82; "Some Attitudes toward Relief in Rural Areas," January 1935, folder 7, box 132, Burgess Papers; Ewing to Bane, FERA, December 11, 1933, 406 CO Field Reports, box 39, FERA Central Files, State Series, RG 69.

55. "Mexicans Charge Discrimination," *San Antonio Express*, December 15, 1933, p. 20; "CWA Is Accused of Discrimination," *NYT*, February 11, 1934, p. E6. Glassberg to Hopkins, February 3, 1934 and February 10, 1935; Glassberg to Hansen, February 3, 1934; Ewing to Bane, December 11, 1933, all in CO Field Reports, box 39, FERA Central Files, State Series, RG 69.

56. Stave, *The New Deal and the Last Hurrah*, 113.

CHAPTER 9

1. Martin Dies, "A Million and a Half Aliens on Relief Cost U.S. $500,000,000 a Year," *Washington Herald*, February 9, 1936, box 194, Division of Information, RG 69.

2. "Macfadden Wants Aliens Dropped off Relief Rolls," *New York Herald Tribune*, September 30, 1936, p. 7; "Woman Patriots Denounce Aliens," *Spokane Spokesman-Review*, June 5, 1937, p. 1, both in box 194, Division of Information, RG 69; "Advocated Taking Aliens off Relief," *North Shore Daily Journal*, January 11, 1938, p. 1, box 195, Division of Information, RG 69; *Statistical Abstract of the United States, 1940* (Washington, DC: GPO, 1941), 100.

3. Amenta et al. only briefly mention that non-citizens were excluded from the WPA. Edwin Amenta, Ellen Benoit, Chris Bonastia, Nancy Cauthen, and Drew Halfmann, "Bring Back the WPA: Work, Relief, and the Origins of American Social Policy in Welfare Reform," *Studies in American Political Development* 12, no. 1 (Spring 1998): 24; Amenta, *Bold Relief*, 158. Goldberg focuses on substantive citizenship, not formal citizenship. Chad Goldberg, *Citizens and Paupers: Relief, Rights, and Race, from the Freedman's Bureau to Workfare* (Chicago: University of Chicago Press, 2007). There are two boxes of articles on "aliens and relief" collected by the WPA's Division of Information, RG 69; Cantril, *Public Opinion: 1935–1946*, 947.

4. Amenta et al., "Bring Back the WPA," 23–24; Katz, *In the Shadow of the Poorhouse*, 236–37.

5. Weiss, *Farewell to the Party of Lincoln*, 168; "Negroes under WPA, 1939," *Monthly Labor Review* 50 (1940): 636.

6. Warren to McBride, September 14, 1938, 311.1215/104, RG 59; Rex Crawford, "The Latin American in Wartime United States," *Annals of the American Academy of Political and Social Science* 223 (1942): 127; Duggan Memo, July 19, 1937, 311.12/504 LH, RG 59; Geiger to Hazelrigg, February 1, 1939, and Beeson to Menefee, February 10, 1939, both in Studies Relating to the Mexican Labor Force in Texas, box 110, Division of Social Research, RG 69; Menefee and Cassmore, *The Pecan Shellers of San Antonio*.

7. Howard, *The WPA and Federal Relief Policy*, 286; Weiss, *Farewell to the Party of Lincoln*, 173–74; Richard Sterner, *The Negro's Share: A Study of Income, Consumption, Housing, and Public Assistance* (New York; London: Harper and Brothers, 1943), 239, 245, 249; Green, *This Business of Relief*, 198–201.

8. WPA of Texas, Excerpts from Social Workers' Reports, August 1940, 2(6), 23, 26, box 2612, WPA State Central Files, TX, 640, RG 69; "Vigilantes in Colorado Take Up Labor War," *Albuquerque Journal*, May 1, 1936, p. 1.

9. Green, *This Business of Relief*, 201; McWilliams, *Ill Fares the Land*, 121, 226; Walsh, "Laboring at the Margins," 413; "Farm Labor Lack Told," *LAT*, March 6, 1936.

10. Mabelle to Perkins, April 8, 1933, "Employment of Aliens," 20/46, RG 174; McElvaine, *Down and Out in the Great Depression*, 198. Linebarger to Johnson, February 5, 1935; Robinson to Johnson, December 14, 1934; Williard to Hopkins, June 28, 1935, all in box 34, FERA State Series, RG 69. "Deny Aliens Given Work on Local WPA," *Akron Beacon Journal*, June 21, 1938, p. 23, box 195, Division of Information, RG 69.

11. Daniel MacCormack, "Immigration and Naturalization Service," *Annual Report of the Secretary of Labor for the Fiscal Year Ended June 30, 1935* (Washington, DC: GPO, 1936), 78–99; Daniel MacCormack, "Number of Aliens in the United States—Legally or Illegally," *Interpreter Release* 12, no. 28 (1935): 242–51; Marshall Dimock, "The Foreign-Born in Times of Crisis," 1939, box 54, Dimock Papers; "The Present Situation in Foreign Communities," *Proceedings of the National Conference of International Institutes, Detroit, MI, June 10–12, 1933*, folder 16, box 270, reel 175, AFII Papers; Marian Schibsby, "Legislative Bulletin No. VII," *Interpreter Release* 12, no. 21 (1935): 188–93; Annual Report of the Director, February 27, 1936, folder 66, box 5, Supplement II, IPL Papers; "The Common Welfare: Aliens Need Their Friends," *Survey Midmonthly* 75, no. 5 (1939): 142; Editorial, "A New Crusade against Foreigners," *Rassviet*, March 29, 1935, folder ID2C, box 49, Foreign Press Survey.

12. Schibsby, "Legislative Bulletin No. VII"; "Alien Defies Court after 6 Year Relief Fraud," *CDT*, February 29, 1936, p. 3; "Alien Reliefer Gets Jail Term for Drunkenness," *CDT*, January 14, 1938, p. 7; "Alien Cheaters on Relief Get Jail Sentences," *CDT*, April 23, 1938, p. 7; "Alien on Relief Tramples Flag; Police Save Him," *CDT*, November 12, 1939, p. 14.

13. On the Bonus March, see Amenta, *Bold Relief*, 71–72, 116–17. "Legion Hears Move to Restrict Immigration," *Evening Tribune*, August 12, 1935, p. 1; "Protests Relief to 3,500,000 Aliens," *Indiana Evening Gazette*, November 9, 1935; "Vets Protest Alien Relief," *El Paso Herald-Post*, March 20, 1935, p. 14; "2 Million Aliens on Relief Rolls in the Country," *Chillicothe Constitution-Tribune*, March 4, 1938, p. 1; "WPA Aliens Are Flayed," *San Antonio Sunday Light*, October 11, 1936, p. 1; Edwards, "N.Y. Supporting Army of Aliens on Relief Roll," p. 5; Edward J. Finan, "A Few Questions about Aliens," *CDT*, June 24, 1937, p. 12; "Purge of WPA of Aliens Asked," *Wilkes Barre Record*, March 5, 1938, p. 17, box 195, Division of Information, RG 69; "Aliens Favored in City Relief," *New York American*, May 20, 1936, p. 13; "Are Aliens Preferred?" *Los Angeles Evening Herald and Express*, June 3, 1936, editorial page, both in box 194, Division of Information, RG 69.

14. Raymond Carroll, "Alien Workers in America," *Saturday Evening Post* 208 (1936): 82.

15. Louis Adamic, "Aliens and Alien-Baiters," *Harpers Magazine* 173 (1936): 561–74; Howard, *The WPA and Federal Relief Policy*, 312, 314; Thatcher, *Immigrants and the 1930s*, 169–71, 182; author's calculation, Gallup Poll #1939-0144; Berinsky, "Public Opinion in the 1930s and 1940s." Data presented with phone weights.

16. FLIS Editorial Committee, "Immigration Problems of To-Day Discussed," 1934, Index No. 3698, May 9, 1934; FLIS Press Releases, Read Lewis, "Making the Alien the Scapegoat," July 26, 1934, both on reel 17, ACNS Records; Adamic, "Aliens and Alien-Baiters"; Schibsby, "The Alien and Old Age Pension Laws"; Morgan, "Foreign-Born on Relief"; Marian Schibsby, "Report of the Ellis Island Committee," *Interpreter Release Clip Sheet* 11, no. 5 (1934): 25–29; Hirst, "Is Citizenship a Fair Requirement in Old Age Assistance Acts?"; Annual Report of the Director, February 27, 1936, folder 66, box 5, Supplement II, IPL Papers; Helen Martz, "The Family and Public Assistance," *Pennsylvania Social Work* 7, no. 3 (1941): 75, in The Alien, the Government and the Social Worker, box 52, Dimock Papers; Fagen, "The Families of Aliens," 3.

17. Morgan, "Foreign-Born on Relief"; Adena Rich, "Naturalization and Family Welfare: Doors Closed to the Noncitizen," *Social Service Review* 14, no. 2 (1940): 237–82; Adena Rich, "Naturalization and Family Welfare: When Is a Client a Citizen?" *Social Service Review* 14, no. 1 (1940): 10–35; Schibsby, "Legislative Bulletin No. III: 73rd Congress"; Elizabeth Behrens, "Time Allowance," *Chicago Daily News*, June 30, 1939, p. 12, box 195, Division of Information, RG 69; Joanna Colcord, "The West Is Still Different," *The Survey* 73 (1937): 243; Lewis, "Making the Alien the Scapegoat."

18. Lewis, "Immigrants and Their Children"; Morgan, "Foreign-Born on Relief"; Schibsby, "Is There an Undue Proportion of Aliens on Relief?"; Schibsby, "Immigrants and Their Children," 213; Thatcher, *Immigrants and the 1930s*, 169.

19. Howard, *The WPA and Federal Relief Policy*, 306n3; Joan Fry, "Aliens on Relief? Have They Any Rights?" *Social Work Today* 3 (1936): 18; "Aliens Have a Pull at Washington," *Spokesman Review*, May 9, 1937, p. 4, box 194, Division of Information, RG 69; CR, 74th Cong., 2nd Sess., May 8, 1936, pp. 6974–75; Frank Kent, "The Great Game of Politics: A Hollow Gesture," *LAT*, September 14, 1937, p. A4; Lewis, "Making the Alien the Scapegoat."

20. Editorial, "Are There a Million Aliens on Relief?" *Saturday Evening Post*, January 23, 1937, p. 22; "1,500,000 Aliens on U.S. Doles, Official Says," *CDT*, April 25, 1935, p. 15; "Five Million Aliens 'On Relief in U.S.,'" *New York City American*, April 30, 1937, p. 3, box 194, Division of Information, RG 69; Edwards, "N.Y. Supporting Army of Aliens on Relief Rolls," p. 5; Edwards, "200,000 Aliens on N.Y. Relief," p. 9; "Alderman Wants WPA Aliens Listed," *NYT*, February 5, 1936, p. 10; "Aldermen Ask ERB to List Aliens Getting City Relief," *NYT*, May 6, 1936, p. 6; "Aliens on Relief Not Known to ERB," *NYT*, May 20, 1936, p. 5; "New York Figures on Relief to Aliens Delayed Further," *CDT*, May 17, 1935, p. 13; Arthur Krock, "In Washington: Why Congress May Take Up Alien Law," *NYT*, December 23, 1936, p. 20; "Would the Figures Be Embarrassing?" *Times-Star*, December 28, 1936, box 194, Division of Information, RG 69.

21. Oscar Armes, "Census Urged of Aliens on Relief," *New York Journal*, January 6, 1936, box 194, Division of Information, RG 69; Edwards, "N.Y. Supporting Army of Aliens on Relief Rolls," p. 5; "Alderman Wants WPA Aliens Listed," p. 10; "Aldermen Ask ERB to List Aliens Getting City Relief," p. 6; "New York Figures on Relief to Aliens Delayed Further," p. 13; "Aliens on Relief Not Known to ERB," *NYT*, May 20, 1936, p. 5; "The ERB Moves Slowly," *New York Sun*, May 20, 1936, box 194, Division of Information, RG 69; "WPA Aliens Exceed Veterans," *New York Sun*, May 21, 1936, p. 6, box 194, Division of Information, RG 69; "Aldermen Imperil TERA Fund to City," *NYT*, May 21, 1936, p. 13; Barbara Blumberg, *The New Deal and the Unemployed: The View from New York City* (Lewisburg, PA: Bucknell University Press, 1979), 36–37; Ronald Bayor, *Fiorello La Guardia: Ethnicity and Reform* (Arlington Heights, IL: Harlan Division, 1993), 104–10.

22. "Hopkins Press Conference, 1/9/36," January 9, 1936, FERA, box 30, Hopkins Papers. Interestingly, Hopkins had previously estimated the number of aliens on relief at "not more than 580,000 (3%) of the total persons receiving relief in October, 1934." Hopkins and Perkins to FDR, "Aliens on Relief," January 21, 1935. Howard, *The WPA and Federal Relief Policy*, 303–4; Senate Committee on Appropriations, *First Deficiency Appropriation Bill for 1936: Hearings on H.R. 12624*, 74th Cong., 2nd Sess. 1936, p. 94; Morgan, "Foreign-Born on Relief"; Eliot to Secretary of Labor, July 2, 1935; Secretary to MacCormack, April 20, 1936, both in Immigration, box 72, RG 174.

23. "Aliens Load Relief Roll," p. 26; "Charity Aids Many Aliens," *LAT*, September 30, 1934, p. 14; "Thomson Tells of Huge Cost of Relief for Aliens," *LAT*, June 6, 1937, p. 2; "Aliens on County Dole Raise Grave Problem," *LAT*, November 8, 1937, p. A2; "Aliens Heavy Relief Burden," *LAT*, November 20, 1938, p. A6.

24. Chester Hanson, "Relief Chief Studies Co-Ordination Plans," *LAT*, January 19, 1939, p. 2; author's calculation, 1940 Census; "Highlights of the Amazing Story behind Relief in California," LA Chamber of Commerce, box 66, #118, Clements Papers; Lester, "Building the New Deal State on the Local Level," 374.

25. Senate Committee, *First Deficiency Appropriation Bill for 1936*, 94–95; House Committee on Appropriations, *First Deficiency Appropriation Bill for 1936: Part II, Emergency Relief—Works Progress Administration*, 74th Cong., 2nd Sess., 1936, p. 221.

26. Senate Committee, *First Deficiency Appropriation Bill for 1936*, 95–96; House Committee on Appropriations, *First Deficiency Appropriation Bill for 1936*, 171, 221; Howard, *The WPA and Federal Relief Policy*, 305; "Aliens Eligible for Relief Jobs WPA Decides," *New York Herald-Tribune*, June 21, 1936, p. 24, box 194, Division of Information, RG 69.

27. LaGumina, "The New Deal, the Immigrants and Congressman Vito Marcantonio"; *CR*, 74th Cong., 2nd Sess., May 8, 1936, pp. 6973, 6976.

28. *CR*, 74th Cong., 2nd Sess., May 8, 1936, p. 6983.

29. Ibid., 6977–78, 6987; Howard, *The WPA and Federal Relief Policy*, 305; "House Ready to Vote 21–3 More Billions Costs," *CDT*, May 9, 1936, p. 1.

30. Charnow, "Work Relief Experience in the United States," 25; Howard, *The WPA and Federal Relief Policy*, 305–6.

31. "WPA Opens Campaign to Oust Aliens," *LAT*, July 3, 1936, p. 1; "Excerpt from 'Works Progress in Arizona," August 1936, Phoenix, and "Excerpt from Narrative Report of Arizona," November 20, 1936, both in 986-A, box 91, Division of Information, RG 69.

32. "Aliens on Relief," *Buffalo Courier-Express*, May 21, 1937, p. 8; "Aliens and Federal Relief," *Shreveport Times*, May 23, 1937, p. 2A; "Example of Alien-Baiting," *St. Louis Post Dispatch*, May 22, 1937, editorial page, all in box 194, Division of Information, RG 69; "Aliens' Relief Jobs Continued by WPA," *NYT*, June 21, 1936, p. 6; Howard, *The WPA and Federal Relief Policy*, 305–6.

33. National Institute for Immigrant Welfare, "Office Memorandum on Actions Taken and Work to Be Done," June 19, 1936, folder 18, box 279, reel 186, AFII Papers. The Stubbs amendment was voted down, 93 to 45. *CR*, 74th Cong., 2nd Sess., May 8, 1936, pp. 6974–75.

34. *CR*, 74th Cong., 2nd Sess., May 8, 1936, pp. 6974–75, 6987; "House Ready to Vote 21–3 More Billions Costs"; House Committee on Appropriations, *Emergency Relief Appropriation Act of 1937: Hearings on H.J. Res 361*, 75th Cong., 1st Sess., 1937, 151–52; *CR*, 75th Cong., May 27, 1937, pp. 5076, 5080. In the Senate version of the bill, aliens with first papers were denied access to WPA employment. FLIS Press Releases, "Aliens to Be Eliminated from W.P.A. Jobs," July 9, 1937, Index No. 4486, reel 17, ACNS Records; Howard, *The WPA and Federal Relief Policy*, 303–13.

35. "Aliens to Be Eliminated from W.P.A. Jobs"; "Robinson Asks Halt on Relief Spending," *LAT*, June 19, 1937, p. 2; Gill to Iffert, December 23, 1938, Administrative Correspondence, box 5, Division of Social Research, RG 69; Howard, *The WPA and Federal Relief Policy*, 307–8; Charnow, "Work Relief Experience in the United States," 25.

36. Lawson to Hopkins, July 14, 1937, box 884, WPA Central Files, CA, 640, RG 69; "WPA Will Oust Aliens," *LAT*, July 13, 1937, p. A1; "5,000 Aliens to Lose WPA Jobs in County," *Los Angeles Evening Herald*, July 13, 1937, p. 6; "Aliens Dropped from WPA Rolls," *Los Angeles Examiner*, July 15, 1937, p. 8, part 2, all in box 194, Division of Information, RG 69; Lester, "Building the New Deal State on the Local Level," 427, 462; Connolly and Hopkins, Transcripts of Telephone Conversations, Alabama–California, July 20, 1937, Containers 71–74, Hopkins Papers. According to Lester, blacks accused Connolly of racial discrimination (436).

37. Lester, "Building the New Deal State on the Local Level," 349, 372–85; Amenta, *Bold Relief*, 182; "Agriculture for Merriam," *LAT*, August 16, 1934, p. A3; Kevin Starr, *Endangered Dreams: The Great Depression in California* (Oxford: Oxford University Press, 1996), 149; Robert Burke, *Olson's New Deal for California* (Berkeley: University of California Press, 1953), 78–79.

38. "Two Courses Outlined, for Needy Aliens in State," *LAT*, July 25, 1937, p. 3; "Meeting of State Relief Commission," July 24, 1937, F2519, Controller—SRA Meeting Files, 1937, SRA Papers; "LACRA Assails Alliance Relief Plea," *LAT*, August 3, 1937, p. A8.

39. "Meeting of State Relief Commission," July 24, 1937; "Proposed Policy Resolution Regarding Aliens"; Cahill to Pomeroy, September 1, 1937; Pomeroy

to State Relief Commission, September 29, 1937; Wixon to Pomeroy, August 30, 1937; Pomeroy to Shaughnessy, August 18, 1937; Pomeroy to State Relief Commission, November 12, 1937; Copland to Triggs, October 28, 1937, all in F2519, Controller—SRA Meeting Files, 1937, SRA Papers; "Aliens on County Dole Raise Grave Problem," *LAT*, November 8, 1937, p. A2.

40. Cahill to Houghteling, January 8, 1938, 55957/456, 85-58A734, RG 85; "California Asks Drastic Laws to Check Aliens," *Reno Evening Gazette*, March 30, 1938, p. 5; "Merriam Urges Expulsion of Undesirable Aliens," *San Francisco Chronicle*, March 30, 1938, p. 14; "Alien Drive Backed," *San Francisco News*, March 30, 1938, p. 12; "Sound Alien Policy Would Admit Only Desirable Ones," *San Francisco Chronicle*, March 31, 1938, all in box 195, Division of Information, RG 69; Houghteling to Cahill, February 16, 1938, April 15, 1938, and April 26, 1938; Cahill to Houghteling, March 31, 1938; "State Urges Strict Alien Laws," *San Francisco Examiner*, March 30, 1938, all in 55957/456, 85-58A734, RG 85; Hoffman, *Unwanted Mexican Americans in the Great Depression*, 158; Hobson Anderson, "Who Are on Relief in California?" F3448-44, SRA Papers.

41. "WPA to Dismiss 5,000 Aliens on Illinois Rolls," *Chicago Daily News*, July 8, 1937, p. 23; "WPA Alien Ban in Effect Here," *Chicago Herald and Examiner*, July 8, 1937, p. 6, both in box 194, Division of Information, RG 69; Report of the Director, April–October 1937, pp. 13–15, folder 65, box 5, Supplement II, IPL Papers; Arthur Evans, "WPA to Remove 5,200 Aliens in Illinois Jobs," *CDT*, July 8, 1937, p. 7; "WPA to Take Workers' Word on Birthplace," *CDT*, July 18, 1937, p. 3; "WPA Drops Plan to Take Aliens Off State Roll," *CDT*, August 10, 1937, p. 4; "Dunham Resigns as Director of WPA in Illinois," *CDT*, January 30, 1937, p. 9; "General Letter No. 147," Hopkins to State Works Progress Administrators, July 17, 1937, F2519, Controller—SRA Meeting Files, SRA Papers.

42. Amenta et al., "Bring Back the WPA," 50, 52; Erie, *Rainbow's End*, 132–35; Lyle Dorsett, *Franklin D. Roosevelt and the City Bosses* (Port Washington, NY: Kennikat Press, 1977); Roger Biles, *Big City Boss in Depression and War: Mayor Edward J. Kelly of Chicago* (DeKalb: Northern Illinois University Press, 1984), 74–77; Gosnell, *Machine Politics, Chicago Model*, 45, 62, 75.

43. Report of the Director, March 1, 1937, folder 67, box 5, Supplement II, IPL Papers; Rich, "Citizenship and Family Security," Indianapolis, May 28, 1937, folder 7, box 67, Abbott Papers.

44. Report of the Director, December 17, 1935, folder 66, box 5, Supplement II, IPL Papers; Wilfred Reynolds, "The Non-Citizen and the Illinois Emergency Relief Commission," in *Illinois Conference on Social Welfare* (East St. Louis, IL, 1935), 145–49; Rich, "Citizenship and Family Security."

45. "WPA in Bay State to Drop All Aliens," *NYT*, July 10, 1937, p. 8; "American Committee for Protection of Foreign Born Campaigns against Discrimination on WPA," July 31, 1937, folder 21, box 50, Subseries 2, Series VII, FLIS Papers. "U.S. Checking Up on Aliens Holding WPA Project Jobs," *Davenport Daily Times*, August 13, 1937, p. 25; "Aliens to Lose Their WPA Jobs," *Macon Telegraph*, October 16, 1937, p. 5; "86 Foreigners Lose WPA Jobs," *Spokane Spokesman Review*, July 18, 1937, p. 1; "Racine WPA Cuts 138 Aliens Off Lists," *Milwaukee Journal*, August 10, 1937, p. 15; "Tax-Supported Aliens to Be on Own

in Wyoming," *Cheyenne State Tribune*, August 25, 1937, p. 1; "500 Non-Citizens Are Dropped by Order from Washington," *Manchester Leader*, August 17, 1937; "Elimination of Aliens on WPA," *Belle Fourche Bee*, August 6, 1937, p. 1, all in boxes 194–95, Division of Information, RG 69; "WPA Denies Aliens Relief," *Republic*, August 28, 1937, and "1,000 Relief Roll Workers Seek Jobs," *Gazette*, August 28, 1937, both in file 986-A, box 91, Division of Information, RG 69; "WPA to Drop Aliens from Payroll Here," *Milwaukee Journal*, July 23, 1937, p. 1, and "Discharge Notices Sent to Aliens on WPA Rolls," *Milwaukee Journal*, July 28, 1937, p. 6, both in box 194, Division of Information, RG 69; "Many Aliens on WPA Lists," *Milwaukee Journal*, August 4, 1937, p. 1, box 195, Division of Information, RG 69.

46. Henry Street Settlement Studies, "Pink Slips over the East Side," 1938, box 88, Hall Papers; "WPA Here to Drop 12,000 Next Week," *NYT*, June 23, 1937, p. 1; Brehon Somervell, "Reduction in Personnel," Bulletin No. 46, June 26, 1937, and Lewis to Hopkins, July 2, 1937, both in folder 21, box 50, Subseries 2, Series VIII, FLIS Papers; "Suit Halts Ousting of Aliens on WPA," *NYT*, July 24, 1937, p. 1; "WPA Will Fire 20,1910 Aliens," *New York Post*, July 2, 1937, p. 9, box 194, Division of Information, RG 69.

47. Department of Welfare, City of New York, *Public Assistance in New York City: Annual Report 1939–1940*, p. 80; Amenta et al., "Bring Back the WPA," 52–53; Erie, *Rainbow's End*, 133–34; Blumberg, *The New Deal and the Unemployed*, 99–100, 116; "Suit Halts Ousting of Aliens on WPA"; "75 End 'Death Watch' on WPA Reductions," *NYT*, July 25, 1937, p. 2; "WPA Here to Drop 12,000 Next Week"; "On Denying Aid to Aliens," *WP*, July 4, 1937, p. B6; "WPA Alien Cuts Halted by Court," *New York Journal and American*, July 24, 1937, p. 1, box 194, Division of Information, RG 69; House Committee on Appropriations, *Work Relief and Relief for Fiscal Year 1942: Hearings*, 77th Cong., 1st Sess., 1941, 405–10; "American Committee for Protection of Foreign Born Campaigns against Discrimination on WPA"; "Relief Rolls Lack Skilled Builders," *NYT*, August 26, 1937, p. 22; Bayor, *Fiorello La Guardia*.

48. Henry Street Settlement Studies, "Pink Slips Overt the East Side"; "WPA Here to Drop 12,000 Next Week"; "WPA Will Fire 20,910 Aliens," *New York Post*, July 2, 1937, p. 9; "12,750 Aliens to Be Dropped by WPA Here," *New York Herald-Tribune*, July 3, 1937, p. 4, both in box 194, Division of Information, RG 69; William Fulton, "Alien Families Form 26.8% of N.Y. Relief Load," *CDT*, June 3, 1941, p. 10; "Relief Dependents off 55.6% in City," *NYT*, June 2, 1941, p. 19.

49. "U.S. Checking Up on Aliens Holding WPA Project Jobs"; "Aliens to Lose Their WPA Jobs."

50. Robert Reynolds, "Displacement of Americans by Aliens," March 1938, *The National Republic*, CR, 75th Cong., 3rd Sess., pp. 989–90; Robert Reynolds, "Undesirable Aliens," NBC Radio Address, February 1, 1939, CR, 76th Cong., 1st Sess., pp. 500–501; CR, 76th Cong., 1st Sess., p. 9028; CR, 74th Cong., 2nd Sess., May 8, 1936, pp. 6973–85; Martin Dies, "America for Americans," Radio Address, May 6, 1935, CR, 74th Cong., 1st Sess. May 10, p. 1935; House Committee on Appropriations, *Emergency Relief Appropriation Act of 1938: Hearings*, 75th Cong., 3rd Sess., 1938, pp. 709–14; CR, 75th Cong., 3rd Sess., May

27, 1937, pp. 5066–80; *CR*, 75th Cong., 3rd Sess., May 12, 1938, pp. 6814–18; Rowland Berthoff, "Southern Attitudes toward Immigration, 1865–1914," *Journal of Southern History* 17, no. 3 (1951): 328–60; Higham, *Strangers in the Land*; Adamic, "Aliens and Alien-Baiters"; Amenta et al., "Bring Back the WPA," 45.

51. Unfortunately, none of the amendments limiting aliens' access to WPA jobs were roll call votes. As a result, I have to gauge support for such policies primarily by looking at those who spoke for or against these measures. LaGumina, "The New Deal, the Immigrants and Congressman Vito Marcantonio," 62; Schibsby, "New York's Foreign Language Newspapers and the Mayoralty Campaign"; Howard, *The WPA and Federal Relief Policy*, 313; Arthur Capper, "Aliens Complicate Relief Problem," *Capper Weekly*, April 18, 1936, file 986-A, box 91, Division of Information, RG 69; "Dismissal of Aliens," *Peoples Opinion*, August 5, 1937, p. 2; "As to Aliens," *Nashville Banner*, August 9, 1937, p. 4, both in box 195, Division of Information, RG 69; Ivo de Capet, "Aliens and Relief," *Baltimore Sun*, June 21, 1937, p. 8, box 194, Division of Information, RG 69; *CR*, 74th Cong., 2nd Sess., May 8, 1936, pp. 6973–77; "120,000 Aliens on Relief, in Hopkins' Office," *CDT*, May 22, 1937, p. 1; "Relief Work Based on Citizenship," *New York American*, February 4, 1936, both in box 194, Division of Information, RG 69.

52. *CR*, 75th Cong., 3rd Sess., February 16, 1938, pp. 2069–70; "Quarter Billion More Relief Is Voted by House," *CDT*, February 17, 1938, p. 2; Willard Edwards, "Quarter Billion Relief Bill Up to Roosevelt," *CDT*, March 2, 1938, p. 5; Howard, *The WPA and Federal Relief Policy*, 308; Report of the Director, April 1938–October 1938, pp. 23–24, folder 67, box 5, Supplement II, IPL Papers.

53. Howard, *The WPA and Federal Relief Policy*, 309–10; *CR*, 76th Cong., 1st Sess., January 13, 1939, p. 338.

54. Senate Report No. 4, to accompany H.J. Res. 83, "Additional Appropriation for Work Relief and Relief for the Fiscal Year Ending June 30, 1939," 76th Cong., 1st Sess., January 21, 1939, p. 3; House Committee, *Conference Report on Resolution Making Additional Appropriation for Work Relief and Relief*, Report No. 15, 76th Cong., 1st Sess., February 1, 1939; Survey of Citizenship, box 45, Records of the Statistics Division, RG 69.

55. Gerstle, *American Crucible*, 158–61; Blumberg, *The New Deal and the Unemployed*, 231; William Leuchtenburg, *Franklin Roosevelt and the New Deal, 1932–1940* (New York: Harper and Row, 1963), 286; Stanton to FDR, August 28, 1938, 55789/979, RG 85; Houghteling to Lewis, April 15, 1938, folder 10, box 7, FLIS Papers.

56. General Letter No. 231, Harrington to State WPA Administrators, February 7, 1939, box 45, Statistics Division, Survey of Citizenship, RG 69; General Letter No. 231, Supplement No. 2, Harrington to State WPA Administrators, April 29, 1939, 23/30675, RG 85; Howard, *The WPA and Federal Relief Policy*, 307–10; Senate Committee on Appropriations, *Additional Appropriation for Work Relief and Relief, Fiscal Year 1939: Hearings on H.J. Res. 83*, 76th Cong., 1st Sess., 1939, 101–3; "Relief Rolls Lack Skilled Builders"; WPA, Division of Statistics, "Terminations from WPA Program Because of Alien Status, March 6, 1939," March 8, 1939, box 45, Records of the Statistics Division, Survey of Citizenship, RG 69.

57. American Association of Social Workers, "A Survey of the Current Relief Situation," March 21, 1938, p. 8, folder 1, box 31, Abbott Papers; "Relief Is Ended for 309 Aliens," *Spokesman Review*, May 4, 1938, p. 6, box 195, Division of Information, RG 69; McWilliams, *Ill Fares the Land*, 226–28; WPA of Texas, Excerpts from Area Social Workers' Monthly Reports, May 1939, Report No. 9, box 2612, WPA Central Files, Texas, 640, RG 69.

58. Batiza to Schlotfeldt, January 10, 1938; Josefe to Whalen, July 21, 1939; Whalen to Commissioner of INS, July 27, 1939; Houghteling to Norton, August 3, 1939, all in 55957/456, 85-58A7 34, RG 85; "Relief for 150 Alien Mexican Families to End," *Kansas City Kansan*, May 29, 1939, p. 1, box 195, Division of Information, RG 69; Menendez to FDR, May 29, 1939, box 17, WPA, Official File, 444c, FDR Papers.

59. "Bill Offered to Ban Relief for Aliens," *Los Angeles Examiner*, January 21, 1939, p. 20; "State Senators Indicate They'll Approve Bill to Restrict Relief to Aliens," *San Francisco News*, January 20, 1939, p. 22; "Antialien Relief Bill Will Be Presented," *Sacramento Bee*, January 19, 1939, p. 6; "State Alien Relief Cut Approved," *Los Angeles Examiner*, June 19, 1939, p. 1; Griffing Bancroft Jr., "Supervisor Assails Alien Relief," *Los Angeles Examiner*, April 12, 1939, p. 10; "Alien Relief Curb Voted," *Los Angeles Times*, June 19, 1939, p. 1, all in box 195, Division of Information, RG 69 ; "Alien Relief Ban Vetoed," *LAT*, July 25, 1939, p. 1; "Olson May Veto Alien Relief Ban," *LAT*, July 20, 1939, p. A1.

60. Report of the Director, November 1938–March 1939, folder 67, box 5; Rich, "Economic and Social Security of Those in Good Faith Believing Themselves to be Citizens," September, 1939, folder 68, box 6, both in Supplement II, IPL Papers; Social Service Department, Reports for February 1939 and April 1939, both in box 20, McDowell Papers; "WPA to Fire 500 Aliens," *Detroit News*, August 2, 1937, p. 6; "Non-Citizens in Local Counties Cut from WPA," *Davenport Daily Times*, January 28, 1938, p. 27, box 195, Division of Information, RG 69; "Two Officials Disagree on WPA Jobs for Aliens," *Baltimore Evening Sun*, September 3, 1938, p. 18; "Mayor Raps Use of Relief Fund for Alien," *St. Paul Pioneer Press*, June 21, 1939, p. 1, both in box 195, Division of Information, RG 69; Schibsby, "Immigrants and Their Children"; Rich, "New Emphases in Services to the Foreign Born," November 12, 1940, folder 68, box 6, Supplement II, IPL Papers. For relief agencies writing to federal officials on behalf of specific relief clients, see Thorson, Levinsky, Caperairo, Sorenson, Reich, and Secreto, 23/30675, RG 85.

61. "University of Chicago Settlement Annual Report for the Year 1939, Marguerite Sylla" and "The First Six Months of 1939 . . . at the University of Chicago Settlement," both in Annual Reports, 1934–1948, University of Chicago Settlement, box 19, McDowell Papers; Henry Street Settlement Studies, "Pink Slips over the East Side"; Henry Street Settlement Studies, "Our Alien Neighbors"; "No Meals for 3 Days, Ends Life," *Akron Beacon Journal*, November 27, 1937, p. 16, box 195, Division of Information, RG 69.

62. "904 WPA Aliens on City Relief," *Chicago Herald & Examiner*, May 22, 1939, box 195, Division of Information, RG 69; Report of the Director, November 1938–March 1939, folder 67, box 5, Supplement II, IPL Papers; Elsie Anderson, Social Service Reports for February 1939, March 1939, July 1939, September 1939, January 1942, box 20, McDowell Papers.

63. Welles to Hopkins, July 21, 1937, 311.12/504, RG 59; Hopkins to Wells, July 21, 1937, 311.12/508, RG 59; Zaragosa Vargas, "Tejana Radical: Emma Tenayuca and the San Antonio Labor Movement during the Great Depression," *Pacific Historical Review* 66, no. 4 (1997): 561–63; Emma Tenayuca and Homer Brooks, "The Mexican Question in the Southwest," *The Communist* (March 1939): 257–68, box 27, #1243, McWilliams Papers; Gutiérrez, *Walls and Mirrors*, 106, 111–13.

64. Adams to President, August 12, 1937, box 1203, WPA Central Files, IL, 641, RG 69; Silvestro to Roosevelt, March 8, 1939, 23/30675, RG 85; House Committee, *Emergency Relief Appropriation Act of 1938: Hearings*, 777–80, 811–12; House Committee, *Work Relief and Relief for Fiscal Year 1942*, 415, 422; Howard, *The WPA and Federal Relief Policy*, 314. The AFL supported alien restrictions. "Exclusion of Alien Workers," 0455, Meetings of August 21–September 2, 1937, reel 7, AFL Minutes; Thatcher, *Immigrants and the 1930s*, 170, 176–77, 196n36. Hundreds of letters from aliens can be found in 23/30675, RG 85.

65. Amenta et al., "Bring Back the WPA," 18; American Association of Social Workers, "A Survey of the Current Relief Situation, Winter of 1938," March 21, 1938, folder 1, box 31, Abbott Papers.

66. "Deny Aliens Given Work on Local WPA," *Akron Beacon Journal*, June 21, 1938, box 195, Division of Information, RG 69; Sterner, *The Negro's Share*, 245; Howard, *The WPA and Federal Relief Policy*, 310–11; Charnow, "Work Relief Experience in the United States," 25.

67. "Mayor Assails WPA Alien Ban," *New York Post*, March 7, 1940; "Glad to Work for Relief Checks," *Syracuse Post-Standard*, February 3, 1938, p. 9; "90 Aliens Now Work to Earn Geddes Relief," *Syracuse Post-Standard*, January 17, 1938; "Work for Aliens on Relief Urged in Bill at Albany," *New York Herald Tribune*, February 4, 1939; "43,252 Aliens on City Relief without Work," *New York Sun*, March 7, 1940; "Mayor Asks Work for Relief Aliens," *NYT*, March 10, 1940, all in box 195, Division of Information, RG 69; Charnow, "Work Relief Experience in the United States," p. 25; Howard, *The WPA and Federal Relief Policy*, 313; Robert Ingalls, *Herbert H. Lehman and New York's Little New Deal* (New York: New York University Press, 1975), 60–63.

68. Author's calculation, 1940 Census.

69. Ibid. The census categorized Mexicans as white in 1940. The figures for Mexicans are based on an alternative measure created by IPUMS. IPUMS imputed Mexican origin using information on birthplace and Spanish surname.

70. Ibid.

71. Erie, *Rainbow's End*, 118–39; Gutiérrez, *Walls and Mirrors*; Bridges, *Morning Glories*.

72. See Geller, De Luca, Manfra, Barone, Diaz, Luna, and Yohner, all in 23/30675, RG 85; Erie, *Rainbow's End*, 129–33; "Who Elects the President? WPA!" *New York Herald Tribune*, November 7, 1937, p. 2, part 2, box 195, Division of Information, RG 69. On machines, the WPA, and new immigrants, see also Luconi, "Machine Politics and the Consolidation of the Roosevelt Majority," 42, 45; Kathleen Munley, "From Minority to Majority: A Study of the Democratic Party in Lackawanna County, 1920–1950" (Ph.D. thesis, Lehigh University,

1981); William Whyte, *Street Corner Society: The Social Structure of an Italian Slum* (Chicago: University of Chicago Press, 1943), 196–97. On patronage-oriented politicians' sometimes tepid support for the WPA program as a whole, see Amenta et al., "Bring Back the WPA," 50–54.

73. Howard, *The WPA and Federal Relief Policy*, 315–17; Steele, "'No Racials'"; Richard Weiss, "Ethnicity and Reform: Minorities and the Ambience of the Depression Years," *Journal of American History* 66, no. 3 (1979): 566–85; Altmeyer to Bigge, February 23, 1942, 533.14, box 231, Central File, Master File, RG 47; House Committee, *Work Relief and Relief for Fiscal Year 1942*, 1–2, 20–21, 260–61.

CHAPTER 10

1. The title for this chapter comes from a speech by the Commissioner of Immigration and Naturalization in 1934 at the National Conference of Social Work. MacCormack, "The New Deal for the Alien." Franklin D. Roosevelt, "Presidential Statement Signing the Social Security Act," August 14, 1935, SSH online; Senate Finance Committee, *Economic Security Act: Hearings on S.1130*, 74th Cong., 1st Sess., 1935, p. 641; Katznelson, *When Affirmative Action Was White*; Lieberman, *Shifting the Color Line*; Quadagno, *The Color of Welfare*.

2. After 1939 the Old Age Insurance program became the Old Age and Survivors Insurance program. Lieberman, *Shifting the Color Line*, 81–82. Using published reports of the 1930 Census, Lieberman estimated that only 62 percent of all workers and 45 percent of black workers were covered under social insurance. But because occupational, industrial, and self-employment classifications often overlap, this method overestimates the proportion of covered workers. Author's calculation, 1930 Census. Bane to Clague, March 22, 1937, "Transmittal of Memoranda Relating to Old-Age Benefits Coverage," 720 Coverage to 1939, box 100, Office of the Commissioner, Chairman's File, RG 47.

3. For some takes on this question, see especially Lieberman, *Shifting the Color Line*; Davies and Derthick, "Race and Social Welfare Policy"; Brown, *Race, Money and the American Welfare State*; Katznelson, *When Affirmative Action Was White*; Alston and Ferrie, *Southern Paternalism and the American Welfare State*; Quadagno, *The Transformation of Old Age Security*.

4. Davies and Derthick, "Race and Social Welfare Policy"; M. M. Libman, "Old-Age Insurance for Agricultural Workers," February 24, 1939, 721.1, Agricultural Labor to 1940, Office of the Commissioner, Chairman's File, RG 47; Edwin Witte, *The Development of the Social Security Act* (Madison: University of Wisconsin Press, 1963), 153; Robertson to Doughton, January 18, 1935, box 393, RG 233; Katznelson, *When Affirmative Action Was White*, 25–79.

5. Davies and Derthick, "Race and Social Welfare Policy," 226; Douglas, *Social Security in the United States*, 9, 100–101, 110–11; Witte, *The Development of the Social Security Act*, 143–44; Martin, *Madam Secretary*, 354; Quadagno, *The Transformation of Old Age Security*, 132–33; "United behind Buck," *Woodland Democrat*, August 24, 1934, p. 8; "Beet Growers to Disband Unless Money Forthcoming," *Woodland Democrat*, June 20, 1934, p. 1; "Re-elect Frank Buck," *Woodland Democrat*, August 27, 1934, p. 8; "W. O. Russell, Leader in County

Republican Ranks, Supports Buck," *Woodland Democrat*, July 9, 1936, p. 1; Sabine Goerke-Shrode, "Pruners' Strike Still Evokes Unease," Historical Articles of Solano County, November 10, 2002, http://www.solanoarticles.com/history/index.php/weblog/more/pruners_strike_still_evokes_unease/; Zelman, "Mexican Migrants and Relief in Depression California." On the alliance between southern Democrats and western Republicans, see Phyllis Palmer, "Outside the Law: Agricultural and Domestic Workers under the Fair Labor Standards Act," *Journal of Policy History* 7, no. 4 (1995): 416–40.

6. Editorial, "Social Security—for White Folk," *The Crisis* (March 1935): 80; Ralphe Bunche, "A Critique of New Deal Social Planning as It Affects Negroes," *Journal of Negro Education* 5, no. 1 (1936): 59–65; Editorial, "The National Conference on the Economic Crisis and the Negro," *Journal of Negro Education* 5, no. 1 (1936): 1–2; Albion Hartwell, "The Need of Social and Unemployment Insurance for Negroes," *Journal of Negro Education* 5, no. 1 (1936): 79–87; George Haynes, "Lily-White Social Security," *The Crisis* (March 1935): 85–86; Clark to FDR, April 11, 1935, CES, box 54, RG 47; Charles Hamilton and Dona Cooper Hamilton, "The Dual Agenda of African American Organizations since the New Deal: Social Welfare Policies and Civil Rights," *Political Science Quarterly* 107, no. 3 (1992): 435–52; Weiss, *Farewell to the Party of Lincoln*, 157–79.

7. Craig Kaplowitz, *LULAC, Mexican Americans, and National Policy* (College Station: Texas A&M University Press, 2005), 26; Vargas, *Labor Rights Are Civil Rights*, 216; Pycior, *LBJ & Mexican Americans*, 29. See also Benjamin Marquez, "The Politics of Race and Assimilation: The League of United Latin American Citizens, 1929–1940," *Western Political Quarterly* 42, no. 2 (1989): 355–75.

8. Katherine Newman and Elisabeth Jacobs, *Who Cares? Public Ambivalence and Government Activism from the New Deal to the Second Gilded Age* (Princeton: Princeton University Press, 2010), 42; Green to Doughton, April 3, 1935, box 394, RG 233.

9. Davies and Derthick, "Race and Social Welfare Policy," 226; Abraham Epstein, "The Social Security Act," *The Crisis* (March 1935): 333–34, 338, 347; Hamilton and Hamilton, "The Dual Agenda of African American Organizations since the New Deal," 441.

10. Weiss, *Farewell to the Party of Lincoln*, 157–79. See also Desmond King and Rogers Smith, "Racial Orders in American Political Development," *American Political Science Review* 99, no. 1 (2005): 77. Even northern legislators deserve some blame for the racial limits of New Deal legislation. Steve Valocchi, "The Racial Basis of Capitalism and the State, and the Impact of the New Deal on African Americans," *Social Problems* 41, no. 3 (1994): 347–62.

11. Dawn Nuschler and Alison Siskin, "Social Security Benefits for Noncitizens: Current Policy and Legislation," Congressional Research Service, 2005; Cantril, *Public Opinion: 1935–1946*, 107. For letters complaining that aliens were getting jobs over Americans, see 20/46, Employment of Aliens, RG 174.

12. Troland to Chairman, Ways and Means, January 30, 1935; Brunner to Ways and Means, March 18, 1935; Boyle to "sir," March 13, 1935, box 393; Pignata to Fitzpatrick, March 29, 1935, box 394; Engel to Chairman, Old Age Pension Committee, April 13, 1935, box 386; Gilman to Millard, March 15,

1935, box 324, all in RG 233; "Conference Backs Social Security," *NYT*, April 9, 1935, p. 9.

13. Witte, *The Development of the Social Security Act*, 64; Committee on Economic Security, *Social Security in America: The Factual Background of the Social Security Act as Summarized from Staff Reports to the Committee on Economic Security* (Washington, DC: GPO, 1937); House Committee on Ways and Means, *Economic Security Act: Hearings on H.R. 4120*, 74th Cong., 1st Sess., 1935, pp. 678–79, 713, 1135; "Old Age pension laws proposed in the 74th Cong., 1st sess.," JP Harris, box 17, CES, RG 47; FERA Research Library, Legislative Bulletin: Federal Series No. 7, 74th Cong., 1st Sess., February 27, 1935, CES, box 29, RG 47; Wilbur Cohen, "Further Comments on the Townsend Plan," box 17, CES, RG 47; House Ways and Means Committee, Report No. 615, *The Social Security Bill*, April 5, 1935, 74th Cong., 1st Sess.; "Questions Received from Foreign Language Readers," folder 2, box 228, reel 141, Common Council for American Unity Papers, Immigration and Refugee Services of America Records, 1918-85, Microfilm. Woodbridge, CT: Primary Source Microfilm; "1,500 Queries an Hour on Security Here," *NYT*, November 26, 1936, p. 34; "Replies to Chief Questions about Social Security," *CDT*, December 1, 1936, p. 4; "Washington," *CDT*, November 8, 1936, p. B11; "Friend of the People: Social Security for Aliens," *CDT*, May 3, 1943, p. 14; "A Correction," *NYT*, February 19, 1939.

14. Senate Committee on Finance, *Amendments Proposed by Social Security Board*, 76th Cong. 1st Sess., April 12, 1939; Senate Committee on Finance, *Social Security Act Amendments of 1939*, Report No. 734, 76th Cong., 1st Sess., 1939, 54–64, 73–75. Carlson's amendment was rejected twice. *CR*, 76th Cong., 1st Sess., June 9, 1939, pp. 6937–39; *CR*, 76th Cong., 1st Sess., July 13, 1939, pp. 9028–30; Carmen Solomon, *Major Decisions in the House and Senate Chambers on Social Security: 1935–85* (Washington, DC: Congressional Research Service, 1986).

15. *CR*, 76th Cong., 1st Sess., July 13, 1939, pp. 9028–30; A. Epstein, "Social Security Policy," *NYT*, July 19, 1939, p. 13. See also Delafield Smith, "Citizenship and Family Security," *Social Security Bulletin* 3, no. 5 (Washington, DC, 1940): 3–9.

16. "A Bad Amendment," *NYT*, July 19, 1939, p. 13; National Emergency Conference, "Latest Congressional Developments on Legislation"; Bernard Conal, "Director's Report to Executive Committee of National Emergency Conference," October 30, 1939, both in folder 10, box 8, Series II.2, FLIS Papers; Erwin Klaus, "Aliens and Social Security," *NYT*, July 27, 1939, p. 14; Epstein, "Social Security Policy."

17. Davies and Derthick, "Race and Social Welfare Policy," 226; Weiss, *Farewell to the Party of Lincoln*, 167; Epstein, "The Social Security Act," 333–34, 338, 347.

18. House Committee, *Social Security Act Amendments of 1939*, Conference Report No. 1461, August 4, 1939, 76th Cong., 1st Sess.; "1939 Marks Association's Greatest Victories," *Social Security* 13, no. 7 (1939): 4.

19. Comptroller General, "Issues Concerning Social Security Benefits Paid to Aliens," 1983, HRD-83-32, General Accounting Office; Gladwin Hill, " 'Wetback' Influx Moves Westward," *NYT*, October 9, 1953, p. 40; Gladwin Hill, "Law Change Seen as Wetback Curb," *NYT*, May 31, 1954, p. 8; Bill Dredge, "Jobless Benefits Law Change Urged," *LAT*, May 31, 1950, p. 4.

20. "Recent Anti-Alien Legislative Proposals," *Columbia Law Review* 39 (1939): 1207–23; Sandy Crank, "The Evolution of Privacy and Disclosure Policy in the Social Security Administration," *Social Security Bulletin* 48, no. 6 (1985): 7–13; Social Security Board, Press Release, "Social Security Board Warns Employers against Circulating Unauthorized Questionnaires Aimed at Revealing Union Affiliations, Religion, and Other Personal Affairs," February, 26, 1937, Washington, DC; FLIS Press Releases, "Social Security Accounts and Those Who Have Failed to Apply for Them," February 17, 1937, Index No. 4392, reel 17; FLIS Press Releases, "36,000,000 on Roll of Social Security," January 8, 1938, Index No. 4559, reel 18, both in ACNS Records.

21. Secretary to Altemeyer, March 25, 1937 and March 29, 1937; Shaughnessy to Jay, April 1, 1937, all in Perkins Files, Social Security, RG 174.

22. Bane to Clague, March 22, 1937, 720 Coverage to 1939, box 100, Office of the Commissioner, Chairman's File, RG 47; Fred Safler, "Tentative Report on Extension of Old-Age and Survivors Insurance to Agricultural and Domestic Workers," December 1940, Bureau of OASI Analysis Division, Economic Analysis Section, RG 47; Witte, *The Development of the Social Security Act.*

23. Joseph P. Harris, "The Social Security Program of the United States," *American Political Science Review* 30, no. 3 (1936): 475; House Report No. 615, *The Social Security Bill*, 74th Cong, 1st Sess.; Schibsby, "The Alien and Old Age Pension Laws."

24. Witte, Suggested Amendments to Wisconsin Old Age Assistance Law, box 11; Witte to Ludlow, January 18, 1935, box 57; Brown to Witte, January 8, 1935, box 55; Witte to Barry, February 7, 1935, box 54; State Old Age Assistance Legislation to Conform to Federal Economic Security Bill, February 6, 1935, Working Papers, box 3; Brown, Summary of Provisions for a State Old Age Assistance Bill, January 24, 1935, box 17, all in CES, RG 47; FLIS Press Releases, "Washington Conference Pleads Justice to the Aliens," Index No. 4256, May 9, 1936, reel 17, ACNS Records; Smith, "Citizenship and Family Security"; Social Security Bulletin; U.S. Federal Security Agency, *Annual Report of the Federal Security Agency for the Fiscal Year 1947* (Washington, DC: GPO, 1948), 115.

25. FLIS Press Releases, "Shall I Become a Citizen? Social Security and the Alien," reel 17, ACNS Records; Rich, "Naturalization and Family Welfare: Doors Closed to the Noncitizen," 249; Illinois Department of Public Welfare, *Annual Report of the Department of Public Welfare, June 30, 1942* (Springfield: Illinois State Journal Company, 1943), 540.

26. Jessie Arndt, "With Funds Short, Problem of Alien Aid Vexes Officials," *WP*, September 7, 1940, p. 13; author's calculation, 1940 Census; National Resources Planning Board, *Security, Work and Relief Policies, 1942* (Washington, DC: GPO, 1942), 197; Federal Security Agency, *Annual Report of the Federal Security Agency for the Fiscal Year 1947*, 115; Abraham Epstein, "Letters to the Times, Social Security Policy," *NYT*, July 19, 1939, p. 13; Ruth Whiteside, *The Impact of the Texas Constitution on Public Welfare* (Houston: Institute for Urban Studies, University of Houston, 1973); Texas State Department of Public Welfare, *Annual Report—State Department of Public Welfare* (Austin, 1951), 10–11; Texas State Department of Public Welfare, *Annual Report—State Department of Public Welfare* (Austin, 1952), 17; *Graham v. Richardson* 403 U.S. 365 (1971); Cybelle Fox, "A New Nativism or an American Tradition? Federal

Citizenship and Legal Status Restrictions for Medicaid and Welfare" (Paper presented at the American Sociological Association Meetings, August 10, 2009, San Francisco, CA).

27. Hugh Carter and Bernice Doster, "The Foreign-Born Population and Old-Age Assistance," *INS Monthly Review* 7, no. 6 (1949): 71–81; author's calculation, 1940 Census; Meriam, *Relief and Social Security*, 23; National Resources Planning Board, *Security, Work and Relief Policies*, 197.

28. Smith, "Citizenship and Family Security," 4; Colcord, "The West Is Still Different," 243–45; Marian Schibsby, "Aliens and Old Age Pensions," *Interpreter Releases* 14, no. 19 (1937): 107–10.

29. Carter and Doster, "The Foreign-Born Population and Old-Age Assistance"; Robert Lowe, "State Public Welfare Legislation" (Washington, DC: GPO, 1939); author's calculation, 1940 Census, 1950 Census.

30. Schibsby, "Aliens and Old Age Pensions"; "New York Would Pay Pensions to Non-Citizens," *Social Security* 15, no. 5 (1941): 5; "A Regrettable Veto," *Social Security* 15, no. 6 (1941): 2; New York State Committee on Old Age Security Amendment, 1937–1938, folder 26, box 50, Series VIII.2, FLIS Papers; Marian Schibsby, "Aliens Become Eligible for Old Age Pensions in New York State," *Interpreter Releases* 20, no. 21–39 (1943): 144–45; Warren Moscow, "Legislators Rush Hundreds of Bills to Adjourn Today," *NYT*, March 18, 1938, p. 1; State of New York, *An Act to Amend the Public Welfare Law, in Relation to Old Age Assistance*, Assembly, No. 2603, March 24, 1937; State of New York, *An Act to Amend the Public Welfare Law, in Relation to Old Age Assistance*, Senate, No. 254, January 14, 1938; "Urge 5 Changes in Relief Laws," *CDT*, January 6, 1945, p. 19. In 1945 Illinois replaced its citizenship requirement with a twenty-five-year residency requirement. Jules Berman and Haskell Jacobs, "Legislative Changes in Public Assistance, 1945," *Social Security Bulletin* 9, no. 4 (1946): 8–15. This residency requirement was dropped in 1951. Jules Berman and George Blaetus, "State Public Assistance Legislation, 1951," *Social Security Bulletin* 14, no. 12 (1951): 3–.

31. Author's calculation, 1950 Census; Colcord, "The West Is Still Different," 244; Douglas, *Social Security in the United States*, 9; National Resources Planning Board, *Security, Work and Relief Policies*, 197. By 1947 average benefit levels for OAA (per recipient) and GA (per case) were roughly equal in the South ($20 versus $17, respectively) as well as the Northeast and Midwest ($39 vs. $43, respectively), but not in the Southwest, where OAA benefits were considerably higher than GA benefits ($47 versus $32, respectively). (GA benefit levels for Florida, Kentucky, Vermont, and Texas were unavailable so these states are excluded from these averages.) Advisory Council on Social Security, *Recommendations for Social Security Legislation: The Reports to the Senate Committee on Finance* (Washington, DC: GPO, 1949), 120–21.

32. Dolores Huerta, Legislative Report, 1961; "Aged Aid Bill Tribute to CSO," *LA Mirror*, July 21, 1961, both in folder 15, box 10, Ross Papers; Huerta to Legislative Committee Chairman, January 12, 1961, folder 8, box 9, Ross Papers; Kaye Briegel, "The History of Political Organizations among Mexican-Americans in Los Angeles since the Second World War" (Ph.D. diss., University of Southern California, Los Angeles, 1967); Mark Brilliant, *The Color of America*

Has Changed: How Racial Diversity Shaped Civil Rights Reform in California, 1941–1978 (Oxford: Oxford University Press, 2010), 127–38, 168–69; Gutiérrez, *Walls and Mirrors*, 168–72.

33. "Highlights of the Amazing Story behind Relief in California," LA Chamber of Commerce, box 66, #118, Clements Papers; McCreery to Hopkins, August 17, 1937, box 893, WPA Central Files, CA, 641, RG 69; California Conference of Social Work, "S.B. 470, Relief Expenditures for Aliens," *The Conference Bulletin* 22, no. 2 (1939): 26; California Conference of Social Work, "Resolution 26," *The Conference Bulletin* 22, no. 4 (1939): 52; Florence Haviland, "A 'Stop' That Means 'Go' in California," box 19, #1243, McWilliams Papers; Carey McWilliams, "California's Olson-Warren Era: Migrants and Social Welfare," *Earl Warren: Views and Episodes*, 1969, 1973, McWilliams Oral History; Brilliant, *The Color of America Has Changed*, 169.

34. Author's calculation, 1940 Census.

35. The relative large fraction of Mexicans with a Social Security number against those working in covered occupations can probably be explained by the fact that some migrant workers worked between harvests in covered industries. Author's calculation, 1940 Census; Bane to Clague, March 22, 1937, "Transmittal of Memoranda Relating to Old-Age Benefits Coverage," 720 Coverage to 1939, box 100, Office of the Commissioner, Chairman's File, RG 47.

36. Author's calculation, 1940 Census; Witte, *The Development of the Social Security Act*, viii–ix.

37. Douglas, *Social Security in the United States*, 163; Frances Perkins, *The Roosevelt I Knew* (New York: Viking, 1946), 293; Sue Ossman, "Concurrent Receipt of Public Assistance and Old-Age and Survivors Insurance," *Social Security Bulletin* 18, no. 9 (September 1955): 3–12.

38. John Corson, "Reasons for the 1939 Amendments to the Social Security Act," *Director's Bulletin No. 35*, January 10, 1940, SSH online; Lyle Schmitter and Betti Goldwasser, "The Revised Benefit Schedule under Federal Old-Age Insurance," *Social Security Bulletin* 2, no. 9 (1939): 3–12.

39. Corson, "Reasons for the 1939 Amendments to the Social Security Act"; author's calculation, 1940 Census; FLIS, 1940, "FLIS Mail Box (VXV)," Index No. 4860, reel 18, ACNS Records.

40. Corson, "Reasons for the 1939 Amendments to the Social Security Act"; Witte, *The Development of the Social Security Act*, 149; Edwin Witte, "The Problem of Extending Old Age Insurance Protection to a Larger Part of the American People," December 1939, 720 Coverage up to 6-30-40, box 100, Office of the Commissioner, Chairman's File, RG 47; Technical Board on Economic Security, Minutes of the Meeting of the Executive and Old Age Security Committee, November 22, 1934, CES, box 1, RG 47.

41. Rich, "Naturalization and Family Welfare: Doors Closed to the Noncitizen," 248; author's calculation, 1940 Census; Hugh Carter and Bernice Doster, "The Foreign-Born Population and Old-Age Assistance," *INS Monthly Review* 7, no. 6 (1949): 71–81; Social Security Board, "Race, Nativity, Citizenship, Age, and Residence of 1,000,000 Recipients of Old-Age Assistance," *Social Security Bulletin* 2, no. 6 (1939): 23–31.

42. Author's calculation, 1940 Census; National Resources Planning Board, *Security, Work and Relief Policies*, 197. These disparities persisted over time (see note 31).

43. Advisory Council on Social Security, *Recommendations for Social Security Legislation*, 120–21; Social Security Administration, *Social Security Bulletin: Annual Statistical Supplement, 1955* (Washington, DC: GPO, 1955), 9, 49; Corson, "Reasons for the 1939 Amendments to the Social Security Act." The 1950 Social Security amendments liberalized OAI benefits, roughly equalizing average benefits under the two programs, and soon after average OAI benefits remained higher than average OAA grants. Social Security Administration, "Table 12—OASDHI and Selected Public Assistance Programs: Average Monthly Payments in Current and 1967 Prices, 1940–67," *Social Security Bulletin: Statistical Supplement, 1967*, 21; E. Eberling, "Old Age and Survivor's Insurance and Old Age Assistance in the South," *Southern Economic Journal* 15, no. 1 (1948): 54–66.

44. Libman, "Old-Age Insurance for Agricultural Workers," February 24, 1939, 721.1 Agricultural Labor to 1940, Office of the Commissioner, Chairman's File, RG 47; Social Security Board, "Race, Nativity, Citizenship, Age, and Residence of 1,000,000 Recipients of Old-Age Assistance"; Advisory Council on Social Security, *Recommendations for Social Security Legislation*, 120–21; Sterner, *The Negro's Share*, 277; Falk to Powell, May 18, 1940, folder 641, box 279, Office of the Commissioner, Executive Director's File Unit, RG 47; Amenta and Poulsen, "Social Politics in Context"; Quadagno, *The Transformation of Old Age Security*, 134, 136–37.

45. Author's calculation, 1940 Census; Social Security Board, *Second Annual Report of the Social Security Board, 1937* (Washington, DC: GPO, 1937), 174–75; Social Security Board, "Detailed Instructions for Preparation of Form RS-201.1, Individual Accepted for Old-Age Assistance," revised June 1937, 630.2, box 93, Office of the Commissioner, Chairman's File, RG 47; California Social Welfare Board, *Public Assistance in California, June 1937* (Sacramento, CA), 27; Menefee and Orin, *The Pecan Shellers of San Antonio*, 42–43, 50.

46. Advisory Council on Social Security, *Recommendations for Social Security Legislation*, 120–21; California Department of Social Welfare, *Biennial Report of the California State Department of Social Welfare, July 1, 1936–June 30, 1938* (Sacramento, CA), 28; California Social Welfare Board, *Public Assistance in California, June 1937*, 27.

47. "Texas Pension Law Fixes Low Grants," *NYT*, November 17, 1935, p. E12; Menefee and Orin, *The Pecan Shellers of San Antonio*, 42–43, 50.

48. Douglas Massey, Jorge Durand, and Nolan Malone, *Beyond Smoke and Mirrors: Mexican Immigration in an Era of Economic Integration* (New York: Russell Sage Foundation, 2002), 35; Otey Scruggs, *Braceros, "Wetbacks," and the Farm Labor Problem: Mexican Agricultural Labor in the United States, 1942–1954* (New York: Garland, 1988); Kitty Calavita, *Inside the State: The Bracero Program, Immigration, and the I.N.S.* (New York: Routledge, 1992).

49. Jessica Walsh, "Laboring at the Margins: Welfare and the Regulation of Mexican and Central American Workers in Los Angeles" (Master's thesis, University of Southern California, Los Angeles, 1997); Calavita, *Inside the State*, 21.

50. Calavita, *Inside the State*, 19.

51. Scruggs, *Braceros, "Wetbacks," and the Farm Labor Problem*; Ricardo Sandoval, "Braceros Get Little Aid in Quest for Lost Wages," *Philadelphia Inquirer*, October 6, 1999, p. A21; Sophie Tareen, "Braceros Can Apply for Wages Withheld in '40s," *San Francisco Chronicle*, October 16, 2008, p. A-6.

52. Selden Menefee, *Mexican Migratory Workers of South Texas: Crystal City, Winter Garden Area, 1940* (Washington, DC: GPO, 1941); Amber Warburton, *The Work and Welfare of Children of Agricultural Laborers in Hidalgo County, Texas* (Washington, DC: U.S. Children's Bureau, 1943), 17–19.

53. Author's calculation, 1940 Census; Social Security Board, *Second Annual Report of the Social Security Board, 1937*, 174–75; Neal to Resnick, May 8, 1937, 610 Legislation, box 65, Central File, State File, Texas, RG 47; California Department of Social Welfare, *Biennial Report of the California State Department of Social Welfare, July 1, 1936–June 30, 1938*, 57–59; Advisory Council on Social Security, *Recommendations for Social Security Legislation*, 120–21; Mink, *The Wages of Motherhood*, 140; Mulliner to Winant, Altmeyer, and Miles, April 7, 1936, 621 Plans–631 State Administration, box 93, Office of the Commissioner, Chairman's File, RG 47. Average ADC benefits for the Southwest were $60 compared to $74 for the Northeast and Midwest and $39 for the South. But this average hides considerable variability in benefit levels within the Southwest: $106 for California but only $48 for Arizona and New Mexico and $38 for Texas.

54. Social Security Board, *Second Annual Report of the Social Security Board, 1937*; author's calculation, 1940 Census; Advisory Council on Social Security, *Recommendations for Social Security Legislation*, 120–21; Nancy Cauthen and Edwin Amenta, "Not for Widows Only: Institutional Politics and the Formative Years of Aid to Dependent Children," *American Sociological Review* 61, no. 3 (1996): 427–48; Reese, *Backlash against Welfare Mothers*, 76–78; Inabel Lindsay and Caroline Ware, "Welfare Agencies and the Needs of Negro Children and Youth," *Journal of Negro Education* 19, no. 3 (1950): 380; Sterner, *The Negro's Share*, 285; Mink, *The Wages of Motherhood*, 142.

55. Social Security Board, *Second Annual Report of the Social Security Board, 1937*, 174–75; author's calculation, 1940 Census.

56. Louis Adamic, "The Old Alien by the Kitchen Window," *Saturday Evening Post* 213 (1940): 27–.

57. Senate Finance Committee, *Economic Security Act: Hearings on S. 1130*, 74th Cong., 1st Sess., 1935, p. 647.

CHAPTER 11

1. Edward Pola and Franz Steininger, composers, "Marching Along Together" (1933); Romare Bearden, "Marching Along Together," *The Crisis* (March 1935): 84.

2. Gerstle, *American Crucible*, chapter 4.

3. Department of Labor, *Twenty-Third Annual Report of the Secretary of Labor for the Fiscal Year Ended June 30, 1935* (Washington, DC: GPO, 1936), 81–82; Department of Labor, *Twenty-Fifth Annual Report of the Secretary of Labor for the Fiscal Year Ended June 30, 1937* (Washington, DC: GPO, 1937), 92; FLIS, "A Sharp Increase in Applications for Citizenship Noted," No. 4203,

February 14, 1936, reel 17, ACNS Records; David Fellman, "The Alien's Right to Work," *Minnesota Law Review* 22 (1938): 137–76; "Aliens, Barred from Relief, in Ohio, Seek Citizenship," *Baltimore Morning Sun*, January 27, 1938, p. 11, box 195, Division of Information, RG 69; "Discloses Rush of Aliens to Win Citizen's Status," *CDT*, March 8, 1935, p. 16; "More Seek U.S. Citizenship," *NYT*, April 12, 1939, p. 48; "36,000 Aided in Naturalization," *NYT*, October 20, 1938, p. 4; Marshall Dimock, "Government and the Foreign Born," June 8, 1939, box 54, Dimock Papers.

4. Lewis, "Immigrants and Their Children"; Rich, "Naturalization and Family Welfare: Doors Closed to the Noncitizen"; MacCormack, "The New Deal for the Alien"; FLIS, "Fewer Persons Denied Citizenship in 1934," Index No. 4063, July 15, 1935, reel 17, ACNS Records; Marian Schibsby, "A New York Naturalization Aid Project," *Interpreter Releases* 15, no. 15 (1938): 145–53; Blumberg, *The New Deal and the Unemployed*, 168–73; Department of Labor, *Twenty-Fourth Annual Report of the Secretary of Labor for the Fiscal Year Ended June 30, 1936* (Washington, DC: GPO, 1936), 90.

5. State County and Municipal Workers of America, "What 'Economy' Means in Pennsylvania," *Social Work Today*, January 1940; "Aliens Again," *The Survey* (June 1939): 185; Elizabeth Campbell, "What Price Citizenship," November 24, 1939; Helen Martz, "The Family and Public Assistance," *Pennsylvania Social Work* 7, no. 3 (1941), all in The Alien, the Government, and the Social Worker, box 52, Dimock Papers. "State Will Deny Relief to Aliens with No Papers," *Philadelphia Record*, December 3, 1939, p. 3; "Aliens Rush to Qualify for Relief," *Pittsburgh Press*, December 31, 1939, p. 1, both in box 195, Division of Information, RG 69. Alexander Stein, "General Assistance and the Alien in Pennsylvania," February 17, 1939, Exhibit P-1, *Graham v. Richardson* (1971), 138a–146a.

6. Rich, "Naturalization and Family Welfare: Doors Closed to the Noncitizen," 245, 276; Marian Schibsby, "Filipinos Declared Ineligible to Preference in Employment on WPA Projects," *Interpreter Releases* 14, no. 54 (1937): 369–72; Henry Street Settlement Studies, "Our Alien Neighbors," 22; Henry Street Settlement Studies, "Pink Slips over the East Side"; "Recent Anti-Alien Legislative Proposals," *Columbia Law Review* 39 (1939): 1223; Wasserman, "'Our Alien Neighbors'"; *Statistical Abstract of the United States* (Washington, DC: GPO, 1931–41); author's calculation, 1930 Census, 1940 Census. The fraction of the adult Mexican-origin population that was non-citizen in 1930 varies depending on the estimate of the Mexican-origin population used: 66 percent using the "Mexican race" question versus 57 percent using the estimate of the Mexican-origin population constructed by IPUMS.

7. Weiss, *Farewell to the Party of Lincoln*; General Accounting Office, "More Needs to Be Done to Reduce the Number and Adverse Impact of Illegal Aliens in the United States" (Washington, DC, 1973), 41–46.

8. Michael Fix and Wendy Zimmerman, "The Legacy of Welfare Reform for U.S. Immigrants," in *International Migration: Prospects and Policies in a Global Market*, ed. D. Massey and J. Taylor (New York: Oxford University Press, 2004), 335–52.

9. Cohen, *Making a New Deal*, 57; Rieder, *Canarsie*, 27–28, 35. Cohen argues that this shame disappeared during the Depression, when many Chicagoans felt entitled to seek assistance from the government (270–71).

10. See, for example, Lieberman, *Shifting the Color Line*; Davies and Derthick, "Race and Social Welfare Policy"; Alston and Ferrie, *Southern Paternalism and the American Welfare State*.

11. Putnam, "E Pluribus Unum"; Alesina, Baqir and Easterly, "Public Goods and Ethnic Divisions"; Goodhart, "Too Diverse?"

12. Michael Walzer, *Spheres of Justice: A Defense of Pluralism and Equality* (New York: Basic Books, 1983), 31.

13. Fox, "A New Nativism or an American Tradition?"

Index

Abbott, Edith, 108, 109, 113, 117
Abbott, Grace, 95, 107
Adamic, Louis, 278
Addams, Jane, 117, 129
African Americans, 2, 3, 4, 21, 117; and
agriculture, 21–24, 191, 195–96, 279, 283;
and assimilation, 122, 283, 290; and black
exceptionalism, 2–3; and black reformers,
118; character and work ethic of, 9, 118,
119; and color, 24–25, 30, 284; and Cook
County, 200; and Democratic Party, 289;
deportation of, 188; discrimination against,
45, 118, 193–99; and disease, 121; and
diversity, 9; and domestic service, 4, 8, 250,
253, 255, 279, 283; education of, 38; and
environment, 118–19; history and condition of, 119; and infant mortality rates, 43;
and labor relations, 4, 11, 12, 21–24, 25, 40,
41, 191, 196, 283, 289; as landowners, 21;
and local government, 291; and marriage,
46; and Mexicans, 2–3, 41, 45, 47, 51, 115,
290; and Midwest, 245; migration north
by, 117, 188; migration to urban locales,
68; mobility of, 22; and North, 17; and
Northeast, 245; and one-drop rule, 19, 25,
44; opportunities for, 118; in peonage, 22;
political exclusion of, 38, 39; and political
power, 96, 283, 289; and political systems,
11; and politics, 25–27, 251; and poll taxes
and literacy tests, 7, 13, 19; population of,
21; and race, 11, 12, 24–25, 30, 45, 283; and
Republican Party, 289; and restrictive housing covenants, 45; and Roosevelt administration, 289; and rural areas, 12, 19, 21, 40,
195, 215, 217, 283, 284; and segregation, 17,
38, 45, 119, 188, 283; and social insurance,
360n2; and social workers, 14, 73, 96, 114–
15, 116–17, 121, 122, 191, 290; and South,
11–12, 19, 23, 83, 114, 115, 116, 120, 123,
245, 283; and southern and eastern European immigrants, 31; standard of living of,
23, 194, 198–99; sterilization of, 200;
as tenant farmers, 12, 19, 21–22, 23–24,
40, 96, 191, 193, 195–96, 198; and uplift,
117–18; voting by, 7, 13, 19, 26, 35, 47;
wages/earnings of, 21, 40; and white
primaries, 13, 19; and working conditions
for, 118
African Americans, and relief, 53, 71; and
almshouses, 114, 115, 120–21; city spending for, 61, 62, 63; in communities with
low benefit levels, 4; and dependency
stereotype, 96, 114–21; exclusion from, 14,
16, 19, 188, 195–99, 288–89; and institutions for feebleminded, 120, 121; less access
to, 17, 83; lower benefit levels for, 13, 194;
lower budgets for, 198–99; lower spending on, 16–17; and migration North, 188;
and political culture and relief spending,
67; population vs. proportion of relief for,
96, 115, 118, 121, 191–92; private agencies
and charities of, 96, 117, 122; and private
charities, 116, 188; and relief sponsorship,
195–96; and Southern spending, 68–69; as
unlikely to use, 96, 114, 119–20, 121, 122,
194–95, 292; unprecedented access to, 188,
190–91; white resentment of, 188, 191–92,
195; and work, 197
African Americans, and relief programs: and
Aid to Dependent Children, 277–78, 289;
and Civilian Conservation Corps, 207,
208, 209; and Federal Emergency Relief
Administration, 190; and federal farm relief
programs, 191; and General Assistance,
289; and means-tested programs, 250;
and Mothers' Pension rolls, 115–16; and
New Deal, 188–89, 281, 292; and Old Age
Assistance, 273–74, 289, 294; and Old Age
Insurance, 273, 279, 289; and Public Works
Administration, 209; and public works
jobs, 245; and Social Security, 4, 7, 250, 251,
252–53, 254, 255–56, 260, 262, 269, 270,
271, 279, 280, 292; and Unemployment
Insurance, 7, 289; and work relief, 211, 288;
and WPA jobs, 215, 216–18, 244, 249
African American social workers, 117–18, 200
African American women, 8–9; in agriculture,
21; and Aid to Dependent Children, 277;
alleged sexual promiscuity of, 119; and
domestic work, 21, 195, 217; private relief

Haynes, George, 117
Henderson, Charles, 201
Henry Street Settlement, 236
Hickok, Lorena, 193–94, 197, 198
Higham, John, 33, 37, 113
Hoffman, Abraham, 129
Hoffsommer, Harold, 23, 67–68
Holland, William, 128, 142, 143
homelessness, 55, 56
home visitors, 79
Hoover, Herbert, 126, 127, 130, 204, 214, 220, 289
Hoover administration, 124, 146, 180, 190, 203
Hopkins, Harry, 195, 199; and aliens, 169, 202, 203, 204, 215, 222, 286; and aliens and WPA, 228, 230, 233; and aliens on relief, 223; and Civil Works Administration, 210; and illegal aliens, 225–26; influence of, 15; and number of aliens on relief, 224; and race relations, 193, 194; and repatriations, 167, 180, 181, 187; and Social Security, 253, 257
Horner, Henry, 241
housing covenants, 25, 33, 45
Houston, Charles, 279
Howard, Donald, 244, 248
Howard University School of Social Work, 277–78
Huerta, Dolores, 268
Hull House, 202
Humphrey, Norman, 184–85
Hungary, 204
Hunter, Robert, 108; *Poverty,* 105–6

Ickes, Harold, 204, 205, 209
Idaho, 206
Illinois, 28; and Aid to Dependent Children, 264; and aliens and WPA, 227, 232–35, 238, 240, 242; and citizenship restrictions, 206; and deportations, 136, 141; and discrimination, 200; and federal relief, 200; and General Assistance vs. Old Age Assistance, 272; Governor's Commission on Unemployment and Relief, 175–76; and Mothers' Pension Law, 54, 61, 112; and Old Age Assistance, 267; and repatriation, 177, 182; and work relief, 200
Illinois Committee on Social Legislation, 140
Illinois Conference of Public Welfare, 136
Illinois Emergency Relief Commission, 139–40, 232, 234, 241
Illinois General Assembly, 234
Illinois State Department of Public Welfare, 136

immigrants: abandonment of culture by, 38, 39; advice for, 109; American-born children of, 206; and barring and deportation of public charges, 131–32; as blamed for unemployment, 125–26; and bonds and commutation taxes, 131; burden of proof of identity on, 145; and California Commission of Immigration and Housing, 49; and civic education, 39, 110; and descriptive representation, 37; and discrimination, 38; and environment vs. hereditary and culture, 108–9; families of, 127, 138; and fear of deportation, 138; in federal government, 37; illegal, 215; and infant mortality rates, 30, 43; and labor market, 105; and labor relations, 108; as less deserving, 1; and national origin quotas, 12; and political machines, 35–37; and racism, 38; and relief spending, 67, 69; and settlement houses, 37; and social networks, 108; in state and local government, 37; voting by, 36–37; white, 67, 69; and workplace political education and incorporation, 37; and YMCA, 37. *See also* aliens
Immigrants' Protective League (IPL), 103, 136; advocacy by, 143–44, 148; and Aid to Dependent Children, 264; and aliens and WPA, 232, 234, 241; and deportations, 145, 335n52; and federal repatriation program, 182; and repatriation, 174, 175, 176; and repatriation in Chicago, 184
immigration, 101; and family studies, 98; fiscal costs of, 98; growth in 1890–1920, 1–2; laws concerning, 96, 121, 125; national hearings on restriction of, 90, 93; and relief spending, 61–64; restricted in mid-1920s from Europe, 87; restrictions on, 126; and social workers, 112–13; and welfare policies, 294
Immigration Act of 1891, 131
Immigration Act of 1907, 101
Immigration Act of 1917, 87, 131, 181
Immigration Act of 1921, 5, 33, 112, 219
Immigration Act of 1924, 5, 33, 87, 88, 112, 219
immigration officials: arbitrary investigations of, 145; cooperation with relief agencies, 124–25, 127, 130–55, 186, 285, 294; and social workers, 14–15
Indianapolis, 102
Indians, 43, 44, 211
industry, 42–43, 95, 260
International Institute, 37, 130, 165
International Institute, Akron, Ohio, 174

Recent Titles

Three Worlds of Relief: Race, Immigration, and the American Welfare State from the Progressive Era to the New Deal
by Cybelle Fox

Building the Judiciary: Law, Courts, and the Politics of Institutional Development
by Justin Crowe

Still a House Divided: Race and Politics in Obama's America
by Desmond S. King and Rogers M. Smith

The Litigation State: Public Regulations and Private Lawsuits in the United States
by Sean Farhang

Reputation and Power: Organizational Image and Pharmaceutical Regulation at the FDA
by Daniel Carpenter

Presidential Party Building: Dwight D. Eisenhower to George W. Bush
by Daniel J. Galvin

Fighting for Democracy: Black Veterans and the Struggle Against White Supremacy in the Postwar South
by Christopher S. Parker

The Fifth Freedom: Jobs, Politics, and Civil Rights in the United States, 1941–1972
by Anthony Chen

Reforms at Risk: What Happens after Major Policy Changes Are Enacted
by Eric Patashnik

The Rise of the Conservative Legal Movement: The Long Battle for Control of the Law
by Steven M. Teles

Why Is There No Labor Party in the United States?
by Robin Archer

Black and Blue: African Americans, the Labor Movement, and the Decline of the Democratic Party
by Paul Frymer

Political Foundations of Judicial Supremacy: The Presidency, the Supreme Court, and Constitutional Leadership in U. S. History
by Keith E. Whittington